HONORING DIFFERENCES

THE SERIES IN TRAUMA AND LOSS

CONSULTING EDITORS
Charles R. Figley and Therese A. Rando

HONORING DIFFERENCES: CULTURAL ISSUES IN THE TREATMENT OF TRAUMA AND LOSS

Edited by

Kathleen Nader, D.S.W.
Nancy Dubrow, Ph.D.
B. Hudnall Stamm, Ph.D.

USA	Publishing Office:	BRUNNER/MAZEL
		A member of the Taylor & Francis Group
		325 Chestnut Street
		Philadelphia, PA 19106
		Tel: (215) 625–8900
		Fax: (215) 625–2940
	Distribution Center:	BRUNNER/MAZEL
		A member of the Taylor & Francis Group
		47 Runway Road, Suite G
		Levittown, PA 19057
		Tel: (215) 269–0400
		Fax: (215) 269–0363
UK		BRUNNER/MAZEL
		A member of the Taylor & Francis Group
		1 Gunpowder Square
		London EC4A 3DE
		Tel: +44 171 583 0490
		Fax: +44 171 583 0581

HONORING DIFFERENCES: Cultural Issues in the Treatment of Trauma and Loss

1 2 3 4 5 6 7 8 9 0

Printed by Edwards Brothers, Ann Arbor, MI, 1999.
Cover design by Nancy Abbott. Images copyright 1999 PhotoDisc, Inc.

A CIP catalog record for this book is available from the British Library.
∞ The paper in this publication meets the requirements of the ANSI Standard Z39.48–1984 (Permanence of Paper).

Library of Congress Cataloging-in-Publication Data

Honoring differences : cultural issues in the treatment of trauma and
   loss / edited by Kathleen Nader, Nancy Dubrow, B. Hudnall Stamm.
       p.   cm. — (Series in trauma and loss)
     Includes bibliographical references and index.
     ISBN 0-87630-934-1 (case : alk. paper).
     1. Post-traumatic stress disorder—Cross-cultural studies.
   2. Psychic trauma—Cross-cultural studies.   3. Loss (Psychology)—
   Cross-cultural studies.   4. Psychiatry, Transcultural.   I. Nader,
   Kathleen.   II. Dubrow, Nancy.   III. Stamm, B. Hudnall.
   IV. Series.
   RC552.P67H66   1999
   616.85'21—dc21   99-11369
                                                                CIP

ISBN 0–87630–934–1 (cloth)

We dedicate this book to recognizing the beauty of individuality and to valuing both the likenesses and differences among humankind.

CONTENTS

11

**Culture, Power, and Community: Intercultural
Approaches to Psychosocial Assistance and Healing**

Michael G. Wessells

CONTRIBUTORS

Elia Awwad, Ph.D.
Palestine Red Crescent Society
West Bank and Gaza, Israel

Dan Bar-On, Ph.D.
Department of Behavioral Sciences
Ben-Gurion University of the Negev, Israel

Phoukham Kelly Bounkeua, M.A.
Graduate Student–Clinical Psychology
Seattle Pacific University

Nancy Dubrow, Ph.D.
Taylor Institute, USA

Lane Gerber, Ph.D.
Department of Psychology
Seattle University, USA

Vello Guluma, M.D.
Physician, Liberia

Anatoly V. Isaenko, Ph.D.
Department of History
Appalachian State University, USA

R. J. Kleber, Ph.D.
Department of Clinical Psychology
Utrecht University, The Netherlands

Camilo Garcia Parra, Ph.D.
Human Development and Family Studies
Iowa State University, USA

Thomas E. A. Macaulay
Christian Children's Fund, Sierra Leone

Carlinda Monteiro, Ph.D.
Christian Children's Fund, Angola

G. T. M. Mooren, Ph.D.
Department of Clinical Psychology
Utrecht University, The Netherlands

Kathleen Nader, D.S.W.
Consultant and Psychotherapist, USA

Quynh Nguyen, M.S.W.
Senior Consultant
Asian Counseling and Referral Service
City of Seattle, USA

Nancy Peddle, M.S.
Taylor Institute, USA

Peter W. Petschauer, Ph.D.
Department of History
Appalachian State University, USA

B. Hudnall Stamm, Ph.D.
Institute for Rural Health Studies
Idaho State University, USA

Henry E. Stamm, Ph.D.
Independent Historian
Pocatello, Idaho, USA

Michele A. Tully, M.A.
Chicago Commons, USA

Carlos G. Velez-Ibanez, Ph.D.
Department of Anthropology
University of California—Riverside, USA

Michael G. Wessells, Ph.D.
Department of Psychology
Randolph-Macon College, USA

FOREWORD

A Cross Cultural Perspective of Traumatology

Honoring Differences opens a new era in the emerging field of traumatology. The book helps us move beyond our Western conceptions of trauma and its consequences and cures. The editors coalesce the various contributions to help paint a complex picture of the cultural perspectives of traumatology. The chapters were each peer reviewed at least twice by two to six experts or scholars in the field. The mission of this book is to help mental health professionals and other helpers enter communities with confidence that they will do more good than harm because they understand the fundamentals of cross-cultural helping. At the very least, they are less likely to do harm because of their insensitivity to cultural values. It is important to realize how far we have come in the helping professions to appreciate the contributions of this book.

☐ Centrality of Culture in Traumatology

Certainly "culture" and all that it implies with respect to human development, human thought, and human behavior should be central—not peripheral—in traumatology research, theory, and intervention (Kleber, Figley & Gersons, 1995). With respect to psychology, this point was emphasized recently by Segall, Lonner, and Berry (1998), three of the most respected cross-cultural psychologists of our time. They and others have argued that without understanding the role of culture in the enterprise and products of science and professional practice we are like a ship without an anchor.

Hermans and Kempen (1998), however, challenge this view as being too simplistic and only thinking in terms of geography and nationality. They note that globalization renders obsolete the conception of cultures as independent, coherent, stable, and geographically distinct phenomena. They further note that when we participate simultaneously in different networks (e.g., educational, financial, ideological, or technological) that are, to a large extent, disjunctive, and we can easily get overwhelmed. Why? Because we are often confronted with uncertainties, contradictions, ambiguities, and contrasting interests. Hermans and Kempen suggest that the only thing that will enable us to find our way cross culturally is an overall integrative knowledge system that helps sort out what is important and places culture above trauma. This integrative knowledge system, one may argue, enables visiting aid workers to translate and accommodate to the new ways of viewing the worlds they visit.

More than a decade ago Higginbotham and Marsella (1988) reported that Western psychiatric care varied little among the largest cities in Asia, in spite of the cultural variations. As a result, local healing opportunities and indigenous health benefits were lost. Bracken and Petty (1998) find that the situation is no different in other parts of the world in terms of humanitarian assistance directed toward postwar recovery. More troubling, however, is the uncritical exporting of Western emphasis on simplistic, quick fix efforts emerging from the field of Traumatology. There is concern that the export of this discourse has tended to "deflect attention from the broader social, emotional, and economic development of children and adults who have experienced extreme suffering and witnessed the destruction of their families and communities" (p. 4).

Summerfield (1998) noted that the emphasis of intervention in developing countries affected by disasters should include rebuilding informal networks for mutual social support, listening to local priorities, and strengthening the family and community structures on which children depend for security and development. It is in sharp contrast to what he calls traditional Western psychiatric approaches which emphasize pathological traumatic memory, in contrast to the political and ideological significance and legitimacy of social memory of people historically affected by conflict.

Bracken (1998) extends this thesis to suggest that Western psychology's effort to export cognitivism, the commitment to reliving the trauma in order to acquire cognitive mastery to eliminate the fear response, is irrelevant in nonwestern countries. These societies are far more focused on cultural traditions, mutual aid, and the spiritual world. In contrast, Western countries have replaced Christianity and other formal religions with science and technology as a "dominant way of ordering our thoughts about the world." Bracken suggests that the challenge of cross-cultural work in Traumatology is to resist quick fix or magic bullet intervention. Rather we need to work with a spirit of humility about what we can and cannot offer.

☐ Local Applications of Global Thinking

In the concluding chapter of *Honoring Differences,* Wessells (1998) emphasizes a central theme throughout the volume: the call to think globally and act locally, a phrase borrowed from environmental activism. We must appreciate and focus on the global, cross-cultural, and multicultural issues that are common to all human beings and then apply them in our every day work. Throughout this book authors address the lessons of applying our understanding of transcultural principals to improving the quality of our work with the traumatized.

Paul Valent (1998) draws upon an enormous amount of cross-cultural data to develop a *triaxial framework* in which he suggests that there are eight fundamental survival strategies consistent with human beings everywhere. By understanding and applying this model we will better appreciate the struggles of human beings that transcend culture and be challenged to effectively assess and facilitate survival among those who seek help. The eight strategies are: rescuing, attaching, asserting, adapting, fighting, fleeing, competing, and cooperating. As we listen and discuss various issues that emerge from the sessions it is important to help construct a set of lessons from our awareness of cross-cultural studies and somehow, as Valent has, apply them to our work on a daily basis.

☐ The Risks to Decontextualizing Culture

Another theme emphasized throughout this volume is that culture is most often decontextualized in traumatology. That is, we view trauma from our own perspective and not from the perspective of the culture. We do this, it is noted, because we are unable to manage the forces of hopelessness, meaning, and perceived control of people not like ourselves.

Judith Herman (1992) has noted that these are the features that are pivotal to trauma of all people. Recovery from trauma and loss requires the reconstruction of meaning, the rebuilding of hope, and the sense of empowerment needed to regain control of one's being and life. The imposition of Western, decontextualized views marginalizes local voices and cultural traditions, disempowers communities, and limits healing. I say this to point out the converse. As traumatologists who are called upon to provide assistance to communities devastated by traumatic events, we can avoid both disempowering and de-contextualizing people who have been traumatized.

We must use our power to situate problems in historic context and to learn about and validate local cultural traditions. My hope is that this book provides the reader with blueprints for effectively empowering communities and providing justifications for using culturally appropriate, sustainable, healing resources. By promoting community empowerment we facilitate regaining control, healing wounds, and building a social-emotional connection to a more positive future.

☐ The Risks of Trauma Lenses

Finally, as briefly noted earlier, there are risks to viewing the world from the perspective of traumatic stress. At the same time that we are concerned about the impact of traumatic events in the lives of people, we must also worry about trivializing the factors that have caused and maintained the trauma response. As Stamm and Stamm (in this volume) point out, the psychological stresses and problems in Native North American communities are inextricably interwoven with a historic context of genocide, discrimination, and marginalization. Similarly, as Vélez-Ibáñez and García Parra (in this volume) points out, the problems of Mexicans in the southwest United States are connected with problems of poverty, unemployment, and oppression. These stressors are chronic and historically rooted.

In a war zone or a disaster situation, many local people may experience problems such as sleep disturbances, flashbacks, social isolation, substance abuse, and so on. For clinical psychologists trained in Western universities, it is quite natural to view these problems through the lenses of trauma and posttraumatic stress disorder (PTSD). For useful reviews, see Friedman and Marsella, 1996; Stamm and Friedman, in press, and van der Kolk, McFarlane, and Weisaeth, (1996). It is tempting in such circumstances to set up mental health clinics or arrange other venues for delivering traumatology services to address traumas.

Although beneficial in some respects, this trauma emphasis encounters serious difficulties when narrowly applied. First, it individualizes the problem. Dominant conceptual frameworks construct trauma as an individual phenomenon, distracting attention from the wider, social elements of the situation. But in war situations, the impact of trauma on individuals cannot be separated from the devastation of families and communities (Reichenberg & Friedman, 1996). Further, in collectivist societies, individualistic approaches may be at odds with the local culture. Second, a trauma emphasis encourages fragmentation of multifaceted problems. Although psychologists naturally look for and address psychological issues, the immediate problems may have more to do with food, security, housing, and survival (Dawes, 1994). It is vital for psychologists to view human problems holistically (Wessells & Kostelny, 1996). Third, emphasis on trauma encourages a historical conceptualization that overlooks the stresses imposed by racism, economic domination, or political oppression. The failure to situate problems historically may lead to oversimplification, diagnostic problems (Dubrow & Nader, in this volume), and the misdirection of resources.

To talk about war affected populations as traumatized, for example, can pathologize the people and medicalize problems that are political and economic. As Vélez-Ibáñez and García Parra (in this volume) notes, profound psychological stress often arises from economic disadvantages. When consultants fail to talk about the historic context of problems, local people often feel demeaned and misunderstood. Consider, for example, the problems associated with focusing narrowly on problems of trauma in the Palestinian context, where victimization has become woven into the fabric of group identity by virtue of the historic situation. In focusing on the trauma of youths who have nightmares and related problems by virtue of having been arrested or shot, a psychologist overlooks the connection between mental health and sociopolitical context (Punamäki, 1989) and tacitly denies the historic oppression that many Palestinians view as the defining feature of their social reality (Awwad, in this volume). Similarly, focus on trauma in the Israeli context may draw attention from the culture of dying, which is grounded in problems of the Holocaust, repeated attacks, and chronic insecurity (Bar-On, in this volume).

Ethically, it is questionable to address traumas in contexts of political oppression without also working to support human rights and constructive political change. Traumatologists must always be aware of the larger cultural and historical context that contributed to the symptoms of the trauma response. Traumatology itself cannot address these wider human needs.

Lasting recovery requires lasting hope and self-sufficiency. Can there be lasting recovery under conditions of ethnic hatred, extreme poverty, oppression, or armed conflict? Gibbs (1997) has noted that jobs and education, bricks and mortar reconstruction, and the resumption of culturally defined routines are more associated with a sense of psychosocial well being than any index of mental health.

To achieve this state of well being, one must work holistically. This requires bridging both the macro- and micro-social levels, and integrating social traumatology work into comprehensive, multidisciplinary programs (Valent, 1998; Wessells & Kostelny, 1996). As cross-cultural traumatologists, we may require many new skills and must have a willingness to go beyond the boundaries of our disciplines.

As a welcomed shift in the field of Traumatology toward a new emphasis in the importance of culture, *Honoring Differences* helps people understand the role of culture in caring for others. Though the book focuses primarily on activities performed by health care and relief agencies following catastrophic or traumatic events, others should read it including tourists, international business professionals, and others who need to understand the customs, habits, and beliefs of particular cultures.

☐ References

Adler, L., & Mukherji, B. (Eds.). (1995). *Spirit versus scalpel: Traditional healing and modern psychotherapy*. Westport, CT: Bergin & Garvey.

Bracken, P. J. (1998). Hidden agendas: Deconstructing post traumatic stress disorder. In P. J. Bracken and C. Petty (Eds.), *Rethinking the trauma of war* (pp. 38–59). London: Free Association Press.

Bracken, P. J., & Petty, C. (Eds.). (1998). *Rethinking the trauma of war*. London: Free Association Press.

Brydon-Miller, M., & Tolman, D. (Eds.). (1998). Transforming psychology: Interpretive and participatory research methods. *Journal of Social Issues, 53*(4),

Danieli, Y. I., Rodley, N. S., & Weisaeth, L. (Eds.). (1996). *International responses to traumatic stress*. Amityville, NY: Baywood.

Dawes, A. (1994). The emotional impact of political violence. In A. Dawes & D. Donald (Eds.), *Childhood & adversity: Psychological perspectives from South African research* (pp. 177–199). Cape Town: David Philip.

Dawes, A. (1997, July). *Cultural imperialism in the treatment of children following political violence and war: A Southern African perspective*. Paper presented at the Fifth International Symposium on the Contributions of Psychology to Peace, Melbourne.

Fals-Borda, O., & Rahman, M. A. (1991). *Action and knowledge: Breaking the monopoly with participatory action research*. New York: Apex.

Figley, C. R. (Ed.). (1978). *Stress disorders among Vietnam veterans: Theory, research, and treatment*. New York: Brunner/Mazel.

Figley, C. R. (1989). *Helping traumatized families*. San Francisco: Jossey-Bass.

Friedman, M. J., & Marsella, A. J. (1996). Posttraumatic stress disorder: An overview of the concept. In A. J. Marsella, M. J. Friedman, E. T. Gerrity, & R. M. Scurfield (Eds.), *Ethnocultural aspects of posttraumatic stress disorder: Issues, research, and clinical applications* (pp. 11–32). Washington, DC: American Psychological Association.

Garbarino, J., Kostelny, K., & Dubrow, N. (1991). *No place to be a child: Growing up in a war zone*. Lexington, MA: Lexington Books.

Gibbs, S. (1997). Postwar social reconstruction in Mozambique: Reframing children's experiences of trauma and healing. In K. Kumar (Ed.), *Rebuilding war-torn societies: Critical areas for international assistance* (pp. 227–238). Boulder, CO: Lynne Rienner.

Gilbert, A. (1997). *Small voices against the wind: Local knowledge and social transformation. Peace and Conflict: Journal of Peace Psychology, 3*, 275–292.

Gurr, T. R. (1993). *Minorities at risk: A global view of ethnopolitical conflicts*. Washington, DC: U. S. Institute of Peace Press.

Herman, J. (1992). *Trauma and recovery*. New York: Harper Collins.

Hermans, H. J. M., & Kempen, H. J. G. (1998). Moving cultures: The perilous problems of cultural dichotomies in a globalizing society. *American Psychologist, 53*(10), 1111–1120.

Higginbotham, N., & Marsella, A. (1988). International consulate and the homogenization of psychiatry in Southeast Asia. *Social Science and Medicine, 27,* 553–561.

Honwana, A. (1997). Healing for peace: Traditional healers and post-war reconstruction in Southern Mozambique. *Peace and conflict: Journal of Peace Psychology, 3,* 293–305.

International Federation of Red Cross and Red Crescent Societies (1996). *World Disasters Report 1996.* New York: Oxford University Press.

Kienle, G. S., & Kiene, H. (1996). Placebo effect and placebo concept: A critical methodological and conceptual analysis of reports on the magnitude of the placebo effect. *Alternative Therapies, 2*(6), 39–54.

Kleber, R., Figley, C. R., & Gersons, B. (Ed.). (1995). *Beyond Trauma.* New York: Plenum.

Lederach, J. P. (1997). *Building peace: Sustainable reconciliation in divided societies.* Washington, DC: U. S. Institute of Peace Press.

Murdock, G. (1980). *Theories of illness: A world survey.* Pittsburgh, PA: University of Pittsburgh Press.

Punamäki, R. (1989). Political violence and mental health. *International Journal of Mental Health, 17,* 3–15.

Reichenberg, D., & Friedman, S. (1996). Traumatized children. Healing the invisible wounds of war: A rights approach. In Y. Danieli, N. S. Rodley, & L. Weisaeth (Eds.), *International responses to traumatic stress* (pp. 307–326). Amityville, NY: Baywood.

Segall, M. H., Lonner, W. J., & Berry, J. W. (1998). Cross-cultural psychology as a scholarly discipline: On the flowering of culture in behavioral research. *American Psychologist, 53*(10), 1101–1110.

Smith, M. B. (1986). War, peace and psychology. *Journal of Social Issues, 42,* 23–38.

Stamm, B. H., & Friedman, M. J. (in press). Cultural diversity in the appraisal & expression of traumatic exposure. In A. Shalev, R. Yehuda, & A. McFarlane, *International Handbook of Human Response to Trauma,* Plenum Press.

Summerfield, D. (1998). The social experience of war and some issues from the humanitarian field. In P. J. Bracken & C. Petty (Eds.). *Rethinking the trauma of war,* pp. 9–37. London: Free Association Books.

UNICEF (1996). *The state of the world's children 1996.* New York: UNICEF.

Valent, P. (1998). From survival to fulfillment: A framework for life-trauma dialectic. Philadelphia: Brunner/Mazel.

van der Kolk, V. A., McFarlane, A. C., & Weisaeth, L. (Eds.). (1996). *Traumatic stress: The effects of overwhelming experience on mind, body, and society.* New York: Guilford.

Wallensteen, P., & Sollenberg, M. (1998). Armed conflict and regional conflict complexes, 1989–97. *Journal of Peace Research, 35*(5), 621–634.

Wessels, M., & Kostelny, K. (1996). *The Graça Machel/UN Study on the Impact of Armed Conflict on Children: Implications for early child development.* New York: UNICEF.

Wessells, M. G. (1998). Humanitarian intervention, psychosocial assistance, and peacekeeping. In H. Langholtz (Ed.), *The psychology of peacekeeping* (pp. 131–152). Westport, CT: Praeger.

PREFACE

Within the United States, mental health professionals must often provide interventions for individuals from a variety of cultures. Wars, violence, or disasters affecting large groups of people nationally and internationally have necessitated mental health interventions for vastly differing cultures (Dubrow, Liwski, Palacios, & Gardinier, 1996). Moreover, many individuals from other countries seek training in the United States creating an additional need for a broad cultural awareness.

Over the years our work with traumatized populations has taken us to many different countries as well as to a variety of areas within the United States. In preparation, we worked diligently to educate ourselves about the special attributes of various cultures relevant to mental health professionals, especially following traumatic events. Identifying sources for information about the social, psychological, political, spiritual, and traditional practices of specific cultural groups entailed a great deal of time and effort. Travel books, textbooks, country reports, and other literature as well as interviews with others who had worked with specific populations were among our sources. Our most informed resources were the people with whom we worked once we were "on the ground." Indeed, this volume can never replace these people-to-people education sessions. However, in writing this book, we did go to these very resources, our colleagues all over the world, for their expertise.

The need for an understanding of specific cultural beliefs has been clearly and repeatedly demonstrated for mental health professionals, for example, when assisting children and adults following traumatic events (Marsella, et al., 1996). Training in the cultural beliefs which may interact with traumatic reactions is important both to accuracy of assessment of traumatic response and to preventing harm in the process of assessing and treating trauma (Nader, 1996). Some issues that are assumed in one culture or group are very different in another. For example, cultural differences may effect the expression of fantasies of intervention (e.g., revenge) or the engaging of support from others that are important to the treatment of trauma. A visiting physician spoke to the grandfather of an adolescent young woman who had been raped in wartime. A year after the rape, she finally had the courage to tell her family. Her brother murdered her two days later. She lived in a culture where a woman who is raped is considered contaminated (Nader, 1996). For the same reason, in Kuwait following the Gulf Crisis, adolescent girls were unwilling to admit a rape experience unless assured of confidentiality and separate record keeping (Nader, 1996).

Understanding cultural differences can be extremely important to individual or group interventions. For effective intervention, a child's or adolescent's beliefs must be recognized, honored, and appropriately addressed. In a training session on children's understanding of death and dying, Liberian counselors discussed the difficulty of talking with children about death in the context of traditional beliefs. Although children had witnessed death, often of a violent nature, and experienced the death of family and community members during the ongoing civil war, traditional beliefs forbade children's knowledge of death. In villages, children were traditionally gathered together and kept inside a designated house so that funeral processions were not viewed. Additionally, among many tribes, chalk was placed beneath children's eyes to prevent them from "seeing" death and to keep the spirit of a dead person from entering the children's bodies. It is believed that a dead person's spirit can harm children. Even talk of death is considered harmful to children. Since the activities of war broke all tradition by exposing children directly to death and dying, Liberian counselors were faced with the necessity of explaining death to children. Sensitivity to this complex dilemma was critical to counselors who were preparing to help children deal with extensive grief, loss, and traumatic memories of death.

Understanding the culture for which services are provided, and understanding the services which are appropriate for the culture, can prevent mishaps and lend to the success of initial and ongoing planning and efforts. When interpersonal relationships and the process of reaching the goal is the primary orientation of a group (rather than the goal itself), methods of goal attainment and time schedules may need adjustment. It is essential in a culture that thinks mental health disturbance may label a family (possibly for generations) to appropriately communicate the normalcy of traumatic response.

We have worked with our colleagues from all over the world to bring to one volume information that is essential to the mental health professional who may enter a different community or culture in order to be of assistance. Our goal is to assist mental health professionals and others honor the valued traditions, main qualities, and held beliefs of the culture or race described. We acknowledge the importance of preparation to the outside mental health professional who intends to lend expertise and needed assistance to a community and we hope this book assists them in entering the community well informed and well equipped to intervene or consult effectively. Finally, we have provided information about issues, traditions, and characteristics that are essential in moving through the phases of posttrauma or other mental health crises.

This book deals with treating trauma and loss, and recognizing and understanding the cultural context in which the professional intends to provide assistance. Among the cultural groups described in this volume, it is apparent that there are many differences in approach to mental health issues. However, traumatic events in the lives of people all over the world cause similar responses of trauma and loss. Honoring differences demonstrates the respect that is necessary to address traumatic events that have already occurred, to prevent future tragedies, and to work toward a more peaceful society.

☐ References

Dubrow, N., Liwski, N., Palacios, C., & Gardinier, M. (1996). Traumatized children: Helping child victims of violence. In Y. Danieli, N. Rodley, & L. Weisaeth (Eds.), *International responses to traumatic stress: Humanitarian, human rights, justice, peace and development contributions, collaborative actions and future initiatives* (pp. 327–346). New York: Baywood Publishing Company on behalf of the United Nations.

Marsella, A. J., Friedman, M. J., Gerrity, E. T., & Seurfield, R. M. (Eds.) (1996). *Ethnocultural Aspects of Post-Traumatic Stress Disorder.* Washington, DC: American Psychological Association.

Nader, K. (1996). Assessing traumatic experiences in children. In J. Wilson & T. Keane (Eds.), *Assessing psychological trauma & PTSD* (pp. 291–348). New York: Guilford Press.

Nader, K. (1997). Childhood traumatic loss. In C. Figley, B. Bride, & N. Mazza (Eds.), *Death and trauma: The traumatology of surviving* (pp. 17–41). London: Taylor and Francis.

ACKNOWLEDGMENTS

We offer our heartfelt thanks to the many individuals who assisted in the making of this book through their efforts and advice. We are deeply appreciative of the efforts of the following individuals who completed many important tasks (e.g., typing, compiling, contacting, sending): Laurie Fetherston, Yolonda Garner, Estelle Gruba, Liz Hahn, Alicia Mersiovsky, Cathy Mullins, Carol Nader, Dr. Sam Nader, Jackie and Foster Smith, Shay Stockdill, and Hal Williams.

We are deeply grateful to the many experts, consultants, and researchers who offered recommendations and assistance regarding the chapters of this book: Dean Ajdukovic, Ph.D., Issan Al-Issa, Ph.D., Ahmad Baker, Ph.D., Jim Baumohl, Ph.D., Carl C. Bell, M.D., Carl Brasseaux, Ph.D., Jeffrey Borkan, Ph.D., Pat Busher, Ph.D., Rafael Chabran, Ph.D., Yael Danieli, Ph.D., Richard Deer Track, LeMyra Debruyn, Ph.D., Holly Delaney-Cole, MSW, Anthony Delgado, Howard Dorgan, Ph.D., Donald Duster, Charles Figley, Ph.D., Lindsay French, Ph.D., Vello Guluma, M.D., Sam Hill, Ph.D., Fayeq Hussein, MSW, Salvatore Imbrogno, Ph.D., Genee Jackson, Ph.D., Marcia Jovanovic, M.D., Sokoni Karanja, Ph.D., Mark Kater, BFA, Susan MacCammon, Ph.D., Bintu Magona and the Sierra Leone KIDS Team, Spero Manson, Ph.D., Bill Meezan, Ph.D., Anica Mikos Kos, M.D., Prexy Nesbitt, Dolores Norton, Ph.D., Rowina Price Jaber, B.A., MIPD, AMREBT, Arthur Rubel, Ph.D., Daniel Scheinfeld, Ph.D., Frank Seever, Ph.D., Arieh Shalev, M.D., Terry M. Thibodeaux, Ph.D., Wilson Watt, Ph.D., Marcellus Williams (Bear Heart), John P. Wilson, Ph.D., William Yule, Ph.D.

CHAPTER 1

Nancy Dubrow, Kathleen Nader

Consultations Amidst Trauma and Loss: Recognizing and Honoring Differences among Cultures

☐ Introduction

Throughout the world, there is increasing concern for the welfare of all human beings exposed to the violence of war, the increase in school and community violence, and a proliferation of natural disasters. Trauma and loss are inevitable not only in any country or community exposed to war or prone to extreme weather conditions but also for those shocked by random or political violence and by changing weather or geographical conditions (e.g., fires and tornadoes resulting from oceanic thermal conditions; broadened flood zones; bombings and other terrorist acts; and school shootings). In May of 1992, Garbarino pointed out that the number of violent deaths in some of our inner cities often exceeded the number of violent deaths in the equivalent time period in areas of civil unrest such as Ireland (Garbarino, 1992). Similarly, across Los Angeles county alone in one weekend, the number of deaths exceeded the number in Bosnia-Herzegovina for the same weekend (The Los Angeles Times, November 1992). Even the nature of war has changed. In World War II, 9 soldiers were killed for every civilian killed. In Bosnia, Kuwait and other recent war zones, many more civilians have been killed, tortured, or otherwise injured than soldiers (UNICEF, 1996). In the past decade, an estimated 2 million children have been killed in armed con-

1

flict and three times as many have been seriously injured or permanently disabled. Countless others have been forced to witness or even take part in horrifying acts of violence (UNICEF, 1996).

Over the years, we have worked as consultants to government, nongovernmental, and intergovernmental agencies responsible for the well being of children on every continent. Our international experiences have challenged us to delve deeply into the cultural, ethnic, religious, and political belief systems of the people engaging our assistance. We have found that simply understanding the cultural context is not sufficient. It is essential to incorporate this knowledge into program design and implementation.

There are certain principles and philosophies which are applicable across cultures. For example, any good intervention requires adequate briefing, masterful problem solving, and skilled timing. Our experiences have demonstrated that there are many differences as well as many similarities among the human family. In the realm of healing interventions, the latter sometimes outweigh the former. We hope that, in addition to offering useful information about cultures, this volume will provide a guide to additional resources for those who work with cultures different from their own.

☐ The West vs. The World

Members of cultures outside of North America, Western Europe, Australia, and New Zealand have often complained about Western thinking and methods related to health and mental health interventions. Westerners are expected to be rigid in their thinking and methods, to have disrespect personal and community beliefs, to lack consideration for the person in context, and to try to treat or deal with only the individual (not his tribe, group, or total situation). These complaints seem to represent a fear that people from the West (which seems to mean primarily the United States and western Europe) will not honor or respect a culture's traditional beliefs or ways of thinking, will look at only the individual and not his or her milieu or circumstances and not attend to all of his or her needs including concrete needs (for example a refugee's needs for food, shelter, and medical supplies), or will belittle mystical or spiritual thinking. There is sometimes an anger that Westerners think they know the whole truth of the universe, and it is not the same truth honored by this particular culture.

We all embrace a set of beliefs (and some disbeliefs). Only some of those beliefs can currently be proved or disproved. Whether or not part of health or mental health disorders can be attributed to, for example, unembodied spirits (e.g., ghosts, evil spirits, gods, elves), invisible forces (e.g., witchcraft, electrical emissions, radiation, psychic imprints, chemical fumes), or microscopic entities (e.g., germs, viruses, parasites, or other toxins), actual and perceived stresses, threats, and/or hindrances must be dispelled or resolved in order for health and mental health to be restored. (The argument has been made that the evil spirits of old are the toxins seen under the microscope or the disturbances in spirit treated today.) We like to enter a new situation with the belief that anything is possible and begin our programs and interventions from where the community, group, or individual is physically, socially and psychologically.

☐ The Dangers of Ignoring Differences

Views toward and reactions to traumatic experiences, and to health and mental health interventions in general, vary across cultures. Understanding beliefs and practices is important to all phases of effective intervention. It is essential to the accuracy of assessment (Nader, 1996a) and to the effectiveness of initial and ongoing interventions. In fact, ignoring beliefs and habits can result in deaths.

Both within this country and elsewhere, what may seem like small details can be of great importance. Jimmy Carter discovered during his presidency the significance of handing an item to somebody in the Middle East with your left hand instead of your right hand. In parts of Asia and the Middle East, the left hand is used for personal hygiene in the bathroom and is considered soiled. Therefore handing something to someone with the left hand is insulting and distasteful. Growing up in Louisiana, "booger" was used as an affectionate term—usually for a young child. The phrase is often used to indicate that the child was very cute or maybe a little mischievous. A national TV and sports commentator was commenting that one of the college football players was called "Booger" by his friends and family. His co-commentator (assuming it meant nasal contents) would not allow him to explain where the name came from which left the audience with disgusting images regarding this young man and his personal habits.

The accuracy of assessment is affected by many things (Wilson & Keane, 1996). It is essential in a culture that thinks mental health disturbance may label a family (possibly for generations) to appropriately communicate the normalcy of traumatic response. The same is true for a culture in which men are disgraced by normal traumatic emotions. In some regions, individuals must be helped to feel free to admit their symptoms and experiences. Following the Gulf Crisis, in the discussion phase of the Kuwaiti school classroom interventions, it was important to reinforce the normalcy, even in men, of traumatic reactions by saying: "We have learned that even the strongest man can be afraid, and that even the strongest man can be so deeply sad or horrified that he feels like crying." In the same country, women may need to be assured of confidentiality in order to feel safe admitting their rape experiences.

Observing cultural practices can be a preliminary requisite to the success of ongoing interventions. For example, in January, 1989, a young man opened fire on children on the Cleveland Elementary School grounds in Stockton, CA, killing 5 and injuring 29 children and 1 teacher. With an awareness of cultural beliefs and practices including religious and medical practices, the school principal invited local clergy including Cambodian and Vietnamese Buddhist monks, a Vietnamese Catholic priest, and Protestant ministers to perform a blessing ceremony upon the school and school grounds. This included the exorcism of spirits including the bad spirit of the man who killed the children and himself and the spirits of dead children who might grab other children and take them into the next world. Children were given chants to use when frightened; children and adults were given factual information to dispel rumors and unfounded fears. These respectful practices addressed fears and other arousal symptoms in the general population. Performing them effectively and appropriately assisted in separating fear related arousal symptoms from ongoing traumatic reactions as well as assisting in making other interventions possible (Nader, 1996a).

Understanding the culture for which services are provided and understanding the services which are appropriate for the culture can prevent mishaps and lend to the success of initial and ongoing planning and efforts. When interpersonal relationships and the process of reaching the goal is the primary orientation of a group (rather than the goal itself), methods of goal attainment and time schedules may need adjustment. For example, after the 1992 Los Angeles riots, planned interventions for children in the Head Start program were stalled because the interpersonal interactions needed and expected by community members before allowing the intervention to occur could not be completed before the Federal Emergency Management Act (FEMA) deadline.

Some issues assumed in one culture or group (for example, the truth of statements) are very different for another. In some cultures inside and outside of the United States, it is polite to be agreeable or to say you will do or even have done something even when it is not a true statement. In some regions of the United States, people graciously and profusely offer assistance but later—when you seek that assistance—are distressed by having to take the time and may even feel guilty about not wanting to assist. Before a trip to Kuwait, the Kuwaiti liaison told a consulting group that he had done everything needed to prepare for their project: he had completed all of the tasks requested by the consultant and bought all of the equipment needed—even coffee cups for each of the administrative staff members. In truth, only the coffee cups were there when the consultant arrived. Several weeks of 16-hour work days were then required so that the project could stay on schedule. The needed computer equipment was not ordered until three weeks after the group's arrival which caused additional problems.

Using practices that work in one culture may lead to failure or adverse effects in another. Diverse cultures have different understandings of specific symptoms, varying tolerances for the expression of strong emotions, and different views of victims. For example, cultural differences in the expression of rage or anger may effect the expression of fantasies of intervention (e.g., revenge, see Nader & Pynoos, 1991; Pynoos & Nader, 1993) or the engaging of support from others (e.g. for a rape victim) which are important to the treatment of trauma.

Training in the cultural beliefs that may interact with traumatic reactions is important not only to accuracy of assessment but also to preventing harm in the process of assessing and treating trauma (Nader, 1997b). Health professionals in the former Yugoslavian republics have reported a variety of harmful effects after survivors of rape were interviewed by journalists, mental health professionals, and other personnel. These effects included suicides and suicide attempts, severe depressions, and acute psychotic episodes (Swiss & Giller, 1993). Failure to understand and honor cultural practices may lead to murder. For example, as noted earlier, in Kuwait following the Gulf Crisis, one clergy explained that Arab females are considered tainted beyond repair if raped. He told the story of an adolescent relative who, after a year, found the courage to tell her family that she had been raped during the crisis. The next day, her brother killed her (Nader, 1996a).

☐ Overcoming Obstacles

It is difficult to predict what barriers there will be to getting started—whether it is getting started with initial efforts or getting started with interventions. Adults and adolescents may need assurance of protection from specific consequences if they become a part of the intervention process. In an area south of Los Angeles, a five-year-old Hispanic girl emotionally described her experience watching a female gang member stab one of her relatives. With extreme fear and upset, she drew a picture of what she had seen and gave a detailed account of the experience. After arriving to pick up her daughter, the girl's mother insisted that the child had only dreamed this experience. The child continued to show extreme distress when the subject was brought up again. In truth, the family was in the United States illegally; they feared discovery and deportation.

When specific things are needed in preparation for the consultant's efforts, it may be best for the consultant to complete these tasks prior to going to the site of intervention. If not, it is important to be certain that these things have indeed been done in advance rather than that someone has just politely said they were done.

What might normally be expected in a consultation is not always what actually occurs. For example, in some countries we have found that the psychiatrists are so thoroughly trained in the use of medication, institutionalization, or practices other than treatment that they may be the most difficult to train in treatment methods. Especially in nations where children are not usually given services, particularly mental health services, the most educated mental health professionals may find it difficult to adjust to methods aimed at children's recovery.

☐ Travel and Preparation

If traveling to a new location to provide consultation, there are a number of practical issues involved in working both nationally and internationally.

National Travel

Travel within the country involves a few simple tasks related to preparation for basic needs (e.g., food and lodging), different geographical circumstances (e.g., the altitudes of Colorado), and new environmental conditions (e.g., variations in weather and air quality). It is also essential to prepare a contact person for your arrival and program needs (e.g., training equipment, copies, conference, and private meeting space) and to make arrangements for contact with those who can aid the success of interventions (e.g., liaisons, elders, community leaders, city or school administrators) (see Nader and Pynoos, 1993). Because of the diverse cultures across the United States, some of the issues related to foreign travel do apply.

International Travel

International travel provides a new set of concerns including those related to documentation, health and safe passage.

Preparation for Foreign Consultation

It is essential to gather information about a culture, its relevant history, and current political situation. The Internet is a rich resource. Travel guides are also a useful place to begin. We have found the Lonely Planet series especially good. In fact, their *Africa on a Shoestring* (Crowther et al., 1995) has been used as a field guide for Peace Corps volunteers. Included in these guides are an historical backround of each country and extensive resource information on local customs, language, religion, and other topics.

A good resource for country reports is the United Nations. For example, UNICEF publishes a variety of reports on the status of women and children in specific countries. To request reports and a current situation analysis, call UNICEF in New York (telephone: 212–326–7000) or Geneva (telephone: 41–22–909–5111) and ask for the desk officer of the country of interest.

If foreign work involves an international nongovernmental organization (Save the Children, Amnesty International, etc.) that is familiar with the particular country situation or that has a field office in the country, they will most likely brief you. Often it is possible to request briefings with in-country staff upon your arrival. Find out the names of other individuals who have consulted or conducted research in the country to which you are traveling. Authors of books and journal articles can be valuable resources. One contact usually leads to a network of people familiar with the country. A good resource for professional contacts in the mental health field are through the membership directories of the World Federation for Mental Health in Baltimore, MD, USA (telephone: 410–938–3180) and the International Society for Traumatic Stress Studies in Chicago, IL, USA (telephone: 708–480–9028).

Clothing

Check travel books and newspapers for weather conditions. This will begin to assist you in packing properly. Clothing is not only weather related but also related to the nature of the job you will perform and to local customs. In some countries in the Middle East, for example, dress is closely tied to gender and religious issues.

Scheduling

Time

Do not expect that people of other cultures operate in the same time frame as you do. In the United States, one will observe people eating a quick sandwich at their desk while continuing their work; in many other countries in the world, lunch is at least a one hour affair. In many warmer climates, the work day is split into two parts: the first until lunch, with a rest of several hours in between and then the second until early evening. As a consultant from the outside, you should not attempt to alter others' normal hours of conducting business. In Muslim countries there will be a need for several specified prayer breaks during the day (and night). In Kuwait the normal workday is 5 hours and people are accustomed to arriving late, taking two prayer breaks, and sometimes leaving early.

Health

Taking care of your health is a key issue for consultants. It is important to remain healthy throughout the consultancy so that you can complete your job assignment. The quality of health care varies from country to country, therefore, some precautions should be taken before departing. Check with your physician or local travel clinic to determine what immunizations are required for the particular area in which you will travel. Latest updates on, for example, malaria, need to be considered so that appropriate prophylactics are taken. Often, if you will be working with small children in crowded conditions, such as refugee camps, immunization against measles and other communicable diseases may be appropriate. Tentanus and hepatitis immunizations are often recommended.

Water is life support, however, in many of the countries we have worked, it has been contaminated or is deadly. Analyze the situation of clean drinking water and follow normal precautions.

In war zones, a consultant should carefully consider entering before the actual cease fire (rather than the official end of war) or before any chemical fires, biological, chemical warfare agents or other toxins are cleaned up (e.g., agent orange, pesticides, dust from radioactive warheads, contaminants in water). Long after consulting in Kuwait, we discovered the effects of having been among the first consultants. Enemy soldiers were not fully purged from the country for two to three months after the official cease fire. Water had been brought into the county in dirty oil tankers. Exposure to this, smoke from oil fires, possible chemical and biological warfare agents, area endemic parasites, and unknown factors resulted in the disabling Gulf War Syndrome. The hardest working and best briefed consultants (i.e., those taken into the thick of things) may be the most vulnerable.

Food

In some cultures, the sharing of food is a ritual of trust and camaraderie. In the war zones of the world, food is extraordinarily important. People starve as a result of war and insufficient food supplies. Therefore, lunch is not just a meal or regular occurrence. It is a symbol of survival. A

Liberian colleague observed a woman on the street and said, "that woman is fat!" Although this would be an insult in the United States, she explained that this was a genuine compliment because the woman was obviously well fed, the sign of good financial status. Bosnian refugees complained that they could no longer give their children occasional treats or have the usual foods that were not necessary to survival. For a consultant to be offered a cup of coffee under these circumstances can be a special gesture of acceptance or an offering of friendship. In the midst of the Intifada, a visit was made to a West Bank family. There were two adults and ten children living in a one room flat. Living conditions were very difficult, however, midway through the visit, cups of freshly brewed coffee were graciously offered in small china cups on a tray.

Safeguards

It is essential to have a round trip ticket and to make sure that all passports and visas are in order before traveling internationally. Especially in war zones, circumstances can change rapidly. Additionally, be certain that the appropriate safeguards are in effect and that there are multiple ways of contacting people on the outside. Consultants are advised to locate and register at their own embassy. In the event of an emergency, such as an evacuation, the embassy will know how to contact you. Contact people within or near the country are essential. These may be other members of the organization sponsoring the trip or individuals well connected to the consultant's own country. Appropriate documentation is essential.

The primary goal of our consultations has always been to assist individuals, families, and communities in repairing the effects of traumatic events. It may be necessary to make some agreements before the consultation, for example, to bring data home to analyze or to arrange funding for the intervention process. In as much as there are cultures that say "yes" to things in order to be polite when the answer is really "no" or make promises that they do not feel obliged to fulfill, it is essential that any necessary agreements be put in writing. (In one consultation to the Middle East following a war, 75 psychologists and social workers were trained in methods of screening children for their traumatic responses. A landmark investigation of the children's reactions was completed. More than 2,000 children, a representative sample in a small nation were screened for their traumatic reactions. All interviewers were trained extensively and their skills as interviewers were tested before they were included in the actual study. The few psychologists and social workers who did not really want to participate in and were not suited for doing the screening were required by the local administrator to participate anyway. Therefore, their data was kept separate and was not a part of the study. When the consultant was at schools with the screening team, the administrator told the data entry person to include the faulty data anyway. Because of his training and at the request of the consultant, the data entry person did keep the faulty data separate. Verbal agreements were made allowing the consultant to take the data home to the United States and have it thoroughly analyzed resulting in both a list of the children who were traumatized and a list of the risk factors for trauma so that a smaller interview could be derived for the remaining children. For political reasons, and because the female consultant did not cooperate in personal ways with the male administrator, the administrator ultimately withheld the data. Claiming each segment was the entire dataset, he reportedly divided and distributed portions of the data to a number of individuals for his own political gain. When university officials from the consultant's location requested the promised data from the administrator, they were asked for proof *in writing* that the data had been promised. The information from this data that could have been used to assist other children exposed to war, and the recommendations for the children interviewed were not attainable.)

Diplomacy

Diplomacy may not be a topic that professionals in the field of mental health have studied formally in universities. However, developing diplomatic skills for international work is absolutely necessary. Diplomatic skills are needed in interpersonal and work relationships as well as a requirement for facilitating collaborative efforts among various organizations for national efforts on behalf of children's welfare.

The cultural context plays a significant role in how one approaches individuals and institutions.

☐ Working with Trauma in Cultures

Working Through a Translator

There is no substitute for good translation. It is important that a translator be fluent in both the native language and the language of the consultant and also proficient at translating and good with the terminology (e.g., psychological or medical) that will be used by the consultant. If the consultation is regarding mental health, mental health professionals can be among the best translators and can learn a great deal by doing so. In Kuwait and Croatia, social workers, psychiatrists, and psychologists fluent in English and the native languages were used as translators. This gave the translating mental health professional chances to observe and to experience, first hand, the methods and results of therapeutic techniques.

Multiple Traumas

Many of the cultures and all of the nations discussed in this book have been through or are going through wars. Some of the groups go through repeated exposures to violence or other traumas—in the inner cities of the United States, for example. Differences have been found between exposed and unexposed children in a violent inner city community after a single act of violence at a school (Pynoos et al., 1987). Therefore, it is important to understand the similarities and differences between a single trauma and multiple traumas when working with these other cultures (Herman, 1992; Nader and Stuber, 1992; Pelcovitz et al., 1997; Terr, 1991; van der Kolk, Roth, Pelcovitz, Mandel, 1992).

Gender Issues

Female consultants traveling in foreign countries may have to deal with several additional issues. Men may be either curious about a woman traveling alone or may have expectations due to things that they have heard about Western women. In some countries women have less power than men for decision making purposes. A female consultant with expertise may be assigned more power in specific areas but not in others. For example, an American female consultant who went to the Middle East worked mostly with a male liaison who had been educated in the United States. The psychologist treated the consultant as an equal as well as an expert in the field. The consultant was shocked one day to walk into the office and find the psychologist ordering the other women around and the women running as though they would be in danger if they did not comply. On the other hand, another male liaison also educated in the United States expected some measure of obedience from his consultant. In Saudi Arabia a female soldier was beaten about the legs because she wore a skirt that was too short. In another country in which women have little power, although the men were in charge, the consultant found that one of her female students was able to get past the red tape to get things done. For example, when some copies were needed and the administrator said it would take two days to have them done, this woman walked them down and copied them herself. Unfortunately instead of being pleased that we were able to get the copies on time, the administrator had the woman removed from her position two weeks later.

Combining Methods

Although local healers are trusted by the community, the aid of outside consultants may be enlisted because of their intervention successes or simply because of the paucity of or the unpreparedness of local mental health professionals to respond to the needs of the population following war, other violence, or disaster. During and after the war in the former Yugoslovian republics, mental health professionals were unused to dealing with the kinds of problems that arose following prolonged exposure to violence and destruction (see chapter 8). In Liberia, West Africa in 1991, at the height of the civil war, the infrastructure of the country was being destroyed. Despite the extensive psychological effect of the war, only one Liberian psychiatrist existed in the entire country and no one was prepared to deal with the extent of the war trauma. Liberian teachers, social workers, health providers, clergy, and traditional healers participated in training sessions with outside consultants discussing the symptoms of posttraumatic stress in both children and adults.

Whether demons are within or without, symbolic or real, the mind is powerful and research demonstrates that strong belief influences both the mind and the body. Of utmost importance is to analyze the safety of traditional practices. Beyond this, when people hold traditional cultural beliefs about dealing with emotional distress and value their curative powers, it is essential to recognize the longstanding effectiveness of these methods within the community. Combining traditional healing practices and current psychological treatments can enhance the effectiveness of each. We have often found the need to enlist from our colleagues discussion of their traditional practices.

Since we have been invited from outside, students from other cultures are often prepared to learn the latest scientific knowledge we have to offer. Some of them fear that we will judge their traditional beliefs as backwards or old. Many cultures have demonstrated their flexibility in approach to a particular problem, employing both traditional and Western practices. For example, the use of feathers under the pillow is a traditional cure for nightmares, (see below) whereas adjusting one's diet may be practiced by Westerners to reduce stress and improve sleep.

The connection between the mind and the body has been well demonstrated. For example, among some Native American tribes, traditional cleansing ceremonies, such as the use of the sweat lodge, have been employed for healing psychological trauma among Vietnam veterans of Native American origin. The Lakota Sioux Indians believe that their stress is caused by evil spirits, which must be sweated out of the body through a process of collectively entering the sweat lodge and enduring extreme heat while a particular ritual ceremony takes place. Research indicates that this form of treatment is highly successful in treating posttraumatic stress among this population (Wilson, 1988).

Interventionists inside and outside the Western world have found it helpful to combine Western and traditional methods of dealing with trauma (see chapter 11). Successful treatment of Cambodian refugees has been reported through the use of traditional ceremonies performed by Budhist monks (Eisenbruch, 1989). For example, extreme depression was diagnosed in a refugee Cambodian woman. She no longer cared for herself or for her young baby; both were on the verge of death. She lived on the top floor of a building and believed that evil spirits had entered her home through the roof. She attributed her distress to these evil spirits. A Budhist monk was requested to enter the home and perform the appropriate ceremonies to rid the house of the spirits. He constructed an alter, lit candles, burned incense, and conducted the known rituals for eliminating evil spirits from a home. Every corner of the house was cleansed. Eisenbruch reports that the woman improved greatly after the ceremony was performed. She began to care for herself and her child. In a more relaxed state of being, she was able to accept other forms of treatment for coping with her past and current traumas.

In one Cambodian refugee camp on the Thailand border, the pharmacy provided large bins full of freshly gathered herbs recognized by the traditional healers as curative. Counselors were also there to provide support (Dubrow, 1990). In Liberia, a Western trained physician (orthopedic specialist) worked with a traditional healer (bone setter) in the local hospital. Working together, using casting and hydrotherapy, produced outcomes that were more successful than if they had provided treatment individually (Guluma, 1992). A few examples of combining methods in the treatment of specific trauma symptoms are discussed below.

Cleansing Practices.   In certain cultures, burning incense, parts of specific plants or resin is used to dispel evil spirits or negative thought forms and sometimes to invoke good or holy spirits (e.g., in Liberian, Hindu, and Native American cultures). This was a part of the cleansing used at Stockton Elementary School prior to additional interventions. In Liberia, dudoo bird feathers are placed at doors and windows to prevent evil spirits or witchcraft from entering the house and incense is burned in the house and, especially, the bedroom to drive away evil spirits who are known to dislike the smell.

Dreams. Long before Freud made dream interpretation popular in the West, interpretation of dreams were imbedded in the cultural, religious, and spiritual beliefs of many cultures. Although some cures and interpretations of dreams differ from our Western understanding and may be indeed beyond our own realm of thinking, they can provide the door to effective dream work. To one who comes to understand them like an insider, they can provide even greater insight.

Specific cultures address dreams in a group or have a specialist who analyzes the dreams and makes recommendations. In the West we usually call these people psychologists, social workers, or psychiatrists. In some cultures they are called by other names such as medicine man or woman, diviner, or curendero (Spanish for healer). For example, most traditional Liberians have a dream interpreter, believing that through dreams, one acquires knowledge. For example, "Climbing a mountain in a dream and failing to reach the peak means that there is a hardship ahead of you in time to come" and "seeing yourself flying high in a dream, while people are running behind you with spears or any weapon trying to catch you, but failing to catch you, means that your spirit is very strong and your enemies are unable to conquer you" (Dubrow, 1993, p. 5).

Liberians have strong beliefs about dreams and how they originate. People in both urban and rural areas attribute bad dreams to evil spirits, witchcraft, or a bad experience that is not verbalized. In the rural areas, members of the witchcraft society are believed to send bad dreams to nonmembers to encourage them to become members. Traditionally, other people believe that dreams occur when a person has had some terrible experience in the day and does not make it known to the public before night. Thus, the experience is recorded in the mind of that person before going to bed. "You can get rid of bad dreams by using the dudoo bird feathers and by burning incense. The feathers are placed at the doors and windows to avoid evil spirits or witchcraft from entering the house. They may also be placed under the pillow, so that the evil spirit does not enter your head. Or, a diviner may prescribe a traditional leaf medicine to rub on the face at bedtime to keep away the bad dreams. Finally, prayer, work, and a light diet will help to cure bad dreams" (Dubrow, 1993, p. 8).

Death and Bereavement. Western cultural practices may conflict with cultural beliefs. For example in some cultures, viewing the body is considered inappropriate. Even in the West we do not all agree.

Some specialists think that all bodies should be viewed no matter how horribly mutilated (Kubler Ross, 1969). Others have found that children's traumatic symptoms have been increased by unnecessary viewings of bodies or of pictures of the mutilation (Nader et al., 1993).

War has an extraordinary impact on culture. Many people die violently from shooting, starvation, fatigue, and illness while fleeing attacks on their villages and homes. In the midst of the chaos, it is impossible to perform, for example, traditional burial rites and ceremonies. For this and other reasons trauma, and grief are inextricably linked. Focused on the violent, traumatic death, many find it impossible to properly grieve the loss (Eth & Pynoos 1985; Nader 1997a). For one young African woman, her inability to properly bury her father after his death was the most difficult part of her war experience. She said, "He was shot on the beach by rebel soldiers. They took his body and others and threw them into the sea, just like that. I am sad for his death, I miss my father, but the worst thing is how they threw his body into the sea. No proper burial. I cannot forget this" (Dubrow, 1992). In her traditional belief, neither the living nor the dead (her father, the ancestors, the spirits) would be at peace because the proper burial ceremony was not performed.

Some traditional child rearing practices concerning death and loss have been completely destroyed in war. In many cultures, including African and Middle Eastern, children do not traditionally participate in burial ceremonies and funeral rites. Believing that their participation is detrimental to their health and mental health, children are kept from viewing dead persons and witnessing expressions of grief by the adult community. For example, in Liberia when there is a death in a village all of the children are gathered together in one house with the windows covered to stop the spirit of the dead person from entering the child and causing him or her harm during funeral processions. Chalk is rubbed under their eyes to keep the spirit of the dead from entering their bodies.

During the war in Liberia, children saw many dead people along the roads while fleeing armed attacks. Many witnessed killings, some of whom were family members and friends. Children were forced to step over dead bodies during flight and, in the worst case, to hide themselves beneath the bodies to avoid their own death. As expected, children began to ask questions about death and dying for which the adult community had no answers. The adults had never considered how to discuss death with a child because traditionally this was never done. This was an extremely unsettling experience for them—tradition had been completely destroyed and it was not in their control.

☐ Ethical Issues

International consultants and other foreign aid workers may often find themselves in contradictory positions. On the one hand they will be viewed as experts with access to information and techniques perhaps not available in-country. In this respect their support will be eagerly sought. It is important to balance the needs of a situation with limited resources with professionally appropriate and focused behavior that is based on sustainability. In particular, opportunities for training and professional development in the field of counseling and therapeutic techniques are both required and requested. Our experience has demonstrated that greater efficiency lies in the remit of knowledge and skills transference through direct training and developing long term coaching and supervision relationships. The goal is to build capacity and national expertise (see chapter 10). However, consultants may be encouraged to work beyond their professional capacity and in ways that may be ethically inappropriate. For example, being ask to provide medical interventions when the consultant is a psychotherapist or to do some other task not in his or her expertise.

☐ Advocacy

In the treatment of trauma, the clinician or consultant becomes an advocate for trauma survivors (Nader, 1994). On November 20, 1989, the United Nations General Assembly adopted the United Nations Convention on the Rights of the Child, a comprehensive international treaty for the protection of children that is applicable at all times—in times of peace and in times of war (NGO Committee on UNICEF, 1993). Children's rights under the United Nations Convention on the Rights of the Child include, for example, the child's right to life; the right to a name, a home, and a family; the right to a nationality; the right to education and recreation; freedom of expression; dignity and special protection and care in situations of armed conflict.

Although most countries have ratified this treaty, effectively adding it to the existing body of international law, recent armed conflicts clearly demonstrate adult neglect and, in many cases, abuse of the human rights of children. Familiarity with the Articles of the United Nations Convention on the Rights of the Child is an excellent public education tool for child development advocacy as well as a framework for child welfare policy. In conditions of war, assistance with primary needs (e.g. safety, food, and shelter) may take precedence over mental health interventions. Although children were eager to discuss their wartime experiences, numerous Bosnian adult refugees in Croatia first needed to address the lack of jobs, personal hygiene items, and food other than their essentials before they could freely discuss their traumatic experiences.

☐ Conclusion

We have known for some time the importance of individual treatment for multiple aspects of the traumatic experience (Wilson and Lindy, 1994; Nader and Mello, in preparation). In this volume, we recognize the importance of incorporating cultural beliefs and practices into treatment. Moreover, we stress the need to go beyond treating the individual to including his or her situation, immediate milieu, and broader community—understanding and assisting the person in context.

Understanding a culture other than your own is a constant work-in-progress; each country, each situation and each individual sheds new light on their unique identities. Mary Catherine Bateson (1990), daughter of Margaret Mead and Gregory Bateson gives an account of the lives of five extraordinary women who "worked by improvisation, discovering the shape of their creation along the way, rather than pursuing a vision already defined" (p. 1). Bateson defines improvisatory art in life as the ability to combine the familiar with the unfamiliar components in response to new situations. To see, in problem situations, solutions and opportunities for growth. As consultants—traveling from one culture to another—constructing knowledge based on the integration of what we know and what we learn along the way, we engage in this type of improvisation. Like the women in Bateson's book, none of us have had a prescribed vision—instead our visions are products of growth and adaptation—not fixed, but emergent.

☐ References

Bateson, Mary Catherine (1990). *Composing a life: Life as a work in progress.* New York: Plume.

Crowther, G., Finlay, H., Cole, G., Else, D., Hamalainen, P., Jousiffe, A., Logan, L., Murray, J., Newton, A., Simonis, D., Swaney, D., & Willet, D. (Eds.). (1995). *Africa on a shoestring* (7th ed.). Hawthorn, Australia: Lonely Planet.

Dubrow, N. (1990). Personal notes. Thailand.

Dubrow, N. (1992). Personal notes. Liberia.

Dubrow, N. (1993). *Traditional Liberian cures and interpretations of bad dreams.* Chicago: Taylor Institute.

Eisenbruch, M. (1989). Health and cosmology among Cambodian refugees. Paper presented at the Congress for Mental Health. The World Federation for Mental Health. Auckland, New Zealand. August 21–25.

Eth, S., & Pynoos, R. (Eds.). (1985). *Post-traumatic stress disorder in children.* Washington, DC: American Psychiatric Press, Inc.

Garbarino, J. (1992, May). *Discussant for the Symposium: The Impact of Violence on Developing Children.* Paper presented at the annual meeting of the American Psychiatric Association, Washington, DC.

Guluma, V. (1992). Personal communication with N. Dubrow. Monrovia, Liberia.

Herman, J. (1992). Complex PTSD: A syndrome in survivors of prolonged and repeated trauma. *Journal of Traumatic Stress, 5*(3), 377–391.

Kubler-Ross, E. (1969). *On death and dying.* New York: Macmillan.

Los Angeles Times (November 23, 1992). 9 Slain, 7 hurt in weekend violence, Metro section. Byline: Andrea Ford.

Nader, K. (1994). Countertransference in treating trauma and victimization in childhood. In J. Wilson & J. Lindy (Eds.) *Countertransference in the treatment of post-traumatic stress disorder* (pp. 179–205). New York: Guilford.

Nader, K. (1996a). Assessing traumatic experiences in children. In J. Wilson & T. Keane (Eds.), *Assessing psychological trauma & PTSD* (pp. 291–348). New York: Guilford Press.

Nader, K. (1996b). Children's traumatic dreams. In D. Barrett (Ed.), *Trauma and dreams* (pp. 9–24). Cambridge, MA: Harvard Press.

Nader, K. (1997a). Childhood traumatic loss: The interaction of trauma and grief. In C. R. Figley, B. E. Bride, & N. Mazza (Eds.), *Death and trauma: The traumatology of grieving* (pp. 17–41). London: Taylor and Francis.

Nader, K. (1997b). Treating traumatic grief in systems. In C. R. Figley, B. E. Bride, and N. Mazza (Eds.), *Death and trauma: The traumatology of grieving* (pp. 159–192). London: Taylor and Francis.

Nader, K., & Pynoos, R. (1991). Play and drawing techniques as tools for interviewing traumatized children. In C. Schaeffer, K. Gitlan, and A. Sandgrund, (Eds.) (pp. 375–389). *Play diagnosis and assessment.* New York: John Wiley.

Nader, K., & Pynoos, R. (1993). School disaster: Planning and initial interventions. *Journal of Social Behavior and Personality, 8*(5): 299–320.

Nader, K., Pynoos, R., Fairbanks, L., Al-Ajeel, M., & Al-Asfour, A. (1993). Acute post-traumatic stress reactions among Kuwait children following the Gulf Crisis. *British Journal of Clinical Psychology, 32:* 407–416.

Nader, K. and Stuber, M. (1992). *A Comparative Study of Children's Responses to Violence and to Catastrophic Treatment for Catastrophic Illness.* Unpublished manuscript. Presented at the annual meeting of the International Society for Traumatic Stress Studies, October 23, 1992.

Pelcovitz, D., van der Kolk, B., Roth, S., Kaplan, S., Mandel, F., & Resick, P. (1997). Development of a criteria set and a structured interview for Disorders of Extreme Stress (SIDES). *Journal of Traumatic Stress, 10*(1), 3–16.

Pelcovitz, D., van der Kolk, B., Roth, S., Kaplan, S., Mandel, F., & Resick, P. (in press). Development and validation of the structured interview for measurement of complex PTSD. *Journal of Traumatic Stress, 10*(1): 3–16.

Pynoos, R., Frederick C., Nader, K., Arroyo, W., Eth, S., Nunez, W., Steinberg, A., & Fairbanks, L. (1987). Life threat and posttraumatic stress in school age children. *Archives of General Psychiatry, 44:* 1057–1063.

Pynoos, R. S., & and Nader, K. (1993). Issues in the treatment of post traumatic stress disorder in children and adolescents. In J. Wilson & B. Raphael (Eds.). (pp. 535–539). *The international handbook of traumatic stress syndromes.* New York: Plenum Press.

Swiss, S., & Giller, J. E. (1993). Rape as a crime of war: A medical perspective. *Journal of the American Medical Association.* 270(5): 612–615.

Terr, L. C. (1991). Childhood traumas: An outline and overview. *American Journal of Psychiatry.* 148(1): 10–20.

UNICEF, *The state of the world's children, 50th anniversary edition* (1996). Oxford: Oxford University.

van der Kolk, B. A., Roth, S., Pelcovitz, D., & Mandel, F. S. (1992). Disorders of extreme stress: Results from the DSM-IV field trials for PTSD. Unpublished manuscript.

Wilson, J. (1988). Treating the Vietnam veteran. In Frank Ochberg (Ed.), *Post-traumatic therapy and victims of violence* (pp. 254–277). New York:Brunner/Mazel.

Wilson, J., & Keane, T. (Eds.) (1996). *Assessing psychological trauma & PTSD.* New York: Guilford.

Wilson, J., & Lindy, J. (Eds.) (1994). *Countertransference in the treatment of post-traumatic stress disorder.* New York: Guilford.

1

CULTURES OF THE UNITED STATES

2

CHAPTER

Michele A. Tully

Lifting Our Voices: African American Cultural Responses to Trauma and Loss

By and by, when the morning comes
And all the saints are gone to gathering home,
We will tell the story of how we overcome
And we'll understand it better by and by.
Traditional African American song (Scanlan, 1994)

African American culture claims space, recognition, and appreciation in a multicultural country. Some common themes emerge from the extraordinary diversity of African American experiences, including the primacy of spirituality and religious faith; the importance of kinship, friendship, and family ties; the centrality of music and dance as expressions of self; the role of women as ones who unite and sustain families and communities; and the importance of community service and self-help. Each of these cultural elements play a role in response to trauma and loss. Insight into these elements may help practitioners work effectively with African American people.

This chapter frames African American culture in the context of a history of trauma dating from slavery to modern times. It has three parts. The first part introduces the context for discussion including the tools of analysis from Judith Lewis Hermans' (1992) work *Trauma and Recovery*. The second section applies these tools in the light of historic and current conditions. The third section looks at cultural accommodations from the perspective of protection from trauma and healing from trauma. These protective and healing mechanisms are *reconnection* to the power within oneself; *witness* through reframing the trauma story, and *commonality* with a supportive community. It also provides advice for practitioners working with African American people.

☐ Context and Tools for Analysis

Who is African American?

African Americans are people who live in the United States whose ancestry derive from the continent of Africa. Currently, African Americans make up 12.8% of the population of the United States, representing more that 34 million people (U.S. Census, 1997). African Americans are considered to be members of a distinct racial group called "Black." Race is commonly associated with physical features including dark skin, brown eyes, curly hair, and a broad nose. However, racial identity is much deeper and more complex than the sum total of physical characteristics. Throughout history, observers have commented upon the amazing variety of hues in skin tones, and of shapes of faces and bodies of African Americans. This rich, colorful variety is born of the mixing of European, Native American and other peoples into the pool of people defined as American Blacks.

Historically, African ancestry supersedes European ancestry as the defining indication of one's social status. This prominence and permanence of the "touch of the tar brush" has separated even the closest relatives by a razor sharp color line—assigning some to the status of White and others to Black. Many African Americans, including some of the most prominent in American history, have had either one White parent (e.g., Frederick Douglas) or significant European ancestry (e.g., W.E.B. DuBois, Malcom X).

Thus, understanding the meaning of racial identity is complex. African Americans' experiences of life are as varied as that of any other group of Americans. African Americans span all regions, socioeconomic classes, family configurations, religions, professions, and tastes. Most African Americans (85.7%) live in metropolitan areas. More than half (54.7%) live in the South. Only 8.6% live in the West. Forty two percent live in the Northeast while 39% live in the Midwestern region (U.S. Census, 1997).

African Americans occupy all professions. The United States Census (1997) reports that by the age of 25, three fourths of African Americans attain high school graduation; nearly 40% have some college experience; and 13% attain a bachelor's degree or higher. Ten percent of Black males and 11.6% of Black females work as executives, administrators, or managers. Black men are most heavily concentrated in service, precision production, machine operation, and transportation occupations. Nearly half (46%) of Black women were employed in administrative support positions (28.2%) and service occupations (17.9%).

Individual experience of racial identity varies considerably. Few African Americans perceive their race in exactly the same way. Some people's lives and habits have very few traces of a distinct African American heritage. Others feel a very powerful connection to an African heritage—to the point of rejecting the dominant American culture. Over the course of life, a person may experience volatility in his or her racial identity. A child who grew up relatively unaware of African American culture may encounter an experience in adulthood that inspires him or her to take an African name. Others may embrace a strong racial identity in youth, yet give it up later, choosing to make their racial identity secondary to other considerations.

Some contexts, such as extreme poverty, may cause people to mistakenly ascribe values to African American culture that are more related to subsistence and oppression than to any habits rooted in African communities. Others may be tempted to claim every aspect of American culture as African. Some find peace in their racial identity and others never do. For some it is never an issue, simply a fact. For others it is a constant irritation. For still other African Americans, identity is a source of pride and evidence of a connection to the strength of generations who overcame unspeakable hardships to build a new world.

However, collective history and current contexts give African Americans some common experiences. Those defined as Black are aware of it. Being Black is a strong social reality comparable to gender, socioeconomic status, and ethnicity. Yet, many African Americans do not consciously connect their habits and experiences to a distinct African American culture. Becoming aware of this culture and embracing it can be a powerful source of healing.

Tools for Analysis: Definition of Captivity

The systems of slavery, segregation, poverty, and isolation are the backdrop to the cultural stage where individual African Americans live their lives. These common traumas have hurt African Americans by causing experiences of personal loss and humiliation. Herman (1992) defines trauma as an affliction of the powerless. She writes, "At the moment of trauma, the victim is rendered helpless by overwhelming force . . . Traumatic events overwhelm the ordinary systems of care that give people a sense of control, connection, and meaning" (p. 31). Trauma, in the form of chattel slavery, stifling poverty, injustice, segregation, and second-class citizenship is pervasive in historical and present contexts. Even for those African Americans whose present lives are not visibly affected by these forces, the history of collective trauma endures.

Captivity, according to Herman, is an opportunity for prolonged repeated trauma. Captivity creates a relationship of coercive control where the captor seeks to achieve not only power over the victim, but also to extract affirmation, gratitude, and even love. These conditions crush the individual's sense of identity and strike at the heart of community.

Captives are forced into surrender so complete that they will do anything demanded by the captors and fail to act against their captors. Surrender is a death of personality and a betrayal of the self. Once forced into surrender, a captive has given up autonomy. Instead of offering joy, the prospect of life is hopeless. The captor is the only source of power. Captives come to doubt their capacity to act and develop an internal sense of guilty self-loathing, often feeling themselves to be reduced to passive animals or even further to "vegetables" or "refuse" (Herman, 1992, pp. 84, 105).

When social systems support captivity, repeated, systematic trauma becomes a way of life for both the captor and the captive.

☐ Applying the Framework of Captivity to Past and Present Troubles

Slavery: The Crucible of African American Culture

Eileen Southern wrote in her work, *The Music of Black Americans,*

> Africans were taken to the New World in chains, stripped to the bare skin, and those that came to the mainland colonies were separated from their families and communities. But though they could bring no material objects with them they retained their memories of the rich cultural traditions they had left behind in the motherland and passed these traditions down to their children (Southern, 1983).

From the late 1600s to 1860, the country now known as the United States operated a system of race based slavery that was "the most consistent system of racial enslavement in the hemisphere" (Segal, 1995, pp.

61–62). The emotional impact of slavery is overwhelming to consider. Slavery was a theft of self. Slave holders owned the life of the slave—every minute of time, every mouthful of food, every breath. The slave had no humanity in the eyes of the law. As less than human, the life of the slave was constantly at risk. Slavery subjugated all human connections of kinship to the whim of the slave owner. Families were broken up by sale. Slaves could not protect themselves or others from assault. Women and men were always vulnerable to sexual exploitation.

Slaves were made to feel degraded through the weariness of labor and the grinding pressure of rules that denied them any recognition as human beings. Ronald Segal, a scholar of the history of the African experience around the world writes, "Beyond the disruption of families, a regime of repressiveness continually explored new ways of expression. It established the offense of insolence, which might extend from raising a hand against a White to "a look," as one North Carolina judge expounded it: "the pointing of a finger, a refusal to or neglect to step out of the way when a White person is seen to approach" (Segal, 1995, p. 62).

Consistent with Herman's analysis, slave holders required a kind of acceptance from the slaves. Slave holders liked to see themselves as parents—givers of civilization, religion, and moral guidance to Africans. Segal writes of middle- and upper-class Southern Whites "inclined to argue, even believe that the paternalism of Southern slavery was accepted by the slaves themselves as being in their own best interests" (Segal, 1995, p. 55). These justifications were built into a repressive legal and social system strongly enforced by individual attitudes.

Slavery happened in family-sized scale with almost half of the slave owners possessing fewer than five slaves each, and three quarters fewer than ten (Segal, 1995, p. 54). Outward surrender was necessary for physical survival. Some risked their lives to revolt, rebel, run away, or to find ways to earn the money to purchase nonslave status. Slaves made psychological spaces for themselves to live. Segal writes, "Between revolt and collaboration was another country, and it was here that most slaves probably spent their lives. They did so to endure with some dignity in a system directed at depriving them of any" (Segal, 1995, p. 64).

The exact role of slavery in producing modern cultural forms among African Americans and the legacy of the trauma of slavery in the problems of African American communities is controversial. Most writings deal with the historical reality of slavery, yet stop short of making connections between then and now. However, it is reasonable to argue that the historical fact of oppression and the continuing low level of socioeconomic status among the African American population produce a profound mistrust and tension between the dominant group and the minority group.

Segregation and Social Isolation Limit Options for African Americans

Forced separation between African Americans and Whites has been a fact in cities of the Northern states since their earliest development. In the South, however, segregation arose in the wake of the emancipation of slaves. Between 1860 and 1920, African Americans went from living in close proximity to their White neighbors in the South to living in nearly homogenous communities in the South or in Black sections of Northern cities. A legal code arose in Southern legislatures (Jim Crow laws) that excluded the intermingling of Whites and Blacks in public and private places. Public schools, transportation, entertainment facilities, restaurants, and workplaces strictly separated the races.

Segregation was the direct descendent of the race caste system that justified American slavery. It went hand in hand with disenfranchisement of African Americans. Without the political power to demand justice, acts of violence, including public torture and execution[1] went largely unpunished.

Segregation and repression in the South shaped many aspects of African American culture. Segregated communities formed close knit bonds in the rural South. These communities united to shield members from the overwhelming force of White oppression and assisted members to endure hardships of poverty and humiliation. In the best cases, community life supported African American farms, businesses, churches, and institutions. Self-help and mutual assistance flourished.

However, the economic pressure, violence, and degradation of the South drove many to look for better jobs and more chances at freedom in Northern cities. The great migration from the 1910s to the 1950s was the largest population movement in the nation's history involving millions of African Americans.

Past Abuses Persist in African American Lives

African Americans have come a long way toward entering the American economic and social mainstream. The United States Census (1997) reports that nearly a quarter (23.3%) of African American families in 1996 earned $50,000 or more. However, 18.9% of African American families earned less than $10,000 that year, compared to only 4.9% of whites. These figures indicate that alarming inequalities between races are real and persistent.

Like all people in the United States, the vast majority of African Americans live in metropolitan areas (85.7%). However, 63.9% of Blacks live in central cities compared to 28.5% of Whites. Only 36.1% of Blacks live outside of central city areas, compared to 71.5% of Whites. While 22.6% of Whites live in nonmetropolitan areas, only 14.3% of Blacks live in nonmetropolitan areas.

Segregation persists throughout the United States. According to Massey and Denton (1993) in their study of segregation and the causes of persistent poverty, "[O]ne third of all African Americans in the United States live under conditions of intense racial segregation. They are unambiguously among the nation's most spatially isolated and geographically secluded people" (p. 77). People living under conditions of segregation are subject to the power of the dominant group. They have limited access to the economic, social, and political networks that make modern cities live. Massey and Douglas state, "Ironically, within a large, diverse and highly mobile postindustrial society such as the United States, Blacks living in the heart of the ghetto are among the most isolated people on earth." (p. 77) Massey and Douglas argue that since 1970, segregation has produced a situation in American cities where horrifying conditions are inevitable. They call these conditions "mutually reinforcing and self-feeding spirals of decline" (p. 2) in African American neighborhoods.

Contemporary African Americans Live in Poverty, Violence, and Deprivation

More than three fifths (63.9%) of the African American population lives in central urban areas (U.S. Census, 1997). Too often, these areas are characterized by intense poverty, crime, and deprivation. Incidents of violence spill over the streets. Gunfire and assault are constant facts of life. In Chicago, for example, homicide is the most prevalent cause of death among young African American men. Children are witnesses to acts of violence from their earliest years. Witnessing violence is traumatic to everyone involved. Danger replaces safety as the "norm."

The most violent urban areas are easily compared to war zones in that the destruction is evident, and the risk to human life is great. However, unlike a war, there is no predictable end in sight. Peace seems impossible within the community. The desperate conditions seem to go on perpetually. The only way to gain peace would be to gain enough resources to leave and to join the unfamiliar world outside.

The never ending assault upon residents of these communities leads to adaptations that reflect those of captive people. Numbing, minimization, identification with the abusive system, self-loathing and an inability to take steps to protect or end the situation are common. Children are robbed by the harshness of their lives of the freedom to play outside, to fearlessly explore their environment, to rest comfortably in the security that they will receive what they need to thrive. The following is a list of outcomes for children living in chronic community violence. For African American children, the added expectation that their race predetermines their inability to succeed is an additional hardship (Gabarino, Dubrow, Kostelny, & Pardo, 1992).

• Difficulty concentrating because of lack of sleep and intrusive images
• Aggressive play including intimidating behaviors
• Bravado and "tough" actions to hide fears
• Severe constriction in activities, exploration, and thinking for fear of re-experiencing the traumatizing event

Inadequate Support for Children's Grieving

Alarming numbers of violent incidents add up to an accumulation of personal tragedy. Adults must shoulder the burden of their own pain and disappointment and live daily with the reality that they are unable to protect their children and loved ones from experiencing similar tragedies. A study by Pedro Martinez and John Richters (1993) found that parents underestimated the level of distress their children were experiencing as result of exposure to violence (Reiss, Richters). Without understanding how to help their children, parents may feel helpless to respond to their emotional needs. Thus the tragedy of pain and loss continues.

Resilience in Children

African American children living in desperate circumstances can cope with stress in a positive way given the support of adults. Resilient children have a sense of personal control, responsibility for their actions, and can master stress rather than retreat from it (Gabarino, Dubrow, Kostelny & Pardo, 1992). They are oriented toward the future, able to find safety in their lives, and see themselves in a positive light (Gabarino et al., 1992). Compared to less resilient children, they are better able to tolerate frustration, handle anxiety, and ask for help when they need it. Several elements of a child's life contribute to resilience. These are:

- Stable emotional relationship with at least one caregiver (parent or other)
- Educational climate that supports development
- Parent who models and encourages constructive coping
- Support from others outside the family (Garbarino et al., 1992)

These elements support the child's identity as a worthwhile human being and give tangible lessons in how to integrate and work through the stresses of life without becoming overwhelmed. Children with support may not internalize as deeply the messages of powerlessness prevalent in their communities. Rather than assume they can do nothing, they look instead to what they can do to make their circumstances better.

☐ Cultural Accommodations and Advice for Practitioners

African American Culture Protects and Heals

What do African Americans do to defend themselves against the array of traumatizing forces from a repressive society and from the personal experiences of loss? How do they make for themselves a freedom denied them? African Americans have been answering this question for hundreds of years. Traditions of deep spirituality, dedication to family, and the communication of thoughts, feelings, and social commentary through music and storytelling permeate the experience of oppression and appear in the contemporary experience of millions of African Americans.

Herman argues that since the core experience of trauma is disempowerment and disconnection, recovery is based upon reconnection to one's own power and to the fellowship of others (1992). This article discusses elements of African American culture that a) provide connection to a powerful identity; b) give witness to and retell the trauma story; and c) support commonality and community with family as a means of buffering the effects of trauma and supporting healing.

Connection: Religious Faith Defines a Powerful Identity

One way that African Americans voice connection to the power within themselves is through the expression of religious faith. African Americans historically have been a religious people. According to Billingsley in the National Survey of Black Americans at the University of Michigan in 1979–1980 (the first national representative sample of Black adults in the nation) found that 84% of African Americans consider themselves religious. Seventy-eight percent (78%) indicated that they pray daily. Women outnumber men in this activity 84% to 68% (Billingsley, 1992).

One of the most prevalent aspects of faith is the devotion to a personal, living God. In this world view, God is all powerful. God is the source of all creation. This powerful God dwells within the individual and lends His[2] power to the individual, particularly in times of strife.

For Muslims, Allah is revealed through the Koran. The Koran teaches a pure, holy way of life that emphasizes prayer and praise of God. No power rivals that of Allah.

The power of the self is granted from the infinite source of power—God. Sacred songs are a text from which to draw personal strength. Praise for God is like a bright light that drives away shadows of fear and despair. Appeals to God are direct and from the heart. Rather than rote prayer, most African American traditions rely upon extemporaneous verbal or silent prayer. God knows and sees all. Nothing can separate one from the sight of God. The following lyrics are an example of the close, personal, helping relationship between a person and God:

I once was lost in darkness
And my way was dark as night
I called on Christ my Savior
To lead me to the Light
He heard me, He heard me
When I call Him, when I call Him
Right now, right now I am saved . . .
Whenever you are tempted
Try not to complain
Just call on Christ the Savior
When you need a doctor
Just call on Christ the Savior
When you need a lawyer,
Just call on Christ the Savior
He'll always remain the same
(Scanlan, 1994).

For Christians, Jesus is the source of freedom from sin and from death. Jesus is a compassionate friend who understands affliction, betrayal, loneliness, and death because of his own experience of a death upon the cross. Jesus, God's son, shared in human sufferings. He is the most important friend, brother, and supporter. In addition to being a comforter, Jesus is the rightful king and ruler of the world. His word brings peace to the soul. Faithful people sing, "Whenever the Lord says, 'Peace,' there will be peace, peace on the mountain, peace in the valley. When the Lord says, 'peace,' there will be peace."

What one needs to do in order to become connected to God varies. Generally, one needs to publicly acknowledge God and live according to a moral code that is derived from the teachings of the holy book (the Bible). This code is in opposition to the rules of the sinful world.

Thus faith builds a strong inner life, one that is protected by the power of God, the Creator. The world of oppression is less overwhelming. The indignities and injustices are easier to bear, and the joys of life easier to grasp. Even when one is utterly forsaken, left alone, betrayed, and deserted, God is still there. A song attributed to the days of slavery expresses this, "Lord, I couldn't hear nobody pray, and I couldn't hear nobody pray. Way down yonder by myself, I couldn't hear nobody pray. In the valley on my knees, with Jesus, my Savior, Chilly water in the Jordan, I couldn't hear nobody pray" (Scanlan, 1994).[3]

A common theme in making a connection to Jesus is being saved or born again. A saved person is cleansed of sin, forgiven, and blessed with the authority to speak of God's works. In many traditions, one becomes saved in a discrete moment of spiritual ecstasy where one physically receives the spirit of God.[4] This event is marked by movement, speaking in tongues, or other expression. Salvation is accompanied by song, dance, and celebration. A saved person is expected to live an exemplary life, according to the principles of the Bible. People who are born again literally know themselves to be transformed by the power of Jesus. They must testify to the reality of God in their lives and live each day as a celebration of God's blessing. Salvation is an anointing with God's divine protection and is a shield against the corrosive power of the world. A saved soul is protected, nurtured, and maintained by the power of God.

Many African Americans pursue a spiritual life without attending worship services or ascribing to an established religion. Individual meditation and a peaceful connection to oneself and to the earth nourish one's identity and creates a safe place within as a haven against the stresses of the world.

This personal safe space may be found in personal rituals such as gardening, fishing, cooking, crafts, artistic expression, dance, song, and other pursuits.

Witness: Retelling the Trauma Story

Witness means telling the whole truth. Nothing goes unsaid. Traumatized persons require a witness to join with them in decrying the truth of the traumatic event and to support them in their healing. Witness is the first step to justice. Bearing witness is a critical theme in African American song, literature, story, art, and humor.

The audience for this witness is the African American community itself. Songs particularly speak to God and to friends. They are heard, but are often misunderstood by the enemies they criticize. Spirituals achieve this disguise masterfully. They were carefully designed to be heard by Whites, but understood only by those with the capacity to understand. Humor is a particularly powerful tool for witness in that it both presents the reality and ridicules the power of the oppressor. It is a means of mastery of a situation that redefines the situation and reduces it to a manageable proportion.

Witness Takes the Form of Songs, Stories, and Humor.

Witness takes place in many contexts and is used both to show the negative and to praise the positive in life. For example, one can be both a witness to the power and glory of God, and a witness to the evil of humanity. The African American songs from the earliest slave composed melodies to the newest rap and hip-hop tunes perform this function. One pervasive characteristic in the power of songs and stories is that they recreate the true emotion of the experience. A single tone, without words, causes one to experience the joy or sadness of the music makers. Frederick Douglass writes of the songs he heard as a slave child:

> [The songs] breathe a prayer and complaint of soul boiling over with the bitterest anguish. Every tone was a testimony against slavery, and a prayer to God for deliverance from chains . . . I have frequently found myself in tears while hearing them. The mere recurrence of those songs, even now afflicts me; and while writing these lines, an expression of feeling has already found its way down my cheek (Douglass 1845/1995).

Songs called the blues are about witness. They declare the depth of feeling in the singer and musicians. They cry out in agony, pain, loss, rage, and occasionally in lusty ecstasy. They claim the freedom, humanity, and vivacity of the Black soul. Richard Wright spoke of the blues this way:

> Yet, the most astonishing aspect of the blues is that, though replete with a sense of defeat and downheartedness, they are not intrinsically pessimistic; their burden of woe and melancholy is dialectically redeemed through sheer force of sensuality, into an almost exultant affirmation of life, of love, of sex, of movement, of hope. No matter how repressive was the American environment, the Negro never lost faith in or doubted his deeply endemic capacity to live (Oliver, 1960).

Rap and hip-hop music are contemporary versions of ancient traditions that testify to reality and challenge the world. The music puts oppression on display. Tricia Rose, in her study of rap music analyzes the text of a rap song, noting that the artists are keenly aware of the role they play as truth tellers and their connection to their ancestors. She writes, "In this way, rap is 'nothing we ain't did before.' Slave dances, blues lyrics, Mardi Gras parades, Jamaican patios, toasts, and signifying all carry the pleasure and ingenuity of disguised criticism of the powerful" (Rose, 1994, p. 99). Currently, these songs speak of the hostility and tension between the police and Black youth and reveal the inner dynamics of the pain within Black communities. The songs challenge, brag, defend, and confront. They are the voice of urban African Americans articulated forcefully and boldly. These works provide insight into perspective on life, and even while speaking the crudest and hardest language, they declare power and vitality within the African American self.

Storytelling bears witness, warns, reviles, and inspires the listeners. As descendants of Africans, African Americans retain an oral tradition. Spoken words are highly valued. The speaker and listener engage with one another. To listen to a story (or sermon or prayer) is a joy and a comfort. Listening styles are active, with a listener responding to the call of the teller. What may sound like an interruption is an affirmation ("I hear you," "keep going," "Amen," "say it," "make it plain"). The speed and pace of conversation varies. Hands, arms, eyes, and whole bodies are involved in the engagement of the story.

African American stories tell hard truth and face oppression head on. Ossie Davis speaks of the dual purpose of the stories he calls "history" and the others made for fun. He writes, "History was a warning. History was a rope that kept trying to save little boys from quicksand. How to avoid confrontation with the Klu Klux Klan and being lynched . . . But it was to storytelling that I ran, as fast as I could, laughing in advance at the thought of the pleasure and surprise that was surely waiting for me" (Goss & Goss, 1995).

Traditional stories use humor to teach lessons about survival. The "signifying monkey" and "Brer' Rabbit" come from African traditions of using animals as the actors in tales. Usually the protagonist overcomes difficulty through some kind of trick or is shown up for foolishness.

Like all people, African Americans' folk tales have veiled the harshest truths in images and double meaning. However, in the written tradition, starting with the narratives of slaves from Frederick Douglas to Linda Brent, the most harrowing of trauma stories are retold with searing language. African American poets and writers from Phyllis Wheatly to those of the present day are not shy about exposing violence, sexuality, exploitation, death, or trauma. With power and grace African American writers tell tales that educate, move, and warn the reader. The reader is placed at the foot of the overseer as he wields the lash, in the bedroom of the female slave as she hears the steps of the master approach[5] These stories are told as bold statements of the trials African Americans have endured and the burdens yet to be overcome. They are a witness to the inner and outer life of a people.

Commonality and Community: Family and Friends Guard Against the Effects of Trauma

Family and friends are another important source of protection from trauma and a source of healing after a traumatic experience. Family ties are vitally important. Families provide the basics of life including food, shelter, love, guidance, and identity. The National Survey of Black Adults showed that "what makes African American women and men feel good about themselves is having good relationships with their family members and friends. This pattern of expressive relations helps cushion the inequities of life inflicted upon them by the greater society" (Billingsley, 1992). Families come in many varieties, from traditional married couple households to families where no parent is present and children are raised by grandmothers, aunts, or other relatives. Extended family networks provide resources for child care, child rearing, economic support, and shelter as well as recreation and moral support. While marriage rates have declined precipitously in some communities, most dramatically among the poorest African Americans, the value of kinship is strong.

Families don't necessarily live together. The bonds of mutual obligation and care holds them together even across great distances. Children may spend significant portions of their childhood living with relations in different parts of the country. Mothers and fathers[6] in the North may send their children to live with grandmothers or aunts in Southern towns. Children may not bond most strongly with their biological parents, instead bonding with the member of the family with whom they have the strongest link of love. Some African Americans will speak of having a play mother or second mother who is not a blood relation, but has a very special tie to them. Unrelated families may intertwine so closely that they become indistinguishable. Persons of similar ages become friends and supporters. It is a source of great joy when cousins solidify their blood relationships with the bonds of friendship.

Families Teach Children to Cope.   Another function of the family is to socialize children to cope with the realities of being Black in a society dominated by Whites. By doing this job, they function as a buffer between their children and a racist world (Billingsley, 1992). These lessons take hold in the personalities and identities of children. Understandably, parents may pass on self-doubt and self-loathing with their desire to educate their children. They may teach them to limit their dreams to those appropriate for a lower station in life. Or families, particularly those who have themselves succeeded, teach children to take pride in themselves and their heritage and to rely upon their sense of self-worth to combat the negative messages from the world. James Baldwin takes on this task in his "Letter to my Nephew on the 100th Anniversary of the Emancipation,"

> I keep seeing your face, which is also the face of your father, my brother. Like him you are tough, dark, vulnerable and moody—with a very definite tendency to sound truculent because you want no one to think you are soft. You may be like your grandfather in this . . . he had a terrible life; he was defeated long before he died because, at the bottom of his heart, he really believed what White people said about him. . . . You are of another era. You can only be destroyed by believing that you really are what the White world calls nigger. I tell you this because I love you, and please don't ever forget it . . . I know how black it looks today, for you. It looked bad [the day you were born] too, yes, we were trembling. We haven't stopped trembling yet, but if we had not loved each other none of us would have survived. And now you must survive because we love you, and for the sake of your children and your children's children (Goss & Goss, 1995).

Becoming Tough Combats:
The Overwhelming Nature of Trauma

In addition to comfort and care, some African Americans also seek to toughen themselves and their children to confront the world. For example, these strategies may include use of corporal punishment and relentless teasing. The purpose is to produce endurance and forbearance essential for survival and to connect the person to the identity within the family or community.

Once again, it is important to emphasize that every person's background differs. These strategies are not unique to African Americans, and may reflect a broader context of other peoples living under oppressive social and economic conditions.

For many children the consequence for misbehavior and/or disobedience is some form of physical punishment. Mothers are often the disciplinarians. In close knit communities, caring adults may participate in monitoring children's behavior and, occasionally, in physical discipline of children.

Playing the "dozens," "ribbing," and "talking trash," are games of personal insult played by children and adults. Players take turns saying bad things about one another in humorous ways. This kind of talk is a way of establishing dominance—the one who can take it best and who can re-turn it best wins. Wordplay and the creative use of language is a highly prized skill. One gains prestige and respect through the use of words to form and shape the world. Name calling and calling people out for a con-frontation requires more than brute meanness. It requires mental agility and skill. Many people think of it as harmless, even building up the ego against insults. But it can also become an outlet for real feelings of ag-gression, inadequacy, and shame.

Being tough minded may also include negative attitudes toward Whites and others. By asserting the superiority of the Black race, one builds up status. In some sectors, Whites are called blue eyed devils, and ascribed all the worst characteristics of humankind. "Never trust a white person—know who you are" is taught from generation to generation. In addition, stories are handed down of the actual atrocities and realities of oppression. In this context being tough means resisting trust and social contact with others in order to protect oneself from potential injury and to prove allegiance to one's own kind.

These toughening mechanisms can deeply injure self-esteem and perpet-uate a shallow identity at the expense of a real connection to oneself. Being tough may mean creating an emotional seal over difficult feelings. Uncon-sciously, toughening tears down rather than builds relationships and feel-ings of self-worth. It reaffirms the powerlessness that is at the heart of trauma. In seeking to defend against hurts, family and friends intensify it.

It is very important to understand that the experiences described, though painful, are more complex. Instead of fracturing the identity of the person, the experience may fit into a larger context. In fact, learning to integrate violence into one's identity without becoming overwhelmed may be the goal of toughening.

It is important to emphasize that violence takes a long lasting toll on the psyche and that toughening is a convenient excuse for terrorizing and abusing others. This is particularly true when the pain inflicted reaf-firms the oppression and powerlessness in an abusive relationship or when it serves to reassert one's inferior position in a social system. The impact of being bound tightly to an identity (as a member of a family or race of people) that one also believes to be flawed or inferior is also hurt-ful to an identity. Resolving these conflicts of love and pain may be an important part of making a true connection to oneself.

Building Strong Communities

African Americans yearn to build communities where families are sup-ported, children are raised, and elders enjoy the respect that they deserve. Social service and community self-help are some of the oldest traditions in African American life. The ethic of service, expressed through institutions and associations, infuses the community with energy. Community members, particularly children, find in these organizations the external social support critical for building resilience to stress.

From the earliest days of slavery to the present, African Americans have contributed to the care of one another. Volunteer organizations, churches, nonprofit organizations and informal helping networks have been until recent decades some of the only sources of relief from destitution. These associations include national service organizations such as the Black Women's Health Network, sororities and fraternities, clubs like the Lions, Elks and Rotaries, and nonprofit human service organizations such as community centers, food pantries, and child care centers. This care both provides tangible and moral support to others and reasserts the power of African Americans to help themselves. Giving to others can be a source of healing oneself.

Political Unity

Consistent political unity creates a sense of oneness. African Americans, for all of their diversity, have an extraordinary history of successful collective action. The American Civil Rights movement mobilized peaceful mass action that brought about the end of legal segregation in the South, eradicating from the laws of the United States the vestiges of chattel slavery and color caste oppression. Recently the Million Man March mobilized roughly 20% of the adult African American population to be at the same place at the same time for a day of atonement. They sought freedom from the tyranny of internalized oppression. They sought to reclaim their inner lives for the good of themselves, their families, their communities, and their nation. This demonstration of unity meant many things to many people. At its core was hope for a better future.

This section examined aspects of African American culture that contribute to the critical processes of healing from trauma and loss. The beauty, complexity, and variety in African American experiences and cultural forms are a treasure. Understanding these elements and incorporating them into interventions may provide a means to create a meaningful, healing connection. These cultural forms are evidence of the many ways people have sought to claim their right to live fully. Helping professionals can facilitate the unique processes that individuals and communities make for themselves to address their problems. Empathy, practical assistance, humility, and a sense of humor are valuable assets entering any helping situation. Working in a different cultural context brings these truths to the forefront.

Advice for Practitioners Serving African American People

All practitioners, even Blacks and other non Whites, may be viewed by some African Americans as others or White until they reveal themselves to be real people. Being accepted as "real" may be a challenge, particularly if the people one encounters are not used to dealing with others different from them. Distinguishing one's own personality from the prejudices in the minds of coworkers and clients is a critical task. While it may take time, flexibility, patience, and endurance, it is the basis for rapport.

Whites may encounter hostility if they are seen as coopting the authority of African Americans. A White woman may be required to prove her toughness and to assert her personality. Genuine personal warmth and willingness to share of one's own story and discuss family and friends will help the practitioner to be seen as someone with a life in addition to being a professional. Its important, however to maintain healthy boundaries.

Male practitioners should be aware of the need to distinguish themselves from the prejudices that may face them. They may symbolize oppression, and all the hurts associated with it. In extreme cases, the practitioner may experience outright hostility or harassment. Telling his own story, particularly revealing the reasons for taking on the job at hand, may help to establish that the practitioner is a real person. Also, communicating that his feelings, just like anyone elses, deserve to be treated with respect. This may be surprising to those unaccustomed to seeing Whites as similar to themselves.

Greetings and Etiquette about Feelings

Greetings are very important. A warm smile, handshake, and the use of a formal title and last name demonstrate respect. It is customary to repeat greetings to a person upon every occasion of seeing them, even on the same day. One often recounts the last time one has seen someone. This recognition and greeting affirms a relationship.

It is important to show that one is pleased with the company of others, if it is sincere. Insincerity is a grave insult. It's acceptable to have a bad day or to be in an evil mood. Sharing burdens makes them lighter. However, it is important to laugh more easily than to complain, to smile more often than frown, and to give kind attention to others rather than to drag a cloud over the heads of everyone.

Negotiating Cultural Territory

Crossing traditional lines between White and Black can be jarring. Hearing about their lives, culture, and history from an outsider can feel like a violation. For example, a person may say, "that's mine" or "that's ours" in relation to a fashion, musical style, or saying. In recent years, a popular T-shirt read "It's a Black thing—you don't understand." This stance may be an extension of culture as territory. Hearing a value judgment, even if it is positive may feel like a personal affront.[7] Some people seek to guard African American things for themselves and people like themselves, guarding the space that buffers their identity.

Professionalism

Like everyone else, African Americans may assume professionals are all knowing and have the power to fix things. The personal experience of victimization by the abuse of power and the stories of others who have been mistreated may poison a relationship with suspicion and reluctance to trust. Deep feelings of inadequacy and shame may make a person unwilling to share. This is particularly true in regard to old fashioned or country ways. African Americans may be reluctant to speak of their traditional means of coping or talk openly about what really feels right for them because they feel inferior to the professional's expertise. They may need permission to talk about prophetic dreams, spirits, their religious faith, and their family.

Physical aid, tangible help, and the accomplishment of designated goals increase the legitimacy of the helping professional and build trust. Real help comes from real people. Specific markers of progress are important.

The concept of emotional help as legitimate and real may be difficult. Such help may contradict the values of self-sufficiency and mental toughness. Emphasizing the person's right to experience their feelings freely, and to acknowledge their pain and vulnerability in a safe, healing environment may help put the experience into perspective. Also, it is important to acknowledge the person's courage to make the choice to seek help, and to validate their own unique process of healing.

Confidentiality

Confidentiality is important on many levels. It is the first step in establishing trust, yet it may be compromised in important ways. In some situations, notes from individual client sessions can be used by law enforcement agencies. Most helping professionals are required to report suspected cases of child abuse and neglect. Social workers and psychologists may be asked to testify in court about their interactions with clients. All of these create dilemmas of loyalty, trust, and obligation.

Some common dilemmas result from a lack of confidence in the systems that are involved in the lives of clients. For example, a day care center worker may identify potential abuse yet worry that reporting to child welfare systems may cause the family to withdraw the child, or that the child will be removed from his or her home, causing further psychological stress. A social worker may be reluctant to disclose in case notes the full content of a session where a disturbing or violent incident was recounted for fear of creating evidence used in a criminal proceeding. These issues should be carefully and thoroughly discussed, and professional confidentiality policies should be well understood so that these situations can be handled deliberately when they arise.

☐ Other Important Issues

Medicine in Healing

Healing takes on many dimensions. The body, mind, spirit, and relationships to one's family and community are all involved in the healing process. Healing in one dimension is incomplete without the others. Integration of positive, healthy habits into daily patterns of life should be the ultimate goal. African Americans have been largely on their own in terms of gaining the resources necessary to bring about healing. Access to professional medical care has been limited. Lack of money, lack of information, and a deep suspicion of the motives of the formal medical system contribute to a rift between African Americans and health care professionals.

African medical traditions rely upon the belief that the natural and the spiritual worlds affect mental health and physical health. The consumption of herbs, use of nonfood items (sometimes called pica) from clay to laundry starch, and a search for a spiritual cause for illness are all a part of African American healing traditions (Dixon, 1994). These traditions are not uniform, yet they have consistent themes. Healing may be viewed as an inner process brought about with the facilitation of outside forces. This contrasts with a Western medical model that poses healing as outside the person.

Some African Americans believe in a dichotomy: healing comes from God and sickness comes from the devil (Satan). Thus, God is the best doctor, and in order to get and remain well one must root out Satan. Healing is a gift from God and evidence of His mastery over evil in the world.

Distrust of doctors results from historical and current experiences of racial discrimination, poor health care services, and negative treatment by health care professionals. These attitudes are well founded upon the history of rejection and abuse by the medical profession. Many African Americans have had traumatic experiences of being mistreated, ignored, or experimented upon by medical professionals. Even if this is not their own personal experience, they have likely heard stories of abuse.

This isn't surprising, given that poverty status and race discrimination have consigned African Americans to the lowest tiers as patients. African Americans, particularly poor populations, have been used to study disease processes.[8] Many African Americans suspect that they are used to test new medical products and dangerous procedures.

The medical profession in the United States has a long history of misunderstanding and mistreating African Americans. From the 1800s until the middle part of this century, medical science asserted that Blacks were physiologically very different from Whites and others. Among these assertions were that Blacks had fewer nerves, thicker skin, smaller brains, larger sexual organs, smaller lungs, greater susceptibility to insanity, less intellectual capacity, and a superhuman ability to bear the heat of the sun (Stanton, 1960). Clearly, these assertions had much to do with preserving slavery and the color caste system. However, these assertions still crop up among medical professionals and may influence attitudes toward treatment.

While many are justifiably dubious of their ability to get the help they need, the Western medical model is accepted. Folk remedies passed down through generations are also used. Many remedies came from ingenuity and invention when no money was available for doctors. Healing foods, natural medicines, and a desire to purify or cleanse the body are traditional components of healing.

Purification of lifestyle correlates to physical purification. Purification can come through intense periods of prayer that may be accompanied by fasting and sexual abstinence. It may also come in the form of atonement in personal relationships and in a community. People may return to church for purification with the guidance of a spiritual leader, friend, or family member.

Death

Death is a loss to the living but can be considered a gain for the one who died. Death is sometimes seen as freedom from the trials of life. Many believe in death as a return home to the arms of a loving God. Some refer to death as "Homegoing." In some traditions, the one who died is crowned in glory and receives the dignity, honor, and prestige in death earned in a life of toil.

Grieving is both public and private. Publicly, family members, including children, are expected to express their sadness with friends and others. Friends and family gather at the house of the relatives and bring gifts of food, money, and other necessary items. Family members will travel long distances to attend funerals and be with the grieving survivors. If the deceased is the matriarch or patriarch of a family or a community leader, funeral guests could number into the hundreds.

Privately, death is a hardship because it leaves a gap in the network of family and friends relied upon for support. The loss of a mother or grandmother in particular is not only emotionally hard to bear, but also may mean a significant disruption in daily life for those who depend upon her for child care, food, comfort, and love.

The spirits of the dead may be believed to be quite active. People will say that they talk to deceased loved ones in dreams and speak of feeling the presence of the spirits helping or hurting them. Rather than debate the reality of these experiences, listening for their meaning in the life of the one experiencing them is valuable.

African Americans also speak of "living death" for those who have lost themselves through addiction, criminality, or "total surrender" to oppression. "Going over the other side" can mean both physical death and living death of becoming a criminal or an addict.

Codes of Morality

Morality depends upon the upbringing of the individual. Conservative Christian homes tend to require high moral standards for physical and sexual purity. Muslims are also very strict in their abstinence from mind-altering substances and insistence upon purity of mind, body, and spirit. Many households have very strict rules against profanity. These standards can create a very narrow road from which it is easy to stray and much harder to get back on track.

Other African Americans believe in a liberal tolerance within a framework of common sense values. Lawlessness is rarely condoned. Vices of any kind are largely looked down upon as self-destructive and weakening to the body and spirit. While in some communities criminality is accepted as a way of life, it is not the crime, but the resulting wealth, status, and power generated through crime that is condoned. Crime against others within the Black community is a source of shame.

Given the preponderance of African Americans affected by the law enforcement system, many African Americans do not assume that a person is automatically bad because they have been convicted of a crime. African Americans, particularly men, are arrested and imprisoned disproportionately to their presence in the population. In many communities there is a willingness to see beyond the negative history to the present circumstances, coupled with the belief that people have the capacity to change themselves for the better.

Important Rituals

African American prayer times are traditionally Sunday mornings and may extend into the afternoon. Some traditions also celebrate one night per week (such as Wednesday). Any time may be the right time to pray, however. Community gatherings and public meetings (both formal and informal) often start and close with prayer. These prayers are generally words of praise, giving glory and thanks to the Creator and blessing those assembled.

Rituals celebrate milestones in life such as births, birthdays, weddings, graduations, and funerals. These are often very similar in style and structure to other American festivities. People may drink alcohol, play live music or recordings, dance, talk, eat, and enjoy. Family feasts at Christmas, Easter, and on Sundays are commonly celebrated occasions. Summertime family reunions may reunite hundreds of related people from all over the nation and the world. Occasionally T-shirts, printed materials, and other souvenirs will proudly declare one's kinship.

Families gather at funerals. Death is the only sure event of life, with weddings, lavish Christmases and graduation celebrations missing from the lives of many. The family owes tribute to the one who has died. Failing to honor the dead is considered a wrong that may be paid for by disharmony with the spirit of the one who died. Funerals are important for the completion of a life and repose of a soul. Funerals, even in the poorest communities, are important rituals to say farewell, honor memories, and celebrate the life of the deceased.

Funerals can be very different ranging from somber, silent affairs to uproarious parades with loud music and celebration. Most funerals are celebrated in funeral parlors like other American funerals. Many funerals culminate in a meal at the home of a surviving relative or other gathering place.

Rituals of hospitality are strong, particularly among the elderly. Refreshments are usually offered to guests. Eating is polite and honors the hosts. Requesting guests to eat heartily is a widespread custom. The comfort of the guest is the most important goal. Guests should show their appreciation cheerfully with sincere sharing of joy at being in the home of friends. Occasionally alcohol will be shared at special occasions, and special gifts of food will be made. Having an outdoor barbecue is a honor for special guests.

Style of Approaching Goals

African Americans are Americans. They have been educated in American schools, reared by American television, and held to American rules. In community settings, however, there may be stylistic issues that show a distinct African flavor. For example, punctuality may not be considered very important. The pace of conversations may not be rushed. Relationships are key to accomplishing goals and people's connections must be nurtured. However, American ideals of industry and accomplishment are very deeply rooted.

Powerlessness and deep seated suspicion, not culture, may interfere with meeting goals. Depending on the context, some expectations may be depressed by expectation of failure and inadequacy. A response may be to either overcompensate and overachieve, or assume the worst and underperform. What people want and what they believe is possible may be quite different. Building confidence in the ability to make positive change and demonstrating competency and capacity to do so are valuable ways to go beyond the issues that interfere with attaining goals.

Authority

Persons with authority must earn respect. Because of the abuse of hierarchical power, it may be suspect. Within the culture, power is invested in those who have assumed adult responsibilities. Women gain authority as mothers, grandmothers, and as providers for their families. This role as a leader is acceptable. While male authority is quite respectable, African Americans display quite a bit of power sharing between men and women in and outside of the home. Women unite their families and communities. Elderly women, especially, hold a place of honor and respect.

☐ Conclusion

African American cultural traditions foster coping, resiliency and recovery from trauma. Those who make the connection to this heritage find pride in the struggle for freedom. This call for freedom is common to African peoples around the world. It is a deep expression of the human spirit. African Americans can claim themselves by coming closer to a consciousness of culture and history that goes beyond the trauma of slavery and the humiliation of captivity. Helping professionals willing to stretch their own boundaries can help this unique healing process to happen.

☐ Endnotes

[1]Lynching was a common practice that included not only hanging but also burning, beating, torture, and dismemberment. Lynchings were public spectacles where onlookers took grisly souvenirs. Ida B. Wells, an African American organizer and activist published the Red Record an account of lynching in the South in an effort to bring public opinion to bear against the practice. Please see Duster, Alfreda M. (ed.) *Crusade for Justice: The Autobiography of Ida. B. Wells*, University of Chicago Press, Chicago, 1970.

[2]God is male in the vast majority of songs, images, and teachings, although the power of God is manifest in both men and women. In some expressions, God is also mother-like as in James Weldon Johnson's poem *The Creation* where the author speaks of God "like a mammy bending over her baby."

[3]According to Scanlan and others, slaves sang this song to cancel rendezvous to escape to freedom or to warn of unsuccessful escape attempts.

[4]James Baldwin speaks eloquently of the meaning of being saved in his work *Go Tell it on the Mountain* and of the life of a small congregation of African Americans in the tradition of sanctification in his play *Amen Corner.*

[5]*Autobiography of Frederick Douglas* (mid 1800s) by Frederick Douglas, *Incidents in the Life of a Slave Girl* (mid 1800s) by Linda Brent. Other stories of note include *Quicksand* (1930s) by Nella Larson, *For Colored Girls who Have Considered Suicide When the Rainbow Isn't Enuf* (1970s) by Nikki Giovanni, and *Beloved* (1980s) by Toni Morrison.

[6]Many fathers don't live with their children, yet are very important in their lives. Often a father's family will be just as important as the mother's in providing support and care, even if the parents are separated.

[7]For example, an African American friend of the author took offense at a White person's reference to the Civil Rights movement. She said "[the person] shouldn't even be talking about that. That was us." While she knew intellectually that freedom was the goal of the movement, her gut reaction was one of anger that her cultural territory was somehow usurped by another.

[8]One of the most infamous cases is the Tuskeegee Institute study of syphilis that consigned 400 adult men to years of agony so that the course of the disease would be better understood. The study took place over 40 years from the 1930s through the 1960s and is chronicled in James Jones' (1992) *Bad Blood.*

☐ References

Billingsley, A. (1992). *Climbing Jacob's ladder: The enduring legacy of African American families.* New York: Simon and Schuster.

Dixon, B. (1994). *Good health for African Americans.* New York: Crown Trade.

Douglass, F. (1845/1995). *Narrative of the life of Frederick Douglass.* New York: Dover Publications.

Gabarino, J., Dubrow, N., Kostelny, K., & Pardo, C. (1992). *Children in danger: Coping with the consequences of community violence.* San Francisco: Jossey Bass.

Goss, L., & Goss, C. (1995). *Jump up and say!: A collection of black storytelling.* New York: Simon and Schuster.

Herman, J. (1992). *Trauma and recovery: The aftermath of violence from domestic abuse to political terror.* New York: Basic Books.

Jones, J. (1981). *Bad blood: The Tuskegee syphilis experiment.* New York: Free Press.

Martinez, P., & Richters, J. E. (1993). The NIMH community violence project II: Children's distress symptoms associated with violence exposure. In D. Reiss, J. Richters, M. Radke-Yarrow, & D. Scarff (Eds.), *Children and violence.* New York: Guilford.

Massey, D., & Denton, N. (1993). *American apartheid: Segregation and the making of the underclass.* Cambridge, MA: Harvard University Press.

Oliver, P. (1960). *Blues fell this morning: The meaning of the blues.* New York: Horizon Press.

Rose, T. (1994). *Black noise: Rap music and Black culture in contemporary America.* Hanover, NH: Wesleyan University Press.

Scanlan, M. (Ed.). (1994). *Wade in the water, African American sacred music traditions: Educators guide.* National Public Radio.

Segal, R. (1995). *The Black diaspora: Five centuries of the Black experience outside Africa.* New York: Farrar, Straus and Girox.

Southern, E. (1983). *The music of Black Americans: A history.* New York: North & Co.

Stanton, W. (1960). *The leopard's spots: Scientific attitudes toward race in America 1815–1859.* Chicago: University of Chicago Press.

United States Census Bureau. (1997). *Black population in the United States, March 1997 (update) tables* [On-line]. Available: http://www.census.gov/population/www/socdemo/race/black97tabs.html.

3

CHAPTER

B. Hudnall Stamm,
Henry E. Stamm

Trauma and Loss in Native North America: An Ethnocultural Perspective

He always said "Let's do it!" with enthusiasm to propel those around him. With boiling excitement, he hurried to finish, speaking with friends, doling out this and that, apportioning to each according their gifts. With one friend he played message tag. Then he was off to Providenia for his research trip. In a traditional skin boat, on the Bering Sea with a group of the men from the village, he was experiencing life as it had been for the past thousands of years. This was for "the healing of our people." The boats never returned. Later, his friends gathered to mourn and relate stories of dreams of visits from Bill. As the months passed, many marveled at Bill's wisdom in giving away his work. This chapter, given away by Dr. William Richards, written by the people to whom the call was never made, is dedicated to him, to his trust in the value of integrating traditional and modern healing and most importantly to his dream, "for the healing of our people."[1]

Bill Richards died trying to increase his knowledge of traditional ways. Dr. Richards' life and death plunged him into the heart of Native North America, a legacy filled with cultural and generational trauma brought on by centuries of natural disasters, racism, oppression, warfare, and catastrophic disease. Yet, that legacy also possesses deep pools of protective cultural strength.

After a brief introduction, we proceed in four major sections: 1) Place and time, considering the importance of land, community, and spirituality; 2) The interrelated issues affecting health and interventions; 3) Important beliefs and ceremonies; and 4) Problems of native life and the challenge of balancing culture and science. Examining traditional culture runs the risk of inaccurately romanticizing earlier times as places of few ills (e.g., Calloway, 1997; Fortine, 1992; Kleinman, 1993; Young & Xiao, 1993). Instead, we pragmatically draw from scientific research, traditional stories, and ethnohistory to try to paint a realistic picture.

☐ Introduction

While not every individual Native North American suffers from a painful inheritance of racism, oppression, warfare, and catastrophic disease, its presence cannot be ignored. The Canadian government formally apologized for the damage done to the Aboriginal populations. The soul wounds are real, the loss of and discrimination against traditional culture are endemic and ongoing. Poverty, alcoholism, suicide, diabetes, unemployment, incarceration, and mental and physical disorders, create a high risk environment (Abel, 1995; LaDue, 1994; Manson et al., 1996; Marsella, Friedman, Gerrity & Scurfield, 1996; Robin, Chester & Goldman, 1996; Tafoya & Del Vecchio, 1996). The tension of living in two worlds, of being aware—however strongly or vaguely—of traditional views while being inundated with modern mass media produces cultural conflict. During the Oka Crisis (1990), for example, Mohawks and the Quebec Provincial police (and later the Canadian Armed Forces) were in a deadly standoff over land rights for 78 days before the Mohawks voluntarily withdrew. Conflicts emerge within the native community in the form of tribal or reservation politics (Anders & Anders, 1986), intergenerational relationships (Condon, 1995) or constructing health care interventions (Foulks, 1989; Westermeyer, 1989; Wolf, 1989).

Yet, native communities retain reserves of cultural power—widespread kinship networks, shared language (or world views shaped by language systems even when the language has been lost), and a rich history of stories, songs, ceremonies, and spiritual beliefs. This cultural reservoir adds to the difficulty of discussing trauma and loss in native communities. There are hundreds of different native peoples and languages spread over the geographical diversity of North America—over

250 active languages are native to North America (Bright, 1994; Talbot, 1994). Most importantly, there are wide ranging reactions to collective and individual trauma and loss. Some adhere tenaciously to traditional values, beliefs, and practices; some choose the ways of the dominant Western culture; and some seek models of behaviors that reflect both worlds.

These cultural variations pose problems for those who would work in Aboriginal, American Indian, or Native Alaska communities. Short of long term listening to, watching, and learning from a particular group of people, there are few commonalties for workers to understand native North Americans. "Ethnocultural differences among people are tied to variations in the social construction of reality, the perception of what constitutes a traumatic experience, as well as the individual and social response to it" (Friedman & Marsella, 1996, p. 13).

☐ Place and Time

The Calendars

Ojibwa (Great Lakes)

1. Long moon, spirit moon
2. Moon of the suckers
3. Moon of the crust on the snow
4. Moon of the breaking of snowshoes
5. Moon of the flowers and blooms
6. Moon of strawberries
7. Moon of raspberries
8. Moon of whortle berries
9. Moon of gathering wild rice
10. Moon of the falling of leaves
11. Moon of freezing
12. Little moon of the spirit

Kwakiutl (Northwest Coast)

1. Spawning season/season of floods
2. Elder brother/first olachen run
3. Raspberry sprouting season/no sap in trees
4. Raspberry season
5. Huckleberry season/oil moon
6. Saladberry season/sockeye month

7. Southeast wind moon
8. Empty boxes
9. Wide faces
10. Right moon
11. Sweeping houses/dog salmon month
12. Fish in river moon/month of falling leaves
13. Split both ways

Netchilli (Arctic)

1. It is cold, the Eskimo is freezing
2. The sun is returning
3. The sun is ascending
4. The seal brings forth her young
5. The young seals are taking to the sea
6. The seals are shedding their coats
7. Reindeer bring forth their young/birds are brooding
8. The young birds are hatched
9. The reindeer is migrating southward
10. Amerairui
11. The Eskimo lay down food deposits
12. The sun disappears (Rothenberg, 1986, p. 243–245)

Native peoples are rooted in place. Traditions, beliefs, and customs of bands and tribal groups originated with respect to geography and environmental conditions (Nabokov, 1991). The calendars reveal intricacies of understanding time in relation to place. Compare the names of the months. Raspberries are collected in month seven in the Great Lakes and month four on the Pacific coast. The Arctic calendar includes the disappearance and return of the sun, but says nothing about leaves (because there are no trees). Rice is important in the Great Lakes, reindeer in the Arctic.

Geographical boundaries overlap and cross national borders. While not entirely satisfactory, several authors (Champagne, 1994, Taylor & Sturtevant, 1991) suggest the following culture areas for North American aboriginal lands: Northeast (which includes most of the Great Lakes), the Southeast, the Southwest, the Northern Plains, the Northwest Coast, Alaska, Oklahoma, California, Plateau, Great Basin, Rocky Mountains, and Canada.

Although market economy and the ubiquitous television have irrevocably altered traditional economies, most Indian peoples identify inextricabley with the natural world (Talbot, 1994). Moreover, geographic dislocation can cause severe distress (O'Sullivan & Handal, 1988; Palinkas, Downs, Petterson, & Russell, 1993; Palinkas, Petterson, Russell,

& Downs, 1993). Tribal histories, patterns of agriculture, hunting, family structures, and spiritual beliefs, as well as community and individual interactions are inseparable from the local environment. Even relocated (by choice or force) communities' understandings of their ancestral land affect ceremonies and customs.

For example, a counselor who moves from Pine Ridge Reservation in South Dakota to Kotzebue, Alaska should know that sage or sweetgrass offerings, important to Oglala Lakota ceremonies, have no parallel meaning to Inupiat peoples. Similarly, corn was a vital ceremonial staple to many Southeastern peoples, such as Creeks or Chickasaws, but unknown to residents of the Pacific Northwest, whose lives revolved around salmon fishing (Boxberger, 1994; O'Donnell, 1994). To ignore environmental factors means to ignore the very context from which Native North Americans come and may well inadvertently sabotage effectiveness as a helper (Schmidt, 1988).

Family, Politics, and Tribal Life

> The Creek Confederacy was (and still is) based on so-called towns. These are social and political units more than residential ones. . . . The towns were divided into two groups, sometimes called sides, usually characterized as white and red. The white or "peace towns" were preeminent in civil affairs, while the red or "war" towns were dominant in military matters. . . . The affiliations of a town as either white or red was not permanent, however. A town changed sides if it was defeated four successive times by a town on the other side in the important match ball games. (Sturtevant, 1991, p. 25–27)

Families (or clans) are the backbone of tribal society, even if tribal political organizations follow corporate format. Historically most people told their stories, hunted, fished, and traveled within extended family groups. This lifestyle may be less common today, but consulting with family is still honored (cf. Northrup, 1993). Few native societies invest decision making authority with a single individual. Traditional protocol often requires tribal or band elders to bless both goals and decisions. Thus, councils strive for consensus, because all parties (families) to agreements need to give their consent. On the other hand, factionalism often makes consensus an ideal, not a reality.

This family/community orientation has distinct implications for helping. Western trauma treatment is usually individual, but native communities may require family or tribal interventions (e.g., Manson et al., 1996; Richards, 1989; Stamm & Friedman, in press). Studies involving suicide interventions (Berlin, 1985; Long, 1986), substance abuse interventions (Brady, 1995; Edwards, Seaman, Drews, & Edwards, 1995; Herring, 1994; May & Moran, 1995; Swaim et al., 1993; Wiebe & Huebert, 1996), and family violence therapy (DeBruyn, Lemyra, Hymbaugh, & Valdez, 1988) suggest that activities must involve active participation, if not control, by families, the community, and traditional healers. At the same time, band factions may compete for political power. Successful programs must be sanctioned by all the appropriate groups (Foulks, 1989; Smith & Warrior, 1996; Terry, 1995; Westermeyer, 1989; Wolf, 1989). This means that workers have to seek a fragile balance to achieve tribalwide decisions by finding individuals from competing factions who are willing to work with each other.

Time And The Spiritual Realm

(Saith the Spirit,
    "Dream, oh, dream again,
    And tell of me,
        Dream thou!")
Into Solitude went I
And wisdom was revealed to me.
    (Saith the Spirit,
    "Dream, oh, dream again,
    And tell of me,
        Dream thou!")
Let the whole world hear me,
Wise am I!
    (Now saith the Spirit,
    "Tell of me,
        Dream thou!")
All was revealed to me;
From the beginning
Know I all, hear me!
All was revealed to me!
        (Now saith the Spirit,
    "Tell of me,
        Dream thou!")
(Mun-Kun Na-Wan, Winnebago Holy Song, Curtis, 1905/1994, p. 255)

The past is present among many native groups; time viewed in cyclical or web like patterns has no true distinction between past and present (Schmidt, 1988; Thompson, Walker, & Silk-Walker, 1993). Past events, like the 1864 Sand Creek massacre of Cheyennes, the 1890 Wounded Knee massacre of Lakotas, or the 1918–1919 influenza epidemic among Alaska natives, still burden the descendants of the victims (BraveHeart-Jordon, 1995; BraveHeart-Jordon, & DeBruyn, 1995; Fortine, 1992; Jaimes, 1992a; Rowland, 1995; Stamm, Stamm, & Weine, 1994; Utley, 1984). Some interpret White contact as colonialism and genocide

(Churchill, 1992; Jaimes, 1992b). Centuries of past disasters may be related to current events; long dead ancestors are honored with current ceremonies; stories of powerful leaders are guarded jealously. Tragedies, triumphs, memories, and stories take on a sacred aspect in both familial and tribal perspectives.

There is no word for "religion" per se in traditional American languages (Talbot, 1994) but there are many complex and diverse religious traditions. Two caveats are appropriate. First, the sacredness of beliefs and ceremonies require careful attention to etiquette. Outsiders must be circumspect in asking questions about religious beliefs. Such discussions are best held at private family gatherings, not in public places (e.g., schools, offices, or medical facilities). Second, not all native peoples observe the customs of their ancestors, nor are such customs or beliefs static. Ceremonies changed over time to meet the demands of new environmental, social, and demographic situations. Furthermore, some traditions have been lost, replaced, or destroyed, making it impractical to know what the old ways actually were (e.g., Shimkin, 1953). Yet, many retain at least nominal allegiance to the traditions of the past. Individuals and communities can reject or ignore this heritage, but the spiritual heritage forms a basic core of identity.

Yorlyorl dunivichane nïkëpfuint   nïkëpfuint
Get up, young man, keep on dancing,   keep on dancing,

Nzananï nüsünga.
Good   feel
(Keep getting up [dancing]. . . . This is what you're here for, for your health.)
(H. Furlong, speaking about Shoshone Sun Dance Songs, Vander, 1996, p. 136)

Native groups have essential beliefs that help define them as distinct peoples. For Eastern Shoshones, Arapahoes, Cheyennes, the Lakotas and Dakotas, and other Plains bands, the Sun Dance is the quintessential ceremony that brings health, happiness, and general economic good fortune (Hultkrantz, 1983, 1987; Shimkin, 1953; Stamm, 1996, in press; Talbot, 1994). The Sun Dance (a 3–4 day ceremony of ritual fasts, songs, and dances) brings individual spiritual power, ensures successful hunts, restores health to dysfunctional families, cements friendships, and smoothes fractious feelings. Not participating in the Sun Dance might indicate rejection of the cultural legacy, or point to family or individual problems. Some Sun Dancers believe ill health, poor economy, and malaise stem from non-participation (Clow, 1994; Joe, 1994; Stamm, 1996).

Other essential beliefs among most native peoples include the power and necessity of dreams and visions. For many Eastern woodlands tribes, such as Hurons, Senecas, Onondagas, and Shawnees, dreams are absolutely necessary. Visions and dreams reveal the paths to follow and even suggest ritual guidelines or interpersonal relationships. As windows to the spiritual world, dreamlife carries as much weight as temporal experiences (Dowd, 1992; Talbot, 1994).

Both caring and tormenting actions mark the Christian missionary legacy begun in 1492 (Calloway, 1997; CatholicMobile, 1998; Keller, 1983; Prucha, 1976; Stamm, in press). The Grant Peace Policy (1869–1882) shifted power from government to missionaries to reduce graft and improve the "Indian situation" by Christianizing the Indians. Generalizing, current Christianity exists in three forms. Some reject Christian tenets outright, usually with anger toward the church for its evangelizing. Others reject the old ways and cling to the Christian tradition. Still others blend Christian and traditional ways into a complex belief system that might seem unusual to some modern Christians.

Heaven and hell are remnants of this aggressive Christian missionary work. Yet, dualism can exist in native beliefs. There are spirits that can help you and there are spirits that can harm you. Indeed, the universe is made of spirits who can progress or hinder your way in the world. Finding good or counteracting harm requires proper spiritual preparation and ceremony. Therefore, participation in kiva ceremonies by Hopis or Zunis, dancing the Sun Dance by Shoshones, wearing and praying via masks among the Yup'iks, or seeking interpretation of dreams from an Oneida holy person are all essential aspects of living a healthy traditional life. Proper ceremonies must be enacted when one encounters bad spirits. This might apply when an individual or family undergoes psychological disease from trauma or loss, such as the suicide of a close friend or family member or an alcohol related car accident. As Talbot describes it:

> From time immemorial, Native American religiousness has grown out of encounters with spirit, plant, animal and human "others" who often seemed liked dangerous strangers. . . . What has not been appreciated is that Native Americans have always understood that the world is a dangerous place. If respectful trust exists, it has been earned. Disaster, whether personal, social, military, or ecological, may therefore be the result of the peoples' failings (Talbot, 1994, p. 441).

Many native traditions do not separate body and spirit. To be mentally healthy literally means one is in "good spirits" (Joe, 1994; Schmidt, 1988; Stamm, 1996; Thompson, Walker, & Silk-Walker, 1993). According to Curtis (1905/1994, p. 32), "the English word 'medicine' has come to be applied to what the Dakota Indian calls wakan. Wakan means both mystery and holiness, and is used by the Indians to designate all that is sacred, mysterious, spiritual or supernatural." If a person exhibits signs of mental distress (by the context of their community), many native peoples see this as a spiritual problem, perhaps even caused by witchcraft or a curse.

Treatment, therefore, would be spiritual involving specialized ceremonies, purification rites, or even ritual exorcisms (Joe, 1994; Mitchell & Bitsui, 1995; Silko, 1986; Stamm, 1996, in press; Thompson et al., 1993). Such spiritual approaches take place within a community (e.g., a sweat lodge ceremony), but individual actions are still necessary (such as using traditional medicines or teas, or seeking aid from a medicine person). Generally, the prescribed procedures involve prayer and/or ritual preparations. Healing flows from the spiritual side of life, given by the Creator or beings (like totemic animals or spirit guides) that possess special powers (Hultkrantz, 1983, 1987). Spiritual remedies could include Christian forms such as the laying of hands. In this context, form (prayers, rituals, and ceremonies) is just as important as content (pharmacological ingredients, diet, or therapy sessions). Without proper respect and proper preparation, even powerful native medicines and teas will yield little therapeutic benefit. Directions: Use the language of [traditional healers]. Say "he turned my mind around" & mean "he told me something." (Inuit, Arctic, Rothenberg, 1986 p. 39).

Not all native people believe or practice the spiritual tenets of their traditions. For those who do, Western medicine—psychotherapy or pharmacological prescriptions—may lack the proper spiritual ritual components necessary to be effective. Yet, however well intended, one must not misappropriate or even steal native ceremonies in the pursuit of culturally sensitive interventions. Perhaps the strongest statement against the appropriation of Native American ways is the Declaration of War Against Exploiters of Lakota Spirituality (maple.lemoyne.edu/~bucko/war.html). The negative term "wannabes" is applied to Whites who appropriate the customs of Indians without truly understanding native ways (cf. LaDue, 1994).

☐ Interrelated Issues Affecting Health Interventions

All the members of the animal kingdom were angry with people and wanted to declare war on them for their carelessness and abuse. They complained in council that humankind had little respect for his fellow creatures, spread too quickly over the world, and killed and ate the animals. First the Bears met under Mount Kuwahi [Clingman's Dome, North Carolina] to plan an attack on the people. They intended using bows and arrows as people did but found that their claws became caught in the strings. . . . The other animals were more successful in their plans. They agreed to unleash all sorts of disease to attack people and, except for the interventions of the plants, may well have killed them all. The plants were friendly to people . . . they made every tree, shrub, and weed the antidote for part of the mischief released by the animals. (Based on James Mooney's *Myths of the Cherokee*, 1900, quoted in Murry, 1992).

Generalizations about native life, land, and community lead to questions. How can one learn about a particular culture, tribe, or people? How might family or tribal social structures affect health care systems, caregivers, and educators? How does one find the elders or traditional healers? Is one allowed to know them? How does one get the consent of a tribal or village council for a research or intervention proposal? What specific beliefs affect health and mental health care? Just what kinds of problems affect First Nations, American Indian, and Alaska Native communities?

Indian country is far too complex to explore each of these concerns in one chapter. Moreover, native peoples themselves pose some of these same queries. For example, Dinlishla, the group that inspired this paper, asked two very difficult questions: "How do we identify and certify traditional healers?" and "how do we bill for their services?" No answers emanated. Other solutions will remain just as elusive. Nonetheless, we hope we can alert potential health caregivers and educators to some of the nuances of American Indian and Alaska Native cultures.

Ethnohistory, Ethnography and Literature

The path toward cultural knowledge starts easily but true understanding might be an impossible achievement. Recent scholarship of historians, anthropologists, ethnologists, and ethnohistorians assesses and contextualize the ethnographic detail of particular peoples and tribes. These authors describe government–native relationships, introduce documentary sources of tribal history, and reveal the richness of native oral traditions, including folklore, legends, spiritual beliefs and practices, and political leadership (see Calloway, 1994, 1996, 1997; Hoxie, in press).

Fiction and essays by and about native people are useful. Writers weave stories with words, sights, and sounds of their communities, or offer scathing criticisms of Western life seen from native perspectives. Outsiders seeking work with natives should begin their cultural education about their new world by reading historical accounts (e.g., Coolidge 1917/1984; DeLoria, 1988; Linderman, 1932/1972; Richter, 1992; Stamm, in press; Usner, 1992) and 20th century native literature (e.g., Allen, 1994; Erdrich, 1994; Northrup, 1993; Riley, 1993; Silko, 1986, 1991).

Seemingly contradictory, many people are preserving native culture and traditional ways by using the technology of the Internet. The intellectual freedom of the Internet provides a platform ripe for nondiscriminatory publication of views and beliefs. Discernment is necessary to ferret out the true native North American information from that which has been commercialized. However, the Internet may be the single largest storehouse of information by and about native issues. There are far too many sites to list here; one search engine produced 90,000 sites searching for native American. The following sites can provide a starting point:

> Native American Rights Fund (www.narf.org)
> Native Web (www.nativeweb.org)
> NativeNet (niikaan.fdl.cc.mn.us/natnet)
> The Forth World Documentation Project (www.halcyon.com/FWDP/fwdp.html)
> Canadian Department of Indian Affairs and Northern Development (www.inac.gc.ca/index_e.html)
> U.S. Native American Policies Dataset (ciir.cs.umass.edu/info/envirotext/environew/usnap.html)
> Index of Native American Resources on the Internet (hanksville.phast.umass.edu/misc/NAresources.html)
> Indian Health Services (www.tucson.ihs.gov).

Folktales, Legends, and Stories

Folklore and legends offer powerful entrance into the native world. Here one can discover special meanings attached to birth, death, general life development, and the interrelatedness of physical and mental health. Do not underestimate the importance of stories. They reveal tribal origins, the proper relationships between men and women, the interactions of the spirit world, and the moral expectations (Murry, 1992; Nelson, 1983; Rothenberg, 1986).

> We were happy. Now it seems so long ago. It all changed. . . . Nothing happened after that. We just lived. There were no more war parties, no capturing of horses from the Piegans and the Sioux, no buffalo to hunt. There is nothing more to tell.
> (Two Leggings, Crow Warrior [ca. 1847–1923], Nabokov, 1967 p. 196–197).

This quote, about the Crow Reservation between 1888 and 1923 when the peoples' "hearts were on the ground," poignantly illustrates that loss of heart is synonymous with the loss of stories.

Nobody made it up, these things we're supposed to do. It came from the stories, it's just like our Bible. My grandfather said he told the stories because they would bring the people good luck, keep them healthy, and make a good life. When he came to songs in the stories, he sang like they were hymns. (Koyukon (Alaska) elder, Nelson, 1983, p. 18).

Native stories and folklore are as diverse as are native peoples. However, there are similarities. Many stories feature some form of trickster, a supernatural being who may aid human ambitions but who, just as often, thwarts or injures people. Plains peoples call this character Coyote, while Raven is the nemesis of Pacific Northwest and Southeastern Alaska groups.

When Raven first created the world, the rivers ran both ways—upstream on one side and downstream on the other. But this made the life too easy for the humans, he decided, because their boats could drift along in either direction without paddling. So Raven altered his creation and made the rivers flow only one way, which is how they remain today. (Koyukon story (Alaska), Nelson, 1983, p. 21).

Other prominent creatures—bears, buffaloes, eagles—symbolize human, spirit, and animal interactions. They also depict values like courage, devotion to family, strength, hunting prowess, and honor, all of which still resonate within Native North American cultures.

Elders, Power Politics, and Family Structure

The People had thought themselves to be strong, yet they had been weak. And the two old ones whom they thought to be the most helpless and useless had proven themselves to be strong. Now, an unspoken understanding existed between them, and The People found themselves seeking out the company of the two [old] women for advice and to learn new things. Now they realized that because the two women had lived so long, surely they knew a lot more than The People had believed. . . . So The People showed respect by listening to what they had to say. (Gwich'in Story (Alaska), Wallis, 1994)

Most native communities listen to the admonitions of their elders. Elders might not hold ultimate authority, but their input is expected and valued. In many Alaska villages, for example, village councils consult elders before hiring teachers. Helpers should seek the advice, approval, and public support of their ideas from the elders. Elders and other important community leaders should be included in meetings and events. "You must ask them, even if you know they won't come. That way, no one is left out" (personal communication, Walter Austin, May 1996). Beware, however: not all older people are elders, nor do all in a community agree on who is an elder. Learning the elders of a community, a village, or even a family takes time and patience. Observe who are called on to offer public prayers at festivals such as potlatches, powwows, or in council meetings, or large gatherings or meals of extended families. Ask your coworkers for their opinions about possible elders. Seek introductions through family members.

While elders may be keepers of tradition, doing so may cause them anguish. Elders and other older traditionals find themselves confronted with elements of the modern world that they do not understand how to assimilate. In the Alaska bush, for example, when electricity became available for home heating, elders welcomed not having to haul wood and were delighted with the new found warmth electricity afforded them. They were astounded, though, when a person came to take their homes away. What the elders did not understand was that electricity costs money and the power company had a lien against their home for nonpayment of utility bills. Having never paid for the wood they burned to keep their homes warm, and having never seen a utility bill, the elders were baffled and hurt by the turn of events that made them into "sordid" citizens.

In many family structures, males occupy the titular head but women play important and crucial roles. In Iroquois societies (Oneidas, Senecas, Mohawks, Cayuses, Onondagas, and Tuscaroras) the women's council often selects the head men (Richter, 1992). Observance of protocol is normative, even if such customs carry no discernible weight. In groups that enforce rigid gender roles, it might be customary to seek permission from a husband to speak to his wife.

Certain personal achievements are associated with age or sex. For example, becoming a medicine person requires completion of associated age related steps. Some Native North Americans might refuse to see a therapist whose age would make them ineligible to be a medicine person. From the traditional perspective, how could a young person (like a newly minted M.D. or Ph.D.) possess the necessary wisdom and spiritual power to heal psychic ills rooted in the spiritual realm? Similarly, women helpers may struggle with leading men's groups (Obenchain & Silver, 1992).

Various interactions undergird power and authority. Moreover, political power and authority can involve serious or even deadly conflict. In 1973, the American Indian Movement's (AIM) occupation of Wounded Knee, South Dakota (on the Pine Ridge Reservation), resulted from the call of traditional Oglala Lakota people to remove the elected tribal president. The traditionals claimed the president practiced nepotism and abused political power (Smith & Warrior, 1996). A standoff occurred between AIM and the FBI. During the confrontation, White providers attended wounded Indians within the Wounded Knee community, a service that put them at odds with federal authority (Crow Dog & Erdoes, 1990; Smith & Warrior, 1996). While most providers will not encounter such partisan political violence, inadvertently (or ignorantly) siding with a faction during crisis could undermine healing efforts.

Other issues emerge at the family level. While the family is the basic social unit of American Indian and Alaska Native communities, the definition of family varies, as do parental styles, childhood roles, and gender differentiation. For example, affinal relationships reflect diverse norms. In some tribes, the sister of one's mother is called "mother," while the sister of one's father is "aunt." In Tlingit societies, the uncle (mother's brother) is the person responsible for the education of his nephews. The birth father plays only a minor role in this case. This is also the case among Laguna Pueblos (Riley, 1993). Among Eastern Shoshones, women are responsible for training both boys and girls in traditions and ceremonies, but women are barred from the Sun Dance. Thus, even if one effectively deals with the spiritual issues raised in mental health care, caregiving in native societies involve family, group, or community processes.

Like most people, different age groups or stages in the life cycle can require careful attention. In many native communities, children have much greater freedom of choice and expression than might be expected in typical White middle class families (Sprott, 1994). Yet, the children's roles vary widely. In those societies that seem to have well established ceremonies marking the stages of life, helpers should be aware of the traditional developmental age. For example, Northern Arapahoes, like many Plains people, have age-set and age-grade developmental standards. That is, children advance through life stages in cohorts; various tests and rituals must be undertaken in order to achieve the next level of maturity. Both boys and girls experience group maturation cycles, as well as their own individual growth (Fowler, 1982).

Although many younger native peoples forego ceremonial observations, traditional elders often remonstrate the younger generation for this neglect, blaming the degradation of their families on such disrespect for tribal traditions. Some Eastern Shoshone elders, for example, claim that the lack of vision and personal power among Shoshone men derives from neglect of birth ceremonies (Stamm, 1996). Some elders believe that avoidance or disrespect of proper rituals leads to alcoholism, suicide, unemployment, and other social evils. According to the wisdom of elders of the Six Nations of the Haudenosaunee (Iroquois), the forces of human history are destroying the world and the only salvation is a return to traditional ways (*A Basic Call to Consciousness*, Akwesasne Notes, 1978). Silko's *Ceremony* echoes this theme (Silko, 1986). These harsh assessments of Western worldviews may impede easy interactions between helpers and reservation peoples. Multigenerational experiences of the Western world informed such beliefs so they carry a great deal of weight. In fact, it might be impossible to bridge cultural differences.

☐ Important Beliefs and Ceremonies

Death and Dying

When Raven created humans, he first used rock for the raw materials, and people never died. But this was too easy so he recreated them, using dust instead. In this way humans became mortal, as they remain today. (Koyukon story, Nelson, 1983, p. 20).

Customs and beliefs about death vary widely, but death may have profound spiritual and social significance in ways far beyond the ken of the dominant culture. End-of-life decisions may be at odds with Western medicine. When older natives from traditional villages have been removed to distant long term care facilities (there are rarely facilities close), in addition to the loss of social support, they may find unfamiliar and hostile environments. Among Yup'iks, pale roast beef may be a horrifying food alternative to salmon berries and stink heads (fermented fish heads) and lead to weight loss and depression (personal communications, M. E. N. Agnew, Nov. 1994).

There are other examples. Giveaway ceremonies to honor the deceased are widespread. Giveaways involve gifting funeral guests with food, clothing, or other symbols that show respect for the community relationships and the status of the deceased. Among the Tlingit and Haida, the death of a family member traditionally requires a potlatch one year from the date of the death. The object of the potlatch is to honor the dead by giving away all the possessions (including food) of the surviving family—the more given away, the more honor accrued to the dead person and their family. This ritualized impoverishment also binds the receivers into an obligatory relationship with the mourning family; at future potlatches food and goods are returned in kind (Langdon, 1993).

Some people honor the dead by renaming a relative after the dead person. Others ritually adopt outsiders and give the adoptee the name of the deceased to secure ongoing spiritual power accrued to the name. Conversely, still others greatly fear their dead, believing that the deceased wander the earth as ghosts for a specified time. To speak of the dead invites them to interfere in the community's life, bring bad luck, or imperil the speaker or the speaker's family or community (Langdon, 1993). Therefore, rituals and customs associated with death should make the health care provider wary of openly investigating the feelings of survivors (Manson et al., 1996).

Death may have a powerful effect on the lives of family survivors. For some, death requires ritualistic mourning such as cutting hair, slicing or gashing arms or legs, or other behaviors indicating the depth of grief. An outsider, unfamiliar with local customs, might diagnose such mourning inappropriately. Helpers should be leery of diagnoses based on acute onset of apparent aberrant behaviors in bereaved Native North Americans (Manson, 1997, in press; Manson, et al., 1996).

Sudden or violent death can exacerbate grief responses, similar to reactions among members of the dominant U.S. culture (Figley, Bride & Mazza, 1997; Rando, 1992, 1996, Stamm, 1999a, 1999b). Moreover, some native peoples have a higher risk than do Whites of sudden or unexpected death, possibly stemming from higher rates of poverty and chronic cultural trauma (Berlin, 1985; Kettl & Bixler, 1991; Lester, 1995; May & Van Winkle, 1994). From 1980 to 1989 Alaska Native mortality was 698 per 100,000 people, while Alaska nonnative mortality was 341 per 100,000 people. Injuries or suicide caused one-third of these deaths; alcohol was involved 98% of the time. Although the life expectancy for Alaska Natives has risen from 48 to 68 years between 1950 and 1984, it still lags behind the white U.S. population average of 75 (Middaugh, 1995; Middaugh et al. 1991). Thus, providers should be particularly alert to traumatic grief.

Ceremonies

In the kiva of the chieftain is performed a ceremonial, symbolic corn-planting. The idea in this song seems to be that a ceremonial planting of a perfect corn-ear . . . [that] will procure even such perfect corn-ears in the crop of the next season. Muyingwa is the god of germination and growth. He lives underground beneath the kivas.

Natwanlawu inamu
Ayam Muyingwa
Mongwi kive
Mokwa Kao
Chochmingwum;
Natwantaqo pom nikiang
Bavas nawita stalwunguni.
(Hopi Song [Arizona] Composed and Sung by Lololomai; Curtis, 1905/1994, p. 429).

Traditions developed with respect to individual climate, geography, and economic systems. There is no overarching Indian ritual. Despite the proliferation of burnt sage offerings, sweat lodges, powwows, and other Plains based ceremonies, many people are dishonored by this generic

"Indian-ness." Therefore, providers need to learn the customs of particular Native North Americans.

Nonetheless, learning about rituals may be difficult. While there is good information regarding rituals in the psychological literature, much of it discusses Plains or Southwestern Indian rituals (for example, see Wilson, 1989). Consult ethnohistorical and anthropological sources. Find respectful ways to talk to the elders who are the keepers of the tradition. Offer to drive elders on errands or to meet with each other. Doing chores for elders might also open opportunities. After a time, if the newcomer proves worthy, elders will begin to talk.

Celebrations

> When the dance is over, sweet-heart
> I will take you home with my one eyed Ford
> Wi yo he ya he yo ha
> Wi ho ha wi yo ha yo

> Excerpt from Forty-nine Dance Song, 'One-Eyed Ford' with English words and vocables. Forty-nine dances are young people's social dances that follow Powwows and may last all night. The drums may be replaced with any sonorous surface and words are changed to fit the location.
> (Berlo, 1994, p. 592)

Powwows, potlatches, and other social gatherings (which may have sacred overtones) provide tension relief, escape from routine duties, and other personal expressions of celebration. Participation in these events solidifies tribal identity and yields a chance to swap stories with far-flung friends and relatives. They are safe havens from everyday concerns. For example, current traditions of sober powwows prohibit alcohol or drug consumption. Powwows may also incorporate healing ceremonies for war veterans and honor songs for warriors (White, 1996).

Rituals, taboos, and special ceremonies are important cultural symbols but sometimes provide grounds for discrimination by insensitive or even hostile outsiders. Providers need to be aware of these potential conflicts regarding native beliefs. Native communities still suffer from institutionally sanctioned discrimination, even when federal law prohibits such activities (e.g., American Indian Religious Freedom Act 1994; see Pevar, 1992). For example, members of the Eastern Shoshones have been fired from their jobs for attending the three day Sun Dance (Stamm, 1996). For traditional Shoshones, it is the most important rite of the year and no other obligation has precedence. By comparison, most U.S. and

Canadian communities would not tolerate such blatant violations of Christian or Jewish religious beliefs.

☐ Problems in Native Life

Indian reservations, Aboriginal communities, and Alaskan villages are rife with the after effects of trauma and loss. Health and mental health care professionals, educators, religious leaders, and administrators will contend with the aftermath of suicide, severe and chronic unemployment, substance abuse, family violence, and other social ills in the course of their employment. Moreover, many of these conditions and events occur on a monthly, weekly, or even daily basis. For example, suicide rates for reservations are twice the national average (Kettl & Bixler, 1991; Marshall, Martin, Thomason, & Johnson, 1991; Travis, 1983). High rates of poverty, unemployment, loss of cultural identity and other factors contributing to social instability are comorbid with tuberculosis, diabetes, substance abuse, posttraumatic stress disorder, and other medical and mental health problems (Abel, 1995; Berlin, 1985; Grobsmith & Dam, 1990; Herring, 1994; LaDue, 1994; Lester, 1995; Long, 1986; Manson, et al., 1996; Manson, Ackerson, Dick, Baron, & Fleming, 1990; Robin, Chester, & Goldman, 1996; Stamm & Friedman, in press; Stamm, Higson-Smith, Terry, & Stamm, 1996; Thurman, Jones-Saumty, & Parsons, 1990).

Native children are at risk both inside and outside their families. Native war veterans may have particular difficulties recovering from war related experiences (National Center for PTSD and National Center for American Indian and Alaska Native Mental Health Research [Matsanaga Report], 1997; Mitchell & Bitsui, 1995, Priess, 1995; Rhoades, Leaveck, & Hudson, 1995). Many Indian children are born and grow up in environments where Fetal Alcohol Syndrome (FAS), chronic illness, substance abuse, and violence are common (Abel, 1995; DeBruyn, Lujan, & May, 1992; DeBruyn, Lemyra, Hymbaugh, & Valdez, 1988; May, 1988, 1991; Yates, 1987). The prevalence of problems is so high it is easy to assume that these problems arise from the culture itself (Manson, 1997). Differential exposure to high risk events is a far better explanation. Poverty and interfamilial trauma histories from centuries of cultural trauma create high risk situations. Ongoing discrimination also figures prominently. For example, American Indians were exposed to heavy combat at higher rates than other soldiers in the Vietnam War (National Center for Posttraumatic Stress Disorder, 1997).

Exposure to the justice system is a powerful social risk for Native North Americans. Nearly every family or community has at least one member who is incarcerated. This loss creates a hole in the generational structure. Incarceration rates are higher among Native North Americans than the White culture (Canada Solicitor General, 1997; U.S. Department of Justice, 1995). In Canada, 40% of the prison population is Aboriginal compared with 2% of the general population. Recidivism is 90% and Aboriginal inmates are projected to increase 6% a year for the next 10 years. The scope of the problem and the responses beginning to emerge make it a good example of how traditional culture and modern treatment can be integrated.

Consider the social implications of the problem. Seventy percent of offenses committed by natives are committed in urban centers (Canada Solicitor General, 1997) where people are more likely to be cut off from traditional culture and support systems. Perhaps the loss of cultural contacts spur on these problems. Alternatively, possibly those with the most difficulties leave their villages and go to the city. Higher substance abuse (Grobsmith & Dam, 1990) may also contribute to these problems. One study proposes that misunderstandings of fundamental differences in cultural personality styles of Native North Americans has lead to stereotypical definitions of a criminal personality (Glass, Bieber, & Tkachuk, 1996). Regardless of the cause, significant proportions of people are removed from participation in the normal life of the community.

Alternatives are emerging. For example, under the protection guaranteed by The American Indian Religious Freedom Act (1994), a number of correctional facilities in the United States have hired traditional healers to conduct ceremonies and training in traditional ways. In Montreal, Quebec, the staff of Waseskun House (www.waseskun.net) incorporates ceremonies such as the healing circle and train the residents (Aboriginal inmates) in life skills to help them reconstruct their lives, deal with sexuality, anger management, grief, and cultural trauma. In 10 years, 400 men have participated in the program and 8 out of 10 do not recidivate (George, 1997).

Like the treatment offered by Waseskun House, most sources recommend that interventions—in the community, in prisons, for veterans—account for specific tribal heritages. Western diagnostic conceptualizations can be useful but must be considered carefully in the context of the culture (Friedman & Jaranson, 1994; Kirmayer, 1996; Manson, Shore, & Bloom, 1985; Manson, Walker, & Kivlahan, 1987; Stamm & Friedman, in press). The papers cited throughout this chapter echo the same refrain: respect the cultural legacy, consult tribal councils and elders, and use the talents of the communities' traditional healers.

Coming in From the Outside

In one incident, the Russian . . . lined up a dozen men and fired his musket . . . to see how many Aleuts one bullet killed. The answer was nine. The

> Aleut recognized their inability to succeed against the guns of the Russians. Introduced diseases further reduced their number. . . . By 1799 only an eighth of the pre-contact population remained.
> (Aleut [Alaska] Story; Rowley, 1991, p. 204).

Mistrust of government is part of the social milieu for most reservations and native corporations, despite recent institutional efforts to respect traditional ways and native sovereignty (Indian Health Service, 1996). Because most native peoples in the United States receive their health care from Indian Health Services, a government agency, transcultural barriers exist long before provider and patient meet. Even the most eager and genuine nonnative helper may find obstacles that can only be overcome slowly as relationships based on personal experience replace those of long standing broken trust (Schmidt, 1988; Thompson, et al., 1993).

For outsiders, gaining the trust of Indian peoples is a necessary step if one expects to provide care. Many natives attribute their problems to cultural imperialism and refuse alternative interpretations. Others are unwilling to air their dirty laundry in front of strangers, while still others give lip service to providers' suggestions in order to seem cooperative (Schmidt, 1988; Stamm, 1996). In communities where norms place high value on harmony and smooth interpersonal relationships, saying "yes" on Monday while acting otherwise on Tuesday does not violate protocol if harmony has been achieved in both interchanges. Providers must understand this, or risk continual frustration or worse, falsely accusing patients of noncooperation or other breach of community etiquette (personal communication, A. Crow, November 1995).

☐ Conclusion

Understanding the idioms of distress, the meaning of loss, and the appraisal of trauma requires understanding the people themselves. Perhaps the most effective way to be respectful and to learn the local culture is to listen very carefully to what the people in the community have to say. Revisionist history, ethnohistory, anthropology and native writers provide a vast wellspring of information. Careful searchers can find valuable resources on the Internet. If it is possible, learn from the elders. They are the keepers of the wisdom of the community and often the keepers of the authority for positive sanction of the helper's ability to work in the community. Knowing the history of the peoples and, when possible, learning the language—even the most basic aspects of it—will show respect. Native peoples ask for no more and no less than do any of us—to be respected, to be listened to, to be honored, and to be loved.

I am Anishinaabe,
in the spring we spear fish
rez² government wishes we wouldn't
it makes some white people mad.
That's par for the course
They've been mad at us
since they got here,
rednecks try to stop us
with threats, gunfire, and bombs.
The state attempts a buyout
thinking cash can do anything.
We're valuable to the media
we fill their columns and empty air
good people witness for us.
We thank Munido for fish, for life,
as we praise our grandfathers
and their generational wisdom.
Spearing is more than a treaty
right—it's an eating right.
We do what has been done since
there have been Anishinaabe.
I am one of them.
I spear fish.
("barbed thoughts," Northrup, 1993, p. 136)

☐ Endnotes

[1]We are indebted to Dinlishla, a nonprofit organization in Anchorage, Alaska, founded in part by Bill Richards and dedicated to the "healing of our people." We are grateful to the following people who gave freely of their time to teach us: Walter Austin (in his words, "from the four directions," Athabaskan and Yup'ik and more), Rita Blumenstein (Yup'ik); Lisa Dolckek (Yup'ik) and Max Dolchek (Athabaskan); Zedora Enos (Shoshone); Bob Morgan (Lakota); and James Trosper (Shoshone and Arahapo). Any mistakes made are ours alone. May we listen with more care in the future.
[2]reservation

☐ References

Abel, E. L. (1995). An update on incidence of FAS: FAS is not an equal opportunity birth defect. *Neurotoxicology and Teratology, 17*(4), 437–443.

Akwesasne Notes (Ed.). (1978). *A basic call to consciousness.* Rooseveltown, NY: Akwesasne Press.

Allen, P. G. (1994). *Voice of the turtle: American Indian literature 1900–1970.* New York: One World/Ballantine Books.

American Indian Religious Freedom Act 1994 Pub.L. No. 103–344 (1994).

Anders, G. C., & Anders, K. K. (1986). Incompatible goals in unconventional organizations: The politics of Alaska Native corporations. *Organization Studies, 7*(3), 213–233.

Berlin, I. N. (1985). Prevention of adolescent suicide among some Native American tribes. *Adolescent Psychiatry, 12,* 77–93.

Berlo, J. C. (1994). Native art in North America. In D. Champagne (Ed.), *Native America: Portrait of the peoples* (pp. 549–664). Detroit: Visible Ink Press.

Boxberger, D. (1994). Native peoples of the Northwest coast. In D. Champagne, (Ed.), *Native America: Portrait of the peoples* (pp. 195–214). Detroit: Visible Ink Press.

Brady, M. (1995). Culture in treatment, culture as treatment. A critical appraisal of developments in addictions programs for indigenous North Americans and Australians. *Social Science and Medicine, 41*(11), 1487–1498.

BraveHeart-Jordan, M. (1995). *The return to the sacred path: Healing from historical unresolved grief among the Lakota and Dakota.* Unpublished doctoral dissertation, Smith College.

BraveHeart-Jordan, M., & DeBruyn, L. M. (1995). So she may walk in balance: Integrating the impact of historical trauma in the treatment of Native American Indian women. In J. Aldeman, & G. Enguidanos (Eds.), *Racism in the lives of women: Testimony, theory, and guides to anti-racist practice* (pp. 345–368). New York: Haworth Press.

Bright, W. (1994). Native North American languages. In D. Champagne (Ed.), *Native America: Portrait of the peoples* (pp. 397–440). Detroit: Visible Ink Press.

Calloway, C. G. (Ed.). (1994). *The world turned upside down: Indian voices from early America.* Boston: Bedford Books.

Calloway, C. G. (Ed.). (1996). *Our hearts to the ground: Plains Indian views of how the west was lost.* Boston: Bedford Books.

Calloway, C. G. (1997). *New worlds for all. Indians, Europeans, and the remaking of early America.* Baltimore, MD: The Johns Hopkins University Press.

Canada Solicitor General. (1997). Aboriginal Corrections Report. [On-line]. Available: www.sgc.gc.ca/EPub/EAbocorrlist.htm.

CatholicMobile. (1998). Resources for the Study of Discrimination against Native Americans. [On-line]. Available: www.mcgill.pvt.k12.al.us/jerryd/cm/native.htm.

Champagne, D. (Ed.). (1994). *Native America: Portrait of the peoples.* Detroit: Visible Ink Press.

Churchill, W. (1992). The earth is our mother: Struggles for American Indian land and liberation in the contemporary United States. In M. A. Jaimes (Ed.), *The state of Native America: Genocide, colonization, and resistance* (pp. 139–188). Boston: South End Press.

Clow, R. (1994). Native peoples of the Northern Plains. In D. Champagne (Ed.), *Native America: Portrait of the peoples* (pp. 161–194). Detroit: Visible Ink Press.

Condon, R. G. (1995). The rise of the leisure class: Adolescence and recreational acculturation in the Canadian Arctic. *Ethos, 23*(1), 47–68.

Coolidge, G. (1917/1984). *Teepee neighbors.* Norman, OK: University of Oklahoma Press.

Crow Dog, M., & Erdoes, R. (1990). *Lakota woman.* New York: Grove Weidenfeld.

Curtis, N. (1905/1994). *The Indian's Book.* Avernel, NJ: Gramercy Books.

DeBruyn, L. M., Hymbaugh, K., & Valdez, N. (1988). Helping communities address suicide and violence: The special initiatives team of the Indian health service. *American Indian And Alaska Native Mental Health Research, 1*(3) 56–65.

DeBruyn, L. M., Lemyra, M., Hymbaugh, K., & Valdez, N. (1988). Helping communities address suicide and violence: The special initiatives team of the Indian health service. *American Indian And Alaska Native Mental Health Research, 1*(3), 56–65.

DeBruyn, L. M., Lujan, C. C., & May, P. A. (1992). A comparative study of abused and neglected American Indian children in the Southwest. *Social Science And Medicine, 35*(3), 305–315.

Deloria, E. C. (1988). *Waterlily.* Norman, OK: University of Oklahoma Press.

Dowd, G. E. (1992). *A spirited resistance: The North American Indian struggle for unity, 1745–1815.* Baltimore: The Johns Hopkins University Press.

Edwards, E. D., Seaman, J. R., Drews, J., & Edwards, M. E. (1995). A community approach for Native American drug and alcohol prevention programs: A logic model framework. *Alcoholism Treatment Quarterly, 13*(2), 43–62.

Erdrich, L. (1994). *The bingo palace.* New York: Harper Collins.

Figley, C. R., Bride, B. E., & Mazza, N. (1997). *Death and trauma: The traumatology of loss.* London: Taylor & Francis, Ltd.

Fortine, R. (1992). *Chills and fever: Health and disease in the early history of Alaska.* Fairbanks, AK: University of Alaska Press.

Foulks, E. F. (1989). Misalliances in the Barrow alcohol study. *American Indian And Alaska Native Mental Health Research, 2*(3), 7–17.

Fowler, L. (1982). *Arapahoe politics, 1851–1978: Symbols in crises of authority.* Lincoln: University of Nebraska Press.

Friedman, M. J., & Jaranson, J. (1994). The applicability of the posttraumatic stress disorder concept to refugees. In A. Marsella, T. Bomemann, S. Ekblad, & J. Orley (Eds.), *Amidst peril and pain: The mental health and well-being of the world's refugees* (pp. 207–227). Washington, DC: American Psychological Association.

Friedman, M. J., & Marsella, A. J. (1996). Posttraumatic stress disorder: An overview of the concept. In A. J. Marsella, M. J. Friedman, E. T. Gerrity, & R. M. Scurfield (Eds.), *Ethnocultural aspects of posttraumatic stress disorder* (pp. 11–32). Washington, DC: American Psychological Association.

George, J. (1997, Fall). Separation from Family and Community isn't Such a Bad Thing for Inuit Offenders at Waseskun House in Montreal. *Nunatsiaq News.* [Online] Available: www.nunanet.com/~nunat/week/80109.html

Glass, M. E., Bieber, S. L., & Tkachuk, M. J. (1996). Personality styles and dynamics of Alaska Natives and non-Native incarcerated men. *Journal of Personality Assessment, 66*(3), 583–603.

Grobsmith, E. S., & Dam, J. (1990). The revolving door: Substance abuse treatment and criminal sanctions for Native American offenders. *Journal of Substance Abuse, 2*(4) 405–425.

Herring, R. D. (1994). Substance use among Native American Indian youth: A selective review of causality. *Journal of Counseling and Development, 72*(6), 578–584.

Hoxie, F. E. (Ed.). (in press). *Talking back to civilization: Native American voices in the progressive era, 1890–1920.* Boston: Bedford Books.

Hultkrantz, A. (1983). *The Study Of American Indian Religions* (C. Vecsey, Ed.). New York: Crossroads Publishing Co.

Hultkrantz, A. (1987). *Native religions of North America: The power of visions and fertility.* San Francisco: Harper and Row.

Indian Health Service (September, 1996). Traditional Medicine Initiative Update. [Online]. Available: www.tucson.ihs.gov/2Comm/Tradup.html.

Jaimes, M. A. (1992a). Sand Creek: The morning after. In M. A. Jaimes (Ed.), *The state of Native America: Genocide, colonization, and resistance* (pp. 1–12). Boston: South End Press.

Jaimes, M. A. (Ed.) (1992b). *The state of Native America: Genocide, colonization, and resistance.* Boston: South End Press.

Joe, J. R. (1994). Traditional Indian health practices and cultural views. In D. Champagne (Ed.), *Native America: Portrait of the peoples* (pp. 525–548). Detroit: Visible Ink Press.

Keller, R. H. (1983). *American Protestantism and United States Indian policy: 1869–1882.* Lincoln, NE: University of Nebraska Press.

Kettl, P. A., & Bixler, E. O. (1991). Suicide in Alaska Natives, 1979–1984. *Psychiatry, 54*(1), 55–63.

Kirmayer, L. J. (1996). Confusion of the senses: Implications of ethnocultural variations in somatoform and dissociative disorders. In A. J. Marsella, M. J. Friedman, E. T. Gerrity, & R. M. Scurfield (Eds.), *Ethnocultural aspects of posttraumatic stress disorder* (pp. 131–163). Washington, DC: American Psychological Association.

Kleinman, A. (1993). Several theoretical topics in neurosis research [Commentary]. *Integrative Psychiatry, 9*(1), 10–12.

LaDue, R. A. (1994). Coyote returns: Twenty sweats does not an Indian expert make. *Women and Therapy, 15*(1), 93–111.

Langdon, S. J. (1993). *The native people of Alaska.* Anchorage, AK: Greatland Graphics.

Lester, D. (1995). Social correlates of American Indian suicide and homicide rates. *American Indian and Alaska Native Mental Health Research, 6*(3), 46–55.

Linderman, F. B. (1932/1972). *Pretty shield: Medicine women of the Crows.* Lincoln, NE: University of Nebraska Press.

Long, K. A. (1986). Suicide intervention and prevention with Indian adolescent populations. *Issues In Mental Health Nursing, 3*(3), 247–253.

Manson, J. M. (in press). Culture and the DSM-IV: Implications for the diagnosis of mood and anxiety disorders. In J. Messich, A. Kleinman, H. Fabrega, & D. Parton (Eds.), *Culture And Psychiatric Diagnosis* (pp. xx–xx). Washington, DC: American Psychiatric Press.

Manson, S., Beals, J., O'Nell, T., Piasecki, J., Bechtold, D., Keane, E., & Jones, M. (1996). Wounded spirits, ailing hearts: PTSD and related disorders among American Indians. In A. J. Marsella, M. J., Friedman, E. T. Gerrity, & R. M. Scurfield (Eds.), *Ethnocultural aspects of posttraumatic stress disorder* (pp. 255–283). Washington, DC: American Psychological Association.

Manson, S. M. (1997). Cross-cultural and multi-ethic assessment of trauma. In J. P. Wilson, & T. M. Keane (Eds.), *Assessing psychological trauma and PTSD: A handbook for practitioners* (pp. 239–266). New York: Guilford.

Manson, S. M., Ackerson, L. M., Dick, R. W., Baron, A. E., & Fleming, C. M. (1990). Depressive symptoms among American Indian adolescents: Psychometric characteristics of the Center for Epidemiologic Studies Depression Scale (CES-D). *Psychological Assessment, 2*(3), 231–237.

Manson, S. M., Shore, J. H., & Bloom, J. D. (1985). The depressive experience in American Indian communities: A challenge for psychiatric theory and diagnosis. In A. Kleinman, & B. Good (Eds.), *Culture And Depression.* Berkeley, CA: University of California Press.

Manson, S. M., Walker, R. D., & Kivlahan, D. R. (1987). Psychiatric assessment and treatment of American Indians and Alaska Natives. *Hospital and Community Psychiatry, 38*(2), 165–173.

Marsella, A. J., Friedman, M. J., Gerrity, E. T., & Scurfield, R. M. (Eds.), *Ethnocultural aspects of posttraumatic stress disorder.* Washington, DC: American Psychological Association.

Marshall, C. A., Martin, W. E., Thomason, T. C., & Johnson, M. J. (1991). Multiculturalism and rehabilitation counselor training: Recommendations for providing culturally appropriate counseling services to American Indians with disabilities. *Journal of Counseling and Development, 70*(1), 225–234.

May, P. A. (1988). The health status of Indian children: Problems and prevention in early life. *American Indian and Alaska Native Mental Health Research, 1,* 244–283.

May, P. A. (1991). Fetal alcohol effects among North American Indians: Evidence and implications for society. *Alcohol Health and Research World, 15*(3), 239–248.

May, P. A., & Moran, J. R. (1995). Prevention of alcohol misuse: A review of health promotion efforts among American Indians. *American Journal of Health Promotion, 9,* 288–299.

May, P. A., & Van Winkle, N. (1994). Indian adolescent suicide: The epidemiologic picture in New Mexico. *American Indian and Alaska Native Mental Health Research, 4,* 5–34.

Middaugh, J. P. (1995, July). National Institute for Drug Abuse Alaska State Workgroup meeting. Anchorage, AK.

Middaugh, J. P., Miller, J., Dunaway, C. E., Jenkerson, S. A., Kelly, T., Ingle, D., Perham, K., Fridley, D., Hlady, W. G., & Hendrickson, W. (1991). *Causes of death in Alaska 1950, 1980–1989. An analysis of the causes of death, years of potential life lost and life expectancy.* Anchorage, AK: Department of Health and Social Services.

Mitchell, H. D., & Bitsui, L. (1995). Cultural and ethnic-sensitive issues that service providers must address when dealing with families of Navajo Vietnam veterans. In D. K. Rhoades, M. R. Leaveck, & J. C. Hudson (Eds.), *The legacy of Vietnam veterans and their families: Survivors of war: Catalysts for change* (pp. 129–236). Washington, DC: Agent Orange Class Assistance Program.

Murry, K. (1992). *Footsteps of the mountain spirit: Appalachia: Myths, legends, and landscapes of the southern highlands.* Johnson City, TN: The Overmountain Press.

Nabokov, P. (1967). *Two leggings: The making of a Crow warrior.* Lincoln, NE: University of Nebraska Press.

Nabokov, P. (Ed.). (1991). *Native American testimony: A chronicle of Indian-White relations from prophecy to the present, 1492–1992.* New York: Penguin Books.

National Center for PTSD and National Center for American Indian and Alaska Native Mental Health Research. (1997). *Matsunaga Vietnam Veterans Project Final Report* [Matsanaga Report]. White River Junction, VT: Author.

Nelson, R. K. (1983). *Make prayers to the raven: A Koyukon view of the northern forest.* Chicago: University of Chicago Press.

Northrup, J. (1993). *Walking the rez road.* Stillwater, MN: Voyageur Press.

O'Donnell, J. (1994). Native peoples of the Southeast. In D. Champagne (Ed.), *Native America: Portrait of the peoples* (pp. 93–128). Detroit: Visible Ink Press.

O'Sullivan, M. J., & Handal, P. J. (1988). Medical and psychological effects of the threat of compulsory relocation for an American Indian tribe. *American Indian And Alaska Native Mental Health Research, 2*(1), 3–19.

Obenchain, J. V., & Silver, S. M. (1992). Symbolic recognition: Ceremony in a treatment of posttraumatic stress disorder. *Journal Of Traumatic Stress, 5*(1), 37–43.

Palinkas, L. A., Downs, M. A., Petterson, J. S., & Russell, J. (1993). Social, cultural, and psychological impacts of the Exxon Valdez oil spill. *Human Organization, 52*(1), 1–13.

Palinkas, L. A., Petterson, J. S., Russell, J., & Downs, M. A. (1993). Community patterns of psychiatric disorders after the Exxon Valdez oil spill. 50th Annual Meeting of the Society for Applied Anthropology (1991, Charleston, South Carolina). *American Journal of Psychiatry, 150*(10), 1517–1523.

Pevar, S. L. (1992). *The rights of Indians and tribes: The basic ACLU guide to Indian and tribal rights,* 2nd ed. Carbondale, IL: Southern Illinois University Press.

Priess, T. (1995). Sea worms, northern lights and Vietnam: The other forgotten warriors project in Alaska. In D. K. Rhoades, M. R. Leaveck, & J. C. Hudson (Eds.), *The Legacy Of Vietnam Veterans And Their Families: Survivors Of War: Catalysts For Change* (pp. 218–228). Washington, DC: Agent Orange Class Assistance Program.

Prucha, F. P. (1976). *American Indian policy in crisis: Christian reformers and the Indian, 1865–1900.* Norman, OK: University of Oklahoma Press.

Rando, T. A. (1992). The increasing prevalence of complicated mourning: The onslaught is just beginning. *Omega Journal Of Death And Dying, 26*(1), 43–59.

Rando, T. A. (1996). Complications in mourning traumatic death. In K. J. Doka (Ed.), *Living with grief after sudden loss: Suicide, homicide, accident, heart attack, stroke* (pp. 139–159). Washington, DC: Hospice Foundation of America.

Rhoades, D. K., Leaveck, M. R., & Hudson, J. C. (Eds.). (1995). *The legacy of Vietnam veterans and their families: Survivors of war: Catalysts for change.* Washington, DC: Agent Orange Class Assistance Program.

Richards, W. (1989). A community systems approach to research strategies. *American Indian And Alaska Native Health Research, 2*(3), 51–57.

Richter, D. K. (1992). *Ordeal of the long-house: The peoples of the Iroquois league in the era of European colonization.* Chapel Hill, NC: University of North Carolina Press.

Riley, P. (1993). *Growing up Native American: An anthology.* New York: William Morrow.

Robin, R. W., Chester, B., & Goldman, D. (1996). Cumulative trauma and PTSD in American Indian communities. In A. J. Marsella, M. J. Friedman, E. T. Gerrity, & R. M. Scurfield (Eds.), *Ethnocultural aspects of posttraumatic stress disorder* (pp. 239–253). Washington, DC: American Psychological Association.

Rothenberg, J. (1986). *Shaking the pumpkin: Traditional poetry of the Indians of North America.* New York: Alfred Van Der Marck Editions.

Rowland, M. C. (1995). *As long as life: The memoirs of a frontier woman doctor.* (F. A. Loomis, Ed.). New York: Fawcett Crest.

Rowley, S. (1991). The Arctic. In C. F. Taylor, & W. C. Sturtevant (Eds.), *The native Americans: The indigenous people of North America* (pp. 204–223). New York: Smithmark Books.

Schmidt, S. M. (1988). American Indian health care: An Indian physician's perspective. *South Dakota Journal of Medicine, 42*(2), 13–16.

Shimkin, D. B. (1953). The Wind River Shoshone sun dance. *Smithsonian Institution: Bureau of American Ethnology Bulletin, 151,* 397–484.

Silko, L. M. (1986). *Ceremony.* New York: Penguin.

Smith, P. C., & Warrior, R. A. (1996). *Like a hurricane: The Indian movement from Alcatraz to Wounded Knee.* New York: The New Press.

Sprott, J. E. (1994). One person's "spoiling" is another's freedom to become: Overcoming ethnocentric views about parental control. *Social Science and Medicine, 38*(8), 1111–1124.

Stamm, B. H. (1999). Conceptualizing death and trauma: A preliminary endeavor. In C. R. Figley (Ed.), *Traumatology of grieving: Conceptual, theoretical, and treatment foundations* (pp. 3–21). Philadelphia: Brunner/Mazel.

Stamm, B. H. (1999). Empirical perspectives on contextualizing death and trauma. In C. R. Figley (Ed.), *Traumatology of grieving: Conceptual, theoretical, and treatment foundations* (pp. 23–36). Philadelphia: Brunner/Mazel.

Stamm, B. H., & Friedman, M. J. (in press). Cultural diversity in the appraisal and expression of traumatic exposure. In A. Shalev, R. Yehuda, & A. McFarlane (Eds.), *International Handbook of Human Response to Trauma.* New York: Plenum Press.

Stamm, B. H., Higson-Smith, C., Terry, M. J., & Stamm, H. E. (November, 1996). Politically Correct or Critically Correct? Community and Culture as Context. Symposium at the 12th Annual Conference of the International Society for Traumatic Stress Studies, San Francisco, CA.

Stamm, B. H., Stamm, H. E., & Weine, S. (November, 1994). Genocide and communal identity: Shoshone Indians and Bosnian Muslims. Presented at the 10th Annual conference of the International Society for Traumatic Stress Studies, Chicago, IL.

Stamm, H. E. (October 1, 1996). Oral history interview with James Trosper. Ft. Washakie, WY. Cassette tape in possession of author.

Stamm, H. E. (in press). *People of the Wind River: The History of the Eastern Shoshone, 1825–1900.* Norman, OK: University of Oklahoma Press.

Sturtevant, W. C. (1991). The Southeast. In C. F. Taylor, & W. C. Sturtevant, (Eds.), *The native Americans: The indigenous people of North America* (pp. 12–35). New York: Smithmark Books.

Swaim, R. C., Oetting, E. R., Thurman, P. J., Beauvais, F. et al. (1993). American Indian adolescent drug use and socialization characteristics: A cross-cultural comparison. *Journal of Cross-Cultural Psychology, 24*(1), 53–70.

Tafoya, N., & Del Vecchio, A. (1996). Back to the future: An examination of the Native American holocaust experience. In M. McGoldrick, J. Giordano, & J. K. Pearce (Eds.), *Ethnicity And Family Therapy*, 2nd ed. (pp. 45–54). New York: Guilford Press.

Talbot, S. (1994). Native American religions: Creating through cosmic give-and-take. In D. Champagne (Ed.), *Native America: Portrait of the peoples* (pp. 441–509). Detroit: Visible Ink Press.

Taylor, C. F., & Sturtevant, W.C. (1991). *The Native Americans: The indigenous people of North America.* New York: Smithmark.

Terry, M. J. (1995). Kelengakutelleghpat: An arctic community-based approach to trauma. In B. H. Stamm (Ed.), *Secondary traumatic stress: Self-care issues for clinicians, researchers, and educators* (pp. 149–178). Lutherville, MD: Sidran Press.

Thompson, J. W., Walker, R. D., & Silk-Walker, P. (1993). Psychiatric care of American Indians and Alaska Natives. In A. G. Gaw (Ed.), *Culture, ethnicity, and mental illness* (pp. 189–243). Washington, DC: American Psychiatric Press.

Travis, R. (1983). Suicide in Northwest Alaska. *White Cloud Journal, 3*(1), 23–30.

Thurman, P. J., Jones-Saumty, D., & Parsons, O. A. (1990). Locus of control and drinking behavior in American Indian alcoholics and non-alcoholics. *American Indian & Alaska Native Mental Health Research, 4*(1), 31–39.

U.S. Department of Justice. (1995). Prisoners in 1994. NCJ-151654. Washington, DC: Author.

Usner, D. H. (1992). *Indians, settlers, and slaves in a frontier exchange economy: The lower Mississippi valley before 1783.* Chapel Hill, NC: University of North Carolina Press.

Utley, R. M. (1984). *The Indian frontier of the American west, 1846–1890.* Albuquerque, NM: University of New Mexico Press.

Vander, J. (1996). *Song-prints: The musical experience of five Shoshone women.* Urbana, Chicago: University of Illinois Press.

Wallis, V. (1994). *Two old women: An Alaska legend of betrayal, courage and survival.* New York: Harper Perennial Library.

Westermeyer, J. (1989). Research of a stigmatized conditions: Dilemma for the sociocultural psychiatrist. *American Indian and Alaska Mental Health Research, 2*(3), 41–45.

White, J. C. (1996). *The pow wow trail: Understanding and enjoying the Native American pow wow.* Summerville, TN: Book Publishing Company.

Wiebe, J., & Huebert, K. M. (1996). Community mobile treatment: What it is and how it works. *Journal of Substance Abuse Treatment, 13*(1), 23–31.

Wilson, J. P. (1989). Culture and trauma: The sacred pipe revisited. In. J. P. Wilson (Ed.), *Trauma, transformation, and healing: An integrative approach to theory, research, and posttraumatic therapy* (pp. 38–71). New York: Brunner/Mazel.

Wolf, A. S. (1989). The Barrow studies: An Alaskan's perspective. *American Indian and Alaska Mental Health Research, 2*(3), 35–40.

Yates, A. (1987). Current status and future directions of research on the American Indian child. *American Journal Of Psychiatry, 144*(9), 1135–1142.

Young, D., & Xiao, S. (1993). Several theoretical topics in neurosis research. *Integrative Psychiatry, 9*(1), 5–9.

Carlos G. Vélez-Ibáñez,
Camilo García Parra

Trauma Issues and Social Modalities Concerning Mental Health Concepts and Practices among Mexicans of the Southwest United States with Reference to Other Latino Groups

☐ Introduction

Approximately a quarter of Mexicans (The term Mexican includes US and Mexico-born distinguished by nativity when appropriate.) and Latinos of the Southwest United States, suffer stress and trauma from the effects of poverty, miseducation, and differential treatment. This is a kind of social modality—a distribution of sadness—among a quarter of the population where parts of the population endure certain kinds of mental illness, physical impairments, and social dislocations. A statistical over participation for this segment is apparent in more catastrophic traumatic behaviors such as gang membership, criminality, and a substantial over participation in wars. More noncatastrophic cultural and linguistic stresses also emerge strongly because of institutional and public assimilationist cultural pressures for larger segments of the population. Each condition represents either the effects of stress or trauma or the potential conditional toward stress and trauma.

These sadnesses cannot be sorted as separate phenomena except only in a categorical sense. These are closely associated to the following cluster of factors:

1. Foreign born nativity, non-English language dominance, low educational attainment, and low income closely associated with lack of educational attainment
2. Negative work and environmental selective factors such as physical stress and environmental contamination, and lack of protective mechanisms such as insurance and medical coverage
3. Gender associated roles and accompanying mental distress, cultural and social dislocation because of migration, self-denial, identity contradictions, ethnic psychocultural conflicts, and lack of positive role models
4. Certain types of addictive behaviors such as alcoholism and drug dependence.

How the population handles these myriad sources of stress and their symptomology culturally and socially is the focus of this work. It must be said at the outset, however, that culturally constituted or traditional practices that are used to mitigate these sadnesses are usually of last resort. These are not usually the first preference of intervention. Also discussed are constructed or intentional cultural formations that emerge to which participants associate as if they were part of their cultural heritage. For the most part, these cultural formations are quite outside of the actual historical cultural heritage and experience of the participants. Mexicans using Puerto Rican *Santeria* (African derived spiritualism) have little actual cultural affinity to the practice. Or equally, Mexicans developing 15th century, pre-European Aztec social formations as the basis of self-help voluntary associations in the present, intentionally learn from the literature on the subject to construct them. These are constructed or intentional in the sense that participants resurrect sets of cultural practices from the very distant past or from other populations that have little to do with the actual and originating rationales for their formation.

For the most part, Mexicans and other Latinos in the United States and in Mexico—rural or urban—do not depend on beliefs or specific practices such as spiritualism, or on folk medical practioners as the first practical option. Rather these are generally invoked when other measures have been tried and failed or when the level of indeterminacy in a particular context is so prevailing that such practices and beliefs are finally summoned. Similarly, participating in intentional cultural and linguistic practices to deal with cultural and linguistic trauma can only be partially satisfying since the structural conditions responsible for such trauma are seldom removed as the causative agents. Therefore, while the focus of attention of this work is on culturally constituted mitigation mechanisms, these are not the first line of preference except in those cases in which persons belong to intentional communities.

☐ Underlying Occupational and Cultural Templates of Social Life

Mexican and Latino social life develops largely within working class sectors in which earnings are limited except for a sizeable portion of Cubans in the Miami area. For the most part, most Mexican and Latino households derive their income from working class occupations with only slightly more than 12% occupying managerial and professional status in comparison to 29% of Anglos in the same categories. Thus 88% of employed Mexican men and women are mostly engaged in lower blue collar service, low white collar service, and agricultural labor with only 3.1% of the 88% working in upper blue collar occupations.[1] As well, income is also derived from employment by several household members, members having two jobs, and using scarce resources in innovative and creative ways. Also more Mexican and Latino households contain more adults than non-Hispanic White households, and thus have potentially more earners per household.[2] This advantage, however, is offset by a larger number of children per household, greater unemployment than among the non-Hispanic White population, and, probably for the first 10 years of a household cycle, intermittent employment.[3] Last, only 1 in 5 households is largely part of the primary labor sector; that is, that sector of the labor market that enjoys income well above the poverty level, durable occupational stability, and security of employment due to contract or representation.[4]

In 1992, 27.4% of all Mexican families were in poverty in comparison to 22.5% ten years previously, but it is also the case that in 1992 73% were not.[5] Only 7.6% of all Anglo families were below the poverty line. However, poverty was very much concentrated in the southern U.S. border region so that the probability of low income is closest to the border such as in the Lower Rio Grande Valley of Texas. In Starr county, a Texas county adjoining the Mexican border, the percentage of families in poverty was 45% in 1980 (Stoddard & Hedderson, 1987) and rose to 60% in 1990 (Brokaw, 1993). Yet for the most part such poverty areas are rural and not urban centers and the pattern of poverty is very much a consequence of the organization of industrial agriculture. Therefore, social life for many Mexicans in the United States is strained in terms of income and occupation with all of the attending stress to that reality. Yet it must be said that 73% of households are not in poverty and even those who are poor have a vibrant social life. In the case of the poverty distribution in Starr county cited above, more than 50% were homeowners.[6] Being poor in Mexico does not mean there is less value to home ownership, more obstacles to the establishment of permanent residency, or inability to provide stable home environments despite the lack of income.

The secret lies in the fact that for most Mexican households extended clustered housing and thick social relations are normative. For the most part, Mexicans emerge associated and connected to dense networks of relationships in which exchange and *confianza* (mutual trust) are the key social and cultural element to social life. The social platforms in which children grow contrast to those of non-Mexican children. Mexican children emerge in clustered households with expectations of relationships with more persons and more expected relationships with the same person (Vélez-Ibáñez, 1996). Importantly these social relational characteristics are part of much larger funds of knowledge which provide positively adaptive forms of survival in the most difficult of circumstances (Vélez-Ibáñez, 1988a, 1988b, 1993, 1995, 1996). These funds are the accumulated strategies of survival that emerge out of the labor history and inheritance of individual and collective households.

In addition, the entire complex of platforms and strategies are provided ritual rationalization by an elaborated ritual cycle of exchange in which a series of calendric and life cycle rituals—some of which are secular and others sacred—operate with some regularity throughout the calendar year among many Mexican households (Vélez-Ibáñez, 1996). Roughly, Christmas marks the first half and Easter marks the second half of the calendar year. Dispersed in between, are myraid life cycle rituals such as baptism, confirmation, communion, quincea-eras (15th year debut), marriages, and funerals. In between, celebrations of birthdays, saints days, days of the dead, and Roman Catholic rituals are practiced. These combine with very intense residential visitations, Tupperware parties, participation in rotating credit associations, residential proximity, recreational activities such as hunting, Sunday outings, and picnics. These practices provide the opportunity for reinforcing mutual trust and the relationships of exchange necessary for their maintenance and development.

Of great significance is that this entire complex of ritual, exchange, and reciprocity patterns increase over time rather than diminish with acculturation (Vélez-Ibáñez, 1996, p. 145). These phenomena seem to argue against a kind of cultural assimilationist process of erasure. As will be seen, language may not be the central mechanism for cultural identity but it is critical to social relations. When these thick exchange social characteristics are glued by ritual participation then they seem to have greater impact on the maintenance of cultural identity than language retention per se.

In fact, although Spanish may be spoken in the majority of homes, linguistic assimilation is extremely strong and in one longitudinal study a third of Mexico-born children preferred English in 1992. But by the second survey in 1995, that proportion had doubled (Rumbaut, 1998). Similarly, U.S.-born Mexicans in San Diego doubled their preferences for English three years after the first survey in spite of the fact that the Mexican border is less than 20 miles south of downtown San Diego. Yet, this study clearly shows that self-identity with the national category of Mexican increased in the aftermath of Proposition 187—an anti-immigrant initiative in California—with an accompanying drop in hyphenated preference like Mexican-American, and pan-ethnic labels like Hispanic. Hardly any persons in the sample preferred the label of American (Rumbaut, 1998, p. 9). Therefore, cultural and linguistic conflict also becomes emergent out of daily living for Mexicans and there is no doubt that such cultural conflict then selects for the development of culturally constituted mechanisms to mitigate the resulting psychic trauma from such contradictions.

The importance however, of maintaining or expanding the extended familial relationships cannot be underestimated. Clustered familial households in which families live relatively close by and maintain interaction is importantly associated to cultural mental health. In fact, the single most important causative factor for the increased risk towards mental disorders over time among this population is the erosion of familial social networks, social support, and emotive and psychological nurturance.[7] What must be emphasized is the paramount relationship between the disruption of thick social relationships as stress buffers and their direct effects on mental well being.[8]

☐ Mental Distress Distributions

Two important conflictive and stressful creating conditions become embedded as part of the daily life course for many Mexicans of the United States: limited income and occupational precariousness and cultural, linguistic, and gender conflict (both internal and external). Such conditionals then become distributed among parts of the population as stressors and indicative of some mental distress such a depression. Low socioeconomic status (SES) is correlated with higher rates of depression, greater exposure to stress, clinical depression, and greater hostility as has been clearly demonstrated in a major review of the literature (Adler et al., 1990).[9] Fifty-two percent of Mexican women are in the labor force which is only 7% less than Anglo women. Fourteen percent of Mexican women in the labor force are in upper white collar occupations as managers or in a professional capacity while only 9.3% of Mexican males are similarly occupied. In addition, almost 30% of employed Anglo women are in the same category and Anglo men are a close second with 29%. In spite of a greater percentage of Mexican women in upper white collar occupations, 19% of Mexican women earn between $25,000 (16.7%) and over 50,000 (2.1%) while slightly over 32% of Mexican males earn income in the same ranges (28.4% and 3.8% respectively).[10] This speaks to the presence of a differentiating factor.

The difference in the percentages between Mexican females and males earning less than $25,000 is significant with slightly over 82% of females and slightly less than 68% of males earning less than that amount. Among Anglos, the difference between females and males is more significant but at lower percentages: 62.4% and 35.1% respectively. In terms of distributed income at this level, Mexican males are more like Anglo females. Both are significantly higher than Mexican women but neither approach the low percentage distribution of Anglo males.[11]

The basic conclusions we can reach, however, are that a higher percentage of Mexican males and U.S. females both earn less than $25,000 than Anglo males and Mexican women are much more highly represented as a percentage than either Mexican males, Anglo females, or Anglo males in this category. This factor is quite important in ferreting out a steady but continuous development of the process of the feminization of poverty and its attending mental health issues in which larger and larger groups of women are over represented within the poverty sector.

Language

The distribution of mental distress—such as depression—among Mexicans can be divided between those who were English language dominant and those who were Spanish language dominant. Each show differences in that the latter scored significantly higher in depression than either Anglos or English dominant Mexicans.[12] This group had significant differences within it since females had much higher scores than males. Additionally, educational attainment was not statistically significant, those with lower depression scores had higher educational achievement.[13]

By and large, however, Spanish dominant Mexicans as a group had significantly greater levels of other types of symptoms such as anxiety and scored higher than either Anglos or English dominant Mexicans. Divorced Spanish dominant women had the lowest scores within the group of any marital category, but education was directly related to anxiety scores with those with less than nine years of school having very high symptoms. Among English dominant Mexicans, those with less than four years of education had the highest scores and females had much higher indications than males. Nevertheless, both males and females with the lowest educational attainment had the highest average scores with the reverse being true.[14]

Education

Education played a very significant role within the Spanish dominant group in that the highest level of psychosocial dysfunction scores were found among those with the lowest educational attainment. Those with the lowest scores had more than a high school degree. Again, females within the group had higher scores and married couples had higher scores than either the divorced or widowed persons. Education may be a realizing variable that provides a rationale for greater dissatisfaction having to do with the quality of the marital relationship. Similarly among the English dominant group, Mexican women had higher scores than men and women who had less than nine years of schooling had the highest scores.[15]

When a propensity towards anxiety, depression, or psychosocial symptoms were measured, there was an inverse relationship between formal education and mental health scores so that higher rates of disorder were found among those lowest in educational attainment. Income and education are more closely associated for Mexicans and especially the Spanish dominant segment than other cultural groups.[16] Similarly, other studies have shown the same relationship between depressive symptoms among Mexicans and the lack of educational attainment.[17]

Most studies show that Mexicans have higher depression rates, higher levels of depressive symptoms, and the highest rate of diagnosed mental illness than Anglos or African Americans.[18] However within the population, farmworkers, first generation Mexicans, those with low educational attainment, and those in maritally disrupted relationships are in greatest jeopardy. As well, one study in San Francisco among immigrant Mexican women (Bach-Y-Rita, 1985), showed that unstable economic circumstance such as uncertain employment, low degrees of emotional closeness among family members, and lack of community integration all seemed to be factors in a significant portion of the sample suffering from stress and demoralization. As one of the most recent studies shows, there is an association between length of residence and psychiatric disorders among Mexicans so that the effects of American acculturation is psychologically unhealthy over the long term (Vega et al., 1998).

Youths and Depression

Depression is not limited to adults and, in fact, adult depression affects children. If perceived racial discrimination is related to depression, lack of self esteem and self worth (Vélez-Ibáñez, 1996), then there is a high probability that depression, anxiety, and feelings of worthlessness will also emerge in selected parts of the Mexican population and especially among the unemployed, undereducated, first generation, and maritally disrupted.[19]

For the most part, youths using inhalants had high prevalences of depression and, even more importantly, high levels of familial conflict and low self-esteem.[20] Their mothers especially showed high levels of depression, high levels of anxiety, learned helplessness, and suicidal tendencies. In turn these mothers' symptoms were related to lack of educational attainment, alcohol and drug use, little familial support, unemployment and to their child's depression. It is central to understand the importance of the relationship of depression of mothers and their children. The greater the depression of the mother, the more the children used drugs, were depressed, and made more suicide attempts.[21]

☐ Culturally Stereotypic Stress Behaviors

Certain stereotyped conditions or behaviors among Mexicans and Latinos have been associated with trauma and stress. Among these are *susto* (fright), *males* (wrongs or hexes), and the appearance in dreams of the dead and animals—portents of death. Symptoms are varied so that susto or fright includes shaking, fever, weight loss, loss of appetite, fever, and madness with a gradual decay until death (O'Nell, 1975). Susto is also used as an explanation for symptoms that cannot be explained medically. It is a type of last resort general explanation for such topical symptoms as uncured rashes, bad dreams, unexplainable fevers, or nervousness. In some cases, susto is associated with both nonhuman agents such as animals or objects and spiritual entities such as the dead. Dog attacks, falling objects, and acts of god may be rationalized as the agents which cause susto. Yet susto is clearly symptomatic of broader psychosocial and economic problems that create uncertainty and indeterminacy the consequences of which result in both the symptomology and rationalization of susto.

Males or hexes on the other hand, do have identified agents but males or bewitchment is an end of the line explanation. For the most part, the males explanation like susto is derived from either medical or mental conditions that cannot be explained in the first instance. These sometimes become manifest as the consequence of unexplained events such as a fire, flood, theft, accidents, or broken relationships. Occasionally, males are used as a means of expressing dissatisfaction over individuals whose social status has improved such that the more reciprocal or communal exchange relations become endangered. This use functions as a leveling mechanism but it is very much associated with small rural communities in Latin America and less so for U.S. born or nonnative born U.S. residents.

On the other hand, there will be highly conflictive social points in the structure of relationships between persons that are unresolvable culturally and may be accompanied by the appearance of males. For example, the overwhelming patriarchy of some Mexican and Latino households place women in a distinct subordinate position within a very well defined division of labor such as traditional housekeeping and mothering roles. Simultaneously, the necessity of making a living places women in new roles and men simply cannot cope with their lack of control over their spouses' labor. Men place exacerbated demands on women to perform double occupational roles so that extreme tension and stress emerge within the household. With that, women will suffer depressive symptoms but attribute such feelings to some external agent creating males. This masks the causative agent involved.

When these males appear and are associated with a medical condition that has not been cured by a medical doctor, then a *curandera/o* (traditional curer) is sought out. The curer applies a combination of physical, spiritual, emotional, and medicinal therapy to the alleged source of the mal or hex. It is highly likely that among the central questions resolved by the curer is the identification of the source of the hex including, in some cases, the identification of the person responsible. In such a case, the curer will provide the victim with a protection in the form of an amulet or other sacra that will prevent future hexes from the same source. In some unusual cases, the curer may even provide the victim with the means of retribution against the original agent but this then enters the realm of brujeria or witchcraft which is in contrast to the normative functions of the curandero/a. In an unintended manner, the persons using such an agent prevent what could potentially have become a violent confrontation between the persons involved.

Again, what must be emphasized is that the appearance of males is closely associated with uncertainty and indeterminacy of context, relationship, and standing, as well as medical conditions not conducive to treatment. Such phenomena are often the topic of conversation on Spanish speaking radio that focus on providing advice in some major cities such as in Los Angeles and Houston. Certainly in rural Mexico, very recent research has demonstrated that the complex of susto, males, and curandero is still very much a part of small rural and town communities.[22] The use of curanderos and even good witches to thwart the machinations of hexes is very much in vogue especially given the severe economic turndowns in the areas studied. [23] The feelings of powerlessness and uncertainty certainly give rise to much greater community conflict and with it a concomitant use of more traditional culturally constituted mechanisms. Therefore, it is not surprising that Latino populations in the United States—especially of the first generation—would also rely on such mechanisms when all else is failing to mitigate the socioeconomic stresses they face.

☐ Intentional Social Forms

Intentional cultural creations and reproductions have emerged in the aftermath of economic and cultural stress and trauma on Mexicans and Latinos in parts of the United States. In California especially, modern versions of 15th century pre-European Aztec social formations termed *Calmecacs* and *Calpulli* have recently been created. Although extinct for 500 years, new versions are being organized by Mexican and Latino women who suffer from economic, cultural, and gender repressions. *Santeria* is another intentional culture creation.

Calpulli.   The *calpulli* phenomenon of California is based on a 15th century Mesoamerican (Central Mexico) cultural mechanism which literally means large house (Rodriguez, 1998). In 15th century Mesoamerica, this formation was basically a familial clan organization that held common proprietorship over a designated territory. Directed by an internal body of sages, the calpulli traditionally had legal, juridical, legislative, and executive functions over all the clan members (Wolf, 1959, 1961).

Mexicans in the Los Angeles and San Diego area formed religiously oriented cooperatives called calpullis that largely offered educational, religious, and liberation theology. This latter ideology emerged out of the political struggles of the 1970s throughout Latin America in which religious communities joined with rural peasants and other groups to form self-sustaining communities.

Focusing on youth as well as community development, the San Bernardino calpulli, for example, offers English and theology classes and also owns a travel agency and book store while simultaneously running sewing and garment shops. These intentional cooperatives then provide an alternative social fabric as well as an underlying ideology tied to liberation theology. Yet for the organizers and participants, the calpulli revives long extinct cultural forms that are framed within mythic frameworks of Mesoamerican non-European philosophy. This framework usually involves a great respect for and association with nature, an emphasis on the spiritualism and connection of all living matter—biological and vegetative—and a connection to a much broader universe of forces that are responsible for the creation of the universe. Thus whatever rituals that are practiced in this context are mediums through which harmony between heaven and earth can be achieved (Carrasco, 1982, 1992).

Calmecac. The calmecac, another extinct 15th century Mesoamerican form, originally referred to the special schools for warriors and priests that focused on ritual and religious training and provided the necessary ideology for qualifying for bureaucratic positions (Wolf, 1959, 1961). In the United States, the calmecac was created specifically in the 1980s by Mexican women—many of whom were mental health workers. They recognized the need for spiritual and cultural infusions that stressed communality, creative artistic expression, and promoted psychic and cultural healing from gender exclusion and repression.[24] These calmecac have created a structure of reciprocal relations and formed a community of interests in which common experiences, ideologies, and world views are tested through friendship and confianza. They too, espouse similar world views to that of the calpulli in which there is a ritual stress towards achieving harmonious relationships with the natural world and the broader cosmos as is the case for most Mesoamerican belief systems (Bonfil Batalla, 1996).

Santeria. Among the most widespread of intentional communities directly associated with physical and mental distress is the religious practice of Santeria (Saints Belief). Primarily practiced among Puerto Ricans, Dominicans, and Cubans in the United States, it is in fact a world wide phenomena that reaches back to its original cultural context: West Africa—specifically the Yoruba peoples. In fact, *Santeria* is so wide spread and popular in the United States, that it has its own web page and in 1998, over 100,000 hits or inquiries were made (www.seanet.com/users/efunmoyiwa/welcome).

Santeria is truly a syncretic belief system and much too complicated to do justice in this brief discussion. Its underlying belief structure is truly African with a pantheon of deities called *Orichas* but syncretized with Catholic saint representations. Originally diffused by African slaves in the 16th century throughout Latin America, the belief system begins with adherence to a divine creator *Olodumare* or *Olorun* who is composed of three separate but equal spirits and is the source of *Ash,* the life source which makes up all material and living things (González-Wippler, 1973). Olorun is the main interactive force with nature, human kind, and the material and spiritual world, but conducts this interaction through intermediaries called *Orishas* that rule over all aspects of material and spiritual life. Each of these are associated with different aspects of nature and human conduct such as water, procreation, curative and medical plants, passion, wealth, peace and harmony, and other attributes.

There are two general kinds of participants—the followers, who participate fully in the rituals, healing, and religious practices associated with Santeria, and those who utilize Santeria occasionally to exorcise an evil spell, physical illness, or mental distress. Both might have three practice sites: the various *botanicas* or specialty shops in which both Santeros (practioners and priests) and laypersons provide literature and materials such as candles, statues of saints, ointments and general knowledge to clients; *Centros* or gathering places for the faithful where rituals of many sorts occur and in which talismans, saint images, candles, flowers, and vases of water are used; and domestic altars in individual households not unlike those in some Roman Catholic homes and with similar kinds of artifacts as those of the Centros.[25]

The underlying premise in the use of these materials and rituals in a Puerto Rican version of Santeria called *Mesa Blanca* (white table) is that humans can control their surroundings—natural, spiritual, and material. This is an interactive process with spirits of nature and spirits of humans molding and affecting humans. Evil and Good are intrinsic—one to the other— and part of the dynamic force that provides the impetus for human and natural development (González-Wippler, 1973). Thus, a Santero who works in promulgating negative witchcraft is perceived as one who is manipulating the negative aspect of a positive force (González-Wippler, 1973).

An important treatment modality in Santeria is the exorcism of evil influences that range from the very common everyday sort of events such as interpersonal conflicts to traumas such as automobile accidents, rape, murder, and serious mental distress. It is in this vein that Santeria becomes not only exceedingly important to the solution of traumatic events but also in dealing with the indeterminacy and uncertainty of social life. Many Puerto Ricans and Dominicans in the United States are triply disadvantaged by economic insecurity, racial stereotypification, and linguistic and cultural erasure and Santeria may offer an avenue of temporary relief, long term community identification, and ritual power.

☐ Other Mitigating Cultural Resources and Persona

As has been mentioned the *curandero* (curer or healer) is usually considered a source of last resort in the United States especially for involved physical ailments or perceived symptoms like *susto, males*, and unexplained damaging events and behaviors.[26] The *curandero* usually has an array of skills and powers ranging from broad knowledge of traditional symptology, herbs, massage, and in some cases the ability to call for helpful spirits or identify harmful ones. Most curanderos invoke Catholic liturgy and the appropriate saints depending on the ailment. Not all curanderos have all of these skills. Some specialize in one or more of these abilities—such as women curanderas who specialize in children's ailments—and it is only by word of mouth that specializations become known.[27] Also, although somewhat rare, medically-licensed physicians and psychiatrists may combine their medical skills with homeopathic, spiritual, herbal, and witchcraft knowledge. In rural areas in Mexico, it is also the case that Mexican doctors will cooperate with local curanderos on some matters and in specific cases. Local custom, however, overwhelms the highly professionalized strictures of the American Medical Association.

For the most part the curandero will have knowledge of the supernatural, natural, individual, and social worlds, is always on call and, charges little or nothing for his services. In rural areas, especially Puerto Rico, South Texas, and New Mexico, poultry, pigs, vegetables, and services are often used as the accepted coinage. The curer will often be part of the community or region and will have social and historical information of the social networks and kinship systems to which the patient belongs. This type of knowledge provides the curer with a gauge of the social dynamics in which an individual may be involved, internalized conflict, and outstanding issues regarding the kinship system and networks that may be crucial to a diagnosis. This is especially important for a prognosis in which sustos or males are involved since these are largely socially constituted symptoms.

For most anxiety, distress, or trauma, such as susto, an *alumbramiento* (enlightenment) is provided regarding the etiology of the causative agent. In this process, a combination of artifacts perceived as sacred and having special curative and diagnostic functions are used such as jade or obsidian or both. A common artifact of discovery is the use of an egg as a medium of diagnosis. The process begins with an unbroken egg rubbed over the body of the client. The egg is then broken and placed in a dish next to the sacred stones. The first time the egg is broken, it is not unusual for it to have a fetid smell and have other objects drop out such as wires, feathers, and an overripe chick. This provides the curer with a pattern of the ills and evils concerned and thus makes diagnosis more predictable. For a number of weeks the same routine is repeated with new eggs. Each time, the objects that emerge decrease and the odor subsides until the egg is clean and with it the curing of the patient.[28]

For traumatic symptoms like susto, the treatment calls for techniques analogous to behavioral desensitization or successive approximations. In the case of an automobile accident, the curer would ask the patient to return to the location of the accident, and after reciting certain prayers and dispelling formulas, the curer would select a few artifacts from the site including soil if any was available. Therapeutic sessions would follow including *barrida* (sweeping) which consists of lightly stroking the patient's shoulders and head with branches of different medicinal plants. Barrida is designed to reduce any fevers and psychological stress and literally to sweep the ills away. The final stage may involve the patient declaring a promise to spirits or saints by showing gratitude in the form of a donation to the church, prayers, or some other type of obeisance such as sponsoring a feast to one of the many Catholic saints in the liturgy. In the latter case, invitations are sent to close members of the family and friendship network to participate. This marks the end of the process.[29]

While curers vary in technique, skill, and approach, they all combine spiritual, physical, herbal, and social aspects that may lead to relief. When they do not, then certainly the curer's reputation suffers. It is not unusual for a patient to seek the advice of other curers after a treatment has failed. In this sense, like the reputation of a medical practitioner that wanes and waxes with success, a curer is open to the same dynamics.[30]

☐ Reading of the Gospels, Spiritualism, Evangelicalism, and Other Healers

The reading of the Gospel according to Saint John by a Spanish speaking priest to the patient is another therapeutic modality for those suffering from trauma and mental distress. Usually associated with very serious, terminal illnesses, the reading of the Gospel is an attempt to invoke the power of Christ to eliminate the illness. It is not an attempt to call up mediating spirits as would be the case among traditional curers. Its function usually, however, is to alleviate the distress, panic, anxiety and loss of control due to the illness itself. Although not promoted by the Catholic Church, this practice is probably strongly associated with more rural regions such as south Texas, northern New Mexico, and rural areas of Mexico.

Spiritualism is a practice used especially with traumatic experience in which there is a loss of an immediate relative or friend. Participation in these practices, although not approved by the Catholic Church, still occurs. There is little formalism, or membership, involved other than providing a fee to a medium who establishes communication with the dead person. Since there seems to be some indication among Catholics that spirits such as saints and angels play some role in the life of the living, spiritual communication and practice becomes importantly linked to attempted explanations because of sudden death.

The medium, usually a woman, functions somewhat like the Internet in cyberspace—as the communications linkage. The process itself usually involves the affected living person sharing with the medium his or her anxiety, loss of control, and strong desire to speak to the departed. The medium establishes the communication with the dead for a period of perhaps three hours, depending on the availability of the departed and its willingness to communicate.

The affected person will ask the dead questions through the medium. The following example illustrates one case in which one of the authors was involved:

> Caller: What do you want? Why do you not leave me in peace? You know that I cannot sleep since you died?
> Dead: I want you to distribute all my belongings to my children. If you do not do it, you will be called to follow me in this work.

Some of the characteristics of such a communication include the fact that the medium will use the tone of the departed. If a woman is the medium and the dead person is a male, a masculine voice will be heard and those present may feel the presence of the departed one. For the most part, the living person will report a sense of strong relief and resolution. Obviously the purported conversation serves a therapeutic function of relieving anxiety and stress.

Evangelical practices serve equivalent functions of those of Santeria, and the reading of the Gospel, and have some aspects of the spiritualist as well as revitalization functions of intentional communities. These collective rituals may assist persons with trauma and serve as curing practices. They include testimonials in a public venue such as an auditorium. Witnesses provide reference models for those wishing relief and solution. Normally witnesses recite similar life histories which represent a conversion process that started as the aftermath of serious illness or psychological disease and concludes with the witness testifying about their relief or resolution. The afflicted person then models him or herself after the witness and learns to embrace a new life way. In fact, like the witness, he or she goes through a revitalization or born again experience and if originally Catholic will convert to the new religion.

What is most interesting in this process is that conversion—especially to Evangelical religions—is a very important mechanism for the relief of social stress due especially to migration, cultural incertitude, or loss of networks. It is estimated that between 60,000 to 100,000 Latino Catholics convert yearly.[31,32] Recent work by Marín and Gambia (1993) clearly shows that most conversions were associated with welcoming and positive social conditions of the new host church. Much of the success of conversion to evangelicalism is the success of small community based approaches for the conversion of Hispanics.[33] The Marín and Gambia/Gamba study points to the fact that large percentages of the converts studied converted because of the need for a welcoming community.

This not only illustrates the extreme sense of social and cultural loss due to migration and dislocation, but also the dissatisfaction with the institutionalized and formal interactive patterns found in the Catholic Church—especially hierarchical relationships to priests and their irrelevancy.[34]

Therefore the role of the Catholic priest, although traditionally suggested as one of the major community resources in dealing with traumatic experiences, is becoming less so. This does not suggest that the priest is irrelevant. Nevertheless, a major reason for the dropping numbers of Latinos as Roman Catholics in the U.S. in the past 25 years (from 90% to an estimated 70–75%) has been the lack of connection of priests to the daily lives of most Latinos that is of central importance.[35]

☐ Central Issues for Institutions and Mental Health Practitioners

Most Mexicans and Latinos live within contexts that are characterized by expanding consanguineal and affinal kinship networks and the underlying cultural principle of *confianza* (mutual trust) which defines expectations of and for relationships. Through ritual and in the daily course of living, most Latinos rely on the ability to establish exchange relationships within very large networks so that sets of obligations are established and favors, labor, information, childcare, money, and support of many sorts are exchanged. Of course, situational conditions may not support either the connections nor the economic basis for these to emerge. Yet the general expectation for Mexicans and other Latinos of the United States is one based on social thickness and not highly individualized expectations (Vélez-Ibáñez, 1996).

Average institutional models providing psychological services, except in highly communalized social service agencies, are focused on the individual's self-improvement and insight as the means of dealing with psychological distress and trauma. This can become problematic especially if the institutional mind set does not consider the manner in which Latinos are expected to interact with significant others, or realize that in-house mental health resources may be available. Bureaucratic procedures, restricted hours, nonuser friendly paperwork, out of the way locations, and lack of Spanish speaking staff serve as barriers that discourage utilization particularly in the case of traumatic experience.[36]

Although methods will vary regionally and by locality, it could be suggested that the more localized the agency concerned is then the higher the probability that the curandero and the mental health practitioner or physician will be more alike than different in the attention paid to context and social relations. A social relational issue may become a serious issue if no overlap exists between the mental health practitioner and other parts of the client's sets of relationships. The local curer depends on these for knowledge, insight, and guidance for diagnosis and prognosis. In a more limited manner, so should the practioner.

Similarly, for the curandero the lack of a fixed rate to charge, and many times gauged to the income of the patient, provides an added layer to the establishment of a social relational tie rather than an instrumental income tie and exchange. It will not be unusual for the curer to be a part of the network of relations in the local arena of exchange so that charging a fee may interfer with relations other than those involved in the treatment process.

As well, kinship and friendship relations with the client's family are relatively common so that the curer is generally available for home visits. This added layer of relationships provides the curer with invaluable allies and sources of information to come to a diagnosis. Such information also establishes the means to advise on the proper course of treatment. Some professionals depend heavily on objective information and seek emotive distance from their patients. This may be a counterproductive strategy to employ.

Finally, the curer has cultural expectations having to do very much with the nonsecular world of the sacred and calls upon images, sources, and elements of the supernatural world for guidance as well as to establish a course of treatment. It will be most certainly in this arena that the greatest challenges will be posed to the traditional mental health practitioner.

☐ Suggestions and Solutions

To become as knowledgeable as possible of the various cultural issues, the practitioner must approach this task as would a student broaching a difficult and demanding subject for the first time. While the practitioner will be considered as expert in the treatment of trauma and mental distress, he or she must shed as much of the professional veneer accumulated and truly become a child willing to become instructed in the complexity of the many options discussed here.

The process would begin by bringing the mental health professional into the household clusters and networks of the cultural populations that he or she is interested in serving. These households contain rich funds of knowledge that are composed of accumulated strategies and practices that have helped households survive (Vélez-Ibáñez, 1988a, 1988b, 1993, 1995, 1996). The knowledge of these funds becomes absolutely crucial to utilize as resources to amend and mitigate the impact of trauma from whatever source it may emerge.

The mental health practitioner would then begin to become engaged within the various networks composing a community of relationships. As a student of social life, the practitioner would be treated with respect but also would be expected to listen to the teachers—members of the household. This exchange between professional and community would open the helping relationship. In time, the practitioner will learn what is of value and what is not and will be able to discard, keep, and embellish the household resources and their funds of knowledge for the benefit of the client. Even in cases of organically caused mental trauma, the cluster of household network would be imperative to maintain. At some future point in time, the practitioner would be accepted as a valued member of the networks beyond the institutional license of practitioner.

Certainly, an open mind toward the local curer should be maintained as well, although it is understood that a magical model and medical model may come into total opposition. From whatever source emerges a solution to the painful and debilitating pain of trauma for the client, the central core of understanding is to investigate and to experiment. In experimenting changes will occur that will become a part of the daily life course of the practitioner and the community from whence her or his clients emerge. It is not necessary for the practitioner to become a curer, but only that he or she recognize his or her own limitations in relation to the client's central cultural core of operation and the various cultural options and mechanisms available.

☐ Conclusions

We have sought to provide a glimpse of the underlying social basis of the cultural life of Mexicans and other Latinos in the United States. It is a population that lives within thick social networks of household clusters. The expectations of relationships with others are very much defined by these social fixtures. Sets of rituals are calendric, cyclical, and create the basic templates for social interaction. When these are made inoperable or if the dynamics of the household and broader community are made inoperable, then local knowledge is put to use to try to explain the resulting stress as well as the sources for such stress. As well, the economic and social context—which is largely working class with a sizeable percentage of households in poverty—engender a greater distribution of depressive symptoms. These symptoms, at times, are correlated with sustos or frights as well as with males or hexes when medical or mental health explanations or treatments fail.

We have strongly suggested that the basis of articulating treatment among Mexicans and other Latinos lies in capturing the core elements of social life. These consist of confianza, funds of knowledge, and the various culturally constituted remedial sources like the curandero, spiritualist, and santero. It is also imperative to understand the various intentional communities and revitalization movements and organizations that have appeared for many years and the manner in which the mental health profession may interact with and among these.

We have recommended that the professional enter the various networks and consult some of the culturally constituted practices of their clients. The acquisition of these funds of knowledge and the relationships entailed could influence the relationship of the client and professional to one in which the professional is student and the client and his or her networks are the teachers. For practioners, this change would greatly enhance his or her relationship to one of mutuality. In this manner, an experimental and experiential dimension of understanding and possible action could be tried out that would be much more inclusive of networks and community. While the clinician constantly learns from the patient in many kinds of therapy, and certainly the cycle of transference and countertransference are constantly in play, the type of learning described here transcends the interactive relationship between two persons. What is being proposed here is a process of network engagement in which the clinician becomes cognizant of the networks of relationships beyond the client.

In the final instance, the treatment of stress and trauma is and must be an undertaking emerging from community and household dynamics. Whether it is trauma resulting from sexual abuse, dislocation, grievous accidents, poverty, cultural conflict, or any other cause, it is the broader community that must be generated to recoup the terrible losses inflicted on and suffered by individuals. The institutional professional alone cannot be made responsible for prolonged treatment among Mexicans and Latinos. No amount of acquired sensitivities or multicultural training will be sufficient to offset the necessity of rallying and arousing community and social network involvement to mitigate, as well as counter, the deep psychic effects of the real sources of the many males facing these cultural communities. But understanding our limitations and strengths does provide us with the balance that is needed to improve our practice.

☐ Endnotes

[1]See J. M. Garcia (1993). Table 2, p. 14.

[2]See F. Bean & M. Tienda (1987).

[3]See Bean & Tienda (1987) for data on household income origins and discussion of household size, p. 199. From Vélez-Ibáñez's work (1988a) in Tucson, AZ.

[4]See E. Ginzberg (1976). For Ginzberg, the essential characteristics of the secondary labor market include lack of occupational stability, security of employment, and above-average earnings.

[5] See Garcia (1993). Table 3, p. 19.

[6] See C. G. Vélez-Ibáñez (1996). Note 11, p. 298.

[7] See W. A. Vega, B. Kolody, S-E. Gaxiola, E. Alderete, R. Catalano, and J. Craveo-Anduaga (1998).

[8] See M. S. Rodriguez and S. Cohn (1998). Page 539.

[9] See N. E. Adler, T. Boyce, M. S. Chesney, S. Cohen, S. Folman, R. L. Kahn, and S. L. Syme (1994).

[10] Garcia (1993). Table 2, pp. 16–17.

[11] Garcia (1993). Table 2, pp. 16–17.

[12] See G. J. Warheit, W. A. Vega, J. B. Auth, & K. Meinhardt (1985). Psychiatric symptoms and dysfunctions among Anglos and Mexican Americans. *Community and Mental Health*, 5, 3–32.

[13] Ibid.

[14] Ibid 17.

[15] Ibid 17 and 20.

[16] Ibid 20.

[17] See J. M. Golding and A. M. Burnam (1990). The community survey offered in both English and Spanish revealed that 538 Mexican-Americans (MAs) born in the U.S. reported more depressive symptomatology than 706 MAs born in Mexico. Immigration status differences (ISDs) in socioeconomic status (SES), stress, and social resources did not account for ISDs in depression. Low educational attainment and low acculturation were associated with depression for US-born Ss but not for Mexico-born Ss. Possible explanations for ISDs in depression include selective migration and relative deprivation.

As well, further analysis by William A. Vega, George J. Warheit, and Kenneth Meindardt indicates similar patterns when applied to marital status and depression. However, this effect was primarily due to the effect of economic stress as reflected by low educational attainment. See Vega et al. (1984). Marital disruption and the prevalence of depressive symptomatology among Anglos and Mexican Americans, *Journal of Marriage and the Family*, X, 817–824.

[18] See S. Vernon and R. Roberts (1982). Prevalence of treated and untreated psychiatric disorders in three ethnic groups. *Social Science Medicine*, X, 1575–1582; L. Radloff (1977); J. Endicott and R. A. Spitzer (1978); and R. Frerichs, C. Aneshenel, and V. Clark (1982).

[19] See M. E. Barrett, G. W. Joe, and D. D. Simpson (1991). Pages 271–272.

[20] Ibid 272.

[21] S. S. Smith et al. 1991:274.

[22] Vélez-Ibáñez carried out research in 1997 and 1998 in the southern rural areas of the western coastal state of Sinaloa, Mexico in two small separate communities of 300 persons each as well as in a larger sized town of 30,000.

[23] For the last 10 years, anthropologist Maria L. Cruz Torres has conducted fieldwork in rural Sinaloa noting various economic practices and has also verified the persistent use of localized versions of mental and physical health practices. In 1998, Vélez-Ibáñez conducted fieldwork in the same area and strongly supports and confirms Cruz Torres' own data. Both interviewed curanderos, patients, and highly knowledgeable community persons in the same area regarding the use, function, and distribution of local practices such as curanderismo, witchcraft, and mental and medical health.

[24] See L. Medina (in press).

[25] See L. Diaz (1998).

[26] In describing the preference of Mexicans for the curandero 35 years ago, see W. Madsden (1964).

[27]Maria L. Cruz Torres (personal communication) reports that in one of the impoverished rural communities she was studying that the curandera was the first choice of preferred treatment care for children since the cost of medical care was so high.

[28]These details of the egg breaking ritual were part of data Vélez-Ibáñez assembled from original ethnographic fieldwork first among Mexican students in a high school in Tucson, AZ in the early 1970s, and from a curandero from a small agricultural village in the Mexican state of Sinaloa in 1998. There were insignificant variations between the two sources. The use of precious stones was data provided by coauthor, Camilo García Parra.

[29]This description is from ethnographic data provided by coauthor Camilo García Parra.

[30]This is a generalized statement concluded from extensive fieldwork carried out by Vélez-Ibáñez and García Parra. There is little in the printed literature that provides these insights.

[31]See K. Christiano (1993). Page 60.

[32]Hispanics (1995). *Catholic Alamanac,* cites the 100,000 figure.

[33]See G. Marín and R. J. Gambia (1993). Pages 368–369.

[34]See Marín and Gambia (1993). Page 364.

[35]Latinos Shift Loyalties. (1994).

[36]See A. Padilla, R. Ruiz, & R. Alvarez (1975, 1971).

☐ References

Adler, N. E., Boyce, T., Chesney, M. S., Cohen, S., Folman, S., Kahn, R. L., & Syme, S. L. (1990). Socioeconomic status and health. *American Psychologist, 49* 15–24.

Bach y Rita, E. W. (1985). An Ethnographic and Psycho Social Study of Latin American Women Migrants in the San Francisco Bay Area. Unpublished Dissertation, Wright Institute Graduate School of Psychology, San Francisco.

Barrett, M. E., Joe, G. W., & Simpson, D. D. (1991). Acculturation influences on inhalant use. *Hispanic Journal of Behavioral Sciences, 13*(3), 267–275.

Bean, F., & Tienda, M. (1987). *The Hispanic population of the United States.* New York: Russell Sage.

Bonfil Batalla, G. (1996). *Mexico profundo: Reclaiming a civilization.* Austin, TX: University of Texas Press.

Brokaw, T. (1993). Incomes in poorest U.S. counties hard to believe, *Arizona Daily Star, 3.*

Carrasco, D. (1982/1992). *Quetzalcoatl and the irony of empire.* Chicago: University of Chicago Press.

Christiano, K. (1993). Religion among Hispanics in the United States: Challenges to the Catholic church. *Archives De Sciences Sociales Des Religions, 83,* 53–65.

Diaz, L. (1998). A Structuralist Analysis of Puerto Rican Santeria. [on-line]. Available: www.t0.oreat/On text/ldsanter.htm.

Endicott, J., & Spitzer, R. A. (1978). A diagnostic interview: Schedule for affective disorder and schizophrenia. *Archives of General Psychiatry, 35,* 837–844.

Frerichs, R., Aneshenel, C., & Clark, V. (1982). Prevalence of depression in Los Angeles county. *American Journal of Epidemiology, 113,* 691–699.

Garcia, J. M. (1993). *The Hispanic Population in the United States: March 1992.* Current Population Reports, Population Characteristics. Washington, DC: U.S. Department of Commerce.

Ginzberg, E. (1976). *Labor market: Segments and shelters.* Washington, DC: Government Printing Office.

Golding, J. M., & Burnam, A. M. (1990). Immigration, stress, and depressive symptoms in a Mexican-American community. *Journal of Nervous Disorders, 178*(3), 161–171.

González-Wippler, M. (1973). *African magic in Latin America.* New York: Julian Press, Inc.

Hispanics. (1995). *Catholic Almanac.* Patternson, NJ: St. Anthony's Guild.

Latinos shift loyalties. (1994). *Christian Century, 111* 344–345.

Madsden, W. (1964). Value conflicts and folk psychotherapy in south Texas. In A. Kiev (Ed.), *Magic, faith, and healing studies in primitive psychiatry today* (pp. 420–440). New York: Free Press of Glencoe.

Marín, G., & Gambia, R. J. (1993). The role of expectations in religious conversions: The case of Hispanic Catholics. *Review of Religious Research, 34*(4), 357–371.

Medina, L. (in press). Los espiritus sigen hablando: Chicana spiritualities. In C. Trujillo (Ed.), *Living Chicana theory* (pp. xx–xx). Berkeley, CA: Third Woman Press.

O'Nell, C. W. (1975). An investigation of reported "fright" as a factor in the etiology of susto "magical fright." *Ethos, 3,* 41–63.

Padilla, A., Ruiz, R., & Alvarez, R. (1975). Delivery of community mental health services to the Spanish speaking/surnamed population. In A. Alvarez (Ed.), *Delivery of services for Latino community mental health* (pp. 94–101). Los Angeles: University of California.

Radloff, L. (1977). The CES-D scale: A self-report depression scale for research in the general population. *Applied Psychological Measures, 1,* 385–401.

Rodriguez, M. (1998). *Mito, identidad, y rito: Mexicanos y Chicanos en California.* Mexico, D.F.: Editorial CIESAS/Miguel Angel Porrua.

Rodriguez, M. S., & Cohn, S. (1998). Social support. In H. Friedman (Ed.), *Encyclopedia of Mental Health* (pp. 535–544). New York: Academic Press.

Rumbaut, R. G. (1998). Immigrants continue to shape America. *NEXO, The Newsletter of the Julian Samora Research Institute, 6*(3), 1–24.

Stoddard E. R., & Hedderson, J. (1987). *Trends and patterns of poverty along the U.S.–Mexico border.* Las Cruces, NM: Borderlands Research Monograph Series, New Mexico State University.

Vega, W. A., Kolody, B., Gaxiola, S-E., Alderete, E., Catalano, R., & Craveo-Anduaga, J. (1998). Lifetime prevalence of DSM-III-R psychiatric disorders among urban and rural Mexican Americans in California. *Archives of General Psychiatry, 55,* 771–778.

Vega, W. A., Warheit, G. J., & Meindart, K. (1984). Marital disruption and the prevalence of depressive symptomatology among Anglos and Mexican Americans. *Journal of Marriage and the Family, X,* 817–824.

Vélez-Ibáñez, C. G. (1988a). Networks of exchange among Mexicans in the U.S. and Mexico: Local level mediating and international transformations. *Urban Anthropology, 17*(1), 27–51.

Vélez-Ibáñez, C. G. (1988b). Forms and Functions among Mexicans in the Southwest: Implications for Classroom Use. Paper Presented to Invited Session of the American Anthropological Association, Washington, DC.

Vélez-Ibáñez, C. G. (1993). U.S. Mexicans in the borderlands: Being poor without the underclass. In J. Moore, & R. Pinderhughes (Eds.), *The barrios: Latinos and the underclass debate* (pp. 195–220). New York: Russell Sage Foundation.

Vélez-Ibáñez, C. G. (1995). The challenge of funds of knowledge in urban arenas: Another way of understanding the learning resources of poor Mexicano households in the U.S. southwest and their implications for national contexts. In J. Freidenberg (Ed.), *The anthropology of lower income urban enclaves: The case of East Harlem* (pp. 253–280). *749.* New York: Annals of New York Academy of Sciences.

Vélez-Ibáñez, C. G. (1996). *Border visions: Mexican cultures of the southwest United States.* Tucson, AZ: University of Arizona Press.

Warheit, G. J., Vega, W. A., Auth, J. B., & Mainhardt, K. (1985). Psychiatric symptoms and dysfunctions among Anglos and Mexican Americans. *Community and Mental Health, 5,* 3–32.

Wolf, E. R. (1959, 1961). *Sons of the shaking earth.* Chicago: University of Chicago Press.

Lane Gerber,
Quynh Nguyen,
Phoukham Kelly Bounkeua

5

CHAPTER

Working with Southeast Asian People Who Have Migrated to the United States

The purpose of this chapter is to educate clinicians that work with Southeast Asian refugees. Clinicians who know something about the history and culture of the people with whom they work are better able to understand why their patients respond in the ways that they do and what interventions and healing practices might be useful. This chapter will offer the reader information regarding the peoples and cultures of Cambodia, Laos, and Vietnam. While the sections on each of the three countries contain some clinical perspectives, specific suggestions for working with Southeast Asian people are included at the end of the chapter. We will begin with some of the commonalties that exist among these peoples and then proceed with sections that describe some of their differences.

☐ Introduction

Cambodia, Laos, and Vietnam were all part of French Indochina from the mid-19th century until the 1950s. Each of these three countries experienced its own unique communist revolution initially promulgated as an attempt to regain national autonomy in the aftermath of this colonial experience. The death and violence from these revolutions and accompanying heavy American military interventions were among the reasons people decided to flee their homelands from the mid-1970s through the 1980s. While the trauma experienced by the refugees from each of these three countries was unique, each group suffered extreme trauma before and during their flight. After coming to this country, each group also experienced many hardships with culture, customs, employment opportunities, government, and language so different from their own.

The religious beliefs of Southeast Asians tend to be a pluralistic combination of traditions—e.g., Buddhism, Hinduism, and animism in the case of Cambodians; Confucianism Buddhism, and Taoism for Vietnamese—that have had profound manifestations in their understandings of modes of living, causes of illness, and treatment (see Kitigawa & Cummings, 1989; Overmeyer, 1986; Reat, 1994; Smith, 1994). Many of these peoples, especially the older generation, believe that illness is brought on by the influence of god or spirit. This could be because of misdeeds in one's past life or because a spirit with malicious intent has been offended. Thus, one would go to a monk to seek the cause and cure for this illness, or one might pray at an ancestral altar (in the case of the Vietnamese) asking for the intervention of ancestral spirits. Ignoring such beliefs or explaining behavior solely in terms of psychological reasons would demonstrate a Western ethnocentrism that would jeopardize treatment and the therapeutic relationship.

Given that refugees from these countries often witnessed and experienced extreme violence and cruelty before, and often during, their escape and internship in refugee camps, many of them experience symptoms of posttraumatic stress disorder (PTSD) and depression. In addition, while refugees fled from intolerable conditions, they left friends, family, customs, and places that were extremely meaningful to them and are now gone. Therefore, they also experience a cultural bereavement. The symptoms for these difficulties can be varied. They include mourning; extreme sadness and emptiness; inability to concentrate; difficulty sleeping; intrusive thoughts and images; flashbacks to traumatic events; panic and startle reactions; sudden flashes of anger and/or violent behavior; inability or unwillingness to trust anyone or be close to anyone; and headaches, body aches or other physical complaints. Coping with these often extremely debilitating symptoms and obtaining help for them is not easy for any of these refugees. This is especially true in an American culture that often does not understand them, their historical antecedents, and that their pain is expressed in somatic rather than in psychological complaints. Western Cartesian understandings of the world have split mind and body into separate realms while for Southeast Asians body and spirit are much more intimately connected.

Refugees from Southeast Asia also have common difficulties adjusting to living in American culture. Refugees from Cambodia and Laos, and the later refugees from Vietnam, were often rural rice farmers. Many of these people were nonliterate in their own language. As they settled in this country and had children who attended American schools and grew up learning to read and write (and in a language foreign to their parents) a large and painful gap was created between generations. In addition, Southeast Asian cultures respect age in a very different way than American culture. Older adults are traditionally respected and obeyed by younger people who, in their country of origin, would not dare question their elders. Now these same elders must ask their children to make telephone calls for them or to translate letters that come from the offices of a variety of government, social service, or utility agencies.

The children thus are thrust into positions of considerable power in the family. At the same time, parents want them to act with the same kind of deference to parental wishes as children have historically shown in Southeast Asian cultures. Children have power but must not show it. Parents suddenly have much less power and feel that loss very acutely.

Also, there are the very different American emphases on independence and on early socialsexual behavior in teenagers that are anathema to Southeast Asian parents, but part of the lives of their children who go to American schools and are immersed in American society. These different emphases further exacerbate the generation gap.

The difficulties in adjustment for the people from these countries are also demonstrated in the changes in the positions of men and women vis-a-vis each other. In the U.S., women are able to get jobs, bring home a salary, and feel important in their own right. The opportunities and expectations for women in America are very different from those in Cambodia, Laos, and Vietnam. For men, however, who are used to having the power in the family, not having land to farm or a language that comes easily to the tongue can be devastating. This results in a huge loss in status for men. This includes well educated men who may have held important jobs in their country, but who typically are not able to find comparable work in this country.

These dislocations are very disruptive to the individuals involved, their families, and their communities. Husbands and wives can become adversaries, neither trusting the other. Domestic disputes can turn into abuse. When this happens, the law typically supports the wife, but the community typically supports the husband, leaving the wife isolated.

The health professional that works with Southeast Asian refugees and their families must be aware of the above commonality of experiences as well as the differences in experiences of the people who come from Cambodia, Laos, and Vietnam.

☐ Working with Cambodian People

The population of Cambodia is approximately nine million. As noted earlier, Cambodians, or Khmer, have been subsistence farmers in the countryside, small shop owners in the villages, or dwellers in the country's main cities. The gulf between people who came from the countryside and those who were raised in the city was and is substantial in terms of education, status, and income. Cambodians who survived the terror of the Khmer Rouge genocide (1975–1979) and fled first to the refugee camps in Thailand came to the United States mainly in the 1980s. The largest numbers settled in California, Massachusetts, New York, and Washington (Mollica, 1994).

Recent Cambodian history is separated by the Khmer Rouge genocide into two periods: the period prior to 1975, and the period afterwards. During the Khmer Rouge regime between one and two million Cambodian people were killed outright (this figure can only be an approximation) or died of torture, illness, starvation, or exhausting, brutal physical labor in work concentration camps throughout the country. A majority of the population moved from their homes to other places in the countryside where they worked as virtual slaves to *Angka* (the organization) the name used by the Khmer Rouge for itself. This extended period of time during which so many Cambodians lost loved ones, were tortured, or even died, resulted in significant physical and emotional difficulties for the survivors (Boehnlein, 1987; Kinzie, 1985; Mollica, Donelan, & Tor, 1993; Muecke, 1983a, 1983b). While most brutal killing ended in 1979, fighting continued as the Khmer Rouge and other resistance factions attacked both refugee camps and settlements villages within Western Cambodia and Thailand.

Since a peace agreement was signed by the Khmer Rouge and other military factions in 1991—an agreement from which the Khmer Rouge subsequently withdrew—fighting in Cambodia diminished considerably. Banditry, however, grew in the countryside and in Phnom Penh. News of such violence is frequently on the minds of Cambodians now living in America, most of whom still have relatives in Cambodia. This news sometimes exacerbates their symptoms of depression and PTSD.

The extreme savagery of the Khmer Rouge regime decimated the leadership and infrastructure of the country. While the government and the educational system have been restored, neither function at a high level and the country is fraught with many factional disputes. In 1997, violence increased again sparked by the conflict between the two Prime Ministers, Hun Sen and Prince Norodom Ranariddh, who shared power. These disputes among rival political factions are often mirrored in disputes within the Cambodian communities that exist in the United States.

Religion and Culture

The vast majority of the population in Cambodia practices a Theravada Buddhism similar to that practiced by the people in Laos and Thailand. Hinduism was brought from India to Cambodia in the fifth century and has been incorporated into Cambodian religious and spiritual beliefs along with Buddhism and an indigenous animism. During the height of its civilization, from the eighth to the 15th century AD, when Cambodia occupied most of the Indo-Chinese peninsula, Angkor Wat was its most important religious and cultural site. This site, the largest of scores of other *wats* (temples) represented the connection between heaven and the Cambodian god-kings (Keyes, 1990). Angkor Wat remains a focal point of Cambodian culture, identity, and pride with its image portrayed on many different articles from the Cambodian flag to symbols used for Cambodian-American clubs to articles sold in stores in America.

Before 1975, there were temples throughout the country and many monks who lived and taught school within the grounds of these temples. The monks and the temples were important parts of the culture. Although most temples were destroyed and many monks were killed by the Khmer Rouge, there has been a rebuilding of the temples and an increase in the number of monks within the last ten or fifteen years. While the Khmer Rouge atrocities challenged the most basic assumptions Cambodians held about the world in which they lived, Buddhist beliefs and practices have been critically important in helping Cambodians come to grips with their experiences. Cambodian communities in America, however, are caught between the desire to preserve deeply held cultural and religious beliefs and practices, and the need to adapt their lives to American culture and religion. This dilemma is most clearly reflected in conflicts between the generations.

Culture, History, Explanatory Models and Clinical Work

My (LG) first session with a Cambodian client was with a 50-year-old woman who was referred because she had not improved after many medical interventions. After our hour long session, my client had the following conversation with her husband which was translated for me by an interpreter.

Husband: What medicine did he give you?
Wife: He didn't give me any.
Husband: What did the doctor say was wrong with you?
Wife: He didn't say anything.
Husband: What did you do in there for an hour?
Wife: We talked.
Husband: Is that all that happened? I don't think you should go back. He is not a good doctor.

After a pause in their conversation, the wife added that while the doctor had not given her anything or told her what was wrong, she wanted to come back because she thought that "perhaps he could be trusted and talking was okay." It was apparent that while the wife was willing to try talking in an open ended way, that did not fit with cultural expectations, at least not until much greater rapport and understanding were established.

In Seattle area clinics, Cambodian patients who are seen for therapy often tend to be women who were, before 1975, from rural Cambodian farms. Most of these refugees, who left Cambodia in 1979 after the Vietnamese invaded, spent years in refugee camps in Thailand before coming to the United States. Most of these patients have lost at least one child and numerous other family members during the Khmer Rouge period. Regardless of the reason for their referral, many of these patients complain of chronic headache, often associated with other physical symptoms such as chest pain, coughing, palpitations, and muscular or joint pain. In an interview, patients will most frequently want to talk about these physical symptoms and to describe them in detail.

Although Western psychology often labels this emphasis on physical symptoms as somatization, Southeast Asian and Cambodian cultures do not share the Western idea of a mind-body split (Kleinman & Kleinman, 1985). If one continues to talk about the specifics of the physical symptoms with a Cambodian patient, one is frequently led to the emotional factors that are associated with them. Thus, a therapist may hear about the symptoms of chronic headache and muscle or joint aches accompanied by the Cambodian phrase *pruiy chiit* (Headley, 1977). An approximate translation of pruiy chiit is a worried or sad heart and refers to feelings of extreme sadness that become manifest in one's body as well as one's thoughts and spirit (Handelman & Yeo, 1996). The physical symptoms, together with the sadness, can refer to remembering the pain of living as a starved and tortured slave under the Khmer Rouge. It carries with it a sense of loss of loved ones who were killed before one's eyes and/or a sense of bereavement over the loss of one's country, community, and culture (Boehnlein, 1987; Eisenbruch, 1988; Eisenbruch & Handelman, 1989).

Many Cambodians who are middle-aged and older believe an imbalance in their systems causes their symptoms. For example, imbalances among the four elements of the body (wind, soil, fire, and water) or in hot or cold are believed to cause ill health and bad feelings (Handelman & Yeo, 1996). Interpreters, monks, or other community leaders can serve as cultural consultants to the clinician in these situations discussing the implications of the specific imbalance.

Cambodian religious beliefs also play a part in many Cambodian patients' understanding of their suffering. Buddhists believe that all of one's actions in this and other lifetimes create reactions. One's circumstances and health in this lifetime thus reflect past deeds in this and previous lifetimes. This belief, called Karma, "determines the overall nature or fate in one's life and therefore affects one's general state of health" (Handelman & Yeo, 1996, p. 273).

Monks and traditional healers (*kru khmer*) perform certain healing ceremonies and practices for physical, emotional, and spiritual pain. These include washing the client with holy water, coining (scraping a coin on the skin), and cupping (burning oxygen under a cup and putting it on the skin at the pain site). These practices are for cleansing and blessing and for drawing out impurities in a particular area of the body. A therapist's awareness of such practices and his or her willingness to include a monk or *kru* as part of the overall treatment can be comforting to the patient and helpful in increasing rapport in therapy sessions.

Finally, it should be noted that for Cambodian refugees who experienced the terror of Khmer Rouge, there often remains a sense that talking to someone else about their feelings and experiences, past and present, can not only stir up very painful memories, but also be dangerous. This relates directly to Khmer Rouge edicts that forbade showing emotions and talking with others. A violation of Angka's policies was punishable by death. While the killing fields of 1975–1979 may seem far away to those who did not experience them, they, and their rules, often remain alive within the minds of the majority of Khmer. Factional disputes within American Cambodian communities only exacerbate these feelings. Therefore, the clinician working with Cambodian patients must create an atmosphere of safety and trust in the therapy setting and anticipate some appropriate wariness on the part of many patients (Chung & Okazaki, 1991).

☐ Counseling Laotians

Laos, known today as Lao People's Democratic Republic (PDR), is a small mountainous country with one of the lowest population densities in Asia: 4.8 million people in 89,984 square miles (Emerging Markets Companion, 1998). As small as the country is—it is just a bit smaller than Utah—Laos is made up of people of many nationalities and ethnic groups totaling 68 different traditions and customs. In spite, or perhaps because, of their diversity, the people of Laos live together quite harmoniously. The population can be divided into three main groups. These include the majority lowland Lao (Lao Loum); the seminomadic peoples who live on the mountain slopes (Lao Theung); and the hill tribes, who are among those least affected by Western influences, including the Kmhmu, Hmong, Lu, Mien, Thaidam, Thaideng, and Yao. About 85% of the population are farmers living in the fertile plain surrounding Vientiane, the capital city (Thongsith & Bouaravong, 1991).

While this section will concentrate on the lowland Lao who comprise the majority of the population, it should be noted that tribes like the Hmong and Mien, who have languages and beliefs different than the lowland Lao, and are significant groups in the U.S. The Hmong, for example, are mountain dwellers whose religious beliefs are animistic. Many Hmong in the U.S., however, have converted to Christianity, at least nominally, for a variety of social and practical reasons. The first wave of Hmong refugees to come to the U.S. consisted of a large number of people who had been leaders in Laos and whom subsequent groups of refugees have looked to for instruction and leadership.

Lao is the common language spoken by two-thirds of the people; however, Laos has been influenced by many other cultures and English, French, Russian, Thai, and numerous tribal languages are spoken. Laos was influenced by French colonialism, although the French invested less in terms of transportation, education, or health care in Laos than they did in Vietnam or Cambodia. Independence from France, negotiated by three brother princes, occurred in 1949. The brothers split into rival factions, however, with one brother making contact with Ho Chi Minh and setting up the Communist Pathet Lao. This resulted in Laos being used as a major supply line for North Vietnam to move troops and supplies into South Vietnam in the 1960s and 1970s. Because of this involvement in the Vietnam War, there were massive American bombings over two-thirds of the country creating 600,000 refugees who had to flee their homeland (Kitano & Daniels, 1988). Many Laotian refugees sought asylum in Thai refugee camps. With the help of the United Nations High Commission for Refugees, Laotians were able to be repatriated to a third

country. An estimated 150,000 ethnic Lowland Lao refugees were resettled in the U.S. The majority of the Laotians entered the United States
between 1979–1980 fleeing Communist persecution. Subsequent Lao
refugees came to flee poverty or to be reunited with their family members (Bounkeua & Viradet, 1995).

Religion and Culture

Ninety percent of the Lao population practices Theravada Buddhism,
and like Cambodians and Vietnamese, the Lao people's values, customs,
and rituals are deeply influenced by their religion. Their cultural values,
which evolved from their religion, may prevent them from seeking help
from outsiders (i.e., counselors) for their personal problems. Laotians
have come to accept that they cannot control their own destiny and that
suffering is a part of the natural process of life. Thus, they may feel that
no amount of outsider intervention can help.

Laotians are known for their love of peace and for their relaxed attitude toward life. There is a saying in Laotian that supports this belief,
Bopen gnang (pronounced "Ball-bin n-Yan"), which means "it does not
matter" or "it is not too important" (Outsama, 1977). When things are
going badly for a Lao person, the belief is that he or she will eventually
find a solution, but for the moment, should not worry about it.

For many Laotians, Buddhism is also deeply influenced by traditional
animistic beliefs (Outsama, 1992). For instance, before Laotians partake
in traveling, vacationing, moving into a new home, and taking any type
of test, a little ritual must first be performed. The ritual is performed by
preparing a dessert tray with beetle nut, tobacco, a cup of water, flowers,
and candles and asking in prayer for *Maa tall lend nee,* or Mother Nature,
for protection and luck in the new situation.

Rituals and Celebrations

A rite of passage for a young man, if he is Buddhist, is to become a monk
before he is to be married. By becoming monks, young men bring honor
and provide credits to their parents to ensure they are allowed into
heaven. If the parent is already deceased, but living in the spirit world
somewhere between heaven and hell, this credit serves like a passport to
lift him or her to heaven. The young man who completes this ordination
process is considered a very good and loyal son by all.

One of the most important and widely practiced Lao customs that is
still carried over to America is the ceremony of prayers and good wishes

called *Baci*. The ceremony serves many purposes for the Lao people's life experiences. *Baci* are used in ceremonies of marriage, welcome, farewell, achievement, thanks for recovery from illness, and for good luck in the New Year.

Beliefs about Death and Dying

Dreams or visions about past relatives who have died are not uncommon. When one has a dream of a past relative, it means the relative has some reason to be restless. It is taken as a sign of a problem and living relatives should act to amend it. "Unmistakable emotional disturbance, however, is usually attributed to possession by spirits of malicious intent; to the bad luck of familial inheritance, or for Buddhists, to bad karma accumulated by misdeeds in past lives" (Muecke, 1983b, p. 838). Dreams of the dead are said to be the first sign of the dead's unrest. It is believed that if you ignore the dream and do not act, the spirits will produce a more drastic sign. The Laotian often believes that illness or bad luck, such as a car accident, could be a drastic sign sent to them by their dead relatives. If one does not find a way to help the ancestors, it is believed that their ghost or spirit will haunt the individual and will not leave him or her alone.

A person who has a dream or vision of the dead must go to the Buddhist temple to seek the monk's assistance. The person gives offerings of food, water, and money to the monk to transfer blessings to the ancestor who has been visiting them in dreams or through signs. When the ceremony is completed, it is believed that bad luck will disappear since the ancestor's spirits are now happy and satisfied.

Customs, Morality, and Taboos

Laotians do not believe in expressing their emotions verbally. As children, they have been taught by their parents and others that it is not acceptable to express emotions openly. For instance, at the age of four and six, a sister and brother might ask each other who they liked for a girlfriend or boyfriend. Their parent, upon hearing them, would say, "you should keep your feelings to yourself. Who you love or like should not be expressed to others."

Although the Western form of greeting with a handshake is increasingly becoming more popular for Laotians, the traditional way of greeting is the "*Wai*." This consists of joining one's own hands "together and raising them more or less as high from the chest to the head as the degree of respect you wish to express. From equal to equal: up to the chest. To a superior: up to the face. To a teacher or parent: up to the head. To god: over the head. . . . A Laotian greets the head of a family or an older person first. In a group he must greet the most important person first" (Outsama, 1977, pp. 6–7).

The most important cultural taboo regards the body. The body is considered something very sacred that must be respected because every part of the body is said to be inhabited by a soul. The importance of the soul increases as one moves from the feet to the top of the head. Therefore, it is absolutely forbidden to touch the head of someone without permission. This cultural rule explains why one must never touch or point at a higher part of someone else's body with a lower part of one's own body.

Unlike the American custom, looking directly into someone's eyes is considered disrespectful. Laotians also prefer to talk about a subject using an indirect approach to come to a particular point. In addition, a smile can have many meanings. It can mean happiness or sorrow, agreement or disagreement, understanding or misunderstanding (Outsama, 1977). Finally, it is very important that outsiders realize that often times a Laotian will say "yes" to a question out of respect for the asker when they would prefer to say "no."

Roles of Men, Women, and Children

As noted earlier in this chapter, men have more prestige than women and children in Lao culture. In the wedding ceremony, for example, the song march is "here comes the groom" while the bride waits for him. The role of women in American culture can lead to an upsetting of traditional family roles and to much family turmoil. Two important aspects include the necessity for both husband and wife to work in America, and the fact that wives often know more English than their husbands.

Lao parents often give up trying to learn English, saying they are too old to learn or understand. They maintain their cultural and religious heritage and customs by listening to Lao and Thai songs or watching Thai soap operas found in ethnic supermarkets (Bounkeua & Viradet, 1995). They choose to live in ethnic enclaves socializing mostly with their own people, rather than struggling to integrate into American society. Their children, however, do not have this option. They must function in both the world of their parents and the world of their peers, and they experience the conflicts between the two cultures acutely. "The children are deeply disturbed by the attitude of their parents and are caught off balance between their own cultural heritage and the way of life in the U.S. They are expected to be Americans at school and Lao at home" (Tomasi, 1993, p. 28).

Finally, children as old as ten years of age often sleep with their parents. This is a common practice in both America as well as Laos. Children having their own room is a Western concept and also requires a family income few Lao enjoy in the U.S. When they get older, children usually share the room with their siblings, including those of the opposite sex.

Family Relationships and Expectations

The traditional family structure consists of the father as the head of the household and decision maker and the mother as budget manager and child and household caretaker. The family ties are tight with values that stress obligation to the family and filial piety (i.e., respecting one's elders). The traditional expectations are for the middle generation to take care of their own children as well as their parents. The family's reputation is to be guarded at all costs and there is a great emphasis put on not shaming or making the family lose face.

In the Lao family, there is a sense of keeping the family structure intact without letting the "bird out of the nest before it is time." Lao children are expected to live with their parents until they are married, "and sometimes, even after marriage if they are not self-sufficient or if their parents are too old, or for other reasons, need their presence" (Outsama, 1977, p. 11). These expectations can cause problems as they clash with American expectations that allow children independence at age eighteen.

The Lao sense of family extends to the community. Since Laotians tend to live in ethnic enclaves or close to someone else who is Laotian, they often depend on each other to watch their children while they are at work. Thus, without the money for daycare or sitters, they often leave their small children (as young as eight years old) at home.

Laotian people as well as other Southeast Asia peoples have become wary about how to discipline their children. Children are constantly being told by the media and their teachers to report if they are being abused in any way. Children can and do threaten their parents with reporting them, for real abuses, or to gain power and autonomy in the family. This causes fear and resentment in the community and increases the gap between generations (Lee, 1988; Zane, Takeuchi, & Young, 1994).

Parents are told by Americans to discipline their children by taking away privileges from them. When the parent generation was growing up in Laos, however, they did not have many material possessions. Now that their situation is improving economically, they may feel they are depriving their children if they are to take these things away from them.

Therefore the parents' dilemma is that it is confusing for them to parent in this Western way and it can be dangerous, given some parents' fear of being reported to the authorities, if they discipline in other ways.

Power and Authority

Lao people greatly respect those in positions of power and authority such as police officers, teachers, and government officials; they typically do not consider themselves in a position to question their authority. This characteristic leaves Lao people especially vulnerable to the abuse of power, however. Avoiding eye contact while talking is a sign of respect and an attempt to avoid offending the person in authority.

Although Laotians view spousal abuse as being wrong, they consider the problem to be a family matter between husband and wife, and, given the status of males in the community, often assume the wife to be at fault. Like many other domestic violence victims, Laotian wives feel at fault and are unlikely to leave their husbands. Given this sense of fault, and a community that blames the wife, she may feel helpless and forced to let the situation continue. Sometimes these women come to community health clinics with somatic complaints that are an expression of the physical and psychological pain they feel but cannot express directly.

☐ Working With Vietnamese Clients

Since the fall of Saigon to the communist North Vietnamese in 1975, a large number of Vietnamese refugees have been resettled in the United States. They came in three waves. In 1975, 130,000 people arrived. These were mostly professional people, government officials and military personnel associated with the South Vietnamese government. They were generally well educated, young, urban dwellers accompanied by their nuclear and, in some cases, extended family members.

The second wave (1979–1983) consisted primarily of 250,000 "boat people." These people were generally less well educated, less literate, of rural origin, and much more traumatized by their escape. An additional 200,000 boat people died at sea having been robbed, assaulted, raped, and killed by pirates (Knoll, 1982). The survivors stayed for years in overcrowded and unsanitary refugee camps on neighboring shores with the constant fear of being sent back to Vietnam. The trauma and high death rate of the boat people led to the creation of the Orderly Departure Program (ODP) with the help of the United Nations (The United Nations High Commissioner For Refugees, 1998) and the U.S. government (Foreign Relations Authorization Act). This program provided a means for qualified individuals to leave Vietnam for resettlement in the U.S. under safe conditions.

The third wave of refugees after 1984, a result of the ODP, included those refugees from Vietnam with relatives in the U.S., and approximately 12,000 Amerasian children (children of Vietnamese mothers and American fathers; see 1987 Amerasian Homecoming, Act 101 Statutes-at-Large 1329). Between 1992 and 1996 South Vietnamese soldiers, officers, and political figures imprisoned by the communist regime for up to 12 years also were allowed to come to the U.S. with their families.

Religion and Spiritual Beliefs

Before the French occupation of Vietnam, there were three main religions in Vietnam—Confucianism, Buddhism, and Taoism. The Roman Catholic religion was brought in by French colonials. The Vietnamese typically incorporated into their way of life ideas from their three religions, earlier animistic concepts, and later Western philosophical ideas. These teachings have had a profound influence on Vietnamese values and modes of living—including explanations about causes of illness, manifestations of symptoms, help seeking behavior, and expectations from treatment.

A main influence on the social interactions and patterns of Vietnamese people is Confucianism. Here interpersonal interactions are determined by prescribed roles, obligations, and duties including especially the notion of "filial piety." The Vietnamese concept of filial piety is a bit different than the Cambodian or Laotian version in that Vietnamese feel a strong sense of family that is passed down from generation to generation. Cambodians, on the other hand, rarely know many of their relatives beyond their grandparents.

Like the other Southeast Asian cultures, Vietnamese child rearing places an emphasis on interdependence, familial affiliation, and relatedness over individuality. When a child does something that is considered wrong, for example, the child's mother does not say "you brought shame on yourself for your behavior," but rather, "you brought shame on the whole family because of your behavior." Consequently, the motivation for children to fulfill their obligations toward their parents and elders is strong.

When a person in a family gets sick, he or she can seek help from Western medicine, Eastern medicine, and also from the temple priest or church priest who might say a prayer for the patient and include the name of the individual within the ritual ceremony. In addition, when people become severely ill, they may pray at an ancestral altar and ask the ancestor spirit for help. When relatives die, especially in traumatic circumstances, most Vietnamese believe that their souls or spirits wander around and cannot live in peace or get to heaven. It, therefore, is the duty of the family members who are left to perform the appropriate religious and spiritual rituals that will enable the ancestral spirits to get to heaven and find rest. This also enables the living relatives to regain their own spiritual and psychological equilibrium.

While other Southeast Asian cultures also emphasize the duty of living family members to perform the appropriate religious and spiritual rituals for the dead, the Vietnamese culture, with a Confucian emphasis on ancestor worship, finds it especially important for ancestors' graves to be tended to and for recently deceased relatives to be buried in the family plot. Thus, for the Vietnamese there is a special pain in leaving their homeland because they are abandoning the graves of their ancestors.

A fundamental religious, spiritual, and cultural belief for Southeast Asians is that nature maintains a balance in all things. This relates to the concept of yin (associated with cold, the moon, and the feminine in both men and women) and yang (hot, the sun, and the masculine in both men and women). Yin-yang represents one manifestation of the notion of a complementary dualism of life in contrast to the Western view of an antagonistic dualism. Southeast Asians see people as a microcosm within the macrocosm of the larger universe, with the energy of one interconnecting with the energy of the other. An imbalance or disturbance of this energy (e.g., associated with excessive stress and lack of harmony with the world) can cause the body to become more susceptible to disease. Natural medicines and traditional healing techniques are concerned with the attempt to restore the body to greater balance, rendering it less susceptible to disease.

Loss and Trauma

In the 35 years before their migration, the Vietnamese people lived through a generation and a half of war (1940–1975). Many people died during this time. The first refugee movement occurred after 1945 when France tried to reoccupy Hanoi after the defeat of the Japanese (who had occupied Vietnam since 1940) in World War II. The French were opposed by Vietnamese Communists led by Ho Chi Minh. Many Vietnamese fled into the jungle during the fighting. The second migration occurred in 1954 after the defeat of the French at Dien Bien Phu by Ho Chi Minh's forces. One million people from the north of Vietnam had to leave their homes and families and move to the south. During this time landowners, who were considered to be enemies of the Communist effort, were killed or persecuted and farms began to be collectivized (Knoll, 1982). The next migrations, as noted above, followed the U.S. war with Vietnam.

Refugees who left Vietnam and arrived in other countries mourn very significant losses. The separation of the family tears at the very fabric of being of a Vietnamese person—missing parents, children, or other family members means that the connections and relationships so important in the Vietnamese way of life have been changed forever. Moreover, as noted above, leaving their homeland means leaving their ancestors' graves, a most painful and significant personal, cultural, and religious loss.

It is important to reiterate that the process of adjustment to the Western way of life is different for every surviving member of the Vietnamese (and every Southeast Asian) family. People do not change at the same rate so a gap in values is created between people of different generations or different genders. This values gap creates conflict and increases stress within the family. The reactions to the accumulated losses, traumas, and attempts at acculturation can include rage, aggression, despair, guilt, grief, hopelessness, and sometimes suicide and homicide. One depressed Vietnamese woman who came to the U.S. with her son complained that when they lived in Vietnam she gave him the most beautiful room in the family home. Now that they are in America, "He put me in the basement, the most cold place in his house."

Assessment and Treatment Interventions

Case Study: "Tran" was brought to a physician with the following physical symptoms: abdominal discomfort, rapid heart rate, sweating, weakness, loss of appetite, and frequent nightmares. Because he had many symptoms associated with depression and posttraumatic stress disorder, the physician referred him for psychotherapeutic treatment. Tran, however, did not want to talk about his traumatic experiences, but instead, wanted to respond only to questions about his physical complaints.

Q.N. made an appointment for Tran with a psychiatrist for medication to treat nightmares and sleeplessness and to provide something tangible to make him feel more comfortable. In addition, because of Tran's discomfort with going to a mental health agency, Q.N. visited him at his apartment. Q.N. and Tran talked about aspects of Tran's daily life as well as his physical symptoms. Q.N. shared some of his own experiences with Tran in an attempt to create greater trust and rapport. Eventually Tran began to talk about his wife.

Tran tried to flee the fighting in Vietnam with his young wife and baby after years of preparation and planning. On the way across the water to Malasia, they ran out of food and water. Their boat then was boarded by a group of heavily armed Thai pirates. Everything of value on the boat was taken by the pirates who also chose some of the Vietnamese women refugees to rape. Tran was handed the baby as he watched helplessly while the pirates tore off his wife's clothes and raped her in front of everyone on the boat. Afterwards, with blood all over her body, his wife staggered to the side of the boat and jumped into the sea. Tran handed their daughter to another refugee and jumped into the sea to rescue her. One of the pirates shot Tran in the shoulder. He was not able to continue after his wife, but could only struggle to the back of the boat and hold on. Tran eventually survived and came with his daughter to the U.S.

Tran said that he usually dreams about his wife and the way she died with all the blood on her body. He said he still does not know why he was alive after the death of his wife. Tran tries not to think about all these events, but he cannot stop himself from doing so. He says that he does not want to be with or meet other people. Tran thinks that because of the way his wife died, her spirit or soul is still wandering around with no place to stay. Sometimes he says he hears his wife cry, "save me."

Q.N. discussed with Tran the usefulness of a religious ceremony at a Buddhist temple for the soul of his wife. By doing this ceremony perhaps he could give his wife's soul some rest and the possibility of going to heaven. Q.N. also asked if his wife were here would she say that she wanted him to die with her, or for him to be healthy and take care of their daughter. "Perhaps the reason that you (Tran) did not die with your wife the day she jumped into the sea was to enable you to care for your daughter whom she could no longer care for."

Tran's physical symptoms eased and he became calmer. Q.N. also encouraged him to attend the Buddhist temple for the reason of building good karma that would benefit his wife and daughter. This behavior also reduced his estrangement from other people in the community and his sense of isolation. If Tran had been given this latter reason (i.e., to help himself) instead of a reason that emphasized his family, it is doubtful that he would have complied given his guilt about his inability to save his wife as well as the Southeast Asian emphasis on family over individuals. The counseling process together with his reconnection with his religion and his community enabled Tran to make significant improvement.

☐ Clinical Suggestions for Working with Southeast Asian People

1. In working with Southeast Asian clients, emphasize the interpersonal relationship rather than a specific procedure (Uba, 1994).

2. Make contact with community and spiritual leaders who can serve as cultural guides, part of the treatment team, resources during times of sickness and death, and who can enhance a therapist's credibility with the community and its clients (Lin & Lin, 1978; Egawa, 1982).
3. Ask the client for the correct pronunciation of names.
4. In addressing someone from Southeast Asia, use mister and then the first name for men, and use missus and her first name or the first name of her husband for women.
5. Introduce yourself by giving your name and profession to help establish credibility and trust in you as a professional. It is also helpful to have the interpreter with whom you will be working give some information about you before your first meeting.
6. During sessions, it is inappropriate for the Southeast Asian client to be seated opposite the therapist. Looking directly at the therapist is considered neither comfortable nor polite.
7. Know something about the interpreter's position in the community to be sure that she or he is an appropriate person to be working with the client. Also ascertain whether the client trusts the interpreter. A woman client may be hesitant to speak openly in front of a male interpreter, for example, or a client who knows the interpreter in the community may be fearful that confidentiality may be broken.
8. Take time to cultivate your relationship with your interpreter. He or she can be a very important cultural consultant giving context to a client's comments and enabling the comments to take on deeper meaning.
9. It is especially important that the therapy hour be guided by what the client seems interested in talking about and not by a preexisting agenda. Often this means starting with physical complaints. If a physical check-up is needed, the goal of the counselor is to understand the symptoms as they are perceived by the client. At first, this may mean a focus on symptom reduction through medication or spiritual ceremony, or both. It is important to remember that mental health typically has been considered only for "crazy" people and thus many Southeast Asian people are not comfortable talking with strangers, especially those who work in mental health, about anything that seems strange. "Mental disturbances are highly stigmatized. . . . Mental illnesses are believed to reflect poorly on one's family and one's heredity because they are regarded as signs of personal weakness. These beliefs cause Asian Americans to avoid seeking advice outside the family for psychological problems" (Chung & Okazaki, 1991, p. 110).

10. It is more important to show that you care through your actions, tone of voice, and facial expressions than your words.
11. Allow the client to talk about their suffering; they are interested and able to do so.
12. Avoid taking notes, especially in an initial interview. This will seriously limit your client's openness. They may fear your notes will be passed on to the authorities.
13. Normalizing the context and symptoms (e.g., by saying that many people have the same type of problem) may increase comfort and encourage openness.
14. When obtaining information about a client's emotional problems, it is very important to understand the individual's own view of the problem and his or her expectations of the problem's effect on his or her life. Also, with the client's permission, it may be important to check with a family member or friend to see how they think the client is dealing with matters that the therapist considers to be traumatic. Any past solutions provided by the client and family members are useful information.
15. If using existing assessment tools, consider whether the question to be asked is culture specific. For example, asking about a marriage date to test for memory is culture specific. In most Southeast Asian cultures, the couple does not celebrate the anniversary of their marriage. Therefore, people do not remember that date. Consult with an interpreter or culture expert to ascertain the cultural appropriateness of an assessment question.

☐ References

Amerasian Homecoming Act, 1. [On-line] Available: http://www.ins.usdoj.gov/legislative history/563.html.

Boehnlein, J. (1987). Clinical relevance of grief and mourning among Cambodian refugees. *Social Science Medicine 25*, 765–772.

Bounkeua, P. K., & Viradet, S. (1995). *Laotian cultural influences on their expression of emotions*. Unpublished manuscript, University of Washington at Seattle.

Chung, R., & Okazaki, S. (1991). Counseling Americans of Southeast Asian descent: The impact of the refugee experience. In E. Lee, & B. Richardson (Eds.), *Multicultural issues in counseling* (pp. 107–126). Alexandria, VA: American Association for Counseling and Development.

Egawa, J., & Tashima, N. (1982). *Indigenous healers in Southeast Asian refugee communities*. San Francisco: Pacific Asian Mental Health Research Project.

Eisenbruch, M. (1988). 'Wind illness' or somatic depression? A case study in psychiatric anthropology. *British Journal of Psychiatry, 143*, 323–326.

Eisenbruch, M., & Handelman, L. (1989). Development of an explanatory model of illness schedule for Cambodian refugee patients. *Journal of Refugee Studies, 2,* 243–256.

Emerging Markets Companion (1998). Laos. [On-line] Available:http://www. emgmkts.com/research/country/asia/laos.htm.

Foreign Relations Authorization Act, SB 1160, Lautenberg Ammendment #376 [On-line] Available: http://www.senate.gov/~rpc/rva/1011/1011134.htm

Handelman, L., & Yeo, G. (1996). Using explanatory models to understand chronic symptoms of Cambodian refugees. *Clinical Research and Methods 28,* 271–76.

Headley, R. (1977). *Cambodian-English dictionary,* vol 1. Washington, DC: The Catholic University of America Press.

Keyes, C. (1990). The legacy of Angkor. *Cultural Survival, 14,* 56–59.

Kinzie, J. (1985). Overview of clinical issues in the treatment of Southeast Asian refugees. In T. Owan (Ed.), *Southeast Asian mental health: Treatment, prevention, services, training, and research* (pp. 113–135). Washington, DC: U.S. Department of Health and Human Services.

Kinzie, D., Frederickson, R., Rath, B., Fleck, J., & Karls, W. (1984). Post traumatic stress disorder among survivors of Cambodian concentration camps. *American Journal of Psychiatry, 141,* 645–650.

Kitano, H. L., & Daniels, R. (1988). *Asian Americans: Emerging minorities.* Englewood Cliffs, NJ: Prentice Hall.

Kitigawa, J., & Cummings, M. (1989). *Buddhism and Asian History.* New York: Macmillan.

Kleinman, A., & Kleinman, J. (1985). Somatization. The interconnections among culture, depressive experiences, and the meaning of pain: A study of Chinese society. In A. Kleinman, & B. Good (Eds.), *Culture and depression* (pp. 138–145). Berkeley, CA: University of California.

Knoll, T. (1982). *Becoming Americans: Asian sojourners, immigrants, and refugees in the western United States.* Portland, OR: Coast to Coast Books.

Lee, E. (1988). Cultural factors in working with Southeast Asian refugee adolescents. *Journal of Adolescence, 11,* 167–179.

Lin, T., & Lin, M. (1978). Service delivery issues in Asian-North American communities. *American Journal of Psychiatry, 135,* 454–456.

Mollica, R. (1994). Southeast Asian refugees: Migration history and mental health issues. In A. Marsella, T. Bornemann, S. Ekbland, & J. Orley (Eds.), *Amidst peril and pain* (pp. 83–100). Washington, DC: American Psychological Associates.

Mollica, R., Donelan, K., Tor, S. (1993). The effect of trauma and confinement on functional health and mental health status of Cambodians living in Thailand–Cambodia border camps. *Journal of the American Medical Association, 270,* 581–586.

Muecke, M. (1983a). Caring for Southeast Asian refugee patients in the USA. *American Journal of Public Health, 73,* 431–438.

Muecke, M. (1983b). In search of healers—Southeast Asian refugees in the American health care system. *Western Journal of Medicine, 139,* 835–840.

Outsama, K. (1977). *Laotian themes.* New York: Board of Education of the City of New York.

Outsama, K. (1992). *The Europa world year book* (33rd ed.) 11 (K-2). London, England: Europa Publications Limited.

Overmeyer, D. (1986). *Religions of China.* San Francisco: Harper & Row.

Reat, N. (1994). *Buddhism: A history.* Berkeley, CA: Asian Humanities Press.

Smith, H. (1994). *World's religions.* San Francisco: Harper.

Thongsith, V. S., & Bouaravong, P. (1991). *Welcome to Laos. Laos traditions and customs.* Vientiane, Lao PDR.

Tomasi, L. F. (1993). Laotian Catholic refugees in the United States. *Migration World, 21,* 24–28.

Uba, L. (1994). *Asian Americans: Personality patterns, identity, and mental health.* New York: Guilford Press.

The United Nations High Commissioner For Refugees. (1998). Briefing Book. [On-line] Available: http://www3.itu.ch/MISSIONS/US/bb/unhcr.html#odp

Zane, N. W., Takeuchi, D. T., & Young, N. J. (Eds.). (1994). *Confronting critical health issues of Asian and Pacific islander Americans.* Newbury Park, CA: Sage Publication.

INTERNATIONAL CULTURES

Nancy Peddle,
Carlinda Monteiro,
Vello Guluma
Thomas E. A. Macaulay

6

CHAPTER

Trauma, Loss, and Resilience in Africa: A Psychosocial Community Based Approach to Culturally Sensitive Healing

"It is a people's culture,
their shared creativity and struggles
as they have evolved over time and space,
that defines their essence.
If there is no shared culture, there is no group, no unity, no solidarity."
(Hilliard, 1995, pg. 10)

☐ Introduction

Violent acts against people and nature are on the rise challenging the conscience and resources of our global village as never before (Wallace, Giri & Serrano, 1995). Over the past several decades, as humanitarian emergencies have increased, the international community has developed remarkable response mechanisms for coping although the ability and resources to handle the increasing number is still dramatically short of what is needed (Wallace et al., 1995). The aftermath of these traumatic events—physical harm, displacement, loss, and human rights violations—result in large numbers of people, especially children, who

121

suffer from psychological wounds (Dubrow, 1995; Machel, 1996; Wessells & Kostelny, 1996).

The work that is done in response to the emergency and in working towards recovery must take into account the whole person including both basic needs and psychosocial needs (Christian Children's Fund, 1998; Machel, 1996; Suzic, Patel, & Doran, 1995; UNICEF, 1997a). The measures implemented should include long term resettlement, rehabilitation, reconstruction, and plans for future, sustainable development (Annan, 1998; Suzic et al., 1995). In addition, community based approaches that take into consideration traditional practices for healing should be encouraged (Dubrow, 1995; Evans, 1996; Fozzard, 1995; Green & Wessells, 1997; Herbst, 1995; Levy & Sidel, 1997; Machel, 1996; Peddle, 1998; Save the Children Alliance, 1996; Wessells, 1996).

This chapter presents a synthesis of backgrounds, cultural beliefs, and values found in many areas of Africa and examines in-depth two African countries, Sierra Leone and Angola, in an effort to encourage expatriates use of culturally sensitive, community based approaches that respect the local culture and community and avoid historic patterns of Western domination and derogation of traditional African practices. "For four hundred years, the slave trade, colonization, segregation, and racism—highly sophisticated systematic strategies of oppression—have been the massive political and economic forces operating on African people. These forces have affected the culture, the socialization process and the very consciousness of West African people" (Hilliard, 1995, p. 7). Add to this the disruptive effects of more than 30 wars since 1970 (Annan, 1998) and the extensive intermixing of ethnic groups and we find that traditions, cultural practices, and views described in this chapter are ever changing. Nevertheless, they must be taken into consideration when working with loss and trauma.

This chapter cannot do justice to the vast and immense diversity the continent of Africa holds and the uniqueness of each community. It is only a beginning. In order to create interventions, related to loss and trauma, that are truly effective and appropriate one must have an understanding of the local history, customs, traditions, power structures, and the events that have taken place. The more you know, the more likely you are to avoid making blunders or possibly reharming the people you have come to work with (Evans, 1997; Suzic et al., 1995).

Despite the differences one finds in Africa, the sources of origins of the conflicts are connected by some common themes and experiences related to their historical legacies, internal and external factors, economic motives, and particular situations (Annan, 1998). Today, exposure to the violence of armed conflict on a large scale, deprivation, and poverty are predominating causes of trauma in African people (UNICEF, 1997b) and are undermining Africa's efforts to secure long term stability, economic growth, and peace (Annan, 1998). In May of 1997 in Sierra Leone, "the chance to plunder natural resources and loot the Central Bank reserves was a key motivation of those who seized power from the elected Government" (Annan, 1998, p. 4). This chapter starts with one of the author's personal experience of this event (Peddle, 1997).

May 16, 1997

My flight from Amsterdam to Sierra Leone, West Africa was packed with both people and baggage. I took this as a good sign: one that supported peace initiatives and looked toward the future. The outward signs: an influx of tourists, more roadside stands, plentiful food supplies in the market, and an increase in development, suggested better times. But other events such as stronger government censorship of the news media, random attacks on expatriates' compounds, targeting of a UN vehicle, conflict between the military and civil defense groups, and organized violent attacks in new areas were also occurring. The latter events ultimately created a pattern that led to the following.

Sunday May 25, 1997

4:00 a.m. the sound of AK 47s, G–3s and RPGs shattered the early morning calm and continued throughout the day bringing chaos to Freetown. Offices and houses were looted and destroyed. People were injured and killed. Hotels were ransacked. The World Food Program's (WFP's) warehouse was pillaged. Vehicles were hijacked and driven recklessly throughout town.

I sit listening to the sound of gunfire grappling with this potentially life threatening situation and these incomprehensible acts of violence. I cannot believe this is real even though I have come here to work through Christian Children's Fund, UNICEF, and the Government of Sierra Leone with children exposed to violence. The air conditioning muffles the disturbance. A friend at the hotel calls to check on me and says, "don't think about going out." I am confined to my villa with little outside communication. The day moves by. No word from my local colleagues.

Acts of wanton destruction were perpetrated throughout Sierra Leone. The Central Bank and the Ministry of Finance were destroyed. 3 RPGs hit the U.S. embassy. Gun fire between soldiers and Nigerian troops left casualties on both sides. *Focus on Africa* reported 10 deaths and 40 people wounded. The actual death toll was far higher; an eyewitness reported seeing 35 bodies in the morgue, mostly civilians. This count included several Indian and Lebanese businessmen, targets due to their wealth. Women were raped. Small boys were drugged and given guns bigger than they were with instructions to "go get revenge on those who steal from our country."

At approximately 9:30 p.m. the air conditioners no longer drown out the sounds of guns. I go to the bathroom to brush my teeth when an RPG is fired outside the window. The force of the shot reverberates throughout the villa. This can't be happening. For almost two hours guns fire and dogs howl just outside my door. I am so close I see flashes of light coming from the guns as they are fired. My heart is pounding. My awareness is keen. I hear the distinct sounds each gun makes. I pray and reflect on my life. I ask God's angels to protect me and my vehicle from danger. We had performed traditional Sierra Leonean libations on the receipt of the car, paying respect to the Spirits and asking for their blessings. I have every confidence that the Spirits are protecting me and the car.

The shooting stops a little after 11:00 p.m. I pull the mattress off the bed and into the hall where there are no windows. I finally fall asleep. At 1:00 a.m. the shooting starts again for a half hour. I curl in a ball and pray it ends. Again I coax myself back to sleep to be jolted awake once more. It is only an intense thunderstorm, but it reactivates the fear.

Monday 26 May

A coup led by the disenfranchised military and rebels had taken place. The Minister of Defense lived in the villa next door until 5:00 a.m. the morning of the coup. Some angry rebels had proceeded to shoot up his villa despite the fact that he was gone. Looting and random acts of violence continued throughout Sierra Leone. Sporadic gunfire could be heard in the distance.

I venture out to see the destruction. I need to physically go into the building that has been shelled to see the destruction; look at my villa to see that there were no bullet holes; and feel my car to make sure that my eyes accurately register the fact that there is no damage. The unreality of the situation gives me the need to connect with that which is real and tangible.

Evacuation is on everyone's mind. Expatriates, especially U.S. citizens, have the privilege of leaving Sierra Leone. Most nationals will not have this luxury.

Ready for evacuation. Waiting. Tense. Nervous energy. I hear stories of the atrocities people faced, false laughter, tears, and questions of what is happening outside the Cape Sierra Hotel. The UN security officers are cut off from Freetown. Conflicting information is reported. The city is relatively quiet. The phone rings. It's a friend from the U.S. I feel more calm, connected. People are sending their thoughts and prayers this way. This connection is very important and reassuring. I can actually feel the energy. Still no contact with colleagues here.

My initial shock passes and I sleep well for a short time. I wake thinking, this is why I am here; children have just experienced more violence. I have a new understanding and empathy for the people who live with war. I want to act on these thoughts and feelings, but this is not the time. I wonder how the local people are experiencing these last two or three days. Can I really understand?

☐ Background

Africa is a vast and diverse continent consisting of 55 countries with 750 tribal languages (Davidson, 1992). It stretches from the Straits of Gibraltar to the Cape of Good Hope. Within this expansive domain one can find the world's largest desert, extensive rain forests, and the largest game reserves anywhere (Crowther et al., 1995). It is regarded as the birthplace of humanity and considered home to one of the cradles of civilization (Crowther et al., 1995). No where else on earth will you find such a mixture of cultures, scenery, cities (ancient, traditional, and modern), and politics amid roaming big game. Where a visa is required, you must present it to gain entry into the country no matter what, or how important, the mission. A travel guide for Africa or the African countries (e.g. Lonely Planet Publications or the Sierra Leone web site) can provide specific visa information, vaccinations required, and health precautions. For example, some malaria medicine must be taken a week before arrival.

Specifically, Sierra Leone is located in western Africa, between Liberia and Guinea just north of the equator. It covers an area of 27,925 square miles, and is a little smaller than the state of Maine with a population of 4.6 million people (http://www.odci.gov/cia/publications/factbook/sl.html) Angola is situated on the West coast of Southern Africa covering 481,350 square miles, with a population of approximately 12 million (http://www. odci.gov/cia/publications/factbook/ao.html). Both countries' population have been in a state of flux between rural and urban settings and have intermixed different ethnic groups since their respective conflicts began. In 1991 civil war in Liberia spilled over its borders into Sierra Leone and rebels took advantage of the situation (Annan, 1998); in Angola, war erupted in 1961 against the Portuguese colonial regime. Armed conflict always causes population movements (Evans, 1996; Levy & Sidel, 1997) with displacement, either internally or as a refugee. It shatters one's social bonds of trust and feelings of safety and has a profound physical and emotional impact which increases one's vulnerability (Machel, 1996; Wessells & Kostelny, 1996).

A staggering amount of people—estimated at 57.4 million around the world—are displaced by war. At least half of them are children (United Nations Department of Information, 1996). Africa, with eight countries at war and others experiencing conflict (Annan, 1998), has its share of internally displaced people and refugees. Refugee camps and camps for displaced persons "have become the modern day international equivalent of the clinician's emergency department" (Levy & Sidel, 1997, p. 197). The ongoing hardships the survivors of violence and terror are forced to endure are critical factors in trauma healing and mental health. If displaced people and refugees are not traumatized by the violence of war, months, and even years, of living in camps can take its toll (Wallace et al., 1995). Chronic conditions can induce trauma (Erikson, 1976). These people have been reduced to surviving in a world with no money, small allocations of food, and only the possessions they could carry on their heads as they ran from their burning homes. "Not enough in my belly to play or sing," explained one young Sierra Leone refugee when asked to participate in the singing and dancing that is a part of the Christian Children's Fund 'Kids in Distress' psychosocial project. Camp homes are makeshift with dirt floors and unsanitary conditions, including bugs, rats, and leaking ceilings. Disconnection from kin and community adds to the stressful situation (Erikson, 1976). For internally displaced people, the threat of safety is still real as they may be located close to zones of conflict. Rebuilding trusting relationships is incredibly difficult (Green & Wessells, 1997) when each person is immersed in his or her own fight for self-survival.

The Religion and Politics Factors

Religion and politics both run the full gamut, with unanticipated days off for religious holiday celebrations or changed work patterns due to fasting for Ramadan. One can find religious beliefs from Islam to born again Christians as well as traditional beliefs (Collins, Burns, & Ching, 1994b). Politically, oppressive dictators to democratically elected governments govern countries. In addition, there can be clashes in the individual countries' leadership between, "the inherited privileges of chieftaincy and the acquired privileges of education" (Davidson, 1992, p. 103). One cannot count on political or social stability in many countries even when outward appearances are calm. An eye on the newspaper and an ear to the radio and local talk can alert one to any indicators of change or upcoming turmoil. Angola has struggled between war and peace for over 30 years fluctuating between military dictatorship and democratically elected leadership. During one author's consultancy in Sierra Leone from January 1996 to May 1997 two coups d'etat's occurred, one democratic election was held, one model peace accord was signed and an eruption of conflict necessitating evacuation of the United Nations and expatriates took place.

Historical Legacies

Africa hosts many contrasts and contradictions. It is home to some of the greatest cultural and architectural achievements in the world (the pyramids, for example) where civilizations and empires flourished and floundered and subsistence villages practice traditions dating back thousands of years. Not even with the advent of colonization and then the slave trade could the strength and the legacy of the past be destroyed. Colonization brought its legacy of both benefits and harm leaving its mark on the continent (Annan, 1998; Blyden, 1994; Collins, Burns, & Ching, 1994a, 1994b; Crowther et al., 1995; Freund, 1984; Hilliard, 1995).

Only two countries in Africa, Liberia and Ethiopia, were not officially colonized at some time in their history and they were heavily influenced by the U.S. and Italy, respectively. Colonization shaped and dramatically changed the geography, language, religion, culture, customs, political structure, economics, and way of life for Africans. Colonialism and its political heritage influence tried to weaken or even eliminate the culture of the colonized people (Collins et al., 1994a; Guluma, 1996). Colonists considered Africans inferior and, thus, engendered in them complexes of inferiority, psychological problems, serious traumas and feelings of alienation often resulting in further submission to demagogues and charlatans (Blyden, 1994; Collins et al., 1994a; Freund, 1984). Both contemporary information and historical information are needed to best understand and work with the people.

> Remember your roots your history and the forbearers shoulders on which you stand.
> (Edelman, 1992, p. 73)

In order to make the most of your time and resources when you go to Africa pack only what you can carry, some gifts to give, and bring plenty of determination, patience, stamina, and flexibility. Spend more time listening than speaking when you arrive. Be aware of and respect people's customs, traditions, and sensibilities and you will be treated with the hospitality that is part of the African nature.

☐ Language, History, Cultural Beliefs, and Rituals

Language

The spoken word is the predominate mode of communication throughout Africa. Many African languages are not written (Richmond & Gestrin, 1998). Bantu languages are the most widely spoken languages in Africa (Collins et al., 1994b). English, French, and Portuguese are widely spoken in urban areas of their formerly colonized countries along with Arabic and Swahili in the south (Crowther et al., 1995). But do not expect the people from the villages to speak the national language: most people in the villages speak their tribal language. Ghana, with its population of 13 million people, has 64 languages alone (Kater, 1995).

The official language in Sierra Leone is English and it is taught in the schools. Yet virtually no one uses it as a first language. However, most Sierra Leoneans are trilingual and know many words in the more than

14 languages that are spoken. In the capital of Freetown, Krio is the first language of the majority of Freetonians.

Angola is made up of 13 ethnolinguistic groups of which the Bantu group is the largest. In fact, the Bantu group dominates almost the entire African continent (Collins et al., 1994b). Portuguese is the official language of Angola and is taught in schools, but one should not assume that it is spoken throughout Angola. In these countries, as in much of Africa, there is a rich verbal heritage of conveying knowledge through storytelling, song, and drama in the person's first language (Finnegan, 1992; Kater, 1995; Richmond & Gestrin, 1998), which can be drawn on for psychosocial interventions (Dubrow, 1992; Dubrow & Peddle, 1997; Fozzard, 1995; Green & Wessells, 1997; Macksoud, 1993; Save the Children Alliance, 1996; Wessells, 1996).

History

Africa's ethnic groups were divided, first by arbitrary colonial boundaries at the congress of Berlin in 1885 by the colonial powers and then inherited by the newly independent African States in 1960 (Annan, 1998). These inherited dividing lines had, in some cases, been designed to exploit local divisions. Thus, the task of nation building fell to often disparate and competing communities in the first years of sovereignty (Annan, 1998). "Ethnicity is at the heart of African diversity" (Richmond, 1998, p. 12).

Sierra Leone is comprised of 18 ethnic groups. The Temne in the North and the Mende in the South comprise over 60% of the population. The Creoles represent less than 3% of the population of Sierra Leone and are largely Western educated urban dwellers who have had considerable political and economic power (Goverment of Sierra Leone, 1990). In Angola, as a result of the enforced mobility due to the length and nature of the war, the mixture of different ethnolinguistic groups with each other and with the Portuguese makes it difficult to talk of pure groupings.

Between 1789 and 1800, freed enslaved African's came from England, Canada, and Jamaica to found Freetown under British authority. These Africans had adopted many Western ways such as Christianity, monogamy, living a European pattern of living, and even adopting an English name (i.e. Cornelius Williams and Maude Peacock) and were called Creoles (Government of Sierra Leone, 1990). After 1807, when the British outlawed slavery, slave ships coming from the West coast of Africa were intercepted and sent to Freetown. This added to the population of the Creoles and created a new society along Western lines, but with African characteristics (Government of Sierra Leone, 1990). Their assimilation to

Western ways and education gave them status and financial rewards with the British. They occupied many government jobs, holding positions of power and influence. Creoles regarded themselves as superior to the indigenous Africans (Blyden, 1994). Today many top civil service jobs are still held by Creoles and vestiges of this status remain (Government of Sierra Leone, 1990).

Angola has a 500 year history of being colonized by the Portuguese, gaining independence in 1975. Super power rivalries undermined Angola's government (and many other African governments) and fuelled one of Africa's longest and deadliest conflicts (Annan, 1998). Successive wars have been waged either interethnically or against the colonial power. Independence did not stop the war that has led to a death toll of many thousands and has left the country in an emergency situation dependent on external forces.

For decades, the Angolan people have lived with suffering, death, mourning, and loss. Knowledge and understanding of the history, philosophy, culture, and religion of the Bantu are essential in order to establish aid channels and to help in the psychosocial recuperation of the Angolan people. Psychosocial assistance projects must consider not only the current state of scientific knowledge, most of which has been constructed in Western cultures, but also the cosmology, values, and practices of the Bantu culture.

Cultural Beliefs and Rituals

The ravages of war, influence of colonial powers, degradation of slavery, and enforced uprooting have all affected social interactions and traditions (Blyden, 1994; Collins et al., 1994a; Hilliard, 1995). Through all this turbulent history there are still deeply held beliefs and traditions. Imported lifestyles are supplanting traditional ways in urban areas, while more traditional patterns, beliefs, rites, and practices concerning dress, funeral rites and ceremonies, child care, eating habits, and dance (Guluma, 1996; Kater, 1995) are held onto in rural areas. Examples include Fullah men wearing a specially designed dress for dance, and the Konos' distinctive marital rights allowing a man to have sexual relations with all the younger sisters of his wife, if she is the eldest. A basic precept of the Bantu culture is that life must be lived on a communal, joint basis and not individually (Annan, 1985). Emphasis is on the family and community. However, the rights and responsibilities of the individual are defined. One may be linked to the network of customs and traditions of the group, yet an individual is free to act on a spontaneous basis as long as it does not risk the cohesion of the community or violate traditional ethics.

In setting up any form of psychosocial intervention, it is essential to develop a good understanding of traditional rituals which occur at different stages of life: birth, puberty, marriage, and death as well as about ceremonies that cleanse spiritually or psychologically. Traditional African belief considers the ancestors to be the real chiefs of the community. They may take revenge if the community does not apply the obligatory rites and customs and they ensure that customs are properly maintained. Ancestors play a vital role in the major individual and social events rituals (Blyden, 1994). Different ethnic and religious groups within each country may have different practices, therefore it is important to avoid generalization.

Integration of current Western thinking in child development, mental health, and child rights with traditional beliefs and practices may require time and a deeper knowledge of the community's specific rites, ceremonies, and customs (Save the Children Alliance, 1996). However, the results will more likely be effective and sustainable in meeting people's psychosocial needs. Without specific local knowledge, people from the outside coming to provide aid can make mistakes that inflict harm. This was the case in Rwanda where more than one aid organization hired local staff to assist and protect Tutsi children without being aware they had hired a Hutu extremist. Yet, to the children they were providing care for, it was obvious (Save the Children Alliance, 1996).

Families, Social Systems, Values, and Beliefs

Unlike Western industrialized societies, which are based on an individualist philosophy and nuclear family, individuals from traditional African societies focus their lives around the extended family (Blyden, 1994; Richmond, 1998). The familial and kinship aspects of village life bring meaning to community. Their social lives are community-oriented both in daily life and in spirit. No one has to carry his or her burden or grieve alone. Sekou Toure, a renowned student of African affairs and culture, affirmed that "solidarity is the greatest wealth of the African people and the cardinal quality of the Negro race" (Senghor, 1970, p. 3).

The primary loyalty to the extended family or kinship group and strong community ties create a natural support system to trauma victims (Evans, 1996; Fozzard, 1995). The group interests are of paramount concern and override the individual's interest. Tradition plays an important part in the prescribed rites and duties that family members have to their kin and community. An individual who starts to isolate herself may be quickly noticed (especially in the rural areas). Those who have money, food, clothes, and other resources, are expected to share with those who do not (Blyden, 1994). People not displaced give aid to those who are displaced. On the one hand this situation alleviates total helplessness in those traumatized and trying to survive. On the other hand, it brings stress to those who have more resources.

Many of the social systems were set up to maintain conformity and fulfill obligations to the group through external rules. Military dictatorships can thrive in this atmosphere. Secret societies (bush schools) were set up to preserve and pass on the traditions, values, and responsibilities of the society. The basic emphasis was on the rights and powers of the elders and obedience to authority (Government of Sierra Leone, 1990). Secret societies establish strong bonds between members and are found throughout Africa. At one time boys and girls went to bush school for at least three years to learn about the life that would follow and the systems under which they would live (Blyden, 1994). With the coming of Western designed schools the use of bush schools declined, but secret societies remain. Children are still initiated into these societies. These are protective measures in a subsistence society. Struggling to survive limits one's creativity and thus, one's choices (Brookfield, 1987). Following the rules is a way of life. Conforming and obedience are highly valued and enforced. Curiosity, critical thinking skills, and internal control are not nurtured or developed (UNESCO-UNICEF, 1981). Individual self-esteem is not encouraged. In the villages, where everything is shared, this makes sense. However, in the urban areas and where Western ideas are being fostered, lack of self-esteem hinders the effective coping mechanisms of the individual. In the urban areas, material possessions, wealth, and status receive a higher value and are more closely tied with self-esteem. A person raised in the individualistic system who loses his or her wealth in conjunction with a traumatic event, may feel the trauma more dramatically than one who came from a more communal sharing of resources tradition (Blyden, 1994; Arroyo & Eth, 1996).

Understanding the nature of the community based lifestyle in Bantu culture is a prerequisite to an appreciation of Bantu institutions and behaviors. Padre Altuna, through research on Bantu culture, concluded that the basic principle is that of participation in the same life or the union of lives. This concept of the union of lives includes the lives of descendants, siblings, clan siblings, direct relatives, elders and a god. For the Bantu people, "the world is like a spider's web, in which you cannot move one thread without affecting the whole structure" (Tempels, 1965, p. 40).

Rites of Initiation and Puberty

The secret societies have such a long history that it is not known when they did not exist (Blyden, 1994). They once taught young boys and girls about domestic work and how to fulfill their marital and family obligations. Additionally, the societies passed on cultural traditions, expectations, and initiation rites and celebrations. It has been observed that as a result of the war and imported lifestyles supplanting traditional rituals, they are no longer practiced in Angola or other places in their original form. The cultural and celebratory piece is being lost; the initiation rites remain. However, this shift has not been formally researched. Interestingly, many adults report to team members of the Christian Children's Fund's Angolan province based war trauma project, that children no longer obey them. They are forming links between children's behavior and unfulfilled initiation rites. Discontinuity of traditions and ethics may be another casualty of war.

Initiation Rites: Feminine

Rites of passage for girls are aimed at preparing them for marriage and motherhood and are performed in the Society for girls. The Society has various names depending on which part of Africa you are in. In Western Africa it is the Bundo Society, further north it's the Suna Society (Blyden, 1994), and the Sande Society or Sande Bush School in Liberia (Guluma, 1996). After going through these rites, girls are considered to be adult women.

Madam Tolka, in Sierra Leone, initiated women into the Bundo Society, the most ancient order of women (Blyden, 1994), where it is customary for girl children to be circumcised. Sierra Leone has one of the highest rates of circumcision (also called female genital mutilation) in the world (UNICEF, 1997b). The practice is deeply ingrained in the social and economic fabric of this society. In 1996, UNICEF and PLAN International, an international nongovernmental organization (NGO) cosponsored a conference on female genital mutilation. A 1997 Reuters article reported that 600 young girls had been circumcised without anesthesia at a displaced persons camp.

In Angola, initiation ceremonies for girls exist in various groups (Ganguela, Tshokue, Nhaneca-Humbe, Ambos). Most commonly, girls go through the initiation ceremony at the time of their first menstruation. For some groups the timing is earlier, while others wait until the time of marriage. The length of time and setting of the ceremonies varies by group, but normally girls should be virgins, and female relatives are expected to attend the rituals.

Initiation Rites: Masculine

It is strictly forbidden to discuss or disclose any secret society ceremonies to nonmembers. The rites end with solemn promises: "You don't even tell the woman you sleep with, even if she asks you, what you saw and learned in the *mkanda* . . . You mustn't say anything—if you speak, you will die!" (Redinha, 1973). The boy child is trained to maintain and perpetuate the traditions. The school for puberty rites is group based. He learns individual and social ethics, notions of politics, education, hygiene, hunting techniques, agriculture, fishing, the history of various groups, why and how to behave in specific situations, the danger of inappropriate behavior, and the significance of masks and disguises. They are trained to obey the authority of the elders, to maintain rituals and customs, and to become independent of maternal authority.

Young men also learn about ceremonies and practices as well as the significance of symbols and rites, the meaning and practice of magic, the hierarchy of ancestors, and ethical norms through practical application. Pupils are subjected to a rigorous regime and difficult testing during the rites of passage. The group also receives a complete sexual initiation, which is viewed as a form of preparation for marriage and procreation. Sexuality is considered to be in the service of the goal of full participation in life and procreation.

There is a hierarchy in most of the societies with the most superior person being the most respected and knowing the most secrets. Initiation into the Porroh or Poro Society, the main secret society for boys the age of six and over (Blyden, 1994), occurs among the Temne in Sierra Leone and many ethnic groups in Liberia (Guluma, 1996). Circumcision is customary as part of the initiation into the secret societies. To become a paramount chief, a Temne must belong to the ruling families and be a part of the secret society.

Rituals for Death and Mourning

In Africa, death due to the war, malnutrition, inadequate health care, famines, malaria and other infectious diseases, water, and sanitation problems, as well as other factors is a common occurrence (UNICEF, 1997b; Wallace et al., 1995). The death may come from these natural causes, but the underlying belief is that it is an unnatural event and is caused by an external agent. The person must have been bewitched or the ghosts of his ancestors have punished him for something he did wrong or omitted. Death is considered to be associated with solitude, which is a disaster in Bantu terms and the greatest disturbance in the life pattern. The words, fatalism, resignation, disgraceful, impotence, absurd, regretful are alone not adequate to describe the feelings of Bantu peoples against death. Death of the elderly, surrounded by numerous descendants and enjoying reasonable material wealth is the only form of death considered natural. These elders die happy because they lived well and will move into life with their ancestors.

Traditionally, people have rituals, ceremonies, support systems, and coping mechanisms to accompany death. They are built into the natural rhythms of life and are constructed to appease and create harmony with the spirit world (Blyden, 1994). When this process is interrupted the healing takes much longer.

Funeral rites, along with puberty rites, are the most solemn and frequently observed types of ceremony in Bantu society (Altuna, 1985). In the case of funeral rites, all family members are obliged to participate together with the wider community, and it is here, through solidarity of all its members, that the Bantu exhibit their most profound cultural roots and religious beliefs. Through birth, the Bantu passed into the world and through puberty rites, into society. In the end, funeral rites provide people with a sense of communion.

In Sierra Leone, all major life events have specific rites and ceremonies for contacting the ancestors. Invoking the ancestral spirit by the graveside creates these links. For example, a person who is unemployed and finding life difficult or is involved in a court case will take kola nuts, rum, and water to the graveside and perform a ceremony to summon the spirit of either his dead mother or father to clear the ill luck. Bereaved families prepare *awujor,* a form of ancestral sacrifice, for the dead. Specialty dishes, such as foo–foo and orbiata, are often made and served together with rum to invited guests. A small hole is dug where portions of the food and drinks are deposited after calling the names of the dead. If a person is not allowed to perform awujor or have a proper burial, the concern for not worshiping the ancestors compounds the trauma. This traditional belief is carried over into the Christian and Muslim traditions. For example, a Methodist woman from Sierra Leone and her family were under rebel attack. They had to flee quickly into the bush with only the possessions they could carry. During this time the woman's father died. When she recounted the story she did not dwell on the hardships of the days in the bush, of being displaced, or even her father's death. The trauma, by her own report, centered on the pain of not being able to bury her father properly. Her new church in Freetown was able to conduct a ceremony without the body to put closure on the death, but when she describes the experience the critical aspect of improper burial remains her foremost concern. The survivor gives meaning to the event and, in order to help the trauma, must be understood in relation to the individual survivor and his or her culture (Janoff-Bulman, 1992; Herman, 1992).

For the Bantu groups there are agents who manage the transition to death. They may be ancestors who are angry because they were never honored in the way they felt they deserved or are just naturally wicked. A diviner should try to identify the guilty party, analyze his motives, and name the penance for reparations that placate the dead. In most cases, it is the diviner who discovers the identity of the black magician by consulting his magic artifacts. In Liberia this is done by the Zoe who is instrumental in bringing healing to the family through the identification and punishment of the wrong doer (Guluma, 1996). Ceremonies are surrounded by dances, singing (Kater, 1995), and speaking in tongues, which are aimed at frightening those who are watching—one of whom may be the guilty party. If the ancestors are blamed, sacrifices will be made in order to placate and calm the inhabitants of the visible world.

In the funeral rite, the body is washed, dressed, and perfumed. This preparation is a form of honoring the family, but more importantly, allows the dead person to maintain dignity alongside the ancestors at the point of transition. Placed with the deceased are personal objects such as clothing and items that will be needed for the journey. The community eats, drinks, and dances for several days as a means of helping the dead person manage the change in his or her life.

If the funeral rites are applied according to tradition and the wishes of ancestors, the dead person will arrive safely at his or her destination. If not, the dead person may wander around lost and disgraced wreaking vengeance on the living and causing harm to the community. The shared anxiety of the community about the possible negative influences of the ancestors leads to a permanent sense of disquiet and religious practices born of fear. However, it is just this anxiety that maintains the Bantu ethic. If the fear of reprisal did not exist, the social and moral value system of the society might be at risk of disintegration. Tradition demands absolute obedience. The elders of the community do not allow innovation or change.

The family and community promote the dead person to the class of ancestors, avenge the cause of the death, reestablish solidarity and social order, and press for peace and harmony within the community. These actions help guarantee and reinforce friendly relations between the two worlds and a happy existence for those who remain in the visible world.

Only those persons who behaved well in life are honored at the time of the funeral. The solemnity of the rites is proportional to the social prestige and position of the dead person. The community is not obliged to worship children and young people in the same way as adults.

In Liberia, death and grief is shared by friends and extended family. For example, the role of distant nephews and nieces, when there is a death in a family, is to take the immediate family's mind off the death (Guluma, 1996). They dress themselves as clowns. Simply, their appearance can turn the tears of the family to laughter. They play funny jokes, sing funny songs, and dance in a manner to amuse their audience. They usually tell the bereaved that the person who has died is not dead but just sleeping. The bereaved family is never left alone during the period of bereavement.

☐ Political Factors

Political factors play a very important role in the stability of the country (Austin, 1990) and the policies that are in place to support mental health (Wallace et al., 1995). Religion exerts a significant influence on the political systems in some counties as well (Austin, 1990). During the period between 1956 and 1983, 43 new nations emerged in sub-Saharan Africa (Collins et al., 1994b; Davidson, 1992). These new nations experienced great political turmoil, instability, and changes in leadership through assassinations and military coups d'etats (Austin, 1990). Elections create a great deal of tension in countries as frequently the winner has power, wealth, resources, prestige, and other privileges that come with the office (Annan, 1998). Elections in both Sierra Leone and Angola have led to bloodshed, coups d'etat, and war.

Since gaining their independence in 1961 from Britain for Sierra Leone and 1975 from Portugal for Angola, both have had political instability with numerous attempts and successful coups d'etat occurring, not unlike many other African countries. In April 1996 in Sierra Leone while rebels were still making their presence felt by mutilating civilians, the women, religious leaders, and paramount chiefs turned down a request for peace before elections. Democratic elections ensued using international UN observers to validate the vote. The civilian party won. A shift from a military government that rules by external force, to a democracy that requires internal self-rule takes time and education in democratic process to be achieved (Austin, 1990; Brookfield, 1987; Freire, 1990). At the time of this printing, anarchy reined in Freetown and no one political force was ruling.

Widespread corruption is another factor leading to conflicts and coups in Africa (Annan, 1998). Davidson talks about the need for "vigilance and moral courage" to withstand the constant temptations of taking "temporary personal advantage" because of the pervasiveness of bribery and corruption in Africa (Davidson, 1992, p. 163). The spouse of a parliamentarian in Sierra Leone voiced this difficulty when she shared with one of the authors that, "only people who have money should hold political or government jobs because the pay is so small you are vulnerable to bribes." Poor economic conditions throughout Africa contribute to this dilemma.

☐ Economic Factors

West, Central, and Southern (i.e. Sierra Leone and Angola) African countries have some of the highest mortality rates in the world (UNICEF, 1997b). Poverty is a silent killer in West and Central Africa (UNICEF,

1996; UNICEF, 1997b; Wallace et al., 1995). This is not always due to lack of resources but due to the distribution of those resources. Many a war has been fought over the control of natural resources (Annan, 1998). Women and children are the hardest hit by war and in the distribution of resources (Dubrow, 1995; Evans, 1996; Fozzard, 1995; Guluma, 1996; Levy & Sidel, 1997; Machel, 1996; Save the Children Alliance, 1996; UNICEF, 1996; UNICEF, 1997b; United Nations Department of Information, 1996; Wallace et al., 1995; Wessells & Kostelny, 1996).

> Poverty, even where blatantly apparent, does not exist simply because some have worked hard to change their lot in life and others have not. Poverty always serves social purposes. That is, the interests of someone, somewhere, are being met through the disadvantage of others.
> (Lynch & Hanson, 1992, p. 131)

Sierra Leone is the third poorest country in the world (UNICEF, 1996; UNICEF, 1997b). The per capita GNP is U.S. $190. The wealthiest 5% and the poorest 40% of the total population are outside this statistic. The population growth rate is 2.6% with the poorest group growing at the fastest rate. Angola is not far behind Sierra Leone with a per capita GNP of U.S. $730 and a population growth rate of 2.7%. But both of these countries and many other are rich in natural resources such as diamonds, timber, oil and other raw materials (http://www.odci.gov/cia/publications/factbook/sl.html and /ao.html). There are many individuals who profit from the ensuing chaos war brings (Annan, 1998).

The 1980s started Sierra Leone's economic decline due to an inefficient trade system and poor public sector management. That led to the 1990s political discord and rebel attack (civil war) with large spending going toward military hardware (Thorpe, Smart, Sesay, Bao, & Dupigny, 1995). International arms dealers are on the top of the list of those who profit from war (Annan, 1998). At the same time, Sierra Leone needed to cope with 20% of its citizens being displaced, as well as an influx of Liberian refugees equivalent to 5% of the total indigenous population. The resultant effect on the economy has been devastating (Thorpe et al., 1995).

The cost of imported goods in Sierra Leone is exorbitant. The slogan, "Grow what you eat, eat what you grow" is posted on billboards throughout the country. Anything indigenous is relatively inexpensive, labor is the cheapest commodity. Everyone works, including the children. Having someone cook, do your wash and cleaning, as well as having a driver for a month is approximately equivalent to the price of a sack of rice, a Sierra Leone staple. The state of the local economy can be seen at the market. A market geared to small quantities—a matchbook, a cup of rice, and half a cake of soap—is evidence of fewer resources. Buying in bulk is very expensive, yet buying in small quantities is even more costly in the long run.

☐ Religion

Religion (traditional African religions, Christianity, Islam and other religions) and spirituality is an intricate thread woven through the daily social fabric of many African societies (Blyden, 1994). Religious beliefs have a strong role in shaping the attitudes and actions of the individuals. Historically, Islam, marked by its use of war as a means to spread the faith, has carried out many a *jihad* or holy war in Africa (Collins et al., 1994b) and was the vehicle that spread Islam through Western Africa. The religious beliefs greatly affect the values of the countries, and in many cases, the politics. Separation of church and state may be blurred or may not exist (Austin, 1990). Whether Muslim or Christian, traditional beliefs permeate the peoples' ways of life (Blyden, 1994) and sorcery and witchcraft continue to play a role in society (Government of Sierra Leone, 1990). The values, beliefs, rites, ceremonies, music and way of doing daily business are intertwined in spirituality and culture. This strong faith perspective can be used in building psychosocial programs through the use of prayer, song, and story.

In Sierra Leone, over 50% of the population adhere to indigenous religions while 40% are Muslim and 7.5% are Christians. Christians have a disproportionate amount of power due to the Western educational system set up by Catholic and other Christian missionaries. Islam, with a 1,000 year history in Africa, is gaining in strength nationally possibly due to the jihads and its ability to blend traditional African beliefs of prestige, warriors, and victors and its allowance for multiple wives in its practices (Government of Sierra Leone, 1990). Becoming a Muslim does not always require a major conversion like becoming a Christian (Government of Sierra Leone, 1990) although that is changing and new Muslims are more strident in their religious beliefs (Collins et al., 1994b). The traditional Africans honor a Supreme Being or God. The beliefs and practices are closely tied to the land and kin—both those living and dead (Blyden, 1994). (See also Rituals for Death and Mourning, this chapter.)

Communication with ancestral spirits is very important. For the Bantu, the invisible world is made up of a god and founder of the clan, former heroes, spirits, geniuses, chiefs, hunters, warriors, magicians and all other ancestors. Ancestors can be good or bad and intervene in the visible world, which is made up of humans, animals, plants, stars, and other natural phenomena. Dreams, omens, music, and spirits are used to carry messages and offerings between the spirit world and the visible world. Life on earth and life beyond have a strong sense of continuity and are interdependent and permanently interrelated (Blyden, 1994).

No living thing exists in isolation—everything and everyone is susceptible to an increase or decrease in his or her life forces (Guluma, 1996; Monteiro, 1989). Happiness or misfortune depends on this relationship with the invisible world. That which the Western world would describe as the cause of an event is attributed in Bantu culture to the invisible world. The living are in constant fear of upsetting their ancestors and attempt to please them to win favors. This union of life forces which brings individuals together is not broken by death but is a continuum. These beliefs are the basis of Bantu religions and constitute one of the most important spiritual and social forces. The individual risks annihilation if he damages his relationship with the ancestors and other members of the community and if he does not transmit the essence of this knowledge to future generations. Elders are greatly respected in most African countries for their wisdom, advice leadership, and passing on of essential knowledge.

The belief that the dead continue to live through their descendants forms the basis of the conviction that it is essential to procreate. In the same way that death is inevitable, so too is it inevitable that life is maintained through descendants. To live is to give life. To procreate is obligatory, and to fail to reproduce is a betrayal of the ancestry.

Religion fosters the collective emphasis in the society. Singing provides a means of communicating with God or the Supreme Being of any faith tradition, and with one another (Kater, 1995). Songs provide a source of comfort, expression, and creativity (Finnegan, 1992) and can be created to fit the situation:

> Bye Bye Trauma
> Bye Bye Trauma
> Trauma go oh-o, oh-o, oh-o
> We nor want for see you nar ya (repeat)
> You can for gee we Pwell at
> You can for gee we Broke at
> You can for gee we Chest pain
> You can for gee we Make we worry
> Bye Bye Trauma
> Trauma go oh-o, oh-o, oh-o
> We nor want for see you nar ya
> (Dubrow & Peddle, 1997)

Songs can also be drawn from religious traditions such as "Tell God Tanke Tanke, Oh Papa God Tanke," a song in Sierra Leone. Songs, as well as dancing, are used effectively in helping children deal with the effects of violence (Dubrow & Peddle, 1997; Fozzard, 1995; Green & Wessells, 1997; Suzic et al., 1995). In the midst of deprivation, the soul comes shining through in song, and a closeness to the Divine is evident. Religious differences do not cause friction as in many parts of the world, and people of different religions coexist in harmony (Lynch & Hanson, 1992).

☐ Education and Literacy

Western education is offered at all levels, but fees and lack of facilities limit access to primary and secondary schooling. Although traditionally, "every ethnic group was educated in the context of his or her society" (Collins et al., 1994a, p. 189) free, in most developing countries more boys are being educated than girls (UNICEF, 1996). An estimated 21% (male: 31%, female: 11%) of Sierra Leonean's are literate (Thorpe et al., 1995). Urban dwellers are much more likely to have access to Western-oriented schools and remain in them longer than rural dwellers (UNICEF, 1997b). Throughout Africa, since the 1970s, there has been a tendency to cram classrooms so full of pupils that teachers are no longer in any position to give them any real education (UNESCO-UNICEF, 1981). The use of colonial languages, foreign curriculum not adapted to African traditions, and the sociocultural environment in the education system are key contributors to the high failure rate. The tension between the traditional and the new literacy—which is the culture and language of the cultural and sociopolitical elite and opens doors to universities whether one is in Ibadan, Paris, or Berkely—is evident (Collins et al., 1994a). One may criticize this situation; but no one can deny its existence as the driving motive behind the ordinary people's demand for access to the dominant culture and the dominant language even at the expense of the wisdom of the traditional learning (UNESCO-UNICEF, 1981).

☐ Health and Healing

Countries in conflict have the highest mortality rate for children under five in the world with Sierra Leone and Angola being in the top three (Levy, 1997; UNICEF, 1997b). Short life expectancy, an average of 48 years in the 22 lowest income African countries (Austin, 1990), and high sickness rates still plague developing counties despite massive inroads during the last few decades. Resources are being directed to the improvement of the physical health of children and their families through international organizations such as UNICEF, the World Health Organization (WHO) and nongovernmental organizations (NGOs). "The assumption seems to be that as long as the child is physically healthy, the quality of that life does not matter nor if the child grows up to be a deviant or delinquent" (UNESCO-UNICEF, 1981, p. 43). To save a child from tuberculosis, childhood diseases, and starvation is an incredible service. Neglecting the mental health of children exposed to poverty, war, child exploitation, and child labor is an abomination. Addressing children's psychosocial needs, while continuing to meet the physical needs, has recently appeared in goals and initiatives taken by NGOs (Dubrow, 1992; Evans, 1996; Fozzard, 1995; Christian Children's Fund, 1998; Green & Wessells, 1997; Herbst, 1995; Peddle, 1998; Save the Children Alliance, 1996; Wessells, 1996) and UN and UNICEF programs (Machel, 1996; Macksoud, 1993; UNICEF, 1997a; UNICEF, 1997b; UNICEF, 1998; Wessells & Kostelny, 1996) worldwide. Sierra Leone, Angola, and Liberia have implemented holistic community based psychosocial programs through coordinated efforts of the Taylor Institute, Christian Children's Fund, UNICEF and USAID.

Western.   "Shortage of medical personnel and a geographic imbalance of services characterize the health infrastructure. Pneumonia, malaria, tuberculosis, gastrointestinal diseases, anemia, and childhood diseases are serious health problems exacerbated by diet deficiencies and unsanitary conditions; infant mortality is very high" (Government of Sierra Leone, 1990, p. 63). People in Freetown and in other urban cities in Sierra Leone are more likely to go to a Western trained physician as their first source of a cure.

Two psychiatrists exist for all of Sierra Leone. They are considered the experts in regard to extreme cases of trauma identification and healing. The Department of Social Services has been in a constant state of flux since the independence of Sierra Leone leaving a shortage of social workers who are trained and have a focused direction. The Christian Children's Fund, UNICEF, and Government of Sierra Leone Kids in Distress (KIDS) Project is training workers to fill in these gaps in a culturally appropriate way (see also Community based strategy for healing, this chapter).

Traditional.   Traditional healers still have a very important role in the health care of Africans (Altuna, 1985; Dubrow, 1995; Green & Wessells, 1997; Kater, 1995; Redinha, 1973; Wessells, 1996). The beliefs vary depending on urban or rural living, education, and rate of success. In addition, the lack of Western health care services and expertise contribute to the continued strong use of herbalist, soothsayer, sorcerer, and medicine men in the rural as well as the urban areas. A woman told a personal story of not receiving satisfaction on the healing of a broken bone attended to by Western practice. She went to a traditional healer who had her buy three chickens that were part of the rituals he performed. Her leg completely healed. Some medical personnel are now combining traditional and Western practice in response to people's beliefs.

It is commonly believed that most illness in children is caused by witchcraft whose practitioners are capable of either sucking the blood of children or putting a bad spell or curse on them. In this cause and effect society, if a child has a problem it is probably the result of something they did. Many children are considered bad if their behavior is deemed bad. For example, the following traditional story about a bad boy was told by a rebel exchild-soldier in his attempt to reconnect from being a bad boy.

Stubborn Child

Once upon a time there was a stubborn boy child who liked to go swimming in a very big river where the devil (Western label that has stuck) of the area is living. Each time this stubborn boy leaves to swim his mother warns him to stay away from the stream but this stubborn boy continues to disobey his mother. One day the devil caught him and took him to his mother. The mother told the devil that if at any time this stubborn boy goes to swim he should be killed by the devil. A few weeks go by and this stubborn boy went back to swim in the same stream. There he was caught and killed by the devil who later displayed his head on top of a very big iron stone. The following day, some women went to fetch water from the stream and to their great surprise they discovered the boy's head on the stone. These women went back to report the ugly incidence to the town chief. The mother upon hearing this sad story wasted no time in reaching the stream. At first sight she refused to accept that her son's head was lying on top of the iron stone. Again she looked, and finally accepting the fact her son was dead, burst into tears. She was going to the stone every day where she would cry and cry. She usually sang very sorrowful songs. She did this for many weeks until one day while she was crying the devil carefully rejoined the stubborn boy's head and took him to her house. The mother upon her arrival home found her son alive. (as told by Thomas E. A. Macaulay)

Mental health problems are often handled and managed by either Alphas or medicine men. One of the most recent practices is to attend spiritual churches thereby bridging traditional religions with modern religions. At times, mental patients are admitted in these churches for prayers and other rituals. Some causes of disorders and their treatments are found in table 6–1.

A traditional healer's power in the Sierra Leone culture is inherited through apprenticeship and repetition of certain rituals. Knowledge and skills are sometimes acquired through dreams or water. It is also true, as in Liberia and other African countries, that twins are endowed with supernatural power and as a result their parents should perform certain rituals (Guluma, 1996). The supernatural powers of twins are often linked with good or bad omens of their parents.

TABLE 6–1. Spiritual Treatment of Disorders

Cause of Disorders	Treatment
Spiritual Possession	Spiritual Cleansing
Hexing or Witchcraft	Confession/Vomiting of the Witch
	Beef after eating special ritual foods
Punishment from God	Prayer

Mental health cannot be viewed in the Bantu context in Angola in terms of individual adjustment to the social milieu. In Bantu cosmology, life is a conversation between the living and the ancestors, and everything that happens in the visible world is attributed to events and meanings associated with the invisible world of the ancestors. Further, the individual is not of primary importance. One's existence reflects the will of the ancestors, and one's highest responsibility is to fulfill the obligations to the spiritual community. Spirituality is at the heart of mental health in the Bantu context. Western psychologists trained in a scientific mode that marginalized spirituality will need to make a significant adjustment in their analysis and practice before work can be undertaken responsibly in Angola.

Community Based Strategy for Healing

The resilience of the people in Africa, their efforts to promote healing, and their ability to rebuild their lives time and time again is powerful. The importance of working with the skills, support, and resources that the community brings cannot be highlighted enough (Evans, 1997; Garbarino, Dubrow, Kostelny, & Pardo, 1992). The communal system for family, work, and society creates a strong foundation for the community based approach to flourish. Creating long term successful and sustainable programs depends on the communities' participation (Dubrow, 1995; Evans, 1996; Fozzard, 1995; Freire, 1990; Herbst, 1995; Machel, 1996; Monteiro, 1989; Peddle, 1998; Save the Children Alliance, 1996). The community must accept the program as its own.

Paulo Freire stated, "One cannot expect positive results from an educational or political action programme that fails to respect the particular view of the world held by the people. Such a programme constitutes cultural invasions, good intentions notwithstanding" (Fozzard, 1995, p. 6).

The Taylor Institute, the Christian Children's Fund and UNICEF have worked together in creating community based programs since 1995 to address the psychosocial needs of children affected by violence in Angola (Province Based War Trauma Team–PBWTT) and in Sierra Leone

(KIDS) through a blending of Western and traditional practice. Each project is based on the specific needs and assets of the country in which it is operating, mobilizes community members to participate, and transfers critical skills and knowledge to local community based workers. Much of the knowledge transferred is in helping the local community based workers understand how their traditional cultural practices of singing, dancing, storytelling, and healing ceremonies are relevant to the healing process. A curriculum which contains basic principles of child development, the emotional impact of war on children, families and communities, traditional and Western methods of assisting children affected by violence, and conflict resolution and peace education, is the template for the training in both countries as well as for a program in Liberia (Dubrow, 1992). Trainers in the country, based on the country's specific needs, rewrite this curriculum (Dubrow & Peddle, 1997) so that the transfer of knowledge and skills will be appropriate to the setting and context of the people. Nancy Peddle and Carlinda Monteiro (chapter authors) have been heavily involved in implementing the projects.

Evaluation of the interventions in both countries and interviews with amputee victims at Connaught Hospital in Sierra Leone in May 1998, have shown: improved child–child relations; decreased sleeping problems; reduced bedwetting, stress reactions, and aggressive behavior; diminished concentration problems and social isolation; and improved future orientation (Green & Wessells, 1997).

☐ Summary and Recommendations for Interventions

The Golden Rule
Be the matter what it may,
Always speak the truth.
Whether at your work or play,
Always speak the truth.
Let this golden rule prevail,
And sink deep within your heart.
Even from this heart of ours,
We must speak the truth.
Beatrice Jones, Sierra Leone

Considering the wide range of values, roles, and other important variables associated with different cultural groups and taking into consideration what has already been said about traditional African cultures, we must consider that any intervention in the psychosocial area, whether in the context of peace or war, should always work holisitically with individuals in the context of their community and culture. Phenomena such as stress and trauma can be understood only within the context of the people's belief systems and spiritual practices. These may not be readily disclosed to people from the outside since they may be regarded as obvious, backward, or not for public discussion with outsiders. Conveying a sense of openness and willingness to hear and learn from locals may help in building the trust needed to do the work.

When dealing with people we should take into account their convictions and their cultural and religious beliefs and try to work within the reality of their systems even if we do not agree with them. If we try to diminish or ignore their convictions, efforts will only end in failure. Respect for other peoples' cultures and beliefs, means that we do not accept negative values which lead to obscurantism and which delay development. To give into the thinking that each culture should not be open to inquiry could be as dogmatic and harmful as that which led to colonialism.

Although there are numerous negative aspects of colonialism, contact with other cultures and peoples also involves positive aspects, which have led to significant changes in health, sanitation, and technology to name a few (Austin, 1990). An intermixture of different African ethnic groups, Western cultures, and Eastern cultures influences African cultures. The amount of influence on each individual will depend on a variety of factors including the development of the overall country, exposure to Western education, urban or rural dwelling, and religious traditions to name a few. It is essential to respect the ancestors and understand the explanations that are viewed locally as laws of nature and that define a psyche that may appear quite foreign to psychologists from other counties. However, at the same time it is important to generate mechanisms that lead us to programs that promote positive growth and development. Thinking in terms of how to positively impact future generations who will emerge from countries which have suffered such long conflicts and difficult situations is imperative to achieve long term stability and contribute to peace in the world.

Paraphrasing a scholar of African culture we finish by saying, We should not let someone who does not want to know Africa come near her. How can one love her if we do not know her real face? How can we really help her to free herself if we do not know her soul (Altuna, 1985)?

Recommendations for Interventionists

1. Coming from the outside one is given power and privilege not accorded to insiders. You might be able to side step protocol, but those

you are working with cannot. They will remain when you leave. Outsiders have different questions, specialized skills, and a new perspective to bring to old problems, but cannot know the cultural nuances to come up with the final answers.

2. The power of colonial rule remains a factor in working with the people of Africa today. France, England, Portugal, and Italy, to name a few, had colonies in Africa each exacting influence on the politics and culture of the land they colonized. The colonial rule manifests itself in the national language, status, religion, political structure, institutional structures, and culture.

3. Honor and respect the faith perspective of the people. Sharing your own faith tradition through a prayer or any means that feels comfortable is accepted and appreciated.

4. Understand and recognize what the differences are between cultural, ethnic, and racial differences and differences that are attributed to poverty (Lynch & Hanson, 1992).

5. Find out how each person you work with would like to be addressed. Age, position, and ethnic group all play a part in how a person may be addressed. If a doctorate or medical degree has been earned, always use the title. Erring on the side of formality is preferable.

6. Adapt your therapeutic interventions to the community taking into consideration their culture, learning styles, socioeconomic status, first language, formal or nonformal education and degree of trauma to which they have been exposed. In addition, whether individuals come from rural or urban areas will greatly impact the type of interventions you may develop (Lynch & Hanson, 1992).

7. Before beginning any work get to know both the formal and informal power structures in the community and who holds the power—Secret Societies, the elders, paramount Chief, village Chief, midwife, medicine man, and/or Women's Society. They are highly respected and their blessing may be the difference between success and failure. Remember to benefit from the strong informal networks of family, church, mosque, and community in developing and implementing interventions.

8. Become acquainted with the resources the community has to offer regarding trauma healing and the therapeutic techniques you will be using. Working with the traditional healer on how he or she cures trauma may cut down your work dramatically (Suzic et al., 1995).

9. The orientation to time can be different depending on which groups of people you are working with. Many meetings start promptly with people coming in up to an hour later. Other meetings and functions do not start until everyone is in attendance. Try to be prompt and use

the time you may wait for informal communication. People in rural areas may not have access to knowing the exact time. Flexibility may be required if you are working within a tight time frame. Process and relationship can be more important than the minutes on the clock.

10. Refrain from stereotyping all Africans based on any one group.
11. Use multidisciplinary and ethnically diverse training teams where possible.
12. Unity and solidarity are shown through the wearing of uniforms or a particular color, fabric, or design. For example, after a funeral a women's group may where the same dress for a week to show solidarity with their deceased sister and Friday is traditional dress day in Sierra Leone. A foreigner wearing African dress in Sierra Leone is appreciated.
13. Take into consideration the heat if you are going to the Sub-Sahara or equatorial areas. The heat saps one's energy. After a while every little gesture and thought becomes harder. Most Africans go home to heat filled houses, which plays havoc with their sleep.
14. In a war zone, some of the main stresses come not only from direct exposure to violence, uprooting, and loss, but also from the disruption of traditional practices and the inability to meet one's solemn obligations to the ancestors. The inability to perform the appropriate burial ritual for a Bantu is not only an individual stressor but places the entire community at risk (Redinha, 1974).
15. Effective intervention may require the restoration of harmony with the ancestors. This entails conducting the appropriate rituals and participating in appropriate patterns of living as defined by the elders.
16. Secret Societies, kin, community, faith, religion, and traditions all play a vital role in trauma healing (Blyden, 1994). They provide individuals with support networks, coping mechanisms, common bonds, and strong attachments.

☐ References

Altuna, P. R. (1985). *Cultura tradicional Banto.* Luanda: Edição do Secretariado Arguidioc esano de Pastoral.

Annan, K. (1998). *The causes of conflict and the promotion of durable peace and sustainable development in Africa* (Report of the Secretary–General to the United Nations Security Council A/52/871-S/1998/318). New York: United Nations.

Arroyo, W. & Eth, S. (1996). Post-traumatic stress disorder and other stress reactions in Apfel, R. J. & Simon, B. (Eds.). Minefields in their hearts: The mental health of children in war and communal violence. New Haven: Yale Univeristy Press.

Austin, J. E. (1990). *Managing in developing countries: Strategic analysis and operating techniques.* New York: The Free Press.

Blyden, E. W. (1994). *African life and customs.* Baltimore, MD: Black Classic Press.

Brookfield, S. D. (1987). *Developing critical thinkers: Challenging adults to explore alternative ways of thinking and acting.* San Francisco: Jossey–Bass Inc.

Christian Children's Fund. (1998). *The CCF approach to psychosocial development and children's well-being.* Richmond, VA: Christian Children's Fund.

Collins, R. O., Burns, J. M., & Ching, E. K. (Eds.). (1994a). *Historical problems of imperial Africa.* Princeton: Markus Wiener Publishers.

Collins, R. O., Burns, J. M., & Ching, E. K. (Eds.). (1994b). *Problems in African history.* Princeton: Markus Wiener Publishing.

Crowther, G., Finlay, H., Cole, G., Else, D., Hamalainen, P., Jousiffe, A., Logan, L., Murray, J., Newton, A., Simonis, D., Swaney, D., & Willett, D. (Eds.). (1995). *Africa on a Shoestring* (7th ed.). Hawthorn, Victoria: Lonely Planet Publications.

Davidson, B. (1992). *The black man's burden: Africa and the curse of the nation-state.* New York: Random House.

Dubrow, N. (1992). *Children exposed to violence: A psychosocial view.* Chicago: Taylor Institute.

Dubrow, N. (1995). *Children of war: Psychosocial and educational needs.* Paper presented at the Armaments, Children and World Population, September 30–October 2, 1993. Montreal.

Dubrow, N., & Peddle, N. (1997). *Trauma healing and peace education training manual* (2nd ed.). Chicago: Taylor Institute.

Edelman, M. W. (1992). *The measure of our success: A letter to my children and yours.* Boston: Beacon Press.

Erikson, K. T. (1976). *Everything in its path: Destruction of community in the Buffalo Creek flood.* New York: Simon & Schuster.

Evans, J. L. (1996). Children as zones of peace: Working with young children affected by armed violence. *Coordinators' Notebook: An International Resource for Early Childhood Development, 19,* 1–26.

Evans, J. L. (1997). Both halves of the sky: Gender socialization in the early years. *Coordinators' Notebook: An International Resource for Early Childhood Development, 20,* 1–27.

Finnegan, R. (1992). *Oral traditions and the verbal arts: A guide to research practices.* New York: Routledge.

Fozzard, S. (1995). *Surviving violence: A recovery programme for children and families.* Geneva: International Catholic Child Bureau.

Freire, P. (1990). *Pedagogy of the oppressed* (Myra Pergman Ramos, Trans.). New York: The Continuum Publishing Company.

Freund, B. (1984). *The making of contemporary Africa: The development of African society since 1800.* Bloomington, IN: Indiana University Press.

Garbarino, J., Dubrow, N., Kostelny, K., & Pardo, C. (1992). *Children in danger: Coping with the consequences of community violence.* San Francisco: Jossey Bass.

Government of Sierra Leone. (1990). Area Handbook for Sierra Leone. Freetown, Sierra Leone: Ministry of Education.

Green, E., & Wessells, M. (1997). *Mid-term evaluation of the province-based war trauma team project: Meeting the psychosocial needs of children in Angola* (Evaluation report). Richmond, VA: Christian Children's Fund.

Guluma, K. (1996). An Introduction to Liberian Culture. Monrovia: UNICEF.

Herbst, L. (1995). *Children in war: Community strategies for healing.* Durham, NC: Duke University.

Herman, J. (1992). *Trauma and recovery.* New York: HarperCollins.

Hilliard, A. (1995). *The Maroon Within Us.* New York: Black Classic Press.

Jannoff-Bulman, R. (1992). *Shattered assumptions: Towards a new psychology.* New York: The Free Press.

Kater, M. (1995). *The use for drumming and dance in the traditional healing arts: The Akan ethnic group Ghana, Africa.* Legon: University of Ghana.

Leite, F. (1991). *Bruxos e magos Africa, revista do centro de estudos Aficanos.* S. Paulo.

Levy, B. S., & Sidel, V. W. (Eds.). (1997). *War and public health.* New York: Oxford University Press.

Lynch, E. W., & Hanson, M. J. (Eds.). (1992). *Developing cross-cultural competence: A guide for working with young children and their families.* Baltimore: Paul H. Brooks Publishing Co.

Machel, G. (1996). *UN study on the impact of armed conflict on children* (Report of the expert of the Secretary-General, Ms Graca Machel A/51/306). New York: United Nations.

Macksoud, M. (1993). *Helping children cope with the stressors of war: A manual for parents and teachers.* New York: UNICEF.

Monteiro, A. (1989). *Angola, Que Saida.* Luanda.

Peddle, N. (1997). Caught in the coup. Chicago: Nancy Peddle (Personal communication).

Peddle, N. (1998). National kids in distress project. *United Nations Chronicle, 35(1),* 46–47.

Redinha, J. (1973). *Praticas e ritos da circuncisao entre os quiocos da Lunda.* Luanda: Fundo de Turismo e Publicidade.

Redinha, J. (1974). *Etnias e Culturas de Angola.* Luanda.

Richmond, Y., & Gestrin, P. (1998). *Into Africa: Intercultural Insights.* Yarmouth, Maine: Intercultural Press.

Save the Children Alliance. (1996). *Promoting psychosocial well-being among children affected by armed conflict and displacement: Principles and approaches* (Working Paper No. 1): Save the Children, Working Group on Children Affected by Armed Conflict and Displacement.

Senghor, L. S. (1970). *Libertad, Negritud y Humanismo.* Madrid: Tecnos.

Suzic, D., Patel, M., & Doran, C. (1995). *An evaluative review of psychosocial programme studies and documents* (Evaluation Review of psychosocial programmes in ESA region). Nairobi: UNICEF ESARO.

Tempels, P. (1965). *La Philosophie Bantoue.* Paris: Presence Africaine.

Thorpe, C. A., Smart, N. D. J., Sesay, A. B., Bao, D. S., & Dupigny, A. C. T. (Eds.). (1995). *New education policy for Sierra Leone.* Freetown, Sierra Leone: Department of Education.

Toole, M. (1997). Displaced persons and war. In B. S. Levy & V. W. Sidel (Eds.). *War and public health.* New York: Oxford University Press.

UNESCO–UNICEF (Ed.). (1981). *African thoughts on the prospects of education for all.* Geneva: UNESCO-UNICEF.

UNICEF. (1996). *The progress of nations 1996.* Oxford, England: UNICEF.

UNICEF. (1997a). *Psychosocial care and protection: Children in armed conflict.* Paper presented at the Psychosocial Care and Protection—Needs of Children in Situations of Armed Conflict, *April 29–May 3, 1997. Nairobi, Kenya.*

UNICEF. (1997b). *UNICEF Annual Report.* New York: UNICEF.

UNICEF. (1998). Position paper on psychosocial interventions for children in need of special protection. In Child Protection Committee (Ed.) (pp. 6). Freetown, Sierra Leone: UNICEF.

United Nations Department of Information. (1996). Too soon for twilight, too late for dawn: The story of children caught in conflict. *United Nations Chronicle, 33,*7–14.

Wallace, H. M., Giri, K., & Serrano, C. V. (Eds.). (1995). *Health care of women and children in developing countries* (2nd ed.). Oakland, CA: Third Party Publishing Company.

Wessells, M. (1996). Assisting Angolan children impacted by war: Blending western and traditional approaches to healing. *Coordinators' Notebook: An International Resource for Early Childhood Development, 19,*33–37.

Wessells, M., & Kostelny, K. K. (1996). *The Graca Machel/U.N. study on the impact of armed conflict on children: Implications for early child development* (Working Paper). New York: UNICEF.

7

CHAPTER

Anatoly V. Isaenko,
Peter W. Petschauer

Traditional Civilization in the North Caucasus: Insiders and Outsiders

☐ Introduction

The collapse of the Soviet Union was one of the major events in world history; a great power slipped out of existence with a minimal number of casualties. The disappearance of this super power in 1991 has created immense opportunities and untold miseries throughout the region. On the positive side are hope for democracy, greater freedom of expression, and business and investment opportunities for Russians and non-Russians alike. On the negative side are unpaid salaries, minuscule pensions, unheated apartments, increased crime, and unresolved traumas of the past repressions, to mention but a few (Chinn & Kaiser, 1996; Conner, 1996; Demko, Zaionchkovskaya, Pontius, & Joffe, 1997). For a time, Europeans, Americans, Japanese, and many other outsiders were flocking to Russia to take advantage of the opportunities and to alleviate the misery. To give a considered impression of the complexity that outsiders may encounter in Russia, this chapter concentrates only on one area, that of the North Caucasus.

The most appropriate designator for the North Caucasus derives from geography, i. e., it is the region of the high mountains and the northern slopes and valleys of the Caucasus Mountains, a region that borders the steppe and the black earth belt of southern Russia. Three types of landscape make up this area: the low coastlines along the Black and Caspian

Seas, the fertile plains and low hills, and the high mountains. In the west, the mountains rise out of the Black Sea; in the east, a narrow coastline parts the Caspian Sea from the mountain slopes. This narrow access to Transcaucasia (and some dangerous highways in the center of the range) has been the first goal of invaders: the power that controlled these roads could call itself the master of the Caucasus. The region attained some cultural and historical unity from its important position as a mountain range between two seas and a crossing point of international trade routes, especially the famous Silk Road. Aside from an unusual geography, the mountains were characterized by unique survival techniques of its inhabitants. Animal husbandry and grazing, combined with handicrafts, the harnessing of natural energy sources, and terraced cultivation, characterized the traditional mountaineers' economy. Nomadic or seminomadic horse- and stockbreeding, together with trading and farming, prevailed into the nineteenth century. Along with herding and cultivating the soil, looting of neighbors and nonmountaineers was a way of life and stayed alive until at least the late nineteenth century. Due to similar living conditions, many of the people in the North Caucasus developed and shared similar cultural patterns and values, the so-called laws of the mountains, or *Adats*. During wars against outside powers, as well as in-fights with each other, the North Caucasians gained a reputation for being fierce warriors. They handled their horses and daggers excellently. Many foreign travelers saw them, and paintings showed them, as slim, handsome, fearsome and dark, very hospitable, proud and fearless, and almost impossible to subdue (Dumas, 1859/ 1962; Potozki, 1829; Smith & Dwight, 1834; von Klaproth, 1812–1814). Now the Caucasians have left the high stony peaks and most of them speak Russian aside from their many native languages. As a byproduct of this transformation, the society offers opportunities to men and women, and one encounters women in the higher political strata and academic positions.

Equally characteristic and formative of the Caucasus and Caucasians is that the region has been both a battleground and a place for mixing peoples, cultures, and religions since ancient times. Scythians, Greeks, Romans, Persians, Arabs, Turks, Mongols, and Russians have been involved in the area, fought over it, and left part of themselves. The outsiders, or conquerors, and the locals, or conquered, traded with each other, lived side by side, spoke each others' languages, married each others' sons and daughters, and adopted each others' religions and philosophies. Nevertheless, those who were settled in the mountains, be they natives or newcomers, gradually developed a powerful story about the conquering and oppressive outsiders, perceiving themselves under constant attack. The latest of these attacks, the Stalinist terror and the recent Russian at-

TABLE 7–1. Ethnic Groups in the North Caucasus

Name of State	Size in km2	Number of Inhabitants	Capital	Major Ethnic Groups in Percentages
Abkhazia	8,600	548,000	Sukhumi	Abkhazians: 20; Georgians: 80
Adygeia	7,600	432,000	Maikop	Adygeans: 22; Russians: 68
Chechen-Ingush	19,300	1,270,000	Grozny	Chechens: 58; Russians: 23; Ingushi: 13
Dagestan	50,300	1,802,000	Machachkala	Avars: 28; Dargins: 16; Kumyks: 13; Lezgi: 11; Russians: 9; Lak: 5
Kabardine-Balkar	12,500	754,000	Nalchik	Kabardians: 48; Balkars: 10 Russians: 32;
Kalmykia	75,900	323,000	Elista	Kalmyks: 45; Russians: 38; Dargin: 4
Karachai-Cherkes	14,050	415,000	Cherkessk	Russians: 42.4; Karachai: 31; Circassians: 10; Abkhazians: 7
North Ossetia	8,000	632,000	Vladikavkaz	Ossetes: 53; Russians: 30; Ingushi: 5
South Ossetia	3,900	99,000	Tskhinval	Ossetes: 66; Georgians: 29

Brooks, 1995.

tempt to subdue Chechnya, left a most profound mark and traumatized families and individuals. It also united many ethnic groups in the region.

The North Caucasus minorities live mainly in eight republics of the Russian Federation (Dagestan, Kalmykia, Chechnya, Ingushetia, North Ossetia, Kabardino-Balkar, Karachai-Cherkass, and Adygeia) and in former autonomous republics and districts in Georgia (South Ossetia and Abkhazia). Table 7–1 gives an overview of the area by some principal characteristics.

Because of the complex web of ethnic intermingling that characterizes the region, ethnic groups do not necessarily live in the administrative units that bear their name, and all administrative units are inhabited by more than one ethnic group. Furthermore, Russians live in most of the republics in the North Caucasus, especially in the cities and industrial centers in the central and western part of the region.

In spite of the recent changes, traditional gender relations and family (patronymic) patterns remain, and men and male values and ways prevail in public and private life. One of the ways of asserting male pre-eminence may still be experienced today at some formal eating arrangements in Ossetia. One major reason for the continuation of these traditions is that the native people in the North Caucasus are still distinct from the mainstream of Russian society, both in terms of their own sense of identity and in the perception of their contemporaries. They remain distinct because all ethnic groups of the North Caucasus have struggled for their languages, traditions, and values, and their ethnic territories, usually in opposition to dominance from the outside. We suspect that many people hope that the reestablishment of almost forgotten customs and traditions will somehow allow them to manage the latest changes entering their area.

The many conquests of the region and the repeated oppression and assimilation of Caucasians are now exacerbated by a whole new set of difficulties. Caucasians, like people throughout the territories of the former Soviet Union, speak in terms of democracy, political competition, human rights, free markets, and free flow of information, but these concepts are inadequately understood and often exploited as slogans to attract outside support or discredit rivals. In these societies, the understanding of democracy is neither deep nor widespread. The art of compromise and accommodation, the process for peaceful resolution of differences and setting of priorities, the rule of law as an inclusive and systematic set of legal procedures, and human rights as being a respect for everyone is neither deep nor widespread.

☐ The Past

Most peoples of the North Caucasus consider themselves descendants either of one of the great conquering tribes or of one of the conquered tribes. Ossetes claim to stem from the Alans, Kumyks from the Khazars, and Nogai from the Golden Horde. Arab, Persian, and Turkish (Ottoman) domination have also left an influence. Each of these affiliations began from outside incursion and domination of the area and speaks volumes about the complex cultural heritage of the North Caucasus. Thus, some of the recurrent intrusions must be mentioned because they played a significant role in the formation of ethnicity, ethnopsychological perceptions, and the underlying traumas of North Caucasians.

The Scythian and Sarmatian penetration into the area infused one unique aspect into the culture (Edwards, 1996a). The Alans were one of the most powerful Sarmatian tribes. Like many of the later conquerors, they mixed with the native population and became one of the principal powers in the Caucasus during the entire early medieval period. The most popular subject among North Ossetian scholars and the populace alike is the search, restoration, and study of the traditional *Alanic* epic folklore, beliefs, and symbols (The Legends of the Narts).

While both Greek and Roman colonists settled at the Eastern shore of the Black Sea, the Huns and the Avars reached Europe in the first centuries AD and subordinated the Alans. Some of the Alans moved west (Bachrach, 1973), and others continued under Hunic rule in the Caucasus in more or less independent tribal federations. These Alans later created a strong feudal state that continued until the devastating raids of the Mongols and Tamerlane in the thirteenth and fifteenth centuries (Kuznetsov, 1993).

Beginning with the fourth century, many people in the western part of the Caucasus converted from paganism to Christianity. In the meantime, the eastern parts of the Caucasus first came under the influence of the Iranian Sassanids, and then, after the fall of the dynasty to the Arabs in the second half of the seventh century, these Caucasians converted to Islam. Out of Turkish and Iranian tribes, defeated Huns, and indigenous Caucasians emerged a new people, the Khazars; by 650 A.D., they established a stable state with trading routes across the Caucasus and accepted Judaism (Vernadsky, 1943).

Genghis Khan's troops crossed the Caucasus from the south and forced the local population into the high mountains (Edwards, 1996b). Then, in the first half of the 13th century, Genghis Khan's son and grandson, Juchi and Batu, ended the domination of Adygeans and Alans and created the Golden Horde north of the mountains. Their state lasted from the mid-13th century until the end of the 15th century (Halperin, 1987).

The Mongolian invasion and the rejection or the accommodation of the various local and migrant groups is one of the anchors around which different ethnic identities were formed. The Mongol dominance reduced the Alan population from more than two million people to barely one-eighth of this number by the end of the 15th century. The survivors were pushed from the plains and foothills of the Northern Caucasus into the gorges of the center of the mountain range. Some Dagestanian groups suffered similarly devastating consequences in that their flourishing kingdom, Savir, was almost totally subdued (Isaenko & Kuchiev, 1995).

Although the Mongols attempted to crush the resistance of the remaining mountaineers, those who endured never fell under their dominance. The mountaineers barricaded themselves in the gorges and highland valleys behind huge stone embattlements and in numerous castles and fortresses. They repulsed practically all attempts to seize their strongholds. From their secure places, they engaged in lightening raids on Mongolian settlements in the open plain. The outsiders were able to strike back successfully only under Timur when they broke through the fortresses into the western part of Ossetia, the Digoria. The memory of these heroic and tragic times lingers to this day among the common people and is reflected in their folklore. For example, every child in Ossetia knows these words from the ballad, *The Cry of Zadaleski Mother:* "Bloody rain is falling on the land of Digoria" (Magometov, 1968).

The stark ruins of the ancient mountain castles and cities speak to locals and outsiders alike; they gave the American coauthor a sense of the immense power they exert on every regional ethnic group. For example, many people's connection to the Alans stems from the ruins of the mountain cities, the eerie necropoli, and the abandoned fields. Most people in the area have visited these ancient sites, stepped over their piles of stone, peeked into the houses of the dead in which a few bodies of mountaineers still lie, and have surveyed the fields where traces of long forgotten boundaries remain evident. Yet most people know little about these remarkable vestiges beyond that they are the remnants of brave people of their distant past. Only some specialists and informed authorities, including a number of heads (seniors) of local clans of the Ossetian, Ingush, Chechen, Kabardian, and Daghestan peoples who preserve family legends and traditions concerning their origins, know more than is visible to the naked eye in the mountains.

Since the Mongolian intrusion, a sense of victimization by conquering powers has become a strong, if not the dominating, element in Caucasian identity. The groups who retreated into the mountains continuously elaborated on the terrible defeats suffered at the hands of the Mongols. To them, these defeats were so devastating that they could not resolve them. Vamik Volkan calls these unresolved defeats chosen traumas (Isaenko & Petschauer, 1995; Volkan, 1991; Volkan, 1997). These are the traumas that linger for centuries and form the very essence of a society's understanding of itself, such as the battle of Kosovo in the Middle Ages for Serbs.

Russia entered the picture after the Golden Horde had disintegrated and became involved in the steppes north of the Caucasus in the 16th century. Firuz Kazemzadeh noted that the conquest of Astrakhan in 1554 enabled Moscow to influence the affairs of the North Caucasian peoples, including the Avars and the Kumyks of Dagestan, the Chechens, the Ossetes, the Kabardians, and the Circassians (Kazemzadeh, 1974). But at this early point, these groups retained many of their past ways. They were independent and remained unconquerable before the introduction of modern weaponry. Year after year, century after century, the mountaineers formed intricate alliances among themselves and with the Crimeans, Turks, and Persians. As successors of the Khanate of Astrakhan, the contemporary Muscovite princes and later Russian tsars, inherited these local conflicts and ways of being. They tried to resolve the conflicts, but they did so in a manner not understandable to the mountaineers whose customs and lifestyle were quite different from those of the Russians. A good example of this pattern is the treaty that some Kabardian chieftains signed with Tsar Feodor I (Ivanovich) in 1588. The tsar extended his protection to the chiefs by promising that he would aid them against all enemies. The chiefs in turn promised to remain faithful to him and his successors. Both sides entered this treaty with very different attitudes. The Russians had already begun to build a centralizing state; the Kabardians still lived in the context of a loose military democracy. The Russians had an autocratic tsar, a formal system of written laws, and the beginnings of a functioning bureaucracy; the Kabardians had no state, no written law, nor the concept of sovereignty. To the Russians, the chief Kabardian negotiator was his people's tsar; to the Kabardians he was no more than one of the chieftains.

With every misunderstanding between insider and outsider, the unresolved memory of the earlier Tatar invasions and occupation was reinvigorated. In addition, each lost battle not only reopened past wounds and insults, preserving them in the minds of leaders and populace alike, but each loss also played an important role in recreating and redirecting the image of the untrustworthy outsider. For many years, the outsider, the enemy, had been the Persians, Turks, and Mongols; now these outsiders were the Russians. The perception that these latest outsiders were no different than previous outsiders forged the psychological link between Mongols and Russians and inspired subsequent mountaineer generations to seek holy revenge against their latest enemy (Isaenko & Petschauer, 1995; Kazemzadeh, 1974). The memories and the losses created a trauma whose depth over time formed the very essence of being Caucasian.

After several retreats, Russia gained access to the areas in the lowlands at the foot of the mountains and, between 1763 and 1793, built a line of fortresses (McCarthy, 1992). Practically all the cities and towns in the region originate with these fortifications. Parts of Dagestan, Ingushetian, and Chechen territory became battlefields in the 1780s and resulted in desperate resistance under local religious and political leadership (1785–1791). This resistance was the first organized military enterprise that unified the North Caucasian peoples. Chechens, Ingushi, Kabardians, Circassians, and Dagestani fought to remain free under the leadership of Sheikh Mansur. He was defeated and captured by the Russians (Akhmadov, 1992). A new imperial campaign began in the late 1820s and ended in 1839 with the defeat of the movement in Dagestan. Another war erupted in 1840 through a Chechen rebellion. It did not end until 1859 when the Imam Shamil, the famous leader of the Caucasian War, was caught. Sporadic uprisings of mountaineers continued in the

Western Caucasus until 1864 when the Caucasian War was concluded. During the campaign, the Russian army lost more than 500,000 soldiers (MacKenzie, 1974; Umarov, 1991).

After the war, approximately 1.2 million Caucasians emigrated from the conquered territories and 800,000 of these lived to settle in Ottoman dominions. Many of the people who stayed were forced to move from their settlements in the valleys to the slopes where they were easier to control (Brooks, 1995). These losses, the changes in lifestyle of the mountaineers, and the memories of them fed and reinvigorated the original fear of and hatred toward intruders, especially in Chechens. This fear and hatred was complicated by fears of total engulfment of their ethnic culture by the lifestyle, laws, and rules of the dominating outside power.

Half a century later, the Russian Revolution of 1917 inspired some North Caucasians to reassert the independence of the region. After the Bolshevik victory, a Terek-Dagestan government declared its secession from Russia. At the same time, left wing radicals established a Terek Republic that was soon overthrown by the pro-imperial White army commanded by Anton Ivanovich Denikin. Once again mountaineer villages were burned to the ground (Maliev, 1988).

By the end of 1919, the mountainous part of Dagestan, Chechnya, Ossetia and Kabardia was again declared an independent state: the North Caucasian Emirate under Islamic slogans. This step caused a serious split between Christian Cossacks and mountaineers and exacerbated the conflict between Cossacks, some of whom sided with Denikin while others sided with the Bolsheviks. Sheikh Uzun-Hadzhi, the leader of the Emirate, as well as Chechen and Ingushetian authorities, soon flirted with the Bolsheviks who used contradictions between mountaineers and Cossacks to their advantage. Their leaders, Gregory K. Ordshonikidze and Sergei M. Kirov, persuaded mountaineer troops to eradicate and deport about 70,000 Cossacks from their settlements on the Sundza and Terek rivers (1918–1920). Ingushetian historians now claim that the number must be less (Alieva, 1993).

After the Eleventh Army defeated the White rebellion, Josef Stalin took control of the situation. To undermine the Caucasian Revolutionary Committee, he proclaimed a Soviet Republic of all Caucasian mountaineers. Those in charge agreed to recognize Soviet power on the condition that *Adats* and *Shariats* (Islam based traditional mountain laws) were the sole legal foundations of the new autonomous republic. Stalin agreed and the Autonomous Soviet Mountain Republic was formed in January, 1921. But Stalin did not fulfill his promises. By the mid-1920s, he had established a hierarchy of ethnically defined autonomies that were headed by local socialist leaders. Without the peoples themselves being involved, specific groups were selected to realize Stalin's plan of national-cultural construction (Stenographic Account, 1992). As if to make things worse, in 1928 Stalin started his program of collectivization; farming land was confiscated, the *Shariats* and *Adats* were forbidden, and the population was disarmed. The prohibition of wearing weapons, including daggers, was perceived as personally humiliating to the mountaineers for whom small arms were considered an indispensable part of clothing. The Caucasian political and intellectual leadership was accused of bourgeois nationalism and consequently annihilated or deported. This critical situation stabilized only in 1936. In a further blow, between 1938 and 1940, the authorities replaced earlier alphabets with the Cyrillic alphabet and barred access to written historical sources.

Some Caucasian peoples characterize events that happened during the Second World War as their third catastrophe; that is, following the Mongol invasion and the Russian war in the 1830s. As the soldiers of the German *Wehrmacht* pushed along the Caucasus and occupied some districts, they closed collective farms, reopened mosques, and promised sovereignty to those people who were willing to cooperate. Stalin thought that the Chechens and Ingushi would side with the enemy. However, the linkage was not made because Soviet troops stopped any further German advance into the Caucasus. All the same, entire populations of some North Caucasian ethnic groups were rounded up, loaded into tens of thousands of cattle wagons, and transferred to Central Asia (Conquest, 1970). Nothing expresses the anguish of these people better than the report by Ruslan G.:

> It was cold, and the floor was coated with hoarfrost. The soldier who came into the house didn't want to bend down. He raked the hut with a burst from his tommy gun. Blood trickled out from under the bench where a child was hiding. The mother screamed and hurled herself at the soldier. He shot her too. There was not enough rolling stock. Those left behind were shot. The bodies were covered with earth or sand, carelessly. The shooting had also been careless, and people started wriggling out of the sand like worms. The NKVD men spent the whole night shooting them all over again.
> (Radzhinsky, 1996, p. 503)

Table 7–2 gives an idea of the magnitude of these deportations.

When the remaining exiles returned to the region in 1956–1957, they found that much of their land had been taken over by people from neighboring areas. Their hostility toward these settlers was not mitigated by their knowledge that these peoples had themselves been forcibly resettled at Stalin's behest. For the Chechens, the return from exile was bitter; however, in their reflections they did not take into account their role in the 1918–1920 campaign against the Cossacks, the forced settle-

TABLE 7–2. Deportations

Date	Ethnics	Population in 1939	Loaded on Trains, 1943–44
November, 1943	Karachai	75,737	69,267
December, 1943	Kalmyks	134,271	93,139
February, 1944	Chechens	407,690	387,229
	Ingushetians	92,074	91,250
March, 1944	Balkari	42,666	37,103

Conquest, 1970; Radzhinsky, 1996; Alieva, 1993; Krag, Funch, table

ment of their neighbors, and their own compensation by Nikita S. Khrushchev with land in the fertile districts of Stavropol.

Historical events, particularly Russian colonization policies of the 18th and the 19th centuries, Soviet deportation practices toward the end of World War II, subsequent unprepared returns to the area in 1957, unconsidered legislation that affected the territorial rehabilitation of 1992, and the Chechen War play a decisive role in current claims and grievances of North Caucasian peoples. This troubled history also serves as an underpinning and identifies and legitimizes ethnic identities.

Every new pain Russians inflicted in the area, especially the deportations and the resettlement on nontraditional lands, added more fuel to a trauma that had by then fully permeated the ethnic identity of these peoples. Having been defeated and abused so many times before, they readily transferred all of their past hostility from earlier to the latest generation of outsiders. Knowing of the deportations and the mountaineer loyalty to land, the full extent of this tragedy may be seen in one example—virtually every Chechen now over age 35 was born in exile. This fact alone accounts for some of the fierceness and loyalty of Chechen fighters to their cause during the latest war between themselves and the Russians (Cuny, 1995). For example, each Chechen fighter vowed to kill at least three Russian soldiers if his father had been deported.

☐ Traditional Customs

During the Soviet period, national and regional histories were falsified in order to attain the ideal of an ethnically unattached Russian–Soviet type of person, sometimes called the new Soviet man. This concept was one of the greatest hopes of the Soviets and is one of their harshest legacies. The resultant confusion fostered inadequate research and a scarcity of information about the Caucasus and its peoples. Furthermore, this manipulation of history gave rise to the formation of myths, the use of guesswork, and the abuse of facts in political debates. Consequently, the authors included in a recent publication a historical sketch that focused on those periods, events and aspects that primarily shaped the formation of individual identity and collective ethnicity (Isaenko & Petschauer, 1995). Today, some specialists who deal with the Caucasus are inclined to estimate all calamities that shake the region (such as the recent national conflicts) as manifestations of a total crisis of traditional Caucasian civilization (Abdulatipov, 1995).

Ramazan G. Abdulatipov, one of the most informed and perceptive analysts in the region, argues that today's crisis are a manifestation and result of a whole series of complex historical mistakes and injustices activated and permitted by different powers toward all the ethnic groups living in the region. Some of these ethnic groups, in turn, are only able to solve modern problems violently. "The ethnical and political elites, as well as many intellectuals," he writes, "proved themselves unable to elaborate and realize adequate sociopolitical, economic, ethno-cultural, and moral mechanisms of self preservation . . . because they closed themselves off in their own highly narrow political interests" (Abdulatipov, 1995, p. 55). The authors of this chapter, like other North Caucasian analysts, counter that the traditional Caucasian civilization, possibly because of the many great transformations and injustices it suffered during periods of intense crisis, has still not exhausted itself (Isaenko & Petschauer, 1995). Additionally, other ways of resolving problems and healing injustices have become available.

One of the main characteristic features of traditional Caucasian civilization is the intensive interaction of different and unique cultures of almost all known world religions. One of the important levers of traditional rapprochement of different Caucasian peoples are the very similar norms and unwritten laws, the *Adats,* that dominated and defined the lifestyle of Caucasians of all ethnic groups over centuries. Each clan and community, and entire ethnic groups, managed to elaborate an integral system of commonly recognized norms of social behavior. These norms interacted with the behavioral patterns of the upper classes in the Caucasus, be they Turks, members of the Golden Horde, or Russians. Because of Russian pressure and recent modern incursions, such as television, these norms currently maintain no more than a shadowy existence. Nevertheless, being aware of them in the most general terms helps outsiders be alert to behavioral patterns that are all too readily overlooked and misunderstood.

Most of these norms and their long standing stability originated within the clans or extended families and may be traced to the nomadic and semi-nomadic forerunners of the modern Caucasians. Homer already used the terms *nomos,* pasture, and *nemo,* to pasture. Thus the original ancient Greek term for nomads was pastoral people. This form of survival and life brought forth wise people, that is, clan elders and tribal notables, whose duty it was initially to distribute pastures and later shares of land among members of each clan and family. These men, or men of name or prestige, played a decisive role in the life of the tribes and clans of the mountaineers. Interestingly, in Ossetian the word *nom* still means both personal and family name and fame. If someone asks a young mountaineer, "what is your name?", he will most likely think that the questioner wants to know his personal name. However, for an older person, the question implies an inquiry about the family name and fame of his clan.

Kinship formed the main basis on which mountaineer societies were constructed. It was the main channel for continuing these societies. The living members of a clan considered themselves to be under the effective protection of its dead members, thus the principal sacred duty of the living members of a clan was to produce offspring in order to preserve the clan's ability to worship the dead and assure its future. The terms for living members in Ossetia are *myggag* and *rvadalta;* in Chechnya and Ingushetia, *teip* or *teipa,* in Dagestan, *tukhum,* and in Kabarda Adygea, *k'uae.* Therefore, one of the most strictly observed norms of the *Adats* was an obligatory marriage after young men and women reached the appropriate ages. With the spread of a money economy in the region and an increased stratification of rich and poor toward the end of the 19th century, some young men were unable to collect the appropriate amount of money for marriage. Young men were thus encouraged or forced to leave the Caucasus for Russia and other places abroad, including the United States, to earn the money required for marriage. As might be expected, not all young men returned to the Caucasus and those who did were changed. All the same, and to this day, senior members of families (especially the elders in rural areas) still play a major role in organizing marriages for young representatives of their clans. Without being at least somewhat alert to the lingering power of clans and elders, outsiders may not be aware of the need to spend considerable time in creating an environment in which the head of a clan and other elders feel comfortable in their presence.

The biological force that keeps the clan alive, representing its living underpinning, is the sperm. Clan members believed it to be the link between past, present, and future generations. It is no accident that the Ossetian word for clan or family, *myggag,* originates from the stem *myg,* sperm. Historically, the continuity of noble families and clans has been preserved and protected by the mountaineer laws and expressed through the idea of one blood and one bone. Members of each clan or family constituted a blood community (Vernadsky, 1943). According to one Malsagov family member, his clan has about 20,000 living members and should he meet someone of this massive group, even in a faraway place like Siberia, they will treat each other as brothers and help each other under all circumstances (Central TV (ORT), 1996). To impinge on the rights, dignity, or property of even the poorest member of a family, even if the offense was no more than a rude comment or a man's awkward touch of a woman during a folk dance, could provoke a sharp reply by relatives and lead to a long and bloody vendetta against all members of the offender's family (Field, 1953). Such vendettas are pursued in the late 20th century. For example, the Chechen fighters' desire to avenge the deportation of their fathers indicates that the custom still flourishes.

These strong relationships date from the times when the *Adats* were still in full use. A particularly important aspect of the *Adats* was the rules of mutual guarantee. Today the system of mutual guarantees allows people to survive by relying on their more successful relatives when, for example, they have become unemployed. The guarantees also mean that clan members help each other in modern industrial, educational, and artistic settings, posing a genuine inhibition to hiring the most competent persons. Mutual guarantees may also lead to criminals being protected by a powerful and strong clan from the judicial system. An outsider unaware of these guarantees can draw assumptions and make statements about counterparts in positions of power that question their appropriate background and training and overlook the much more powerful clan connections.

Each clan and extended family has an ancestral home in the highlands and valleys where the clan or family originated, which include dwellings, towers, cemeteries (in the Eastern Caucasus) and crypts (in Ossetia, Balkaria, and Kabarda). Although many of these homes were abandoned after the Russian invasion and then again during the Soviet deportation and rural outmigration, the admiration for them still lingers in modern Caucasians. The Ingushetian towers in the highland valley, Targim, are being preserved very well. They are slender and esthetically pleasing, and striking to the imagination of outsiders. Most Ingushetian and Chechen families still bury their dead in their mountain clan cemeteries, even if the individuals lived all their lives away from their homeland. Thus, for example, two of the most powerful Ingushetian families, the Malsagovs and Plievs, have been able to preserve their clan cemetery untouched by intruders (especially during the period of deportation) and bury their dead there. Caucasians are very proud of these ancestral places and are always eager to show them to outsiders. People still give their oath by the native place, by the graves of the ancestors, or by the sacred old religious monuments, even when they enter a modern business deal. Such oaths are esteemed to be more reliable than the procedures established by state law. Visitors are thus well advised to arrange for visits into the spectacular mountains. The gratitude of their hosts will open history and heart.

Knowing this background, one can understand why Ingushetian society showed such a sharp negative reaction when the Russian military recently blew up an ancestral tower in Jeirakh hollow under the pretext that weapons were being kept there. Such an action is reminiscent of the artillery bombardments in the 1830s in the cities in the Kurtatin valley of Ossetia. Today, some groups remember this war as no more than an occurrence in the distant past. However, others see it as one more reminder of the losses inflicted by outsiders (Isaenko & Petschauer, 1995). More significantly, the loss of the tower at Jeirakh reinforced earlier traumas and validated the outsiders' inability to understand the psychological depth of the mountaineer. With such traumas come not only hostility toward the outsider, but also reinforcement of strong values, local customs, and beliefs among the insiders.

By the 1930s, small families (of two or three generations) continued to supplant the remnants of the clans and extended families. Only some of them remained in rural and highland areas. According to tradition, complete small families were headed by the person who was its oldest member; before the Russian Revolution, the elder was usually a husband or grandfather. After the Revolution, a number of households in all ethnic groups were headed by widows and divorced women, who in former times and according to *Adats* would have had to return to their clans. During collectivization, most of the clans lost their traditional productive functions because their private farms were united into collective farms. However, the greatest shift came from 1950 to 1980 when practically all women worked either on collective farms, in industrial enterprises, or in a host of different institutions, leaving their children at day care centers or in kindergartens. This involvement of women in work beyond the household, the removal of children from the clan environment, and other drastic changes undermined many traditional norms of family and social etiquette. All the same, many of these norms are still functioning and undergoing rejuvenation. Indeed, the majority of the male representatives of all families preserve the memory of their origin, belong to a definite clan, know the clan's history and ancestral places in the mountains and are aware of all the relatives and families that constitute the greater patronymy.

☐ Traditional Behavioral Norms

According to the traditional Caucasian clan norms, the most important custom was honoring or respecting elders. Already in the 18th century, in Kabardian, Ossetian and Dagestani societies and among Chechens and Ingushi, the term elder (in Kabardian, *N'achydz;* in Ossetian, *Hyshtar;* and in Chechen and Ingush, *K'hel*) referred not only to biological age, but also, and more importantly, social position. Thus, the position of elder was reserved for men of definite social maturity and in turn was determined by personal merits, social status, wealth, kinship, and age.

First, one needs to acknowledge some general points about chronological and social age. Folklore assigns the following characteristics to different ages:

> At the age of 5 he jumps and plays like a goat;
> at the age of 20 he catches everything like a wolf;
> at the age of 40 he becomes strong and healthy like a lion;
> at the age of 60 he is an old lioness-calm and wise;
> at the age of 80 he looses all strength and wit;
> at the age of 100 everything in him blurs like in the rotten egg.
> (*Predania o Zabagy, 1965, pp. 51–2*)

As if in refinement of this outline of biological ages, Kabardian terminology distinguishes two forms of seniority in men or women. The first is given to all persons over 60, the second is offered to all those who may be younger than 60 but have attained the qualities mentioned above and are recognized as elders. Thus, older men and women, as well as elders, had an exclusive right to special treatment by their communities.

For a man who wanted to attain fame, esteem, and respect in his society, the most highly esteemed personal qualities were daring, boldness, bravery, and valor (Dubrovin, 1871). K. Koh, an explorer of the Caucasus, noted that at death the highest honor went to warriors who perished in battle (Koh, 1974). Such qualities were highly esteemed by the Adygean (Cherkes) feudal nobility. Along with bravery and courage, the mountaineers valued popular wisdom, experience, proficiency, eloquence, and moral qualities. While describing the lifestyle of Black Sea Circassians, John Bell pointed out, for example, that only those "who proved their proficiency, wisdom, energy, and honesty" enjoyed the greatest power (Bell, 1838, p. 465). One may add Karl F. Stahl's comment that "Circassians called a man who had attained knightly valor, eloquence, and a profound knowledge of customs 'the tongue of the people'" (*tle-gubzyg*) (Stahl, 1900, p. 156). The same standing of eloquent and expert men is affirmed by the Adygean custom of electing only such men as the group enters into negotiations (Girei, 1978). Traditional societies in Kabardia, Ossetia, Chechnya, Ingushetia, and Dagestan also highly valued craftsmanship, ability to heal, writing, forging, the talent to organize and lead a household, and to write and sing ballads. Folk singers (in Kabardia, *dzeguak'uae*) as a rule were illiterate but revered as having a gift from God. They created and recited historical ballads during folk meetings and festivities. They also performed at weddings and extended greetings to guests. The social position of *dzeguak'uae* in feudal Kabardia and Circassia is unique. In both places, people were routinely robbed, killed, or captured and sold as slaves to the Crimea or Turkey. However, the singers could appear without guard or weapons wherever they pleased, enjoying more freedom and personal immunity than clergymen. However, with the spread of Islam in Kabardia and in the Eastern Caucasus in the 19th century, the social status of folk singers diminished. Ultimately the struggle for power over the souls between *dzeguak'uae* and Muslim clergy ended with the victory of the latter at the beginning of the 20th century. With that change, the number of folk singers declined considerably (Naloev, 1978).

By the end of the 19th and the beginning of the 20th centuries, wealth played an increasingly important role in the attainment of social status. As a result of the gradual impoverishment of the nobility and the appearance of wealthy individuals among former serfs, the latter were increasingly placed at the head of elected communities. The Kabardian chronicle preserves the history of the Gaunov family, which emerged from the lower classes and became one of the richest representatives of rural ownership in their area. In 1887, Hachimakho Gaunov, the owner of a stud farm, owned more than 160 horses. Hagundokov, a prince and former owner of the Gaunov family estates, was forced to work for his former peasant (Beituganov, 1989). At the beginning of the 20th century, the heads of the kinship units almost everywhere tended not to be the oldest and noble but the richest members.

Since the incorporation of the North Caucasus into the Russian Empire, another factor has modified the status of elders. Anyone who was elected or placed as an official or functionary—whether it was in the Tsarist administration, the Communist party apparatus, or most recently a modern bureaucracy—could acquire the standing of elder in the community. Personal qualities became irrelevant. But the kinship factor continues to play an extremely important role in defining status in different societal units: family, clan, and society. Proximity to a noble, famous, powerful, and rich family still heightens the social standing of a person.

Traditional etiquette required that older men were treated in the following fashion:

- Younger men were not to be uncivil and rude toward elders, especially not toward old men.
  (*Narty,* 1974)
- Older men were to be treated mildly and indulgently, especially when they were guilty of some transgression. As a rule, those who were in charge of examining conflicts in rural and mediation trials were also to treat older men mildly.
  (Central State Archive of the Kabardian-Balkan Republic)
- Younger men were obligated to render many services to their elders.
- To be seated in the presence of elders was considered unseemly.
  (*Karbardinsky folklore,* 1936)
- To initiate quarrels, or to use foul language, in the presence of elders was utterly forbidden.
- Any senior man could reprimand his junior, and the younger man was to listen politely.
- In houses, elders were to sit at a special place closest to the hearth.
- Only an older man could initiate a conversation.
- Younger men could not enter a conversation with older men until they were asked to do so.
- If a younger man accompanied his elder, he was to be kept on the right side; if there were three travelers, the oldest man was to walk in the middle.
- A younger man could not cross a path in front of an older man.
- When meeting an elder, the junior was to offer him the more venerable right to pass.
- When meeting an elder, the younger man was not to offer first to shake his hand.

While these patterns of etiquette may not be practiced today by everyone, one should be aware of them to show respect for the culture and to understand and respect nuances in behavior.

As we have already shown, Islam, especially its Sufi variety (Muridism) has played a unifying role during the long war for independence in the Eastern Caucasus. The Chechens and Ingushi revived the tradition of Sufism. It served as a force for ethnic networking during the deportation in the 1940s and 1950s. Today, two brotherhoods of Murids towards the right way to God, the *Naqshbandia* and the *Qadiri,* have emerged from revivalist movements and have become part of North Caucasian political movements (Akaev & Khusalnov, 1988). The eastern communities of North Caucasians thus maintain great respect of Muslim clergy. This in turn gives them the unique opportunity to exercise leadership during crisis periods. Among the clergy, as is true in the rest of the Muslim world, those individuals who have performed pilgrimages to Mecca and Medina are particularly respected. Along with the leaders of kinship units, they enjoy most fully attitudes based on traditional forms of etiquette towards the elders.

The western Caucasian republics have adopted a much more secularized attitude toward religious rituals and symbols and their Muslim identity is predominantly cultural. Although mosques and Islamic institutions were opened in several places (Dagestan, Chechnya, Ingushetia, and Karachai-Cherkassia) with the help of emissaries from other Muslim areas, Islamic fundamentalism has had little bearing on the situation until recently. In the last few years, fundamentalist adherents have migrated into many areas, in several cases with the help of outside Islamic powers, and have spawned both a religious revival and terrorism.

Even within this very male dominated setting, senior women could attain the personal qualities, and thus the esteem and reverence, just described for men. The most profound respect was shown toward wise women, especially if they also had the talent for healing (*zelitel*). Women healers knew about traditional healing techniques, including herbs, in an environment in which doctors were not only distant physically but culturally as well. Many of them were Russians, Germans, and Jews, and Caucasians preferred to visit healing women for the ordinary diseases that plagued them. Such women were invited to village (*aul*) meetings by the elders and asked for advice on important social questions.

The etiquette towards married and senior women was similar to that afforded older men. The image of such women is well reflected in folklore: Among them are Satana of the Ossetian Narts, and an older women in the Adygean heroic songs. Until today, the highest compliment one can render a hostess in Ossetia is to compare her to Satana. Nevertheless, several important customs pertaining to women within the family and in the society need to be added. For example, husbands were to treat their wives correctly: neither offend, insult, nor beat them, to take care of them, and to dress them well and beautifully. Until relatively recently, rudeness and violent actions on the part of a husband could lead to ostracism of the offender (Girei, 1978). Rudeness was considered interference in the specially designated part of the domestic sphere, such as the laundry, the kitchen, and the bedrooms. Somewhat in contrast, when a family invites a guest over for a meal, men still prepare the traditional meat dishes, whereas women prepare the round cakes, dressings, sweets, and salads. In spite of the cultural norms against it, violence exists in marriage to this day. In the Eastern Caucasus, exposing domestic violence to the police and other outsiders would deface the family and is rare. The power of a husband over his wife is still sustained by his right to initiate a divorce. He can leave his wife without any explanation, after repeating three times in the presence of a Mullah (Muslim clergy) the traditional formula: "I let you go" (Bell, 1838).

Except young unmarried women and older women, women in most Caucasian societies were not allowed to appear alone in public nor to take part in rural festivities (Girei, 1978). By contrast, in Muslim areas women acquired greater freedom after having given birth to a child. At the beginning of the 20th century, the following norms towards women were commonly recognized and observed:

- When meeting a woman, a man was to offer her the more venerable right side.
- A man could not pass a woman from the left side.
- When accompanying his daughter or sister, or even an unknown woman, a man was to give them the right side, even as his wife followed him.
- At the appearance of a woman, all men were to stop smoking, drinking, or using curse words and quarreling.
- To offend women at a public place through words or actions was totally forbidden and could result in blood revenge against the offending party and his relatives.
- In Kabardia, a host was to offer a woman the most venerable place at his home (i.e., his own).
- While meeting a group of people, a man usually first greeted the women and then the men.
- To give help to a widow or single woman was also welcomed by traditional etiquette.
  (Babich, 1995)

All of these customs have been in place for centuries. In part, they helped the mountaineers preserve their ethnic identity and survive during crisis periods in which outsiders imposed their own norms, rules, and laws. Some of the most significant changes in the traditions of honoring elders and older women, and in the etiquette described, came during the Soviet and post-Soviet period. For example, personal, i.e., moral qualities are not as determinant now as social position, wealth, and connections of relatives. These traditional customs were rarely practiced until recently, although some, such as respect to elders, are now being revived. Outsiders aware of this revival and having knowledge of some of the norms and etiquette will find their interaction with Caucasians enhanced.

Throughout the Caucasus, similar norms characterized the attitudes and duties toward the dead and served the unspoken purpose of overcoming the sorrow associated with death. Traditionally, lavish feasts accompanied funerals in Ossetia to which all relatives, friends, and guests were invited. Mountaineers believed that a meal eaten in memory of the dead would reach him in the other world. This is a ceremony and process not unlike that practiced by the ancient Scythians and recreated with men only at a funeral (Edwards, 1996). They believed that the more abundant the table being offered, the better the deceased's provisions in the other world. Few Ossetian insults are as powerful as, "Let your dead go hungry!" Today some of the more expansive customs associated with funeral meals, for example, horse races and target shooting have disappeared. However, the traditional meal is still lavish with visitors expressing condolences and helping to organize the process. One particular custom that has remained is the preparation by the hostess and other women of round cakes with sheep cheese. At Ossetian celebratory feasts, the three subsections of the cakes may symbolize three major givens of life: the Great Lord-Creator, or the sun, water, and fire; sky, land, and the world of the dead; or priests, warriors, and peasants (Isaenko & Shvili, 1997).

Whether it is a meal with traditional games or a less traditional meal, the purpose of alleviating the sorrow over the death of a member of a clan or a friend is served in the sequence of toasts and foods. At the beginning of a series of feasts to honor a deceased, the elder of a clan opens the ritual feast at which men above age 21 sit in order of their age. In one hand, the elder holds a horn with traditional maize vodka (*arak*) or a specially brewed beer. In the other, he holds a grilled right bottom-chuck of a bull or sheep (*shashlyk*) sacrificed for the occasion. He simultaneously intones a long prayer in honor of the Great Lord and the spiritual protectors of the land. In Ossetia, the usual prayer is: "To the Great Lord, Creator of earth, men, and cattle, we ask blessings on those present. We are also praying to the seven saints and seven angels who protect our holy land; let them preserve Ossetia in peace and quiet and protect it from all evil and enemies. Amen." While listening to the toast, all the men stand and mark every rhyme with a loud, "Let it be!" The table ritual has a very definite and carefully observed order, with a specific number of toasts with different contents for different occasions. If the feast is organized to mark a joyous occasion or an event in the traditional calendar, the elder may vary the number of toasts according to odd numbers. In case of a funeral remembrance, the elder usually proclaims four, six, or eight toasts at the occasion of the 9th day, the 40th day, or a year after a death. None of the other men may interrupt the speech of the elder, propose their own toasts, or leave the table without his permission. This format is reminiscent of the knights' feasts of the ancient ancestors of the people of the Northern Caucasus and the earlier versions may be followed in the Legends of the Narts, especially "The poems about the Heroes" (Uarziaty, 1995).

Meals for the dead recall the many sorrows and traumas Caucasians have sustained over the centuries. As we indicated, they have experienced everything from murder, rape, torchings, loss of friends and family, deportation, and removal from traditional lands. In the past, older women were the designated healers. More recently, political leaders have taken on this role, but by all accounts they are not as well equipped to address the hurt of many clans, families, and individuals. All the same, politicians have for years participated in the May 9th ceremonies that acknowledge the fallen heroes of World War II. Ossetians have found this acknowledgment to be one of the ways in which they could grieve the death of their men. Additionally, healing is provided through the arts. One of the most striking examples is a piece in the repertoire of the North Ossetian State University's Dance Troupe that movingly recreates the deaths of one Ossetian mother's seven sons during World War II. The deaths of these men and their contribution to their society is so exceptionally well choreographed and performed that audiences burst into tears at home and abroad. By reliving one woman's infinite pain, audiences feel genuine acknowledgment of their losses and the associated emotions. Still another way of healing remains the conversations of women who support each other in mourning a death or some other trauma.

Traditional meals are also occasions to celebrate, to receive a guest, to reaffirm the social and gender standing in the community, and to form alliances. The American author and his wife vividly recall the first visit to Vladikavkaz, the capital of North Ossetia. The chancellor of North Ossetian State University received them at the airport and feted them for at least two hours. The stunning meal was an introduction to many similar occasions. In every case, the hosts showered them with many courses of magnificent foods and splendid vodka and champagne. These meals follow the patterns laid down over hundreds of years.

Today not everyone enjoys these meals. The older generation finds greater affirmation in them than the younger generation and non-Ossetes. In the traditional thinking of the Caucasus, a person who had shared a formal meal with another person was perceived to be allied and protected by this person, whereas non-Ossetes from the Caucasus often felt that this tradition had lost its meaning. In some cases, we were told very specifically that a particular meal was not a traditional occasion but rather a normal, or modern meal. Almost all of these meals were held in an intimate setting and in most cases not by Ossetes.

As guests, the American author and his wife were, thus, included in one of several mechanisms that allowed Caucasian groups to prevent collisions between different ethnic communities. Anyone in the Caucasus, who was able to speak the words "I am your guest" to the head of a clan, or family, was received as a friend, even if he had been an enemy. The guest was given the seat of honor, but his host did not ask him whether he would like to eat, as this might be considered an indication of avarice. He simply offered him from whatever stores were available and waited on him personally. To sit down or to eat in the guest's presence was considered unseemly. At his departure, the host accompanied his guest until far beyond his property (*aul*), often as far as to the next hospitable house. In case of an attack by brigands, he defended his guest even at the peril to his own life, and the outrage of his guest compelled him to take revenge, as if the crime had been committed against one of his kinsmen.

Fraternization (*kunac*) served similar purposes. This practice was inherited by the Caucasians from their Scythian and Alan forerunners. The ritual of the ceremony was first described by Herodotus and has not visibly changed since then. The two participants of the ritual dropped some blood and sacred personal items (such as a cross in the Christian parts of the Caucasus) in a cup—which was originally a horn—and drank from it. In this way, they became kinsman and accepted the obligations to help each other's families in all situations. The sacred authority of the ritual was so strong that a newly acquired relative was considered more reliable than a natural kinsman. The protection of the *kunac*'s family, or clan, was generally offered to those who needed it. Thus, almost all ethnic communities had a *kunac* family unit in its midst. Blood revenge between these families was usually forbidden or avoided. Intermarriages and having the children brought up in the *kunac*'s families and estates were welcome. As children, these exchangers learned the other clan's languages and customs. As grown-ups they could become respected and skillful mediators in possible conflicts. This custom was called *atalychestvo* and the children, *atalyks*.

When the peril of an interethnic collision arose, the authoritative elders from such *kunac* families, who were frequently connected to several ethnic groups as a result of numerous intermarriages, were asked to enter into preventive negotiations. During these talks, the mediators asked both sides to articulate their demands openly to each other and to trade insults. They thought that this openness would let the bad spirit— the negative emotions and suspicions—out. Prominent and skillful mediators were greatly respected in all ethnic communities and were invited to reconcile even in blood vendettas. During these talks, the mediators usually defined for each side's elders the form and sum of ransom to be paid by the offending side.

The much more intense feeling is a strong mistrust toward some outsiders. It characterizes not only Chechens but also other groups in the

Caucasus. Outsiders are not necessarily Americans or Europeans, but ethnics originally from outside of the particular region in which one is, for example, eating a festive meal. For example, Russians, who came to the region during the Soviet period, have been considered outsiders. Until very recently, they were perceived as quite different from the so called root Russians or Cossacks, who lived in the region for generations and know the customs of their native neighbors. For the most part, they have been loyal to the region, familiar with its various traditions, practice them in their households, and serve the societies in a multitude of capacities. Still, many of them now repatriate in traditional Russian areas and are even considered refugees in some areas where they have lived for many generations. The most recent clear differentiation of outsiders is not older than five years. The American author noticed in 1994 that non-Ossetian ethnics, including those old settlers, were becoming more and more aware of their separateness. Thus members of the university community characterized themselves as being Azerbaijani or Russian as part of their conversation. By 1995, the Russian author characterized himself and all of his friends and colleagues first by their ethnic affiliation and then by their activities. When I pointed this phenomenon out, he reflected on the Soviet period and how policies in vogue then suppressed statements about ethnic awareness. In the last few years, this differentiation has allowed for the targeting of some Russians for ethnic cleansing and it in turn has led to the outmigration of an increasing number new and old settlers.

Outsiders, thus, need to be alert to not become caught in internal altercations and to avoid situations in which their status as nonaffiliated outsiders aligns them with a traditional enemy of native Caucasians. Being perceived as helping one or the other side may all too easily be interpreted by another side as affiliation, and thus as enmity. It is probably still true, as Aslan Mashadov, a general and president of the Chechen Republic, said in the Süddeutsche Zeitung in late 1996 regarding the murder of Red Cross personnel, "What happened is a terrible tragedy, shameful, for the Chechen people. Even during the war we have never touched a foreigner. We even treated the mothers of Russian soldiers the same way; they, too, were victims of the war" (Süddeutsche Zeitung, 28/29 December, 1996, p. 9).

But a new situation has been emerging over the last two years; this situation makes the area less and less safe for any outsiders, in spite of the long standing wish to be gracious to guests. We are talking about the deterioration of capitalism into gangsterism and terrorism and the decline of traditional and local law and of local law enforcement agencies. This trend has been especially pronounced in ethnically charged areas like Ingushetia, Chechnya, Dagestan, and now Ossetia. There, hostage taking has become a very lucrative business for field commanders and more than 150 bands operating in the area, who have declared themselves independent of local authorities. In Chechnya alone over 100 Russians and about 10 foreigners were recently hostages (Moscow, 1998). According to Magometov Tolboyev, the former head of Dagestan's Security Council:

> Islamic fundamentalists strengthened themselves in the area; they received the skills and experiences of carrying out military operations . . . People are sick and tired of them: raids of brigands, kidnappings, stealing of cattle, murder and assassination . . . I warned the Interior and Foreign Ministries of Russia many times, do not let people come to the North Caucasus region [that is,] Kabarda, Dagestan and Ossetia. I know how [kidnapped] people live there . . . they sit like slaves in dungeons . . . If you want to be kidnapped, go to Chechnya, Dagestan, Kabardino-Balkaria, and Ossetia. Maybe you will be ransomed afterwards, maybe you will not. If not, you will be killed . . . In Moscow the officials do not understand what the Caucasus looks like.
> (Tolboyev, 6 July, 1998, p. 7)

☐ Conclusion

The North Caucasus has been favored by nature as much as any comparable region in the world. In spite of their linguistic and cultural differences, its ethnic groups have managed to elaborate and share similar cultural patterns and values, which have been fixed and preserved in the powerful, albeit unwritten norms and rules of traditional behavior. These came into existence in part because of the similar living conditions; some of these norms (including mutual guarantees, hospitality, fraternization, the establishment of mediators, and mountain etiquette) have served for centuries as effective mechanisms that provided mitigation, reduction of tensions and cessation of hostilities. These norms also remained in place because they helped mountaineers to oppose the dominance of outsiders. While some of the mountain communities freely intermingled with outsiders, others resisted them. All the same, a common pattern of thinking about outsiders emerged. The mountaineers began to believe that the outsiders would exterminate them, relocate them, or assimilate them. Every time an outside force engaged in such activities, this memory was reinforced. Ultimately, the mountaineers cherished and guarded their traditional habits and values, even during the Soviet period. Of course, even in enmity the mountaineers learned from the latest outsider, and their culture changed and became enriched through the acquisition of Russian and Russian customs and values.

Four main points can be offered about the history and reinvigoration of the traditional Caucasian civilization. First, we want to recall the integration into Imperial Russia after a century of fierce resistance. This subjugation was followed by mass resettlement of mountaineers off the mountains that challenged their tribal and clanic style. All the same, the integration into the Empire helped some clans to overcome the land shortage and starvation in the highlands and thus to survive. To their credit, it must be said that the Imperial government learned from the Caucasian War and preserved and protected the traditional *Adats,* sometimes using its authority on their behalf. Second, we want to highlight the forced integration of the Caucasians into the Soviet administrative and political system with its suppression of the deportation of local populations, suppression of the *Adats,* and collectivization of agriculture and industrialization in the 1930s and 1940s. Additionally, Caucasians made unbelievable sacrifices during World War II, suffered mass deportations of entire ethnic groups in the 1940s, and experienced resettlement of some of the same groups in the 1950s. These Soviet assaults on mountaineer life, culture, and essence dramatically changed lifestyles; they left profound scars on ethnic groups, clans, and individuals. Third, the present crisis is shaped by two contradictory tendencies: the reappearance of the traditional culture as part of a general national rebirth and the simultaneous deterioration of old customs under pressure to modernize all aspects of life. In some cases this pressure has turned into a free-for-all that includes gangsters and terrorists. Fourth, the lingering trauma in the North Caucasus is connected to historical experiences. On the one hand is the chosen trauma—the trauma that is based on the many attacks by outsiders. This experience has become an expectation that outsiders will attack, slaughter, maim, and relocate insiders and that one must resist the outsiders at all cost. On the other hand is the more immediate trauma of clans and individuals who have experienced these assaults either in the immediate past or on their own bodies. Because Russian and regional ethnic and political leaders undertook few efforts to alleviate this trauma, issues continue to be resolved through violence rather than through traditional cultural means. Most abhorrent of these means is the gangsterism and terrorism now rampant in some areas. These new phenomena may be linked to a misfiring of capitalism and a net of international terrorists who have established a school for terrorists in Chechnya and who destabilize the area.

Outsiders working in the area will do well to be aware of the trauma of the past, the hostility toward outsiders, the need to remain absolutely neutral, and be cognizant of the new threat of gangsters and terrorists operating in the region.

☐ References

Abdulatipov, R. G. (1995). Kavkazskaya tsivilizatya: Samobytnost y tselostnost [The Caucasian civilization: Originality and integrity], *Nauchnaya Misl Kavkaza (The Scientific Thought of the Caucasus)* (pp. 57–58). Rostov-on-Don: North Caucasian Scientific Center.

Akaev, V. K., & Khusainov, S. A. (1988). O gnoseologicheskikh i nravstvennykh aspectakh sufizma [About the Gnoseological and Moral Aspects of Sufism]. In V. K. Akaev (Ed.), *Iz istorii islama v Checheno-Ingushetii (Pertaining to the history of Islam in Chechnya-Ingushetia)* (pp. 35–66). Grozny: University Press.

Akhmadov, S. B. (1992). *The people-liberation movement of the North Caucasus mountaineers under the leadership of Mansur in 1785-1791.* Rostov-on-Don: University Press.

Alieva, S. (Ed.). (1993). *Tak eto bylo. Nationalnye Repressii v SSSR 1919-1952 gody [This is how it happened. National repression in the USSR]* vol. 1 & 3. Moscow: Insan.

Babich, I. L. (1995). *Narodnye traditsii v obshestvennom bytu Kabardintsev [The folk customs in social life of Kabardians].* Moscow: Russian Academy of Science.

Bachrach, B. S. (1973). *A history of the Alans in the West: From their first appearance in the sources of classical antiquity through the early middle ages.* Minneapolis, MN: Minnesota University Press.

Beituganov, S. N. (1989). *Kabardinskie familii: istoki i sudby [The Kabardian families: origin and the fate].* Nalchik: Kabardian-Balkar State Publishing House.

Bell, J. (1838). Dnevnic prebyvania v Cherkessii v techenii 1837, 1838, 1839 godov [Diary of the stay in Circassia in the years 1837, 1838, 1839]. In (1974) *Adygy, Balkartsy y Karachay v opisaniyakh Evropeyskykh avtorov, 13–19 vekov [Adygeans, Balkars and Karachai in the descriptions of European authors, 13th–19th centuries]* (p. 463). Nalchik.

Brooks, W. (1995). Russia's conquest and pacification of the Caucasus: Relocation becomes a program in the post-Crimean war period. *Nationalities Papers, 23(4)*, 675–686.

The Central State Archive of the Kabardian-Balkar Republic, fund I-6, description 1, opus 64, list 14.

Central TV (ORT). (1996). Program entiled Vainakhi.

Chinn, J., & Kaiser, R. (1996). *Russians as the new minority: Ethnicity and nationalism in the Soviet successor states.* Boulder, CO: Westview Press.

Conner, W. D. (1996). *Tattered banners: Labor, conflict, and corporation in postcommunist Russia.* Boulder, CO: Westview Press.

Conquest, R. (1970). *Nation killers: The Soviet deportation of nationalities.* New York: Macmillan Co.

Cuny, F. C. (6 April 1995). Killing Chechnya, *New York Review of Books,* 15–17.

Demko, G., Zaionchkovskaya, Z., Pontius, S., & Joffe, G. (Eds.). (1997). *Populations under duress: Geodemography of post-Soviet Russia.* Boulder, CO: Westview Press.

Dubrovin, N. F. (1871). Istoria voiny i vladychestva Russkikh na Kavkaze [The history of the war and dominance of Russians in the Caucasus: vol. 1]. St. Petersburg: Department Udielkov.

Dumas, A. (1859/1962). *En Caucase. [Adventures in the Caucasus]* A. E. Murch, transl. London: Peter Owen.

Edwards, M. (September 1996a). Searching for the Scythians. *National Geographic, 190(3),* 60–61.

Edwards, M. (December 1996b). Lord of the Mongols, Genghis Khan. *National Geographic, 190(6),* 9–37.

Field, H. (1953). *Contributions to the anthropology of the Caucasus.* London: Cambridge University Press.

Girei, K. (1978). *Zapiski o Cherkessii [Remarks on Circassia]* (p. 122). Nalchik: Institute of Humanistic Studies.

Goldstein, A. F. (1975). *Bashni v gorakh [The Towers in the mountains].* Moscow: Sov. khudozhnik.

Halperin, C. J. (1987). *Russia and the golden horde: The Mongol impact on medieval Russian history.* Bloomington, IN: Indiana University Press.

Isaenko, A. V., & Kuchiev, V. D. (1995). Necotorie voprosy drevnei istorii Osetin (Some actual questions regarding the ancient history of the Ossetians). *Alanica, 3,* 12.

Isaenko, A. V., & Petschauer, P. W. (1995). The long arm of the dead: Traumas and conflicts in the Caucasus. *Mind and Human Interaction, 6*(3), 104–115.

Isaenko, A. V., & Tinikashvili, V. V. (1997). The Ancient Symbols of the Ossetians. *Darial.* Vladikavkaz.

Kabardinsky folklore (The Kabardian Folklore). (1936). Moscow: USSR Academy of Sciences.

Kazemzadeh, F. (1974). The Russian Penetration of the Caucasus. In T. Hunczak (Ed.), In *Russian imperialism from Ivan the Great to the revolution* (pp. 240–242). New Brunswick, NJ: Rutgers University Press.

Koh, K. (1974). Puteshestvie po Rossii i v Kavkazskie zemli [Journey over Russian and Caucasus lands]. In (Ed.), *Adygeans, Balkars, and Karachai in the descriptions of European authors, 13th–19th centuries* (pp. 621–622). Nalchik.

Kuznetsov, V. A. (1993). *Ocherki istorii Alan [Sketches of Alanic history]* (pp. 253–279). Vladikavkaz: Ir Publishing House.

MacKenzie, D. (1974). *The lion of Tashkent: The career of General M. G. Cherniaev* (pp. 26–28). Athens, GA: University of Georgia Press.

Magometov, A. K. (1968). *Kultura i byt Osetinskogo naroda [The culture and lifestyle of the Ossetians]* (chap. 1). Ordzonikidze: Ir.

Maliev, N. D. (1988). *Revolutia i grzdanskaia voina na Tereke [Revolution and Civil War on Terek]* (chaps. 1, 2). Ordzonikidze: North Ossetian State University Press.

McCarthy, I. The fate of the Muslims, quoted from Paul B. Henze, Circassian resistance to Russia. In M. B. Broxup (Ed.). (1992). *The North Caucasus Barrier: The Russian advance towards the Muslim world* (p. 104). London: Hurst and Company.

Naloev, Z. M. (1978). *Iz istorii kultury Adygov [From the history of Adygaen culture]* (p. 41). Nalchik: Institute of Humanistic Studies.

(1974). *Narty. Adygskii geroicheskii epos [The Narts. The Adygean heroic epics]* (p. 257). Moscow: Glavnaia redaktsiia Vostochnoi literatury.

Neubert, M. (1996). It is Most Important that No One Interfere With Us, (an interview with General Aslan Mashadow). *Süddeutsche Zeitung.* 28/29 Dec. 1996, p. 9

(1996). Officers of the Federal Security Service returned from Captivity, *Argumenty y Fakty (Arguments and Facts).* Moscow. 17, 16

Potozki, J. (1829). *Voyage dans les steps a Astrakhan et du Caucase* (Vol. 2). Paris.

Predania o Zabagy [The legends about Zabagy]. (1965). (pp. 51–52). Nalchik: Institute of Humanistic Studies.

Radzhinsky, E. (1996). *Stalin,* H. T. Willetts, transl. New York: Bantam, Doubleday, Dell.

Smith, E., & Dwight, G. O. (1834). *Missionary researches in Armenia: Including a journey through Asia Minor, and into Georgia and Persia, with a visit to the Nestorian and Chaldean Christians of Oormiah and Salmas.* London: George Wightman, Paternoster Row.

Stahl, K. F. (1900). Altnographichesky ocherk Cherkesskogo naroda [An Ethnographic Sketch of the Circassian People], In *Kavkazskay Kollektsiya [Caucasian Collection].* (Vol. 21, p. 156). Tiflis.

Stenographic Account (9–12 June 1923). (1992). *Tainy nationalnoi politiki TSK RKP: Chetvertoe Soveshchanie TSK RKP s otvetstvennymi rabotnikami natsionalnykh respublik i oblastei v g.* [*The Secrets of National Policy of the Central Committee of the Bolshevik Party*]. Moscow: Insan.

Tolboyev, M. (6 July 1998). Do not come to us in the Caucasus! *Novoye Russkoye Slovo* [*New Russian Word*]. (p. 7). New York.

Uarziaty, V. S. (1995). *Prazdnichnii mir Osetin* [*The festive world of the Ossetians*]. (pp. 6–7). Vladikavkaz: Institute of Humanistic Studies.

Umarov, S. (1991). Islam i voina. [Islam and War]. *Kavkaz*: Ir.

Vernadsky, G. (1943). *Ancient Russia.* New Haven, CT: Yale University.

Volkan, V. D. (1991). On 'chosen trauma,' *Mind and Human Interaction,* (3), 13.

Volkan, V. D. (1997). *Blood lines. From ethnic pride to ethnic terrorism.* New York: Farrar, Straus and Giroux.

von Klaproth, J. (1812–1814). *Reise in den Kaukasus und nach Georgien unternommen in den Jahren 1807 und 1808.* Halle/Berlin.

8

CHAPTER

G. T. M. Mooren,
R. J. Kleber

War, Trauma, and Society: Consequences of the Disintegration of Former Yugoslavia

☐ Introduction[1]

World media images of men locked behind wire in the Serbian concentration camps of Bosnia-Herzegovina and of children from Sarajevo in need of medical help, illustrated the war atrocities in areas that belonged to the former Socialist Federal Republic of Yugoslavia. In Spring 1991, Slovenia and Croatia were the first of the six states of the Republic to declare their independence. In April, the European Community, and then in May of 1992, the United Nations acknowledged the independence of the republic of Bosnia-Herzegovina. Finally, the southern republic of Macedonia declared its independence. Together with Montenegro, Serbia consequently formed a new Federal Republic of Yugoslavia.

Before the war, nearly 24 million people lived in this part of the Balkans. The area of the former Yugoslavian Federation is surrounded by Austria and Hungary in the north, Romania and Bulgaria in the east, and Greece and Albania in the south. In the west, it is bordered by the Adriatic Sea (see inserted map). Besides the six republics of Slovenia, Croatia, Bosnia-Herzegovina, Montenegro, Serbia and Macedonia, prewar Yugoslavia also consisted of two autonomous regions, the Vojvodina

178

in the northeast and Kosovo in the southwest (parts of the Republic of Serbia). This part of the Balkans can be characterized best by its diversity. There are religious, economical, linguistic, and social differences. People belong to six main nationalities: Slovenes, Croats, Serbs, Bosnjaks (Muslims of Bosnia), Montenegrins, and Macedonians or to one of the minorities, such as Albanians (mainly living in Kosovo and Macedonia), Gypsies, Italians and Hungarians. There are different religions, also. Orthodox Christians, Roman Catholics, and Muslims constitute the largest communities. Before the war, the same language (Serbo-Croatian or Croato-Serbian) was spoken in Croatia, Bosnia, Montenegro, and Serbia (with significant differences in dialect). Other main languages were Slovenian, Albanian, and Macedonian. Finally, the old federation was characterized by large economical differences: the industrial north was far more affluent than the south.

The aim of this chapter is to help mental health practitioners understand how culture influences trauma and loss in light of the circumstances and events that led to the disintegration of former Yugoslavia. War has caused enormous disruption to individual lives as well as to the society. The consequences cannot be properly understood without insight into the background and context of the events, both historically and culturally.

The diversity in people and in the historical backgrounds of former Yugoslavia are complicated and, at face value, difficult to grasp. In this chapter a brief historical impression of the appearances of Yugoslavia through-out time will be given. The next section introduces the peoples living in the different countries. There is a focus on three important cultural tradi-tions in the region: the Serbian, Croatian, and Bosnian. The third section of this chapter deals with the experiences of war and the postwar adapta-tion: the enormous disruption of life, the breakup of families and commu-nities, and the massive numbers of refugees, as well as the psychosocial aid that has been provided so far. The chapter ends with a reflection on the importance of acknowledging cultural similarities as well as former Yu-goslavian commonalities for providing psychosocial help.

☐ Former Yugoslavia: A Region in Turmoil

Yugoslavia (translated: land of the South Slavs) has, throughout con-temporary history, existed in three major forms: First, as a Kingdom of Serbs, Croats, and Slovenes constituted after the First World War; sec-ond, as a Federal Republic of six states and two autonomous provinces, bound together by the powerful figure of President Tito; and last, as the recently proclaimed Republic consisting of Serbia and Montenegro. The area has been the scene of numerous conflicts. It has been the prey of different empires which all left their cultural legacy (see Jelavich, 1983a; Singleton, 1985). Today this turbulent region of the Balkans is the homeland of citizens of five different countries: Slovenia and Croatia in the north, Macedonia in the south, Bosnia-Herzegovina in the middle and Yugoslavia (consisting of Serbia—with Kosovo and Vojvodina—and Montenegro) in the southeast.

Former Yugoslavia and Its Rulers

Under Turkish Rule: The Ottoman Empire

In the late Middle Ages, centuries after the first Slav tribes had settled in the area and after a period of different independent kingdoms, Turkish troops gradually invaded large parts of the Balkan region. During its rule of almost five centuries, the Ottoman Empire left an important contri-bution to contemporary culture, especially in Bosnia-Herzegovina. It caused the large scale conversion into Islamic religion. Many words, tra-ditions, and customs (Turkish coffee, for instance) can be traced back to this period. The defeat of the Serbs by the Turks at the Battle of Kosovo in 1389 has been marked as the beginning of the Ottoman occupation. Many Serbs fled north, ahead of the Turkish armies into Hungary or into mountainous areas, such as Montenegro. Throughout the years the Turks were pushed back and forth in northern areas, and parts of Croatia were under Ottoman rule. Only in 1882, after many uprisings against the Turks, did Serbia become an independent kingdom. During both Balkan wars (1912 and 1913), Macedonia was lastly liberated and fought over by Bulgaria, Serbia, and Greece. Furthermore, these wars resulted in the incorporation of Kosovo from Albania by Serbia (Singleton, 1985).

Austro-German and Hungarian Influences: Habsburg Rule

Of former Yugoslavia, Catholic Croatia and Slovenia experienced the authority of the Habsburg house (until 1918) the most (Jelavich, 1983b; Singleton, 1985). Significant for understanding modern Croatia and Slovenia is the period of reform and enlightment during the 18th century. Subsequent emperors ended the suppression of peasants as serfs under the ruling nobility. They attempted (and were partly successful) to reduce the power of these landlords and increase schooling and health facilities. Touched by the French Revolution as a result of conquests by the Napolean armies, feelings of autonomy and nationality were strengthened in this area (Jelavich, 1983a).

The Serbian population of Croatia was in a different position. In the 16th century Serbs had been encouraged by the Austrian rulers to settle along a military border (the Krajina) to form a buffer against Turkish invasion. In exchange the Serbs were given autonomy. This lasted until 1881 when the region was incorporated by Croatia. The Krajina was always one of the poorest areas of the region. Many of the people living in the Krajina worked in the army and police forces (Jelavich, 1983a). In recent years, propaganda stating that a threat existed for the Serbian population among Croats facilitated the recruiting of people for fighting for the Serbian cause (Denitch, 1994; Malcolm, 1994).

Croatian nobilities were often in dispute with Hungarian lords. One of the subjects in dispute concerned the official language. The Habsburg house had proposed the German language as the communal language; the Hungarians strongly urged Hungarian to be the official language. Croatian scholars subsequently introduced the Illyrian movement. Inherent in this movement is the sharing of ancient roots by all Balkan peoples (Illyrians inhabited the region before the Slavs arrived) and a proposition for one Slav language (Jelavich, 1983a).

First World War

The First World War started in Sarajevo with the assassination of Archduke Ferdinand (the Habsburg heir) by a member of an illegal, national movement of Serbs and Muslims in June, 1914. It made an end to the Austro-Hungarian dictate. At the end of the war, a kingdom of Serbs, Croats, and Slovenes was constituted (after 1929 it was called Yugoslavia) with a centralized government in Belgrade. Several groups (including Croatian nationalists) gradually but strongly opposed the centrality of Belgrade. To end political unrest, King Alexander declared a personal dictatorship in 1929. In 1934 he was assassinated (Jelavich, 1983b; Singleton, 1985).

Second World War

The Second World War, started by the German invasion after Yugoslavia backed out of an agreement with the fascists, knew many fighting parties. Not only were there Germans to fight, various groups of Yugoslavs fought each other as well (Singleton, 1985). In Croatia and Bosnia-Herzegovina, a fascist puppet government was set up by the Ustaša movement. The Ustaše were extremely violent in their attempt to expel all Serbs from Croatia to Serbia, murdering at least 350,000 ethnic Serbs, Jews, and Gypsies (estimates vary considerably) (Singleton, 1985). The Communist Party launched a peasant army, the partisans, led by Josip Broz (Tito). A monarchist resistance group, the Četniks, tried to get back at the Croats by massacring them. In all, about one and a half million people died violently in a war that was fought mostly in Croatia and Bosnia-Herzegovina (Jelavich, 1983b; Malcolm, 1994).

A 1943 meeting of the Antifascist Council for the National Liberation of Yugoslavia at Jajce laid the basis for a future communist led Yugoslavia. As a reward for their support, the Montenegrins as well as the Macedonians were given republic status within Yugoslavia after the war. The inhabitants of Kosovo and Vojvodina were denied republics of their own (Singleton, 1985).

Kosovo has been extremely important for Serbia. It has been the home of the Serbian Orthodox Church (at Peć). At the end of World War II communist partisans liberated this region. In 1974, Kosovo became an autonomous province after serious rioting in 1968. Although Kosovo has always been one of the poorest regions of former Yugoslavia, its inhabitants were better off economically than their relatives in Albania, due to financial aid provided by the Yugoslavian government in Belgrade (Detrez, 1996).

The Vojvodina, northern Serbia, formed the second autonomous province within the Federal Republic. Many Serbs sought refuge in this Hungarian controlled area after the Hungarians drove the Turks back across the Danube in the late 17th century. Until 1918, the region remained part of Hungary. During this period, it went through a period of large development. Before 1945, it was probably the most multiethnic region in Europe. It had, for instance, a large German minority (Jelavich, 1983b; Singleton, 1985).

Socialist Federal Republic Yugoslavia

Tito continued to be the dominating figure for Yugoslavia after World War II. He remained president until his death in 1980 (his portrait is still present in many houses of former Yugoslavia). Through his slogan *"Brastvo i jedinstvo"* (brotherhood and unity) he attempted to let the people live as one united people. Many inhabitants felt that they were Yugoslavs, more than Serbs, Croats, or Bosnjak. To lessen the impact of the dominant Serbian citizens, the regions Vojvodina and Kosovo were assigned the status of autonomous provinces within Serbia. Nationalist feelings and political disagreements were not permitted. Any expression of undesirable national prejudices was punished (Pecjak, 1994).

Yugoslavia's communism—or rather: socialism—was unique. In the early 1950s, Tito broke away from the orthodox communism dominated by the Soviet Union (this was financially rewarded by the American and British governments) and created his own independent form of socialism. The Federal Republic (abbreviated SFRY) consisted of six republics with economical and administrative independence. Foreign affairs, economy, jurisdiction, and defense remained the responsibility of central government. Until 1989 there was only one political party: the League of Communists (Jelavich, 1983b; Singleton, 1985).

After World War II, a large scale industrialization process took place. As in other Eastern European countries, it was official policy to turn farms into collective corporations. In the Federal Republic these attempts never succeeded, however, and most of the agricultural land continued to be worked privately by small farmers. Many peasants went temporarily to the cities or even abroad for work (Bringa, 1995; Halpern & Kerewsky-Halpern, 1972; Schierup & Alund, 1987).

Furthermore, characteristic of Yugoslavian socialist economy was the self-management of industry by workers. Factories and businesses were run by councils of elected personnel. Since collectively owned property had no clear owner, it was difficult to enforce economic efficiency or guarantee profits. Initiatives were stifled and employees often used self-management to improve their own financial standing, without feeling any responsibility towards their property. Problems increased when loans were applied for without hope for repayment. In the late 1980s it became clear the Federal Republic was heading for bankruptcy (Singleton, 1985; World Bank, 1996).

The Disintegration of the Federal Socialistic Republic Yugoslavia (1991–1995)

After more than four decades of peaceful coexistence, the people of former Yugoslavia faced a violent beginning of the 1990s. Increasing feelings of nationalism emerged in the turbulent transition from an undemocratic one party political constitution to a pluralistic system, as well as in the process of change from a communistic economy to a free market economy. Feelings of nationalism grew stronger by the propaganda, referring to memories of the Second World War. (For a detailed account of the progress of the war, see Glenny, 1996; Silber & Little, 1995.)

War in Slovenia and Croatia

In June, 1991, four decades of shared socialism ended when Slovenia and Croatia declared their independence. They were officially acknowledged states by the European Community in 1992. After ten days of combat at the border, the army of the Federal Republic left the small, homogeneous state of Slovenia. In Croatia however, the Serbian dominated federal army found more alliance among the Serbian population, concentrated in the southern parts of the state, the Krajina and Slavonia. As a result of heavy fighting, more than a quarter of Croatian territory fell to the federal army and Serbian militias. The strategic town of Vukovar was first besieged and consequently destroyed by the federal army in November, 1991. It was left in ruin. Autonomous Serbian areas were established in the Krajina and Slavonia. In January, 1993, ethnic cleansing had left only few Croats in Serbian Krajina. In 1995, in the shadow of the events taking place in Bosnia, the Croatian army invaded western Slavonia, east of Zagreb. The Krajina Serbs responded by shelling Zagreb. In August, 1995, the Croatian army violently regained control over the Krajina resulting in the flight of almost the entire Serbian population (Glenny, 1996).

War in Bosnia

The events in Slovenia and Croatia boded no good for the multiethnic Bosnia-Herzegovina. Because its inhabitants belonged to one of three major ethnic groups (Croats, Serbs, and Muslims, or Bosnjaks), Bosnia-Herzegovina was best off within a federal state offering home to all of these groups. Serbia, however, was determined to establish a Greater Serbia uniting all Serbian civilians in one state. Croatia tried, on the other hand, to generate a Croatian territory including all Croat pockets. Bosnia, the land in between these two striving powers, was subjected to a politics of pencils and scissors cutting the area into Croatian and Serbian parts (Malcolm, 1994).

Ethnic cleansing had far reaching consequences for Bosnia's population. Six months after the start of local hostilities, more than one third of Bosnia's inhabitants had chosen or been forced to leave their homes (Detrez, 1996). The events that took place in this war—the siege of Sarajevo by the Serbs, the siege of Mostar and the proclamation of the puppet state of Herzeg–Bosna by the Croats, the horrible slaughter of the men of Srebrenica by the Bosnian Serbs, and the fighting in central Bosnia between Muslims and Croats—have effectively led to the establishment of more ethnically homogeneous regions. The civilians of Bosnia-Herzegovina have not only been victims of this war; they also have been the targets and instruments of the bloodiest war of the Balkans, except for World War II (Glenny, 1996; Malcolm, 1994; Silber & Little, 1995).

The international world tried to interfere, and although finally NATO air strikes led to the end of the war, negotiations were directed toward the division of the Bosnian territory among Croats, Serbs, and Muslims. There was no attempt to direct solutions towards coexistence of the different peoples (Detrez, 1996).

Bosnia-Herzegovina was officially acknowledged as an independent state on April 6, 1992. Civil war broke out the next day, after Serb snipers opened fire on unarmed civilians demonstrating for peace in Sarajevo. During 1992, the Serbs were able to occupy a main part of Bosnian land (Detrez, 1996; Malcolm, 1994). Muslim people were virtually prisoners in enclaves like Bihac, Gorazde, Sarajevo, Srebrenica, Tuzla, and Zepa. In 1993, these areas came under the protection of UN soldiers "whose mandate entitled them to return fire, not if the Muslims were shot at, but only if they, the UN soldiers, came under attack" (Malcolm, 1994, p. 250).

In May, 1993, Croat forces in the western part of Mostar began a siege of the Muslim quarter, east of the Neretva River, for ten months. The Croats forcibly expelled thousands of Muslims from the west bank of the Neretva and killed hundreds more. All of the town's 16th and 17th century mosques were destroyed. In November, 1993, Mostar's famous Turkish Bridge (1566) was blown up by Croat artillery (Glenny, 1996; Silber & Little, 1995). Even today the city remains divided by the war because of the Bosnian Croats' persistence in a Herzeg-Bosna in spite of the Dayton peace accord.

In February, 1994, the world was shocked by the news of the Serb mortar attack on the Sarajevo market, which caused the death of 68 people and injured many more. In 1995, the international pressure increased and finally NATO decided on air strikes after the fall of Zepa and Srebrenica. The first air raids were retaliated by the Bosnian Serbs with mortar attacks on Tuzla, killing 71 youngsters on the Day of the Youth, May 25 (World Wide Web, 1997). The peace conference in Dayton, Ohio at the end of 1995 officially put an end to this horrible war that costed the lives of approximately 150,000 people. According to the agreement, Bosnia-Herzegovina is composed of two entities: the Federation of Bosnia and Herzegovina (Muslim and Croatian part, 51%) and the Serb Republic of Bosnia-Herzegovina (49%). Furthermore, the agreement announced the reunification of Sarajevo, the establishment of a Human Rights Commission, and of a War Crimes Tribunal in Hague, the Netherlands (General Framework Agreement, 1995).

Contemporary Former Yugoslavia

The recent, long, and violent (civil) war officially ended with the subscription of a peace agreement in Dayton, November, 1995 (officially signed in Paris, December, 1995). Two entities, a Federation (of Muslim and Croat areas), and the Bosnian Serb Republic form the Republic of Bosnia-Herzegovina (General Framework Agreement, 1995). However, the current situation in the area of the former Socialist Federal Republic of Yugoslavia is far from stable. In 1997, the streets of Belgrade were filled with people demonstrating against their nationalist leader Slobodan Milošovic. Kosovo, with a majority of Albanian citizens, is currently the area of most severe fighting.

Hundreds of thousands of civilians have, as a consequence of ethnic cleansing, sought refuge elsewhere. Huge numbers of people have come to live in cities like Sarajevo and Tuzla where they have had to rebuild their lives and start a new future. Many of them are more used to living in rural areas than in a city. Due to years of war, the economic situation is dreadful (World Bank, 1996). Numerous factories have been destroyed and jobs have been lost. In addition, society faces a transformation from a former socialist economy with major governmental control into a free market economy. Furthermore, the countryside, especially in Bosnia-Herzegovina, is filled with land mines. Only half of the mined areas have been located. Accidents, especially among children and animals, happen daily and will continue to do so for a long time to come.

While peace is still very fragile, a beginning has been made with respect to the rebuilding of communities in these new countries which once belonged to one state. A structure for health services is being developed. Within this context, many international, nongovernmental, and intergovernmental organizations operate. Besides the aid they provide, they contribute to the reestablishment of economic life by providing necessary services and spending money.

Summary

The youngest of wars in the Balkans focused on Serbian versus Croatian territorial claims and was fought on the battlefields of Croatia and Bosnia-Herzegovina. These conflicts have finally resulted in a rather uncertain kind of peace. At the same time, the violent struggle between the Albanians of Kosovo and the Serbian dominators pose, once again, to the international world the complex decision of whether to intervene or not. Furthermore, the most southern republic of former Yugoslavia was declared independent in January, 1992, and, as the former Yugoslavian Republic of Macedonia admitted to the UN in April 1993, without any interference by the federal—predominantly Serbian—army. The international world has shown itself rather powerless in the efficient construction of ethnically more homogeneous regions.

Although a peaceful coexistence of different social and religious groups have existed for many extended periods, history can be characterized to some extent by an ongoing strife for dominance between ethnic groups, religious groups, and nationalities. In particular, Croatia, influenced by the Austro-Hungarian power and the Catholic church, and Serbia, having been part of the Ottoman empire and predominantly Orthodox Christian, have remained rivals in the strife for power. In this respect, the most recent war has been a new version of an old conflict, in which Bosnia performed its own role.

The territory of Yugoslavia has been a theater of various essential borderline issues: those between Roman Catholicism and Orthodox churches, between Christianity and Islam, between the Cyrillic alphabet and the Roman alphabet, between Central European powers such as the Austrian Empire and Middle Eastern powers such as the Ottoman empire. These conflicts have left a tremendous mark on the ideology of the people. Whether justified or not, Croats and Slovenes often consider themselves as characteristic Middle European people, while Serbs are proud of the fact that they have been one of the last strongholds of Western civilization against Islam.

☐ Similarities and Differences among Three Cultural Groups

Cultural Diversity and Homogeneity: Defining Culturally Distinct Groups

Before the war, in all states except for Bosnia-Herzegovina, a majority of one particular ethnic group could be found. However, the population was never homogeneous. Besides Kosovo, where the majority of the population consists of Albanian people, more than half of Serbia's people were Serb. Most people living in Slovenia were Slovenes (90.5%), people living in Croatia were mostly Croats (75.1%), and most inhabitants of the southern areas were Macedonians and Montenegrins (Detrez, 1996). In particular, Bosnia-Herzegovina was a pluralistic republic. The three most numerous groups (Catholic Croats, Orthodox Serbs, and Muslims) lived together reasonably peacefully. In 1991, just before the war started, nearly half of Bosnia's population were Muslim (43.7%), about one-third Serbian (31.4%) and nearly one-fifth Croatian (17.3%). Of the inhabitants, 5.5% considered themselves as Yugoslav (Detrez, 1996). There were many minorities such as Hungarians, Italians, Czechs, Gypsies, Slovaks, Romanians, Bulgarians, Turks, and Ukrainians living in different areas. Before the Second World War, Yugoslavia had a considerable Jewish and German population making Balkan population more diverse.

Religion and Nationality

The idea of nationality was a late 19th century invention in this region of the world, where many different groups had lived together in a sometimes troubled, sometimes harmonious coexistence. The development of nationalities in Eastern Europe differs from the establishment of Western European countries. In the latter, defining a nation was dominated by political, economical, and legal purposes; in the former the concept of nation was more based on peoples' ethnoreligious heritages (Bacova, 1993). This development was complicated by the fact that the different groups lived in the same areas. As Singleton strikingly pronounces: "The cynical definition of a nation as 'a group of people united by a common error as to their origins and a common dislike of their neighbors' has a tragic relevance in the history of the Yugoslav peoples" (Singleton, 1985, p. 23).

In former Yugoslavia, nationalities were based on the major ethnoreligious communities (Detrez, 1996). Serbs, Macedonians, and Montenegrins have been predominantly Orthodox (*pravoslavci*), Croats and Slovenes were Roman Catholic (*katolici*), and there was a growing recognition of the Bosnian Muslims to form a distinct nationality. Detrez (1996) distinguishes further among nations (*nacije* or *narodi*)—referring to people with a state within Yugoslavia—and nationalities (*nacionalnosti* or *narodnosti*)—referring to people with a state outside of Yugoslavia (e.g. Albanians of Kosovo, the Italians in Istria, or the Hungarians in Slavonia and Vojvodina). This difference is important because, according to the law based on this distinction, some peoples could proclaim rights to a separate state while others could not. Serbian nationalistic government used this as an argument to end the autonomy of Kosovo and Vojvodina in 1989 (Detrez, 1996).

Although originally the peoples living in this part of the Balkan had roots that go back to three early Slav tribes that set foot in the area (the Serbs, Croats, and Slovenes), or to even more ancient peoples (the Albanians are presumably descendants of the Illyrians from the pre-Roman period) (Malcolm, 1994; Singleton, 1985), frequent migration, sequential occupation by different Empires, and shared government have homogenized former Yugoslavian inhabitants to a large extent. Distinguishing among different cultural groups and looking for different traditions and expressions of dealing with living circumstances, therefore, may be a somewhat forced enterprise. Nevertheless, in subsequent sections, we describe three societies that are culturally different to some extent: the Croats, Serbs, and Bosnians. These people constitute the largest groups in contemporary Croatia, Bosnia-Herzegovina, and Yugoslavia. Moreover, the most recent war was dominated by a distinction among these ethnoreligious groups.

Serbian Culture: Eastern-Orthodox Influences

"To be a Serb is implicitly to be Orthodox, explicitly to celebrate the slava, and importantly to associate oneself with a heroic tradition of struggle."
(Halpern & Kerewsky-Halpern, 1972, p. 123).

The southwestern part of former Yugoslavia was inhabited by a Slav tribe that exerted influence south- and eastwards in the early Middle Ages (Jelavich, 1983a; Singleton, 1985). In time, the area that came to be known as Serbia, knew different periods of both governmental importance and domination as well as suppression and severe struggle.

Serbian society is usually described as a traditionally peasant society. Only in the 1960s did urbanization come to its full growth and activities and employment were transferred from the rural villages to the cities. Halpern and Kerewsky-Halpern (1972) conducted anthropological research in a small village in the rural area south of Belgrade during nearly two decades. In this period changes in the Serbian society became obvious which could be contributed to industrialization and urbanization. These relatively recent processes had an everlasting impact on family life and rural community structure. Communities used to rely heavily on neighborhoods and extended families and the production of goods took place with only few requirements of professional services. Currently the number of family members living together in one household has started to decline rapidly. The changes in society also resulted in a prolonged education of children and youth, which implied their leaving the village. "Most (youth) reject the traditional village economy, and there is a decline in the prestige of the hard labor required to wrest a living from the soil" (Halpern & Kerewsky-Halpern, 1972, p. 137). It became common for men to have jobs outside the house (mines offered many job opportunities), or even abroad. Private houses were built with the extra money. More and more, women and children were the ones who took care of the agricultural work.

In a description of modern city life in Serbia, Van de Port (1994) provides a similar view. The people of Novi Sad (Vojvodina, northern Serbia) are very much aware of their rural backgrounds, although they attempt to distinguish themselves from people from regions they regard as backwaters (southern Serbia, Montenegro, the Krajina). As opposed to these countrymen, the inhabitants of Novi Sad like to see themselves as civilized, Western European *fini ljudi* (fine people) (Van de Port, 1994). The start of the war put an end to this self-image and many people consequently were bothered by how they—as Serbians—would appear to the world (Van de Port, 1994).

Referring to the urbanization in the 1960s, Van de Port mentions the fact that rather than newcomers forming suburbs in the outer circles of established cities, as happened in most Western countries, cities were ruralized by the arrival of peasants in town. Many urban inhabitants have little gardens besides their houses to grow vegetables.

In rural society, ties with family members as well as ties with people living in the neighborhood are extremely strong. This may have origins in earlier times when households existed of extended families living together (*zadrugas*). Marriages were closed between two families, more than between two partners only (Bringa, 1995; Halpern & Kerewsky-Halpern, 1972). In these "traditional" families, god fatherhood was an honored position. The *kum's* most important duty was to select a name for his godchild and to perform a christening ceremony. He was also expected to be a witness at his godson's wedding (Halpern & Kerewsky-Halpern, 1972). Although weddings, according to old custom, only occasionally take place, they may be adapted to modern facilities (one may be confronted with a tour of cars driving through the city). Furthermore, in modern Serbia, family units are generally restricted to the husband, wife, and children, with rather equal responsibility between both sexes.

Several festivities are important to Serbian people. Traditionally celebrations are accompanied by roasted meat and plum brandy *slivovic* or *rakija*. Some of the feasts have their origins in pre-Christian times, such as the *Slava*, others are Christian celebrations (Easter and Christmas) and still others originated from the socialistic federal period (the First of May, birthdays, and the Day of the Republic) (Halpern & Kerewsky-Halpern,

1972). The *Slava* (derived from *slaviti,* meaning celebrating) is celebrated in order to honor the household's saint (Van de Port, 1994). It involves few religious rituals and it is celebrated at home. According to Halpern and Kerewsky-Halpern (1972), this feast symbolizes the importance of old pre-Christian traditions, celebrated within the most important social system, the family, and with the accordance of the Christian church (Halpern & Kerewsky-Halpern, 1972).

Most celebrations take place at home. Only at Easter, which is considered the most important Orthodox feast, is the church the center of activities. In general, Serbs do not attend church very frequently. Orthodox churches have a modest impact, in physical as well as spiritual appearance.

Although Catholicism and Orthodoxy can be traced back to the same origins, there are differences between both traditions. Besides the use of a different script (the adoption of Latin alphabet by the Catholic church; the use of a Cyrillic script by the Orthodox community), a different calendar was used. For the Orthodox Church, Christmas falls on January 7th (Gregorian calendar), while New Year starts on January 13th. The Socialist Federal Government, however, centralized the celebration and holiday after the Second World War. Christmas and New Year were set according to the Gregorian calendar. The First of May, Day of the Workers—regarded as an important day for socialists and communists—replaced the traditional St. Georges Day as a herald of spring (*Đurđevdan*), and the celebration of children's birthdays was introduced. Furthermore, the day of the founding of the Republic, November 29 is celebrated every year. The Serbian anniversary of the Battle of Kosovo and their defeat by the Turks, is still intensely remembered every year.

The occupation of the territory by the Ottoman Empire, causing large numbers of Serbs to flee into mountainous Montenegro and up north, is viewed with most bitterness. Generally, Serbs take great pride in the battles that were fought and the participation in military service. Serbia's history of ongoing strife against threats from outside and domination has left deep marks in the self-image of the people (Halpern and Kerewsky-Halpern, 1972; Van de Port, 1994).

Gradually, differences between towns and villages have grown stronger. People that were members of the one and only political party, the League of Communists, during socialist years and/or those living in town, are more and more strictly acknowledging the newly introduced or redefined feasts and dates. Rural peasant ideals and values still shape life in contemporary Serbia. Traditional literary themes, folk songs, and dances are still highly appraised, both for reasons of encouragement of tourism as well as for sharing cultural identity (Halpern & Kerewsky-Halpern, 1972; Van de Port, 1994).

Croatian Culture: Under the Spell of Roman-Catholic Austrian-Hungarian Empire

Slav tribes moved into what is now Croatia and occupied two former Roman provinces: Dalmatian Croatia along the Adriatic, and Pannonian Croatia to the north. Since the division of the Roman Empire at the end of the fourth century, the region now known as Slovenia, Croatia and Bosnia-Herzegovina belonged to the Western Roman Empire (Eterovich & Spalatin, 1976; Singleton, 1985).

The two parts of Croatia, either united or separate, as well as Slovenia, have nearly always been under the impact of Western and Middle Europe. Germany, Hungary, Italy, Austria (much of the Dalmatian architecture stems from this period), and France (after the conquest of the Illyrian provinces by Napoleon) have all exerted their influences on the territory throughout history. Until the end of the First World War in 1918, Croatia (and Slovenia) remained under the control of the Austrian-Hungarian monarchy.

The impact of the Western European world and its Roman-Catholicism has unmistakenly determined Croatian culture. Croatians are predominantly Catholic, and they have used the Latin alphabet from the beginning. In contrast to the Serbs and the average Muslim, religion has an important place in Croatian life. According to Eterovich and Spalatin (1976), the Christian faith shaped preexistent general virtues, such as honor, fidelity, tightly knit familial bonds, and a deep love for the native land, as well as vices, such as revenge, envy, and a destructive hatred of the enemy. Based on an analysis of folk literature and song, these authors described the idealization of Croatian morality: the admiration for heroes, the love of God and one's neighbor, brotherhood extending to the value of friendship and the importance of hospitality, and a strong sense of justice. Freedom is highly valued; the long independence of the city-state of Dubrovnik is appreciated as an historical example. At the same time the law of vengeance is regarded as an old custom, dating from the time that blood vengeance was regarded a sacred duty of all members of families and clans (Eterovich & Spalatin, 1976). Of course, these morals and vices are rather idealizing, generalizing, and maybe outdated. And, as Croatians probably differ amongst each other, they may well share these virtues with other peoples living in the Balkans as well.

During the 18th century the Habsburg court introduced a period of enlightment and reform with the intent to improve living conditions of the people. As a result, schools, a university, and better health care facilities emerged. Croatian scholars subsequently started to embrace the idea of a national, independent identity, thereby referring to their Illyrian origins (although these are not exclusively Croatian) (Singleton, 1985). Strong feelings of nationalism seemed to have dominated Croatian rulers, leading to the murderous regime of Ante Pavelic in the Second World War and fueling the most recent war.

Along the Adriatic coast, Venetian influence is most strikingly present. Under Venetian rule, the inhabitants of Dalmatia knew a relatively calm and balanced life. Inspired by the Italian Renaissance, many works of art (sculptures, architecture, and literature) were produced (Singleton, 1985). The city-state of Dubrovnik (Ragusa in Latin) in this region managed to maintain an independent position for most of the time. It flourished due to trade activities (the export of woods, metals, and wool from the inner Balkan lands) (Halpern & Kerewsky-Halpern, 1972; Singleton, 1985).

The citizens of parts of Croatia that experienced strong European influence, have known periods of fortune and prosperity. Croatian peasants under Habsburg nobility, however, were for a time worse off than their Serbian colleagues in Ottoman Serbia and Bosnia. They were dependent upon the good will of their landlord and had no opportunity for self-organization whatsoever (Singleton, 1985).

In former Yugoslavia, the Northern republics, Croatia and Slovenia, were wealthier than the country's Southern states, such as Bosnia, Kosovo, and Macedonia. Still today, in postwar Balkan, both countries recover more rapidly from war investments and damage than their counterparts (World Bank, 1996), due to, for instance, the gradually returning tourists. Spending time at the Adriatic coast is one of the favorite ways of spending holidays by many of the former Yugoslavian inhabitants (if they can afford it).

Bosnian Culture: The Most Heterogeneous of All

Bosnia-Herzegovina, an independent kingdom in the Middle Ages and a territory without any natural borders, has been confronted with the Austro-Hungarian empire on one side and the Turkish Ottoman empire on the other. In this way, it was influenced by Eastern and Western civilizations. Bosnia-Herzegovina remained under Ottoman rule until taken over by the Austro-Hungarian Empire in 1878 (Jelavich, 1983a; Malcolm, 1994).

Influenced by Eastern and Western Christianity and later, by Islam, the people of Bosnia-Herzegovina adhere to all three religions. The affiliation of Bosnian families with one of these three religious traditions was, in most cases, according to Bringa (1995), determined during a period of over 500 years of coexistence. There is historical debate about the conversion of inhabitants of the Ottoman empire to Islam (Bringa, 1995; Krug, 1991; Malcolm, 1994). It seems unclear whether people were pressed to convert to the newly introduced religion or were just being pragmatic, since Islam could lead to more freedom and better positions in society. In the literature it is implied many times that a sect, the (Bulgarian) Bogomils, had acquired adherence among many of Bosnia's inhabitants in pre-Ottoman times. Tombstones were used as an argument for the Bogomil presence in Bosnia. Malcolm (1994) however, disentangles this Bogomil myth and convincingly argues there was an independent Bosnian church that was restricted to some monasteries throughout the countryside. Because of the remoteness of Bosnian country, it must have been very hard to exert large scale influence on the people. Conversion to Islam only took place very gradually throughout Turkish rule (Malcolm, 1994; Singleton, 1985). Sometimes within families, members belonged to different religious communities (Bringa, 1995). Converting to Islam implied changing one's name. Last names often describe a profession or social status of the person who first adopted the name (Bringa, 1995; Malcolm, 1994; Singleton, 1985).

For a long time Muslims were not officially recognized as a separate ethnocultural group within the Federal Republic. Only in 1971 at a national census, were people given the opportunity to choose Muslim among the nationalities offered. At earlier censes they could only choose the category "other" ("undeclared" or "uncommitted"), or, later, "Yugoslav." To distinguish them from, for example, the Albanian Muslims, only those who spoke the central south Slavic (Serbo-Croatian) language were considered to be Muslim in ethnic definition (Detrez, 1996). People with high ranks in the communist state were obviously members of the communist party and therefore atheist or nonbelievers (Bringa, 1995).

In Bosnia, as we have seen for Serbia, religion taken as a whole was not a very pivotal matter in daily life. It is important to emphasize that the Muslims of Bosnia cannot be compared with fundamentalistic Muslims. Only after the recent war did the attendance of mosques start to increase (during socialism, the practice of religion was discouraged). Belonging to an ethnoreligous group was more evident in customs and traditions. Muslim and Croatian inhabitants living in a village near Sarajevo, though peaceful in their coexistence, formed two different societies. Muslim houses would have a picture of a girl in a head scarf praying, while Catholic houses were decorated with images of the Virgin Mary with the child Jesus, and a crucifix (Bringa, 1995). The only outward sign of Muslim identity of village men is their dark blue beret (Bringa, 1995). Furthermore, families were very much opposed to mixed marriages, although Muslims and Croats did visit each other and sometimes took part in joint festivities (Bringa, 1995).

Bosnian practice of Islam occurs according to its own set of rules. Some rituals are officially obligatory (*dženaza* or the burial ceremony and *Ramazan*, Ramadan, the month long fast), and some are signs of good intent and behavior (*tevhid*, prayers for the dead, *sevap*, acts that will benefit after life because it pleases God). Annually, the end of Ramadan, *Kurban-bajram*, and the autumn *mevlud*, honoring the birth of the Prophet Mohammed, are celebrated. The most frequently held rituals (*tevhids* and *mevluds*) are celebrated in private homes, in contrast to other rituals, that require services in the mosque (Bringa, 1995). Men and women perform different rituals. In rural Bosnia, the fast was kept mainly by women, while men had a prominent role in the burial ceremony. *Mevluds* that are celebrated at the home, are held for various reasons, such as moving into a new house, or the birth of a child. *Mevluds* may differ with regard to religious and didactic content. Intermediators (priests, *hodža*, or *bula*) are invited to recite prayers. *Mevluds* serve not only to gain merits in the face of God, they also serve to gain social acknowledgment of Muslim identity and can be considered signs of Bosnian hospitality as they coincide with food and drinks (Bringa, 1995).

In the case of health related problems, after consulting a doctor or psychologist, rural Bosnian Muslim inhabitants may seek the help of the *hodža* or *bula* (priest; lecturer of Qur'an), who, for example, writes an amulet (*žapis*) as treatment. Gypsies and fortune tellers are mentioned as options as well but, in general, they are not taken very seriously (Bringa, 1995).

The wearing of scarves, berets, and the performance of rituals such as carrying a loaf of bread when entering a new house at marriages (stressing household prosperity and fertility) are overt expressions of Bosnian Muslim culture, at least in rural Bosnia (Bringa, 1995). Other such rituals concern the burial of the dead. According to Muslim belief, relatives are expected to behave quietly, not being overtly emotional or crying loudly (as opposed to Orthodox Serbs, for instance) since the death is the will of God and furthermore, overt expression of grief would upset the soul of the deceased (as it is expected to leave the body forty days after the death) (Bringa, 1995). Only men are present at the graveyard when the body is buried: Women stay at home to pray. Sometimes a person who recites at the burial is being paid or given a gift in name of the dead (Bringa, 1995). A *tehvid* for the lost person is held five times at certain times after his or her death. Except for the first one, *tehvids* are accompanied by hospitality and food (Bringa, 1995). (Although according to personal communication, first burial ceremonies are followed by much drinking and eating).

In prewar Bosnian society, the differences between people living in rural and urban areas were probably more important than the distinctions among people along ethnic lines. Traditional customs such as wearing *dimije* (a typical type of trousers for Muslim women), for instance, were considered old fashioned and were seen as signs of backwardness and orientalism, both by the Croatian and the urban Muslim population (Bringa, 1995). Mixed marriages, furthermore, hardly occurred in remote villages but were very prevalent in the large cities. The overall number of intermarriages was found to remain the same over the last three decades (Botev, 1994). Exact assessment is difficult, however, since categories in which people could declare themselves changed repeatedly. For instance, before 1991 it was not uncommon for an urban citizen to have a Serbian mother and a Muslim father and to consider him- or herself Yugoslav. After, one parent had to renounce his or her heritage.

The typical household structure, with the extended family living together, and the *zadruga* had been present in Bosnia as in Serbia. These patriarchal social structures are no longer very widespread (Bringa, 1995). More and more, Bosnian women claim their own households by standing up against their husbands and families-in-law. Moreover, Bringa disagrees with a patriarchal view on Bosnian family life. While the men were away most of the time, the women were in charge of organizing the household and (religious) upbringing of the children.

Differences and Similarities

The federal state of Yugoslavia had always been a heterogenous nation. Not only were there many different peoples, but the republic was also a country with major differences between urban and rural areas, industrial and agricultural areas, and economically affluent and poor areas. These dissimilarities were associated with the distinction between the northern and the southern parts, but not entirely.

In spite of its rather unique character in Yugoslavia, communism had about the same impact on society as in other Eastern European countries. Postwar Yugoslavia went through a large scale modernization process with the focus on industrialization. Many people migrated from rural areas into the cities. The industrialization efforts had a real Eastern European effect: buildings and cities were bleak and bland. The variety of merchandise on sale was meager and people had to wait and save for a long time before they could afford a car or a refrigerator. At the same time, health services and women's rights were sometimes better—and undoubtedly more equally distributed—than in most Western countries. As a result of a lack of jobs in the 1960s and 1970s, many people chose to work abroad as guest workers in Western European countries.

There were regional differences, as well. The northern states of Slovenia and Croatia experienced an economic boom and were far more prosperous than other states. Increasingly, their inhabitants felt they had to pay for the poverty in the other republics. Just before the war started, the socialist system, politically and socially nearly bankrupt, collapsed in 1989 and hesitantly gave way to a new, more market oriented economy and society. This change started slowly and without momentum. War activities started in 1991 after the leaders of the Republic Serbia threatened equality by annexing the formerly autonomous regions of Kosovo and Vojvodina and broadcasting reports in the media of a massacre of ethnic Serbs in Croatia (Malcolm, 1994).

The economic differences between regions have now increased. Slovenia is a comparatively affluent and industrial state. The same holds true for Croatia. Serbia maintains its socialist economic system. Sanctioned by the United Nations, it has been subject to significant inflation and a massive reduction of industrial production and employment. Kosovo with its fertile land remains the poorest area of the Balkans. Bosnia-Herzegovina, one of the poorest regions, had an unemployment level of 80% at the end of the war. Ironically, the industrial and extremely polluted town of Zenica in Central Bosnia, has never been as clean as it is now, since its steel factory was closed due to the war activities.

Before the war, the living conditions of people in the cities of former Yugoslavia were better than those in other Eastern European countries. Although traditionally families used to live together with more than two generations in one house (called *zadruga*), men and women now live in nuclear families. Both partners have jobs (if available) and the birth rate is low. Differences between socialization of men and women are dependent upon the region and religion. In Kosovo, for instance, among the Muslim population, men and women remain at a distance in public, women wear head scarves and parents decided until recently who their children should marry. In the northern areas, as well as in the cities throughout the country, both men and women have jobs outside the home and it is more normal to divide housekeeping tasks and care taking of children (Centraal Orgaan opvang Asielzoekers, 1995).

In general, the people are known to be very outgoing and extraverted. They do not shy away from confrontation and argument. They embrace life in a Mediterranean way: they enjoy celebrating, singing, and dancing. Pecjak (1993, 1994) speaks of a Balkan character typified by an extreme compliance to tradition (with an emphasis on arms, fights, and vendettas) and to authorities (characterized by a patriarchal family structure and by a long past of dependency). As there was hardly a history of democracy and enlightment, these elements led to a rather authoritarian leadership and to a lack of pluralism in political parties. Already in the communist era there was an obsession with enemies and a suspicious attitude towards leaders. This could easily lead to a manipulation of national feelings by propaganda (Siber, German & Millsaps, 1994). These feelings were severely intensified by the horrible and never really well managed memories of World War II. For instance, Pecjak (1994) reports that the notorious war generals, Adzic and Mladic, were traumatized in early childhood when the Ustaša killed their families.

In spite of the differences mentioned, one should be cautious in dividing the people along ethnic lines. In prewar Yugoslavia other distinctions (urban–rural areas) were at least as important. The commonalities were, and still are, large (although now it is not popular to emphasize them). Nevertheless, the war and the resulting ethnic cleansing led to a far reaching increase of the interethnic differences. Before the war, people of different ethnicity and/or religion would live together peacefully, but this has changed. "War changes people and it changes their perceptions of who they are" (Bringa, 1995, p. 197). Bosnian Muslims, Serbs, and Croats are redefining their collective identities by emphasizing differences. Even in reception centers abroad this may result in confrontations. Most of the people used to speak one language, usually referred to as Serbo-Croatian (except for Slovenes, Macedonians, Hungarians of the Vojvodina, and Albanians of Kosovo, who speak their own languages). After the recent war, countries have tried to differentiate between the dialects, adding new words. New dictionaries have been produced which for the most part, serve a political function. As a consequence, there are now three different (but strongly overlapping) languages: Serbian, Croatian, and Bosnian. And while many European countries are about to share one single currency, three different currencies exist within the Republic Bosnia-Herzegovina.

☐ Consequences of the War

Earlier we described the background of the civil war in former Yugoslavia. Authoritarian and opportunistic leadership and long suppressed wishes for control over a large territory seemed to justify ethnic cleansing. The turbulent political history has left a significant mark on the peoples' cultures. There are differences as well as similarities. In this section we report on the implications of the war for the people, as individuals, and as a collective entity.

The Destruction by the War

As a consequence of ethnic cleansing (in Croatia and Bosnia-Herzegovina), hundreds of thousands of people were forced to leave their homes.

TABLE 1. War Stressors

Personal Stressors

Ongoing threat of being killed or wounded
Loss of spouse and/or children
Loss of relatives, friends, and colleagues
Loss of home and property
Loss of freedom, imprisonment
Being maltreated, tortured, humiliated, abused
Limited or no access to health care, food, fuel, and water
Loss of personal items and mementos
Loss of important records and documentation
Loss of usual leisure and recreational activities
Loss of expected future resources

Social Stressors

Shattered trust
Alienation among people
Unemployment and loss of employment opportunities
Disruption of families and communities, e.g. due to migration
Loss of parenting perogatives, e.g. ability to provide for children's basic needs and
    safety

Cultural Stressors

Destruction of historical legacies
Destruction of mosques and churches
Drastic change of original communities as a result of migration
Emphasizing distinctive languages (dialects)
Destruction of landscape

Political Stressors

Lack of optimism about the future
No improvement of economic situation (especially Bosnia, Yugoslavia)
No change of leadership
Witness of large-scale violation of human rights

Slovenia, Croatia, Macedonia, and Serbia all offered shelter to the ones who fled the war. Many others sought refuge abroad in countries such as Sweden, Switzerland, Germany, and the Netherlands. One study among adult refugees in Croatia revealed that the homes of 80% of these people were destroyed. Seventy percent lost important personal belongings. More than half of the interviewed refugees had been exposed to direct bombing and had lost everything they had owned. Many people had family members who had left to fight in the war. Relatives or friends had died, people had been wounded, parents were separated from their children. War was an everyday reality; many had witnessed other people getting wounded, abused, or killed. Some have been tortured and a small percentage reported having been sexually abused (Ajdukovic & Ljubotina, 1995).

Accounts of the horrendous events experienced by many more civilians of former Yugoslavia are numerous. The thousands of women and children who fled the besieged (1992–1995), and finally (in 1995) conquered, city of Srebrenica, eastern Bosnia, are left with little hope for the survival of their sons, brothers, and fathers who vanished after the invasion by the army troops of the Bosnian Serbs. Sarajevo was under siege for several years (1992–1995). Civilians of this once cosmopolitan center of eastern European culture felt oppressed and humiliated by their captivity. Hardly any civilian could leave or enter the city for an extended period. There was a great shortage of food, electricity, and water. For instance, a woman recalled feeling regretful and fearful about cutting the tree in front of her house; it reminded her of earlier times and, moreover, snipers now had a better view on the street. There was indeed a continuous threat of being hit by a sniper. Parents would not leave the house together. If one of them was killed, the other at least would still be around to take care of the children.

Human rights were violated on a large scale. Many people endured imprisonment, lack of basic living conditions, little or no access to health services, maltreatment, murder, theft, rape, and destruction of property. Most difficult to grasp perhaps, were and still are, the ruptures within communities, families, and even marriages. Nothing is more shattering than a war in which a former neighbor turns into one's biggest enemy, capable of the most brutal acts. The fanatic efforts to establish ethnically pure regions has led to disruption of shared frames of reference and social support systems. Curtis (1995) reports that Muslim inhabitants of the Bosnian city of Mostar were refused purchase of bread or flour in the Croatian section of this fragmented city. They were dependent upon non-Muslim neighbors who would smuggle it and, later, upon relief organizations.

War has ruined society in Bosnia-Herzegovina, Kosovo, and other areas. Hospitals have been destroyed, staff have left, and health care has been severely reduced. Factories have suffered the same fate and offer only a limited number of jobs. Furthermore, much of the cultural inheritance has been destroyed. Mosques and churches were specifically targeted in bombardments and shootings. The destructions of the library of Sarajevo and the ancient cities of Vukovar and Mostar are irreversible (referred to as "urbicide").

The postwar period confronts people with the task of building a new society on the ruins of cultural genocide. For a long time to come, the scars of the war will be visible. Although some of the buildings and roads will be repaired reasonably soon, the number of graveyards with their recent graves and the limited access to fields because of mines will remain reminders of the war for a long time. Moreover, this immediate postwar period is in itself not a very victorious time; no enemy has surrendered in this complicated civil war, the same nationalistic political leaders who started the war are still in charge, and there is not enough perspective on economic prosperity.

War Trauma

Research has shown the range and intensity of direct and long term health consequences of war (Bracken, Giller & Summerfield, 1995). For instance, studies of World War II survivors have found signs of serious mental disorders in approximately 15–25% of representative groups of citizens 50 years after the war (Bramsen, 1995; Mooren & Kleber, 1996).

Reactions such as nightmares, recurrent dreams, concentration problems, flashbacks, and numbness will be commonly experienced. Persons may be hampered by feelings of shame and guilt, as well as by a diversity of somatic symptoms (Horowitz, 1986). Such experiences cause a dramatic disruption in an individual's sense of continuity (Lifton, 1979). Subsequently he or she has the difficult task of regaining control over his

---

TABLE 2. War-related Disturbances

Sleeping disturbances
Concentration disturbances
Various stress-related psychological reactions
Acute stress disorder
Panic and startle reactions
Depressive reactions
Loss of trust
Anger and hostility
Suicide (attempts)
Substance abuse
Feelings of alienation
Social withdrawal and isolation
Post-traumatic stress disorder
Complicated grief
Brief psychotic disturbances

or her life and deriving some kind of meaning from the experiences (Kleber & Brom, 1992).

Several authors (Keilson, 1979) use the concept of multiple traumatization or sequential traumatization to describe the long term impact of war. Introducing the idea of sequence to trauma theory makes it possible to understand the chronic problems of people confronted with a prolonged series of extreme events. Moreover, extreme traumatization occurs when the elimination of some members of society by others is aimed at the destruction of the individual, his sense of belonging to the society, and his social activities (Becker, 1995). This process of extreme traumatization develops sequentially. Life has definitely changed and will probably never be the same any more. Extreme traumatization can be applied to the civil war that has raged through the Balkans, with its central focus on discrimination among different ethnoreligious groups and ethnic cleansing.

It would, therefore, be too simple to perceive all health consequences as responses to traumatic stress. First of all, many symptoms can also be conceptualized in terms of loss and bereavement (Eth & Pynoos, 1985; Nader, 1997; Parkes, 1986) especially in the case of chronic warfare. There have been many losses to regret. Husbands, sons, daughters, siblings, friends, or other important persons have died during the war. In addition, people will have to cope with the loss of houses, the loss of expectations about the future, and the loss of faith that the world is a safe place (Eisenbruch, 1991). Therefore, grief processes will be complicated. Secondly, traumatic stress may interfere with acculturation problems. Many war refugees face an intense change of culture (Berry, 1994). They have come to live in a new place, among unknown people without most of their relatives. In Vogosca, just outside of Sarajevo, for example, many women and children who fled Srebrenica and who were used to rural life, came to live. Finally, there is the interaction between traumatic stress and the burden of daily hassles in a (post)war society. Living circumstances are hard at many times, so difficulties with coping with war experiences can only be understood in the context of the daily hardships with which many inhabitants struggle.

Several authors have attempted to measure the cumulative effect of war trauma by comparing refugees with local inhabitants (Ajdukovic & Ljubotina, 1995; Kuterovac, Dyregrov, & Stuvland, 1994; Zivcic, 1993). Using different methods, significant problems have been found in all studies. Refugees and their children reported more negative feelings (Zivcic, 1993), more worries (Ajdukovic & Ljubotina, 1995) and more problems in coping with the war experiences (Kuterovac et al., 1994). A cumulation of drastic events or a combination of trauma and loss was found to increase the risk of health problems.

Nevertheless, psychological responses to war should not be conceived merely in terms of serious mental disorders. Empirical studies as well as clinical evidence (Brom, Kleber, & Witztum, 1991; Yehuda & McFarlane, 1995) have shown that most people do not develop serious disorders, such as posttraumatic stress disorder or major depression, after extreme life events. Although their memories may be painful, they are able to function adequately (Kleber & Brom, 1992). People often show remarkable resilience after having survived the most dreadful circumstances. Intrapsychic as well as interpersonal resources that facilitate maintenance of health are often neglected.

Labelling Health Problems: Western Influences

Some of the first studies (published in English) on the psychosocial consequences of this war were conducted in Croatia (Cop, Ivanovic, & Matek, 1992; Hotujac, Vukelja, & Mahnik, 1992; Koic, Delalle-Zebic, & Bosnic, 1992). These authors worked in hospitals and were confronted with young soldiers who had fought in the Croatian army at the beginning of the war. Peak admission to the hospitals was around December 1991, the period when the fighting in Croatia was most intense. In these early publications, the authors stated that they had no prior knowledge or experience with the type of symptoms the soldiers presented.

> Our generation of psychiatrists was confronted with war and the need for wartime organization of our work for the first time. The initial lack of experience led to an insecurity in our work. We often asked ourselves: What kind of psychopathology can we expect? Our considerations were suddenly brought to an end when our clinic was demolished in one of the great number of attacks on the Osijek General Hospital
> (Koic et al., 1992, p. 277).

Psychology and psychiatry in former Yugoslavia were not oriented toward the field of psychological trauma. Psychiatrists were mainly focused on schizophrenia and inpatient treatment, while psychologists were more concerned with educational and industrial psychology and clinical assessment (Marinkovic, 1992; Pecjak, 1987).

Following World War II, psychology, psychiatry, and other sciences were strongly influenced by Russian theorists, but after Yugoslavia's breakup with Soviet communism, they became more oriented toward the West (Marinkovic, 1992). In publications, symptoms were often labeled in terms of diagnoses based on the Diagnostic and Statistical Manual of Mental Disorders (DSM). Depression and anxiety disorders were frequently observed (Bilanakis, Pappas, Baldic, & Jokic, 1997; Delimar, Korenjak, Sivik, & Delimar, 1995; Hotujac, Vukelja, & Mahnik, 1992; Koic, Delalle-Zebic, & Bosnic, 1992; Nesvadbova, 1995). However, can we use these diagnostic criteria with regard to mental stress in this war stricken and formerly socialist society? Empirical and conceptual studies on the cross cultural validity of psychodiagnostics are scarce (e.g., Kleinman, 1986; Kleinman & Cohen, 1997; Manson, 1997; Marsella, Friedman, Gerrity & Scurfield, 1996), but there are indications that the concepts of the Diagnostic and statistical manual of mental disorders (DSM, APA, 1994) and International classification of diseases (ICD, WHO, 1992) may be used in this part of the world although one should change the content of some concepts. A study investigating the validity of the well known and frequently used Impact of Event Scale (IES) (Horowitz, Wilner, & Alvarez, 1979) in this region found support for its cross cultural validity among displaced and nondisplaced children (in Croatia) (Dyregrov, Kuterovac, & Barath, 1996). In 1992 Nader found a significant difference between children with different exposure and of different ages among refugees in Croatia using the Child Posttraumatic Stress Reaction Index (Nader, 1992). Several other studies are now in progress (Yule, 1998).

Some mental health problems may prevail in this part of Europe. In the hospital in Osijek (Koic et al., 1992) for instance, severe problems with the use of alcohol were seen at least as frequently as posttraumatic stress disturbances. Excessive use of alcohol is mentioned by other authors as well and appears to be considerable compared to the alcohol consumption in other societies (Jukic, Hotujac, & Mandzic, 1995; Lang, 1991; Markovic, Markovic, & Glavic, 1995; O'Brien, 1994). The high acceptance of alcohol in the former Yugoslavian society is only one example of considering the importance of complaints and behavior within a cultural context.

Mental Health Services in and after the War

Although primary health care services in the former federal Republic were well developed, the development of psychotherapy and other mental health care services was rather restricted. The number of psychologists working in clinical practice was limited and not comparable to the number of colleagues in the industrial and educational fields (Marinkovic, 1992). Health care was mainly provided in hospitals, where only specialized medical doctors had high status. In order to receive professional help for mental health problems one had to be referred to a neuropsychiatrist. His (or her) help was mostly restricted to severe disturbances. Hence, seeking psychological help was stigmatizing. Treatment usually involved hospitalization and the prescription of psychotropic drugs. The conditions of patient wards, as well as patient services, were often quite poor.

Due to the war, health services have been severely reduced in the various states. In Serbia, for instance, war expenses and economical boycotts have cut health services drastically (Popovic, 1996).

It is also important to emphasize that health care in war stricken areas has to go beyond the individual level. Western thinking on health and illness is very much based on the individual human being as the basic unit of study. The theoretical emphasis is on intrapersonal processes, in isolation from the social, political, and cultural context. The prevailing view on the responses to trauma as individual centred processes is in line with this tradition. Bracken and colleagues (1995) accuse Western mental health professionals of arrogance if they consider the self and its relationship with the outside world as a given. Traumatic experiences and their implications should be conceptualized in terms of an interaction between the victim and his or her surroundings (Mirowsky & Ross, 1989; Summerfield, 1995a). The ruining of community cohesiveness and political solidarity will have an impact on the way the atrocities of war are experienced and handled. This is obvious in the case of a civil war, where neighbors do not trust each other any longer and communities fall apart. Recovery over time will be dependent upon the reconstruction of social and economic networks, cultural institutions, and a respect for human rights (Bracken et al., 1995).

Despite criticism, trauma is a concept that can appropriately bridge the gap between the single individual and the surrounding society (Herman, 1992; Kleber, Figley, & Gersons, 1995). Trauma threatens the individual's sense of self and the predictability of the world. Basic beliefs in trust, confidence, and the connectedness with other people are shattered (Janoff-Bulman, 1992). Helping people exposed to traumatic events is, in principle, a matter of restoring the bond between the individual and the surrounding society. It is particularly this perspective that is increasingly being used in health care activities in former Yugoslavia. A considerable number of interventions during and after the war, in which individual and collective approaches were integrated, have been conducted (Ajdukovic, 1997). Interventions have a larger chance to succeed when they are family, group, or community oriented (see Popovic, 1996).

☐ Implications of Acknowledging Cultural Diversity

The history of this part of the Balkans tells a complicated and often bloody story. Different empires have ruled over different regions in different times. They have left significant cultural marks on the inhabitants of its territories, that can be recognized in preserved early literature, poetry, and folk songs. Differences between people were stressed more than ever when, after a period of four decades of coexistence within a Federal Republic, feelings of nationalism increased. The way to war seemed irreversible when nationalistic leaders propagated a new ideology, using old painful World War II memories to divide a society with large economical frustrations. Propaganda enlarged the suggested differences among the peoples. But, in fact, the only difference between a Bosnian, a Croat, and a Serb is sometimes nothing more than a difference in family name.

Especially in war, people who come to ask for help, tell stories that are full of the traumatic events they have experienced. Not only did they witness the killing of a neighbor by a sniper, they were also frequently frightened by the alarm that announced bombardments or by the constant fear of snipers. In the immediate postwar period, it is hard to rebuild a new life, because close relatives have either died or fled and because there is no money, and jobs are hard to obtain. In addition, the church, mosque, or club where one would find support among people sharing the same religion or the same dedication, has been destroyed. Being confronted with war takes away all certainty and order in daily life. Intervening with programs based on modern (Western) psychology and psychiatry only makes sense when there is a focus on comprehensive intervention in addition to individual treatment. Also, it is important to respect the strengths and resources within people to cope with their experiences, even in the horrendous circumstances of war in a shattered and demolished country.

The recent war emphasized differences among people, neighbors, or family members according to their ethnoreligious belonging. Due to the war, collective self-images seem to have undergone permanent changes. Formerly Croats, Serbs, Bosnjaks, and the other groups of former Yugoslavian inhabitants used to live together while practicing different customs as well as joining in festivities and ceremonies. Time will tell how the different communities will be able to live, trade, and communicate together.

☐ Endnote

[1]Both authors have visited Bosnia-Herzegovina in recent years as participants in the Mental Health Project of Médecins sans Frontières (MSF). The impressions gained from these visits have inspired this text. The staff of MSF-Holland, in Amsterdam (The Netherlands), Sarajevo (Bosnia-Herzegovina), and Zenica (Bosnia-Herzegovina) are gratefully acknowl-

edged for providing facilities and hospitality. The authors thank Maggie Stroebe, Goran Matković, Asja Mandžić, Lidija Balabanović, and Mihela Murovec for their valuable comments.

☐ References

Ajdukovic, D. (Ed.). (1997). *Trauma recovery training: Lessons learned.* Zagreb: Society for Psychological Assistance.

Ajdukovic, D., & Ljubotina, D. (1995, May). Posttraumatic and depressive symptomatology in refugees: Correlates, predictors and changes. Paper presented at the Fourth European Conference on Traumatic Stress, Paris, France.

American Psychiatric Association (1994). *Diagnostic and statistical manual of mental disorders, fourth edition (DSM-IV).* Washington, DC: APA.

Bacova, V. (1993). Influence of Eastern-Western European state citizenship and ethnic majority-minority membership on the perceiving of ethnic concepts. *Studia Psycholica, 35,* 288–289.

Becker, D. (1995). The deficiency of the concept of post-traumatic stress disorder when dealing with victims of human rights violations. In R. J. Kleber, C. R. Figley, and B. P. R. Gersons (Eds.), *Beyond trauma: Cultural and societal dynamics* (pp. 99–110). New York: Plenum Press.

Berry, J. W. (1994). Acculturation and psychological adaptation: An overview. In A. Bouvy (Ed.), *Journeys into Cross-Cultural Psychology* (pp. 129–141). Amsterdam: Swets & Zeitlinger.

Bilanankis, N., Pappas, E., Baldic, V., & Jokic, M. (1997). Post-traumatic stress disorder in a refugee camp in Serbia. *Torture, 7,* 17–20.

Botev, N. (1994). Where East meets West: Ethnic intermarriage in the former Yugoslavia, 1962 to 1989. *American Sociological Review, 59,* 461–480.

Bracken, P. J., Giller, J. E., & Summerfield, D. (1995). Psychological responses to war and atrocity: The limitations of current concepts. *Social Science and Medicine, 40*(8), 1073–1082.

Bramsen, I. (1995). *The long-term psychological adjustment of World War II survivors in the Netherlands.* Delft: Eburon Press.

Bringa, T. (1995). *Being Muslim the Bosnian way.* Princeton, NJ: Princeton University Press.

Brom, D., Kleber, R. J., & Witztum, E. (1991). The prevalence of posttraumatic psychopathology in the general and the clinical population. *Israel Journal of Psychiatry and Related Sciences, 28*(4), 53–63.

Centraal Orgaan opvang Asielzoekers. (1995). *Former Yugoslavia. Information on prominent countries of origine of asylumseekers in the Netherlands.* Rijswijk: COA.

Cop, J., Ivanovic, J., & Matek, P. (1992). Psychic disorders in war casualties. *Psychologische Beitrage, 34,* 234–241.

Curtis, P. (1995). Urban household coping strategies during war: Bosnia-Herzegovina. *Disasters, 19*(1), 68–73.

Delimar, D., Korenjak, P., Sivik, T., & Delimar, N. (1995). The effect of different traumatic experiences on the development of post-traumatic stress disorder. *Military Medicine, 160,* 635–639.

Denich, B. (1994). Dismembering Yugoslavia: Nationalist ideologies and the symbolic revival of genocide. *American Ethnologist, 21*(2), 367–390.

Denitch, B. D. (1994). *Ethnic nationalism: The tragic death of Yugoslavia.* Minneapolis, MN: University of Minnesota Press.

Detrez, R. (1996). *De sloop van Joegoslavië. Relaas van een boedelscheiding* [The demolition of Yugoslavia. Account of the division of an estate]. Antwerpen, Belgium: Hadewijch.

Dyregrov, A., Kuterovac, G., & Barath, A. (1996). Factor analysis of the impact of event scale with children in war. *Scandinavian Journal of Psychology, 37,* 339–350.

Eisenbruch, M. (1991). From post-traumatic stress disorder to cultural bereavement: Diagnosis of Southeast Asian refugees. *Social Science & Medicine, 33,* 673–680.

Eterovich, F. H., & Spalatin, C. (1976). *Croatia: Land, people, culture (Vol. 1 & 2).* Toronto, Canada: University of Toronto Press.

Eth, S., & Pynoos, R. (1985). Interaction of trauma and grief in childhood. In S. Eth and R. S. Pynoos (Eds.), *Posttraumatic Stress Disorder in children* (pp. 169–183). Washington DC: American Psychiatric Press.

General Framework Agreement (1995). Fact sheet released by the Office of the Spokesman, US Department of State, November 30, 1995. [On-line]. Available: *http://www.nato.int/ifor/gfa/gfa-summ.htm.*

Glenny, M. (1996). *The fall of Yugoslavia.* London: Penguin Books.

Halpern, J. M., & Kerewsky-Halpern, B. (1972). *A Serbian village in historical perspective.* New York: Holt, Rinehart and Winston, Inc.

Herman, J. L. (1992). *Trauma and recovery.* New York: Basic Books.

Horowitz, M. J., Wilner, N., & Alvarez, W. (1979). Impact of event scale: A measure of subjective stress. *Psychosomatic Medicine, 41,* 209–218.

Hotujac, L., Vukelja, D., & Mahnik, M. (1992). Some social-demographic, psychopathologic and clinic characteristics of psychiatrically treated soldiers of the Croatian army. *Psychologische Beitrage, 34,* 224–233.

Janoff-Bulman, R. (1992). *Shattered assumptions. Towards a new psychology of trauma.* New York: The Free Press.

Jelavich, B. (1983a). *History of the Balkans. Eighteenth and nineteenth centuries (Vol. 1).* New York: Cambridge University Press.

Jelavich, B. (1983b). *History of the Balkans. Twentieth century (Vol. 2).* New York: Cambridge University Press.

Jukic, V., Hotujac, L., & Mandzic, N. (1995). Mental health care in Croatia. *Socijalna Psihijatrija, 23,* 23–34.

Keilson, H. (1979). *Sequentielle Traumatisierung bei Kindern.* Stuttgart: Enke Verlag.

Kleber, R. J., & Brom, D. in collaboration with Defares, P. B. (1992). *Coping with trauma: Theory, prevention and treatment.* Amsterdam/Berwyn, Pennsylvania: Swets & Zeitlinger International.

Kleber, R. J., Figley, C. R., & Gersons, B. P. R. (Eds.). (1995). *Beyond trauma. Cultural and societal dynamics.* New York: Plenum Press.

Kleinman, A. (1986). *Social origins of distress and disease: Depression, neurasthenia and pain in modern China.* New Haven: Yale University Press.

Kleinman, A., & Cohen, A. (1997). Psychiatry's global challenge. An evolving crisis in the developing world signals the need for a better understanding of the links between culture and mental disorders. *Scientific American (3),* 86–89.

Koic, O., Delalle-Zebic, M., & Bosnic, D. (1992). Psychic disorders among Croatian soldiers from the East Slavonian front hospitalised in the Psychiatric Clinic Osijek. *Psychologische Beitrage, 34,* 270–279.

Krug, P. (1991). *Oost-Europa in de spiegel: cultuurhistorische en literaire verkenningen* [Eastern Europe in the mirror: Cultural and literal explorations]. Kampen, the Netherlands: Kok Agora.

Kuterovac, G., Dyregrov, A., & Stuvland, R. (1994). Children in war: A silent majority under stress. *British Journal of Medical Psychology, 67,* 363–375.

Lang, B. (1991). Problemi pijenja alkoholnih pica, alkoholizma i drugih ovisnosti u ratnim uvjetima. [Problems of drinking alcoholic drinks, alcoholism, and other addictions in wartime]. *Socijalna Psihijatrija, 19,* 325–334.

Lifton, R. J. (1979). *The broken connection: On death and the continuity of life.* New York: Simon and Schuster.

Malcolm, N. (1994). *Bosnia: A short history.* London: Papermac.

Manson, S. M. (1997). Cross-cultural and multiethnic assessment of trauma. In J. P. Wilson and T. M. Keane (Eds.), *Assessing psychological trauma and PTSD* (pp. 239–266). New York: The Guilford Press.

Marinkovic, K. (1992). The history of psychology in former Yugoslavia: An overview. *Journal of the History of the Behavioral Sciences, 28,* 340–351.

Markovic, H., Markovic, A., & Glavic, N. (1995). Alkoholizam tijekom domovinskog rata u Hrvatskoj. [Alcoholism during the war in Dubrovnik]. *Socijalna Psihijatrija, 23,* 79–87.

Marsella, A. J., Friedman, M. J., Gerrity, E. T., & Scurfield, A. J. (Eds.). (1996). *Ethnocultural aspects of posttraumatic stress disorder.* Washington: American Psychological Association.

McMaster, P., McMaster, H. J., & Southall, D. P. (1996). Personal child health record and advice booklet programme in Tuzla, Bosnia Herzegovina. *Journal of the Royal Society of Medicine, 89,* 202–204.

Mirowsky, J., & Ross, C. E. (1989). Psychiatric diagnosis as reified instrument. *Journal of Health and Social Behavior, 30,* 11–25.

Mooren, G. T. M., & Kleber, R. J. (1996). *Gezondheid en herinneringen aan de oorlogsjaren van Indische jeugdige oorlogsgetroffenen* [Health and memories of the war among child survivors from the former Dutch Indies]. Utrecht: Utrecht University.

Mooren, G. T. M., Kleber, R. J., & Jong, K. de (1997). *The MSF mental health project in Bosnia-Herzegovina: A preliminary report on the effects and coverage of the MSF counselling centres.* Unpublished report. Utrecht University & MSF Holland.

Nader, K. (1997). Childhood traumatic loss: The interaction of trauma and grief. In C. R. Figley, B. E. Bride, & N. Mazza (Eds.), *Death and trauma: The traumatology of grieving* (pp. 17–41). Washington, DC: Taylor & Francis.

Nesvadbova, L. (1995, May). Posttraumatic stress syndrome disorder in the group of teenagers from Bosnia. Paper presented at the Fourth European Conference on Traumatic Stress, Paris, France.

O'Brien, L. S. (1994). What will be the psychiatric consequences of the war in Bosnia? *British Journal of Psychiatry, 164,* 443–447.

Parkes, C. M. (1986). *Bereavement: Studies of grief in adult life.* London: Tavistock.

Pecjak, V. (1987). Yugoslavia. In A. R. Gilgen and C. K. Gilgen (Eds.), *International Handbook of Psychology* (pp. 574–586). New York: Greenwood Press.

Pecjak, V. (1993). Verbal associations with sociopolitical concepts in three historical periods. *Studia Psychologica, 35,* 284–287.

Pecjak, V. (1994). War cruelty in the former Yugoslavia and its psychological correlates. *Politics and the Individual, 4,* 75–84.

Pecjak, V., & Polic, M. (1996). Psychology in Slovenia. *European Psychologist, 1,* 231–233.

Popovic, M. (1996). Refugees in the federal republic of Yugoslavia: Present situation and psychological support. *Medicine, Conflict and Survival, 12,* 325–332.

Port, M. van de. (1994). *Het einde van de wereld. Beschaving, redeloosheid en zigeunercafés in Servië* [The end of the world. Civilization, reasonless and gypsy cafes in Serbia]. Amsterdam: Babylon-De Geus.

Richter, D. (1994). Croatian experience on the care for the displaced and refugee children. *Croatian Medical Journal, 35*(1), 8–11.

Schierup, C.-U., & Alund, A. (1987). *Will they still be dancing? Integration and ethnic transformation among Yugoslav immigrants in Scandinavia.* Göteborg: Graphic Systems.

Siber, I., German, D. B., & Millsaps, S. (1994). Yugoslavia divided: Nationalism, ethnic rivalry and war. *Politics and the Individual, 4,* 85–94.

Silber, L., & Little, A. (1995). *The death of Yugoslavia.* London: Penguin Books.

Singleton, F. (1985). *A short history of the Yugoslav people.* Cambridge: Cambridge University Press.

Summerfield, D. (1995a). Adressing human response to war and atrocity. In R. J. Kleber, C. R. Figley, and B. P. R. Gersons (Eds.), *Beyond trauma. Cultural and societal dynamics* (pp. 17–29). New York: Plenum Press.

Summerfield, D. (1995b). Raising the dead: War, reparation, and the politics of memory. *British Medical Journal, 311,* 495–497.

Terr, L. C. (1991). Childhood traumas: An outline and overview. *American Journal of Psychiatry, 148,* 10–20.

World Bank (1996). Countries and regions. [On-line]. Available: http://www.worldbank.org/html/Welcome.html.

World Health Organization. (1992). *International classification of diseases* (Tenth Revision: ICD-10). Geneva, Switzerland: World Health Organization.

World Health Organization. (1996). War and health: Crossing the bridge to peace. Annual report 1995. [On-line]. Available: http://www.who.dk.

World Wide Web (1997). The scream of Tuzla. [On-line]. Available: http://www.hr/tuzla/english/massacre.html.

Yehuda, R., & McFarlane, A. C. (1995). Conflict between current knowledge about post-traumatic stress disorder and its original conceptual basis. *American Journal of Psychiatry, 152,* 1705–1713.

Yule, W. (1998). World veterans consider needs of children and families. *Traumatic Stresspoints, 12,* 1–11.

Zivcic, I. (1993). Emotional reactions of children to war stress in Croatia. *Journal of American Academy of Child and Adolescent Psychiatry, 32*(4), 709–713.

9

CHAPTER   Dan Bar-On

Israeli Society Between the Culture of Death and the Culture of Life

☐ Introduction

Israeli society has had to struggle for physical and mental survival since the moment of its establishment. Seven wars and several additional armed conflicts have created a reality of death and dying as a major theme in this society. In contrast to the urge to live and survive, a collective legend of "dying for our country" developed during the early phases of Zionism, somewhat similarly to the medieval Jewish Ashkenazi legend of Kidush Hashem (dying for one's faith in God) and to the myth of collective suicide at Massada after the destruction of the Second Temple, during the Roman era. The peace process, especially the Peace Accord with the Palestine Liberation Organization (PLO) at Oslo, introduced into this struggle for survival and its mythology a counterpoint, strengthening the wish for life and living. Though peace has always been the dream, actual confrontation with the psychological implication of redefining oneself not through an enemy is not at all easy for the Israeli society. In this chapter the culture of dying and the culture of living are described and presented as two polarities between which Israeli society has been trying to find its way during the last decades of this millennium.

☐ Cultural Background:
Trauma and Its Recognition

Trauma in the Middle East is deeply (though not only) associated with the bitter struggle of the last 100 years between Arabs and Jews. It is difficult to summarize this long struggle in a few sentences. I will concentrate in this section on the trauma associated with the Palestinian-Israeli conflict. There were about 600,000 Jews and a similar number of Palestinians living west of the Jordan river when the United Nations decided to establish 2 national states in this territory on November 29, 1947, thereby ending the British Mandate (which started after WWI). The Jewish population, which immigrated to Palestine during the last 100 years[1], came from all over the world. Most of the Palestinians[2] lived in this region and some immigrated into it from neighboring countries.[3] The national consciousness of both groups grew systematically in a kind of *implicated relations,* while focusing on the conflictual aspects of the commonly claimed territory (Portugali, 1996).

The Jews viewed their immigration (in Hebrew, *Aliya,* going up) as an act of revival of their national home, which had been destroyed about 2,000 ago by the Romans. They tried for many years to ignore the Palestinian population as a separate social and recognized national entity. Most of the Palestinian leadership soon viewed the Jewish immigration as an intrusion of an alien group, similar to previous intrusions of conquerors or colonialists (Crusaders, Mamelukes, British, and French). Though there were several efforts to develop peaceful relationships between these two developing groups, most of the history of the last hundred years can be characterized by indifference and animosity of two geographically and economically interwoven, but culturally separate, groups, who are at the same time also quite diversified internally.

The Israeli and Palestinian national groups are very different in many respects: historical heritage, religious belief, cultural linkage, socioeconomic status, and community setup. They share, however, some similarities. Though they both come from ancient cultural and religious traditions, they both lack a modern, independent heritage of statehood. This means that they have had to develop the tradition of statehood during, and to some extent through, the violent struggle with the rival national group.[4] Psychologically, they both tended to define themselves as victims of their enemy, which I call their *relevant other,* and through which they reconstructed their own collective identity (Portugali, 1996).

After the UN decision in 1947, the Israelis viewed the Palestinians as part of the hostile Arab countries, like Syria and Egypt. These were later heavily supported, from 1954 on, by the USSR, thereby slowly making the Middle East part of the global Cold War. The Palestinians viewed the

Jews as a powerful hostile group, supported initially by the Western countries, the USSR, and, of course, the Western Jewry. While the Israeli population enjoyed wide political support from the Jewish Diaspora after WWII (mainly in the United States), the violent conflict created a Palestinian Diaspora, which slowly gained strength in the West and in Arab countries such as Lebanon, Jordan, and Kuwait. The Palestinian Diaspora was manipulated by the Arab countries both during the power struggle with Israel and among themselves.

The Palestinian and Israeli conflict spread to different spheres of life (threat to personal safety, ownership of land, housing, and territory, education and cultural autonomy, control over scarce resources such as water, international recognition, and trade). Psychologically, each group addressed the other as the aggressor and saw itself mainly as the victim. For many years (1954–1989) this situation was manipulated by the struggle between West and East, thereby reinforcing the clear cut conflict as perceived by each group. Only after the fall of the communist block, in 1989, and the lack of military resolution (during the Intifada), did the leaders of both sides finally decide to put aside hatred and ideas of elimination and to try and move toward recognition and coexistence. The Jewish population, which arrived in this region prior to World War II, was selective and idealistically oriented toward Zionism. They believed in the secular revival of Jewish national identity in the ancient homeland, after many generations of exile and Diaspora. This had been the dream and subject of daily prayers of religious Jews throughout the years of exile. Now it became a modern, secular vision in light of the pogroms in Eastern Europe at the turn of the century and their disappointment in assimilation in the Western European countries (Kimmerling, 1983). The Zionist movement brought with it the revival of Hebrew as a spoken language (not only as the language of the Holy Scriptures) and the vision of a new, strong Jew who could cultivate and defend his land and himself. This vision was the negation of the weak Jew of the Diaspora who did not live on his own land and could not defend himself. This image was to some extent an internalization of the anti-Semitic perception and hatred of the Jewish middleman in European countries.

One of the first heroes who exemplified this modern, Zionist vision was Joseph Trumpeldor, a Jewish–Russian officer who had lost his arm in the Russian–Japanese war at the turn of the century. He later immigrated to Palestine and settled at Tel Hai (the hill of life, in Hebrew) at the northern edge of the Jewish settlement. He fulfilled the ideal of life by working hard, cultivating the land during the day, and guarding the settlement at night. He was fatally injured by an Arab mob in 1917, and became known for saying shortly before he died: "It is good to die for our country." The collective myth, which developed around this sentence can teach us quite a lot about the atmosphere of those early days. The Jewish Israelis are surrounded by enemies and have to struggle, physically and mentally, for their life and survival. They can succeed only if they are willing to sacrifice a lot, even their lives (Zrubavel, 1986).

This myth of the new secular hero was not such an alien notion for the Jewish heritage. It was, in a way, a natural continuation to earlier heroes and heroes to come such as Bar-Kochva—the Jew who rebelled against the Romans after the destruction of the Second Temple—or the heroes of Massada who committed suicide rather than fall into the hands of the pagan Roman captors. To these were later added other heroes: the Warsaw Ghetto fighters and the Sabra[5] of the 1948 war. It is interesting to see how heroism can be reinterpreted over time. Bar-Kochva was redefined during the late seventies by an Israeli general and historian, Yehoshafat Harkabi. He wrote of Bar-Kochva as being a stupid, fanatical leader who, through his rebellion, caused the destruction of the Jewish population in Judea and the death of about a million peaceful Jewish farmers. Harkabi wrote this thesis at a time when fanaticism again threatened to take over, this time within the modern Israeli society after the shock of the 1973 war. He was part of the moderate Israeli leadership which looked for symbols to warn Israelis of self-destruction (Zrubavel, 1986).[6]

In the early days of Zionism, Bar-Kochva and the fighters of Massada were the symbols of heroism. There was little room for emotional expression of fear or helplessness. Those who could not cope and left the new settlements (or even returned to their homeland) were seen as traitors. Some even committed suicide. Only recently have we learned that during the War of Independence, battle shock of Israeli soldiers did not exist as an acknowledged phenomena. There were only three small and secret units who took care of a few scores of cases, and there is no documentation left of the activity of these units (Wiztum, Levi, Gernak, & Kotler, 1989). The knowledge was there from a few World War I physicians who even wrote about it in a local medical journal in 1948. Officially, however, no Palmach or Haganna[7] soldier was formally treated for battle shock or post traumatic stress disorder (PTSD) (Rom & Bar-On, in press). Those who suffered from such phenomena had to cope with them alone. Some were given labels. They were called degenerates, or cowards or even people who vanished, never to return to the battlefield. In a few cases there are reports of battle reaction and fatigue which was covered up by comrades, enabling the inflicted people to return to their units, unnoticed.

A similar Spartan spirit also existed in the early Kibbutzim, which were the backbone of Israeli pioneering society before the establishment of the State of Israel. Children were brought up in children's houses in harsh conditions, under an educational ideology which emphasized physical strength and saw the expression of emotions, especially fear, as weakness. Psychological clinical services were developed relatively late, mainly to answer the need of children who did not adjust to this harsh and sometimes extreme lack of emotional support. As long as one could cope with the harsh conditions and emotional restraint, they were surrounded and supported by a strong collective bonding (Lanir, 1990).

At the same time, a secular culture of grief and immortalization developed around the heroic losses. It stemmed originally from the traditional Jewish religious rituals of the weekly, monthly, and annual memorial days, including special mourning services and prayers. These are still, for many, the major personal and collective way of expressing grief and bereavement. For example, there is an almost sacred ritual of burial in the Jewish and Israeli tradition. First of all, the bones of the dead have to be buried in a grave. Israel went out of its way to negotiate the return of its dead soldiers during the different wars, even at the price of releasing confined Arab saboteurs. Within the secular part of the society a whole spectrum of other forms of mourning rituals developed, from military practices of memorial days accompanied by poems of Nathan Alterman and Yehuda Amichai, to spiritual sessions of talking with the dead and making them become alive again. These examples represent the extreme form of the culture of death and dying within the secular society of the State of Israel (Wiztum, Malkinson & Rubin, 1993).

During the years of the Israeli national consensus (1948–1982), the culture of bereavement was heavily supported by the state, which psychologically and economically assisted the war widows and orphans, but also heavily burdened them with a normative double bind (Granot, 1976). When the national polarization broke out, especially during the Lebanon war and the Intifada, disputes arose also on the uniformity of grief and mourning rituals. For example, should families be allowed to add personal writings to the standard military tombstone wording? This ritual has recently become the topic of an emotional dispute, reaching even the court, as families demand that they be able to decide what will be written, which stone to choose, and other issues. This became especially disputable for family members of those killed in military accidents, who did not agree that the standard wording of "died while fulfilling his duties" be used.

Similarly, the political dispute between left and right caused extreme opposite emotional reactions to terrorist attacks. While representatives of the extreme right would try to make political gains by inflaming emotional reactions like "death to all Arabs," the political left tried to interpret these acts as a sign that reconciliation had to occur and thereby tried to strengthen the moderate part of the Palestinian society before it became too late. Only during the Gulf war, when the Iraqi Scuds fell on Tel

Aviv while Palestinian citizens danced on their roofs in joy, did the two sides unite in a reaction of anger and despair (Portugali, 1996).

To the original internal and external conditions one has to add the outburst of World War II with the Holocaust and extermination of European Jewry. Suddenly, the European families of those who had immigrated to Palestine from Poland or Russia, as well as other European countries, vanished in the catastrophe—the magnitude of which became known only after it was over. People could not imagine what was going on under the Nazi regime and thought of the events in terms of another pogrom (Segev, 1992). When the first survivors arrived in the late 1940s, many people were in shock and reacted with guilt, shame, and mistrust: "Why did you survive and so many die?" "Why did you go like sheep to the slaughter and did not try to fight?" They were trying to make some sense of the void, imposing their current self-image on the European context. They could not imagine how different it had become from what they remembered. These were also the days prior to the establishment of the State of Israel, during violent conflict with the Arabs, and thus there was not much room for understanding and working through such differences (Hadar, 1991).

A deep cleavage of pain and misunderstanding developed between the two groups (the Sabras and the Holocaust survivors), which has taken two generations to surface (Bar-On, 1995a; Davidson, 1980). For example, two students at Ben-Gurion University researched the early period of a kibbutz in which one of the students lived (Keren & Almaliach, 1994). They found that the kibbutz was composed of two groups: a group of about 40 Sabras who had started the kibbutz and a group of similar size of young survivors of the Holocaust who joined the kibbutz shortly before the 1948 war. The two groups fought together during the war and were taken into captivity by the Jordanian army. During the period of captivity the survivors were due to be granted full membership (after a year of being candidates). However, the Sabra veterans voted against the change in status because the Holocaust survivors were not good enough for that.

"They were good enough to fight and to be together in captivity," write Keren and Almaliach (1994, pp. 111–146), but not to become full members of the Kibbutz because they came from there. This traumatic experience was formally corrected long after they returned from captivity and reestablished their kibbutz. Informally, the survivors were still feeling not good enough in the late 1980s and early 1990s, when they already had children. The latter did not know their personal stories from the Holocaust. This is an extreme example of the kind of emotions that were not acknowledged between subcultures within the dominant Ashkenazi Jewry[8]. But this was only part of the story of the tribal ego system which evolved within the Israeli society during its early days (Moses, 1993).

The establishment of the State of Israel changed many things. A massive *aliya* (wave of immigration) brought to the young state hundreds of thousands of Jews, mainly from the Arabic countries (North Africa and Asia). This was not the idealistically oriented immigration of the 1920s and the 1930s. These were mostly families of traditional background, stemming from a very different cultural and socioeconomic origin. These were Sephardic Jews who differed from the Ashkenazi Jews in many ways. While the European Ashkenazi Jewish culture developed mainly among Christians, the Sephardic Jewry developed mainly among Muslims.[9] For example, they preached different Jewish philosophies of life and death during the Middle Ages. The Sephardic Maronites were Jews who converted to Christianity under duress. Many of them returned to the Jewish faith after two generations. During the Middle Ages quite a few of the Ashkenazi Jews committed suicide for Kiddush Hashem (dying for the sacred belief in God). There were also other differences in terms of obedience to religious laws and practices. The Sephardic Jew viewed these laws as serving them as human beings, while the orthodox Ashkenazi Jew saw the laws of God as being above themselves as people (Wiztum, Malkinson, & Rubin, 1993).

Now, the new immigrants were swallowed up by the young society which was determined to impose its own values and ideals—some of which were different from those of the immigrants. Some of the newcomers were placed in outposts near the borders and had to learn to practice modern agriculture. Others were recruited into the army. Some of the wealthy and honored heads of large traditional clans found themselves planting trees or unemployed and living on social security. The continuous military and economic struggle for survival demanded the primacy of a strong collective identity and mission and these were interpreted within the dominant discourse of Eastern European Jewry (Segev, 1992). Within the general dominant trend dissonant undertones could be recognized within the Ashkenazi culture itself. For example, shortly after the state was established, religious women were released from army service. So were some extremely orthodox Jews who were allowed to study instead. Still, most of the feelings of pain and bitterness dissonant to the ethos of the Sabra had to be repressed and have been denied or overlooked for many years.

The Yom Kippur war of 1973, with its thousands of casualties, created a manifest crisis in the national ethos of the Sabra. The surprise of the attack and initial success of the Egyptian and Syrian armies found many young soldiers in the position of begging for their lives, rather than dying for the common cause. This, in retrospect, suggested that survival in contrast to fighting may have been legitimate also within the context of the Holocaust. This was accompanied by a crisis of trust in the labor government and the rise to power of the right wing parties, in 1977, who were supported massively by the Sephardic population. The Sephardic population had felt suppressed by the labor government, as the major representative of the dominant East European culture, and had now begun to express its voice also on the national political level.

The 1973 war, trauma, and loss helped, paradoxically, introduce the phenomena of nonphysical injuries in war into the public consciousness. It was the first war in which many soldiers suffered and were officially treated for battle shock (Wiztum, et al., 1989). A special military unit was established to treat the psychological after-effects (PTSD) and it be-came legitimate to acknowledge mental trauma as part of the war, not only physical injury or death in the family (Solomon, 1993). Quite a few soldiers were later identified to have suffered from battle shock during the Lebanon war in 1982 (though, objectively speaking, there were less military reasons for trauma in comparison to the 1973 war), because the military unit of professionals was there to absorb these cases and treat them accordingly. Interestingly, the 1987–1993 Intifada created again an adverse effect in this respect. Again, there were no soldiers who were recognized as suffering from mental trauma. It became a political dispute (for and against acknowledging the rights of the Palestinians) and psy-chologists were accused of misusing their professional role when they claimed that soldiers were suffering, emotionally, by participating in mil-itary actions against the Palestinian uprising (Bar-On, 1992; Bar-On, Yitzaki-Verner, & Amir, 1996).

Today, Israel is loaded with layers of trauma which have been trans-mitted intergenerationally (Bar-On, 1995). At each of these critical points—the Holocaust, the War of Independence, the mass immigration during the fifties, the 1973 war, the Lebanon war, the Intifada and the recent terrorist attacks on civilians—new sources of loss, pain, and trauma were created and had to be acknowledged and worked through (Wiztum, Malkinson, & Rubin, 1993). They nourished the struggle be-tween the myth of life and survival, on the one hand and the myth of death and dying, on the other. But the world outside the Middle East has changed and the latter myth receives less and less external support. Fi-nally, the peace process in the Middle East calls for a reevaluation of the relationship between these two myths.

☐ The Peace Process: Trauma or Relief?

What is the impact of the peace process on the question of trauma and its relief in Israeli society? The process actually began in 1977 with the visit of Sadat in Jerusalem and the Camp David Agreement between Egypt and Israel. It reached the unimaginable climax with the Oslo Accord between Rabin and Arafat in 1993. Suddenly, bitter enemies began to see each other as potential partners. The Palestinian–Israeli Declaration of Principles of September 1993 and subsequent agreements initiated a major shift of attitude of the leaders of the two peoples who had been in bitter conflict over this small piece of land known as Palestine and Israel for more than 100 years. The leaders of both national entities decided to recognize the other's right to exist and to search for a compromise which would enable each group to begin living in freedom and peace alongside the other. This dramatic shift in the formal attitude of the leaders of the Israelis and the Palestinians clearly reflected the hope of the majority of the Palestinian and Israeli people, but it was not accepted without severe resistance on both sides.

The peace process brought about two main forms of discourse within both societies. The first, a euphoric kind of discourse, emphasizes the new possibilities for coexistence and peace between the two peoples who have lived through 100 years of conflict and bloodshed. The second, a pessimistic kind of discourse, emphasizes that actually nothing has changed in the relationship between the two societies. There is no open dialogue between these two kinds of discourse. We claim that both kinds of discourse reveal the limited readiness of the wider population to acknowledge the difficulty of moving out of the long phase of violent conflict, with its accompanying fantasies of a total victory for one side and total submission of the other, into a new and more open approach. This new approach requires acknowledging the other and testing the realistic possibilities of coexistence.

The paradox is that the Oslo agreement created a leadership of both peoples which sounded more optimistic than the average person in the Israeli or Palestinian streets. In addition to the top down political process which was now taking place, a bottom up social and psychological process became crucial for the successful implementation of the peace process. In that respect, it became clear that within both national entities there are still extreme groups who are not willing or able to make this shift and continue to ignore the legitimate existence of the other national entity. These extreme attitudes are represented by some religious–nationalist Jewish groups (Gush Emunim) and religious–nationalist Islamic groups (the Hammas and Jihad).

These groups have done their best to sabotage the first stages of the peace process through reciprocal acts of terror and delegitimation. This activity reached a climax with the assassination of Israeli Prime Minister, Yitzhak Rabin, on November 4, 1995, by a young extremist of a Jewish religious–nationalist group, with the Goldstein massacre in Hebron, and with the terrorist attacks in Jerusalem and Tel Aviv in February 1996 by Palestinian extremist groups. All these assassins hoped that their acts of violence would stop the peace process.

Still, resistance was not exclusively the property of the extreme funda-
mentalists. Within the Israeli public there is a real fear of the ambiguity
created by the peace process. This came to international attention with
the elections of June 1996, when the right wing parties, which originally
opposed the Oslo Accord, gained national support and won the elections. It is still an open question if the change of political leadership in Israel has also reversed the process begun in Oslo. Netanyahu, the new
Prime Minister, though he has declared that he will stick to the Oslo
agreements, has up to now not followed the same spirit of mutuality
with the Palestinians which the former prime ministers of the labor
party (Rabin and Peres) started to introduce.[10]

How can we understand how people who have been conflict ridden
for so long, who have carried such a load of unresolved traumas, can resist the hopeful prospect of the peace process? Is it not a paradox that
when the dream becomes a reality, people begin to be frightened and
hesitant? It probably depends on which perspective one holds of such
events. Economists or lawyers may not have a rational explanation for
such a trend, but psychologists do have a ready made perspective for
such paradoxical trends. The responses within the populations to the
peace process suggest that many Israeli and Palestinian people are not
yet ready for mutual acts of dialogue and reconciliation (Bar-On,
1995b). They are still too involved in the conflict on all levels: emotional, cognitive, and behavioral.

Further, Israeli society, being so committed to its struggle for life, and
living through death and dying, is undergoing a severe crisis of identity. It
is the first time since the destruction of the Second Temple and the exile
into the Diaspora that Jewish identity may not center around the struggle
with enemies, the struggle for survival. This is not an easy transformation
for a young nation that has been so deeply involved in its fight for survival. From the myth of "good to die for our country" it now has to address a new myth of "good to live for our country" (or, ourselves) which
is very different in its demands on the collective and the individual.

This is a shift far more complex than one would expect. It is difficult
enough to develop an approach toward the other as a partner, instead of,
or at least in addition to, continuously seeing him as an enemy. It may
suggest that part of the Israeli identity constructions relied too heavily
on the continuation of this conflict and its accompanying myth of death
and dying. This identity was defined, negatively, through hatred of the
enemy, rather than positively through what they are in their own right,
irrelevant of the definition of the other. Suddenly, all the tribal egos,
which were suppressed for the sake of the overriding goal of the struggle
with the Arabs, are allowed to demand attention, as could be seen during the 1996 elections.

When, after the Oslo Accord, Israeli people were asked about their fantasies concerning war and peace (Bar-On, 1995b), different reactions were received. Some subjects wanted it "done once and for all." In Hebrew there is an expression for it: *"Zbeng vegamarnu"* which means "one blow and we finished with it" (never mind at what price or what the outcome).[11] Similarly, while talking with people after a new move toward the next round of peace talks or following the latest assault on an Israeli by an Arab (or vice versa), one heard familiar expressions of fantasies or anger and frustrations, but very little new expressions or discourse related to more moderate and realistic expectations. We interpret this as the difficulty people exhibit in disassociating themselves from their past perspective of warfare.

Certain interviewees spoke openly about their pain, their lives invested in warfare, those who got killed and how it all seems suddenly like "wasted effort and time" that did not "materialize into the expected positive outcome" (Bar-On, 1995b, p. 71). Another reaction we identified was that of floating anxiety identified by fantasies about "them" (how will they react to us after all that we have done to them?), fears about one's own people (we will never be able to integrate into the Middle East society because we are strangers here), even some fear concerning oneself (who am I if I am not the brave Israeli fighting against our enemies). Fears were usually associated with a lack of trust in the negotiating parties who may "try to solve some issues and leave us to live afterwards with all the problems" (Bar-On, Spitzer, & Bukrashov, 1996, p. 21). One person reported dreams of doomsday, in which the peace-process "turns suddenly back on us, but we will not be able anymore to defend ourselves, the way we could until now, as we already have given up our control of the territories" (Bar-On, Spitzer, & Bukrashov, 1996, p. 23).

As in PTSD (Figley, 1986; Solomon, 1993), there is a realistic aspect in each of these attitudes and emotions. However, we begin to view them as traumatic stress when they control one's perspective and do not enable a more relaxed form of reality testing. The main problem is to envision the possibility that "the future will slowly become different from the past (warfare) and from the present (ambiguity)" (p. 74). This intermediate twilight period has its own stresses, just like periods of war and conflict. Therefore, I identified it as a prepeace stress reaction (PPSR), which should be considered separately from more the familiar PTSD wartime reactions (Bar-On, 1995b).

As examples of such a prepeace traumatic reaction, some of our interviewees projected their anger at the political leadership involved in the negotiations. Certain interviewees spoke of the betrayal of the leadership that is tired of wars. Others accused them of their lack of courage to admit past mistakes: "After all, it is the same political leadership which has claimed all these years that they will never sit together with Arafat at the same table" (Bar-On, 1995b, p. 76). Both groups actually expressed the feeling that the leadership has not assisted them in constructing adequate expectations which could help them cope better with the ambiguity of the intermediate phase. "In the past leaders preached that peace will emerge only as a result of each side's strengths and victories. Now we are expected to take the perspective of the Palestinians into account" (Bar-On, 1995b, p. 76).

Some argued that only the previous leadership could help the Israeli public go through this change. However, others argued that this only added to the stress of the situation. They believed that only a fresh political leadership, disassociated from the collective memory of the past, could help the public accommodate the new changes and the ambiguity of the intermediate state. Similar projections were made towards the media and the role it plays in accommodating the peace accord. They have been accused of being pro-PLO and anti-PLO by different interviewees, relating to the same programs from opposite perspectives. It seems that certain parts of the media suffer from an additional difficulty during the ambiguous intermediate phase. It is the part of public media that tends to reinforce simplification, attempting to improve their ratings by presenting clear cut news and sensationalism. They do not view it as their task to help the public cope better with the intermediate gray zone of war and peace.

One could ask if there are more specific reasons or conditions that have made the Israeli public more vulnerable to the intermediate stage—that is more than the usual human difficulty of accommodating change and living with ambiguity. Though striving for peace for many years, Israelis have had to face many realistic hazards which, manifestly, could be associated with a future state of peace. Israel has had (and may have again in future negotiations) to give up territories, a fact that in some future scenarios could endanger its existence. Israel is still surrounded by totalitarian regimes and strong fundamentalist movements. "They" are many and "we" are few and "they" have natural resources upon which the world is dependent.

There are, however, other more latent psychological hazards in a future peace. Many Israelis will have to question and let go of the part of their self-definition that has been achieved mainly through the negative use of the other. This part of their self-definition was achieved through a consistent negative relation to the enemy. Such a definition is, psychologically speaking, more easily achieved than a positive self-determination with no available and negative other. As I mentioned earlier, Jews have been well-trained throughout the ages to define themselves by experiencing the other who persecuted and tried to exterminate them (Keen, 1987). There exists this peculiar combination of the myth of life and living and the myth of death and dying which non-Jews can hardly comprehend.[12]

Let us examine some normative rituals to which the Israeli public is still exposed. For example, education is provided to children in relation to the relevant other. They learn from a very young age that festivals are associated with the other who endangered their existence during different eras. The Jewish calendar year of celebrations in the kindergarten and elementary schools, after the initial Holy days of Atonement, continues with Hanukah (around Christmas), and the festival commemorating the success in stopping the ancient Greeks from taking over the First Temple. This is followed by Purim (usually, in March) which celebrates the success in preventing the extermination of the Jews by the Persians. Then comes Passover (in the spring) when Israelis succeeded in liberating themselves from the Egyptian oppressors, followed immediately by Holocaust Day (the Germans) and Independence Day (the Arabs), each a week apart from the other. Last on the list is the Ninth of Av, the day of the destruction of both Temples (by the Babylonians and the Romans) which happens, fortunately or not (depending on your religious and national conviction), during the summer holidays.

An anecdote (bitter or funny, depending on one's perspective) which could show this general trend was shown on TV during the first school day, September 1, 1993. The Israeli Minister of Education during that time, Prof. Amnon Rubinstein, was shown visiting a kindergarten in Jerusalem. He asked the children if they knew about the peace process and with whom the Israelis were trying to make peace. A few of them reacted spontaneously: "Of course we know." One spoke about the Germans, the other about Egyptians. Only one said "with the Palestinians."

We are not the only people who were threatened by the loss of the enemy. Russia is moving through a painful transition in which they not only lost their enemy but also their own pure ideological identity of a world super power (Zizek, 1989). In a sense, this is a stressful situation because one has to face oneself and one's unresolved problems after being accustomed for many years to defining oneself through negative and relevant others, which is less energy consuming. In the Israeli case, this kind of danger is not yet so acute. Even if the peace process continues, certain others may still be counted on to assume the role of the enemy: the Iranians, Hammas, and Hizbulah. Still, the fear of losing the overriding uniting goal that the enemy provided is already a reality, bringing with it the fear of falling apart as a united people because of internal conflicts (religious-secular; ethnic groups; political orientations).

There are specific groups within our society who may not suffer just from the latent danger of losing an enemy but whose stressful situation is real and practical. Some people have been economically linked to the production of weapons (Kimmerling, 1993). Others are directly linked to maintaining our security. For these groups a future peace may mean personal uncertainty or loss of career. In addition, there is a whole section of Israeli society which moved to the Golan Heights, to the West Bank, and to Gaza for ideological and religious reasons (different from those who went there for economic reasons). For them, even the first steps of the intermediate phase of peace and war have been very stressful. They may have to take into account that the following stages of the peace process will endanger their existence in these places and/or their sense of security.

An additional concern is the people in charge of the helping professions. Within or right after the intermediate phase, those who suffer from latent PTSD from one of the previous wars, and especially those who experienced it during the Intifada, may suddenly show overt PTSD symptoms. Perhaps some of the reactions quoted earlier from the interviews are early signs of this pattern. These people will now be able to express the traumatic experiences they had to deny when the political conflict around the Intifada was still full fledged and did not enable them to relate to their own experiences (Bar-On, 1992). They may find themselves alone with their trauma in the future, because their commanders and the politicians who supported their activity during the violent activities might neglect their responsibility for that period.

Another group which may face additional stress in the intermediate phase of war and peace are those families whose family members died during the long period of warfare with the Arabs. For them, the justification for their loss was that one day peace would come and compensate the living for the dead. Thus, they would not have died in vain. However, this justification was based on the illusion or fantasy of total peace, not on the ambiguous and complex intermediate phase of peace and war. Such a phase may cause them to question the former justification and feel the meaninglessness of the loss: "Did our dear ones die for this kind of peace?" Again, some of the reactions I have quoted before relate to this aspect.

It is usually seen as the task of the political and social leadership to assist the vulnerable groups in the society, as well as the society as a whole, to accommodate the delicate and complex demands of such an intermediate phase between war and peace. They have to help the public confront previous unrealistic expectations which they themselves may have helped develop during earlier stressful and frustrating years of warfare. But, in many cases the leadership itself is stuck in the same prepeace syndrome (Bar-On, 1995b). Can many leaders state openly, for example, that they sent people to live in outposts for the purpose of national security, but now they should leave those places for the same reason because the perspective of national security has drastically changed?

It is not easy to suggest what they should actually do to help the public cope with this ambiguity (Tetlock, 1978). For example, should they prefer to present every new act or situation as an error or as a coincidence, rather than as an anticipated part of a larger process? This may help some people while perhaps distress others. It would help those who cannot cope with the whole process at once, while it may hamper the effort of others who could gain from a wider interpretive map which would help them reduce uncertainty (Lanir, 1990). Some people prefer to receive difficult knowledge about the change in bits and pieces, or even wish it to be presented as involuntary acts—for example, as concessions to American pressure. As the leaders cannot predict the outcome of the process they are leading, they may prefer to limit their own perspective and that of others, rather than show a clear direction and be punished if this fails at some point in the future.

The PPSR concept can be applied to other social contexts in which a sudden collapse of the role of the enemy or an intermediate phase of war and peace can be identified. This is true of the countries which were deeply involved in the cold war (such as the United States, Germany, and Eastern Europe). Other societies, suffering from long and exhausting conflicts (such as North Ireland, Bosnia, Cambodia, and South Africa) and trying to move towards resolving the conflict, will experience a similar intermediate phase like the one described earlier. However, in each social context these factors, and possibly others, have to be assessed separately, according to the specific cultural and historical characteristics of that context.

☐ Mental Health in a Society Between War and Peace

The mental health of a society is comprised of many different elements. It includes its community network, formal and informal institutions, educational system, and value composition. These factors all change over time. The Israeli society concept of mental health has changed radically during its almost 50 years. During the early years, it was based on informal institutions and strong ideologically oriented collective cohesion and combined with a strong demand for denial and suppression of private, emotional needs considered to be weaknesses. Lately, it has moved to almost the opposite extreme. First of all, we can identify different subcultures. A more open expression of emotions has become legitimate within the secular part of Israeli society. In this sector, mental health

now relies heavily on formal institutions, with a decline of the earlier cohesive sense of community. The religious subculture continues to build
on its previous informal structure of ideology and community combined
with the formal rabbinical leadership.

Let us look at the Israeli army as an example of this process. Though a
very modern medical system was an integral part of the Israeli armed
forces from its very beginning, this was not the case with mental health
services. As mentioned earlier, battle shock was not recognized and treated
during the 1948, 1956, or 1967 wars within the Israeli army. It was treated
for the first time during the 1973 war and a field setup for early identification and treatment functioned only during the 1982 war (Wiztum et. al.,
1989). In addition, Holocaust survivors and their families were acknowledged as suffering from PTSD only in the late 1960s to mid 1970s (Davidson, 1980). Though a modern and very egalitarian system was established
right from the beginning to take care of the physically handicapped and
the families who experienced the death of loved ones during the violent
struggle, minimal attention was given to the mentally distressed.

The dominance of technological and medical perspective of body versus soul was quite typical for Israeli society during the early years (Kimmerling, 1993). Mental distress and private emotional expression were
associated, if at all, with womanhood and childhood, while manhood
was supposed to be strong and healthy (Segev, 1992).[13] Still, compensating social mechanisms existed which enabled emotionally needy individuals and groups to receive the necessary emotional support and care.
Small, homogenic, and cohesive communities, such as the Kibbutzim,
which were characterized by a strong ideological motivation and discourse, helped distressed individuals cope with their lot, especially
within the dominant Western population. But, this was always at the
price of conforming to the dominant norm which preached for the new
Jew, the strong Sabra and the higher priority of collective values, sometimes even at the expense of family values and cohesion.

The groups that suffered from this structure of mental support were
mainly new immigrants, minorities, and individuals who were not part of
these cohesive and dominant social settings and discourse (Antonovsky,
1990). Some of these groups developed their own compensatory systems.
For example, Jewish immigrants from Morocco maintained their traditional support systems of healers and rituals around holy saints in parallel
to acquiring modern mental health services. The memorial day of Baba
Sali in Netivot (a small development town in the south of Israel), is a
mass pilgrimage each year. Other holy saints' places from Morocco were
transplanted into Israeli sites through the dreams and fantasies of their Israeli followers (Bilu, 1993). In the recent elections, myth and rationality
were interwoven when Rabbi Kadoorie, a ninety-year-old Sephardic or-

thodox Rabbi gave out coins and blessings while the rational leaders argued for peace and security (Ram, 1997). Similarly, the Arabic-Israeli population and the orthodox Jewish subculture used religiously oriented healers and Rabbis, respectively, to compensate for the lack of public support or their inability to use modern mental health services. Perhaps, in an era of transition and uncertainty, it is best to combine the traditional and the modern methods of support and health because both are necessary and alone neither is sufficient.

Since the Six Day War, and even more so after the 1973 War, Israeli society has slowly but steadily become polarized between the left and right, politically speaking. This polarization became more and more focused on the relationships with the Palestinians and the right to the territory. While the political left preferred to return the occupied territories for a negotiated peace and recognition by the Arab States, the political right advocated the historical right to the promised land and did not trust Palestinians as partners for peace. Paradoxically, the right wing governments had to make the first moves toward peace in 1977, in the Madrid conference of 1991, and lately by legitimating the Oslo Accord with the PLO by the majority of Netanyahu's government. But the main products of polarization were the recent warfare: The Lebanon War and the Intifada, rather than creating an overriding goal which united the society during earlier wars, created a social rift, protest, and even conscientious objectors unknown to Israeli society in earlier warfare. Each side now had a legitimate voice, interpretative systems, and social support groups, as well as its own definitions of enemies, partners, and heroism. This broke the consensus on which the strong, collective, cohesive power was based (Gal & Miesles, 1992).

This change of perspective of collective composition came parallel to the legitimating of private, emotional expression and mental distress within Israeli society. What counts as heroism is undergoing a radical transformation. If, in the past, there was a national consensus on the symbols of heroism (Trumpeldor, Bar-Kochva, the Ghetto fighters, and the 1948 Palmach Sabra), according to their willingness to devote their lives (and sacrifice others) for a national cause, in 1996 many different ideas were voiced concerning the definition of heroism (Golan, 1996). Today it can be a soldier who did not shoot at a child who threw stones at him, or a man who did not use his weapon while being attacked by a mob in the middle of a Palestinian town into which he had entered by mistake. Individual values have become more important in comparison to collective ones and the values of life and living overrule the ideal of dying for one's country unless there is no other choice. If the latter is the case, everyone has a right to question and open issues for discussion.

Young soldiers, who were once expected to restrain their emotions, are now being photographed on the national news program crying during a funeral. Though such a phenomena is still in public dispute (if soldiers should show their feelings in public or not), the mere willingness of discussing it openly is new. As part of this process, much more attention has been provided and services offered to the mentally distressed after terrorist attacks, rocket attacks at northern towns (by Hizbulah), and even during the attack of the scud missiles of the Gulf War. This is part of another process which has transpired simultaneously. During the last two decades violent activity has shifted from warfare between armed forces to warfare in which civilian populations are under fire. This was the case during the Gulf War, the Lebanon war, the Intifada, and the violent suicidal terrorist attacks in Hebron, Jerusalem, and Tel-Aviv during the nineties. This shift from conflicts between armed forces to conflicts involving civilian populations has been recognized, according to the United Nations, as a global phenomena.

One should also remember that over a quarter of the Israeli population is composed of Holocaust survivors and their descendants. We have found that in the third generation the Holocaust has been adopted as a personal legacy also by the descendants of Sephardic immigrants from countries which were not under Nazi occupation (Bar-On & Selah, 1991). The organized trips to Poland to visit the Nazi death camps have become a relatively new ritual, trying to strengthen the secular myth of victimization (Segev, 1992), while also renewing the relationship to the roots from which the Sabra turned away not so long ago. The relevance of the Holocaust to daily events in Israel is being preached almost daily. Two contradictory legends and moral consequences have been drawn from the past to the present: we have to be strong and not trust anyone (Danieli, 1980) and; we have to consider minorities, whoever they are. They were adopted by the political right and left wings to reinforce their current political perspective. This is one of the reasons why it was difficult to reestablish a consensus, a middle way, that would enable the renewal of informal collective support mechanisms and create a basis for a common and agreed upon leadership.

The Holocaust has constantly had its effect on boundary rituals that cannot be implemented in the current conflict because of what they represent from the Nazi era. For example, the use of dogs was proposed several times during the Intifada, to be turned down again and again because of the association with Auschwitz. The ideas of transfer, or of concentration camps, are similar taboos in the Israeli discourse. In this sense, the Intifada created an inner conflict in the moral self-perception. The pictures of soldiers struggling with children and women, located in camps surrounded by barbed wire, were hard on the collective social consciousness (Bar-On, Yitzhaki-Verner, & Amir, 1996). The denial of the role of the victimizer, constantly reliving the role of the victim, was the major form of keeping the Holocaust separate from the local conflict. Only recently, has Israeli society acknowledged and worked through the fact that Arabs were driven out of their homes during the 1948 war and that captives were murdered in cold blood during the early wars (Morris, 1996).

Israeli men are the carriers of the violent struggle with the enemy. Women were fighters in the 1948 war but became backstage supporters after that. Women were more involved in compensating mechanisms of supporting the bereaved and the handicapped. But lately, even this norm is under attack. On the one hand, certain women want to become combat fighters, especially pilots in the air force (Grumer, 1996). On the other hand, the ideal of men being recruited does not continue without being questioned. The role of the army in the social mobility in Israeli society is still very strong, but this norm is slowly changing in some subcultures. Recently, the army aired the issue of motivation to serve, an issue which was not previously acknowledged, though rumors on this subject have existed over the last ten years, perhaps even since the Lebanon War (Portugali, 1996).

In young Israel, male children were emotionally recruited at puberty and urged to begin thinking about their role as fighting men. Even today, groups of teenagers go to Poland each year to learn, first hand, about what "has been done to us when we were weak in the death camps" (Bar-On, 1995a). In Palestinian society the role of women and children has changed drastically since the 1982 war and even more so during the Intifada. They became the backbone of the national uprising with their daily struggle with the Israeli soldiers broadcast on television around the world. In Israel, except for very selective and ideologically oriented groups such as Women in Black and the nationalistically oriented religious Jews, the society as a whole adopted the typical role of the bystander who turns a blind eye. For example, young Israeli women reflected the voice of the consensus as performed by the Greek chorus. Many did not know, or did not want to know, what their boyfriends were actually doing in the occupied territories (Grumer, 1996) and viewed Palestinian women as especially mean and dangerous.

Opening the dispute around national legends and taboos today moves in many different directions. One can identify the Israeli sense of insecurity in other domains. One identifies it in the new neighborhoods, which demonstrate a Ghetto-like psychology in the tendency to live very close to each other, irrelevant if it suits the landscape or not and in many cases even fenced and guarded at night. This becomes obvious when one compares it to the Palestinian housing style which sets each house apart, very much in tune with the landscape, representing a much more relaxed perspective of having a home and living safely. Others will identify it in the way Israeli drivers navigate on the roads: Israel has almost the highest ratio of road accidents in the Western world. The Israeli will listen attentively, almost compulsively, to the news every half hour when a soldier is stabbed in Jerusalem but will almost ignore the annual death toll of over 500 people.

Internal contradictions can probably be identified in the daily discourse of other societies as well. In the Israeli society, however, they center around life and death, here versus there, and moving forward or backward. In a recent group process at our university, a group of veteran Israeli and new immigrants from Russia were asked to place themselves, physically, on a continuum between one wall, representing 100% Israeli and the opposite wall, representing the opposite (Bar-On, Spitzer, & Bukrashov, in press). Almost the whole group placed itself, quite surprisingly, about a third away from the 100% Israeli wall. When the new immigrants asked the Israeli students to account for the fact that they did not place themselves near the Israeli wall, these students started to reflect on their own sense of alienation. They associated it with daily issues—not feeling comfortable as an Israeli. This was a new phenomena which would not have been discussed openly 10 years ago.

As the group process continued, the Israeli group was divided between those who saw the placing of the Israeli students and their following reflections as a regression from the previous idealized local patriotism, while others viewed the same act as moving forward, being able to discuss openly what they felt and did not talk about long ago. It represented for us the recent transitions, mentioned earlier, and the conflicts in identity that they were willing to discuss openly. We write in our report of this event that had these been Arab-Israeli students, probably such openness would not have taken place, in front of the (past) enemy. In order to open internal contradictions in one's identity during such periods of transition trust, support, and leadership are necessary conditions.

This event was not easy for the two facilitators who were themselves Israeli and Russian. They became so involved in the process that they could hardly facilitate the group process. This exemplifies that in such periods of transition, mental health workers are in the same boat as their clients and have therefore little extra internal energy to give support and acknowledgment of the distress of their clients (Bar-On, 1992). The question of the group, "are we moving forward or backward?" is not always easy to answer because there are mixed signs of depression and anger mixed together with hopefulness and creativity. There is no way to promise that "on the other side of the river of death and dying there is a safe shore of life and living" (Bar-On, 1995a, p. 38). In the meantime, we should all learn to swim in this deep and shaky sea of our current life events.

☐ Endnotes

[1]About one million Jewish immigrants, composed mainly of European Holocaust survivors and the Jewry from the Arab countries (Morocco, Iraq, Yemen, and others), came during the first five years after the establishment of the State of Israel.

[2]Though the Palestinian national entity is composed of a Muslim majority and a Christian minority, they are referred to as one entity in the present discussion.

[3]This simple issue - how many Palestinians have lived here for ages and how many immigrated in the last century from neighboring countries is an ongoing dispute between Israeli and Palestinian political scientists. Similarly, there is an ongoing dispute between new and old Israeli historians as to the extent that Palestinian refugees of the 1948 war were actually driven out intentionally by the Israeli army or fled on their own initiative (Morris, 1996). These examples demonstrate how politics and interpretation of historical facts are deeply interwoven.

[4]The 1948 war was defined as the War of Independence by the Israelis (and clearly very differently by the Palestinians). The Intifada (1987–1993) was similarly identified as a national struggle by the Palestinians, but as an uprising or unrest by the Israelis. This demonstrates how these terms are emotionally loaded and have to be used carefully, recognizing their different implications for the parties in the conflict.

[5]Sabra is a nickname for the Israeli born. It is the Arabic name for a wild fruit which has thorns on the outside but is juicy and soft inside. This reflected the public image of the new Jew.

[6]In the spring of 1997, two Israeli high school principals in Jerusalem decided not to let their pupils visit Massada, as part of their annual school excursion, because the people who committed suicide during the struggle with the Romans were fanatic murderers. This is another example how myths are reexamined and reconstructed according to present political disputes.

[7]These are the Israeli armed forces, prior to the State of Israel, who were illegally trained and emerged as the basis for what became the Israeli Defense Forces (IDF) after May 15, 1948.

[8]Thanks to a comment of a reviewer I would like to add that an indirect sign of "not being good enough" can be seen by the fact that Holocaust survivors and their families are close to a fifth of the Israeli population today. They always were, and still are, underrepresented in the Knesset (the Israeli parliament), in comparison to other Ashkenazi or Sephardic segments of the Jewish population.

[9]A. B. Yehoshua recently published a fictional story (1997) in which he tried to show the origins of the contemporary lack of understanding between Ashkenazi and Sephardic Jews, which was associated with the different cultural and religious influences of Christians and Muslims on the two respective Jewish subcultures, long ago.

[10]These sentences were written in May, 1997. When they were written first in November, 1996, they were more optimistically phrased. This shows how fragile the situation is and to what extent it is difficult to predict what the next political developments will be. It is still my personal conviction that the Oslo agreement created an irreversible process and it is only a matter of time and energy, how and at what pace (and, unfortunately, with how many unnecessary casualties) it will move forward.

[11]Dr. Tom Greening suggested the phrase "the temptation of facile fatalism and dreamy optimism" to describe the simplistic solutions some people tend to prefer when faced with the ambiguity of a sudden transition like the one from war to peace (personal communication, December 17, 1993).

[12]Though the Israeli left played an important role in bringing about the beginning of the peace process, the difficulty to give up one's self-definition through the negation of the other is not less difficult for some of them, than it is for politically right wing young people. We observed this process during the encounters of Jewish and Palestinian-Israeli student groups at our University (Zak, Halaby, Sagy, & Bar-On, 1997).

[13]Grumer (1996), using the symbolic meaning of Athena and Phenelopa, found that even during the Intifada, women tended to play a back role, not raising difficult questions and thereby providing emotional and moral support to their male friends during their military activity. A small group of "Women in Black," however, protested openly against this activity.

☐ References

Antonovsky, A. (1990). *The sociology of health and health care in Israel.* New Brunswick, NJ: Transaction Books.

Bar-On, D. (1992). A testimony on the moment before the (possible) occurrence of a massacre: On possible contradiction between the ability to adjust and the maintaining of human moral values. *Journal of Traumatic Stress, 5*(2), 289–301.

Bar-On, D. (1995a). *Fear and hope: Life-stories of five Israeli families of Holocaust survivors, three generations in a family.* Cambridge, MA: Harvard University Press.

Bar-On, D. (1995b). Peace intermediate stress syndrome: the Israeli experience. *Palestine-Israel Journal, 2*(1), 69–79.

Bar-On, D., & Selah O. (1991). The "vicious cycle" between current social and political attitudes and attitudes towards the Holocaust among Israeli youngsters. *Psychologia, 2*(2), 126–138.

Bar-On, D., Spitzer, I., & Bukrashov, Y. (1996). *Internal conflicts in Israeli identity.* Unpublished manuscript, Ben Gurion University of the Negev.

Bar-On, D., Yitzhaki-Verner, T., & Amir, S. (1996). The recruited identity: The influence of the Intifada on the perception of the peace process from the standpoint of the individual. *Journal of Narrative and Life History, 6*(3), 193–224.

Bilu, Y. (1993). *Without boundaries: The life and death of Rabbi Yaacov Wazana.* Jerusalem: Magnes.

Danieli, Y. (1980). Countertransference in the treatment and study of Nazi Holocaust survivors and their children. *Victimology, 5,* 3–4.

Davidson, S. (1980). The clinical effect of massive psychic trauma in families of Holocaust survivors. *Journal of Marital and Family Therapy, 1,* 11–21.

Figley, C. R. (1986). (Ed.). *Trauma and its wake, vol. 2: Traumatic stress, theory, research and intervention.* New York: Brunner/Mazel.

Gal, R., & Miesles, O. (1992). *Anticipating chemical warfare during the Gulf war.* Zichron Yaakov: The Institute for Military Research.

Golan, T. (1996). *Heroism as a changing metaphor in the Israeli society.* Unpublished manuscript, Ben Gurion University of the Negev.

Granot, T. (1976). *Bereaved parents: Phenomena and processes.* Tel Aviv: The Ministry of Defense Publication.

Grumer, K. (1996). *Athena or Phenelopa? Israeli young women talk about their friends' involvement in the Intifada.* Beer Sheva: Ben Gurion University.

Hadar, Y. (1991). The absolute good and bad in the eyes of Holocaust survivors and their descendants. Presentation given at The 8th Family Therapy Conference, Bat-Yam,

Keren, N., & Almalich, D. (1994). A community under siege. In D. Bar-On, & D. Fromer (Eds.), *The second reader—After-effects of the Holocaust on second and third generations* (pp. 111–146). Beer Sheva: Ben Gurion University.

Kimmerling, B. (1983). *Zionism and Territory*. Berkeley, CA: Institute of International Studies.

Kimmerling, B. (1993). Militarism in the Israeli society. *Theory and Critics, 4*, 123–140.

Lanir, Z. (1990) *A young kibbutz in a conceptual crisis*. Hakibbutz Hameuchad: Yad Tabenkin.

Morris, B. (1996). *Israeli border wars, 1949–1956*. Tel Aviv: Am Oved.

Moses, R. (1993). *Persistent shadows of the Holocaust: The meaning to those not directly affected*. Madison, CT: International University Press.

Portugali, Y. (1996). *Implicated relations: Society and space in the Israeli–Palestinian conflict*. Tel Aviv: Hakibbutz Hameuchad.

Ram, U. (1997). The 1996 elections: Images and coins. In *Theory and critics: An Israeli stage* (pp. 199–208). Jerusalem: Van-Leer.

Rom, E., & Bar-On, D. (in press). Battle shock during the war of independence: Was there such a phenomena? In D. Bar-On, *The 'Other' within us: Changes in Israel: Identity from a social-psychological perspective*. Jerusalem: Ben Aurion Print Mosad Bialik (in Hebrew).

Segev, T. (1992). *The seventh million*. Jerusalem: Keter.

Solomon, Z. (1993). *Combat stress reactions: The enduring toll of war*. New York: Plenum Press.

Tetlock, P. (1987). A value pluralism model for ideological reasoning. *Journal of Personality and Social Psychology, 50*(4), 819–827.

Wiztum, E., Levi, A., Gernak, E., & Kotler, M. (1989). Battle reactions in Israeli wars 1948–73. *Sichot, 4*, 65–70.

Wiztum, E., Malkinson, R., & Rubin, S. (1993). Grief and immortalization: The double face of the national myth. In R. Malkinson, S. Rubin, & E. Wiztum (Eds.), *Loss and grief in the Israeli society* (pp. 231–258). Jerusalem: Ministry of Defense Publication.

Zak, M., Halaby, R., Sagy, S., & Bar-On, D. (1997). I am stuck with my own pain: An Arab-Jewish students workshop. Presented at The Geneva Foundation meeting in Annecy, France, January, 1997.

Zizek, S. (1989). *The sublime object of ideology*. London: Verso.

Zrubavel, Y. (1986). The holiday cycle and the commemoration of the past: Folklore, history and education. *Ninth World Congress of Jewish Studies, Magnes, 4*, 111–118.

Elia Awwad

Between Trauma and Recovery: Some Perspectives on Palestinian's Vulnerability and Adaptation

☐ Background

The writing of this chapter came at a stage of rapid change and transition in the turbulent history of the Palestinians. During this writing, the author participated in funerals for youths killed by the Israeli army at one of the checkpoints near the city of Bethlehem. This event took place during the last 4 days of confrontation between the Israeli soldiers and the Palestinians. The conflict erupted on September 25, 1996, following Israel's decision to open the tunnel under the Al Aqsa Mosque in the Old City of Jerusalem. In the end, 89 Palestinians were killed and over 1,000 were injured.

The Green Line with Israel is the armistice line drawn in 1949 between areas under the control of Arab and Jewish forces after the war. It is defined as Jordan to the East, Egypt/Sinai to the South, the Mediterranean Sea to the West, and the Green Line to the North and East (The Palestinian Academic Society for the Study of International Affairs, 1996).

Since the Canaanite era of around 2500 years B.C. until now, Palestine was conquered more than 15 times. Following the 1948 Arab-Israeli war, an agreement was signed in Rhodes which did not affect settlement of the Palestine question. In the course of the war, the Gaza Strip was administered by Egypt and came under the administration of an Egyptian governor. The Palestine West Bank was annexed by Jordan by decree in April 1950, declaring the two banks of the Jordan River as the Hashemite Kingdom of Jordan. Both the West Bank and the Gaza Strip remained under Jordanian/Egyptian rule until 1967 when Israel occupied the areas in the June war, followed by the Israeli military rule over the occupied Palestinian territories. After the 1948 war, Jerusalem was divided into two parts, East Jerusalem for the Palestinians and West Jerusalem for the Israelis. However, East Jerusalem was annexed by the Israeli Knesset to the Western part in June 1980. Israeli laws were imposed on East Jerusalem and its Palestinian residents were issued distinct identity cards. According to Israeli law, they are not citizens, but rather permanent residents, who although born in Jerusalem hold the status of foreigners or immigrants who entered Jerusalem after 1967 (Palestine and the U.N., 1997).

Furthermore, the 1948 war resulted in the demolishing of at least 418 Arab villages. Some 714,000 refugees were forced to flee from cities and towns. The West Bank and Gaza Strip harbored most of these refugees, many of whom fled again in the 1967 war. In the West Bank, there are 19 refugee camps, in Gaza 8. Although nearly half the refugee population has moved out of these camps, they are still severely over crowded with cramped housing, unpaved streets, and open sewers. United Nations Relief and Works Agency (UNRWA) is responsible for refugee camps. It provides health and rehabilitation services, education, training, water, electricity supplies, sanitation, and building control. It is estimated that the Palestinian population in the West Bank including East Jerusalem is 1,571,575 and 963,028 in the Gaza Strip (Palestinian Central Bureau of Statistics, 1996).

In November 1981, Israel established the Civil Administration. This partly differentiated the functions of governing the Palestinian population under occupation from military operations. This initiation was in line with the Israeli autonomy proposals of 1979 and the Camp David Agreement (PASSIA, 1996). The West Bank is also referred to by Israeli officials as Judea and Samaria.

On the 9th of December, 1987, the Intifada—the Palestinian uprising against Israeli occupation—started and continued until 1990, declining by 1992. After 30 years of military occupation of the West Bank and Gaza Strip, Palestinians witnessed for the first time the redeployment of the Israeli troops from Gaza and the major cities of the West Bank. The transfer of authorities took place on the 20th of January, 1996. A legislative council and a President, Yasser Arafat, were elected by the Palestinians themselves. These initial achievements took place as a result of the peace agreement Declaration of Principles (D.O.P.), which was signed on the 13th of September, 1993, in front of the White House.

In 1994, the Palestinian National Authority was declared and the land confirmed for Palestinians was called the autonomous areas or the National Authority Areas. Difficult issues such as Jerusalem, sovereignty, security, water, borders, settlements, refugees, prisoners, and other sensitive topics remained for the final stages of negotiations.

However, the life of the Palestinians is better understood as lying on a continuum ranging from psychological trauma at one end and adaptation on the other. Vulnerability and stress are two psychological processes that are taking place between these two extreme poles.

☐ The Intifada

The Intifada—or Uprising—was a general population event that created a number of changes in the structure of Palestinian society. These included economic and lifestyle changes plus the construction of Palestinian thinking processes in the occupied territories. The Intifada was a national event, involving the entire Palestinian population in a unique action of solidarity, which was a surprise to both Israelis and the rest of the world. The Intifada was not limited to a particular geographical area in the territories, but was an inclusive event. Every Palestinian village, city, and refugee camp was actively involved as were Palestinians from all social strata, class, gender, and age. In itself, the Intifada demonstrated the tremendous psychosocial changes in the Palestinian people.

Previous to the Intifada, the occupied territories had witnessed different types of active resistance against the Israeli military occupation. However, the Intifada was a phenomenal event which started at a grass roots level by the oppressed working classes. The intensity and severity of the violent acts of resistance were the result of accumulated oppression suffered during the military occupation. People of all classes were traumatized and unable to exist under inhumane conditions. The mass population resistance movement of the Intifada lasted for several years, from 1987 to 1992.

The changes which resulted from the Intifada occurred in a relatively short period of time and stemmed from the Palestinian people themselves. The role of the different social classes in the Intifada can be characterized as follows.

Working Class

The start of the Intifada can be traced to an incident in a Jabalia refugee camp in Gaza, where four Palestinian workers were killed by an Israeli military jeep. This was the culmination of many events. At that time

Palestinian workers were suffering from stressful working conditions in Israel, in addition to other humiliations, low wages, and a series of illegal tax deductions. The miserable work and life conditions of the people, together with Israeli violence, harassment, and killings, led to a build up of anger and psychosocial and economic oppression which had no constructive outlet over time. When the Intifada started, Palestinian workers recognized that they would have to sacrifice their own interests, in terms of jobs and salaries, for the interests of all the people. Accordingly, the workers were the first group of people who stopped going to work in Israel at the request of the unified national leadership of the Intifada. As a result, workers' incomes decreased tremendously—estimated by official reports at between 50% to 60%.

It should be noted that about 30% of those who were killed by Israeli soldiers during the first two years of the Intifada were workers. Gaza workers tried to search for employment opportunities within the Gaza Strip. Some managed to find work in small local factories or companies, but with over 70,000 workers in the most condensed area of the world, many found this impossible. The majority were left without any income at all, which increased their poverty and suffering. The Israeli authorities implemented various punitive measures and collective punishments against the people in an attempt to put an end to the Intifada. One of the first of these was the issuing of what are called personal identity cards, and no one was allowed to leave the Gaza Strip without obtaining a red card. By this measure the Israeli authorities were able to achieve the following goals:

- retie the Palestinians to the Israeli civil administration after they had declared civil disobedience
- purse Palestinians who refused to pay taxes
- differentiate between people wanted by the Israeli army for security reasons or for being politically active by providing different identity cards to prevent them from leaving the Gaza Strip
- increase economic pressure on the people and create a state of chaos in the hope that Palestinians would get tired of the hardships and reject the Intifada

Although the workers rejected the policy of the red cards, in the end some accepted them as a means of solving the hunger problems of their families and as a way of coping with the deteriorating economic and political conditions in the Gaza Strip. In order to try and gain control of the Gaza Strip, the Israeli's then issued a new magnetic card to be applied for by anyone who needed to work in Israel. These cards are still in operation in the West Bank and Gaza. During the Intifada, workers faced a conflict situation about whether to accept the imposed Israeli military orders, or to follow the instructions of their leaders. Since the unified leadership was unable to solve the serious socioeconomic problems of the Palestinian people and because of the following difficulties in coordinating between the West Bank and the Gaza Strip, the Israeli military measures began to gain some gradual acceptance by extremely poor and depressed workers. However, this took place only after a very long period of work strike and continuous confrontations with the Israeli army.

During this period of struggle, many Israeli employers fired their Palestinian laborers because they were not attending work daily. Eventually, the unified national leadership of the Intifada, who understood the serious financial problems of the workers and their families, instructed them to obtain the magnetic cards and to work in Israel. An important point to note here is the dependency of the Israeli economy on Palestinian labor. Israeli officials reported a loss of millions of dollars daily as a result of Palestinian workers' strikes.

Peasants

This social class suffered a high price during the Intifada as a result of keeping themselves attached to their land. After the 1967 war and the Israeli policy of establishing settlements in the occupied territories, many Palestinians were forced to leave their lands and join the workers in search of waged employment inside Israel in the construction industry. When the Intifada began, many people joined the peasants in working the land despite the very small subsistence from this. In the first year of the Intifada, the unified leadership called on the people to cultivate the land in preparation for the starvation policies of the Israelis. The importance of the peasants increased when the Israeli authorities prevented any Israeli agricultural products to enter the occupied territories. This coincided with a call from the Palestinian side to boycott these goods. These agricultural products, in spite of the low prices in relation to the efforts made, were the only substitute for Israeli food products. While the national leadership asked all strata of the Palestinian society to respect the strike days, the peasants were the only group to continue working on the land. Masses of the population, including professionals, academics, city dwellers, and others joined the peasants in cultivating areas of land for produce which had been previously neglected. During Israeli curfews, these agricultural products were distributed throughout the population for nothing or at a very low price to help the population endure the suffering of economic and military seizure. The Israeli army began to attack the peasants once they realized their role in sustaining the people against the starvation policies. Strict and extensive curfew periods were issued during the cultivation periods so that people were unable to go to the land to water or care for the produce. Those seen on the land were shot or captured and imprisoned. Through this harsh collective punishment, the Israelis were able to destroy the efforts of the peasants to support the Palestinian economy and resistance, and force them to abandon their lands.

Merchants

This group also played an important role in the Intifada and were often directly affected by Israeli violence. From the beginning of the Intifada, merchants followed the requests of the unified national leadership by closing shops and stores on strike days. Prior to the Intifada, shops and stores had been open from the morning to the late evening. During the Intifada, economic progress declined, and shops were closed each day until 12 in the afternoon. Like the workers, the merchants faced a conflict situation. While attempting to support the Intifada through store closures, they were attacked harshly by the Israeli military who tried to force them to open their stores. Merchants were often imprisoned and suffered violence from the Israelis. In addition, the Israelis imposed severe taxes on merchants and store owners, opened stores without the presence of the owners, and fined merchants who refused to obey the military orders. Hundreds of merchants were put in prison and shops and stores burnt down at night. Despite these measures, the merchants continued their struggle with the rest of the people throughout the years of the Intifada.

Students

Palestinians have a high regard towards learning. They are the most highly educated population in the Arab world. During the Intifada, Israeli authorities recognized that the student population played an important role in the struggle against military occupation. Therefore, all Palestinian schools, universities, and institutions of higher education were closed. Strict closure was maintained for almost three years. An Israeli military order was issued stating that any school or university must apply for a formal request to reopen.

Palestinians realized that this was a deliberate Israeli policy to create a generation of children and youth without education. In response, Palestinians initiated a community movement of popular teaching. Education was conducted in homes, churches, and mosques. Each neighborhood was organized to provide different levels of school classes. In response, the Israelis issued new orders prohibiting the popular teaching and decreed it illegal. To enforce this order, spontaneous home raids in search of any teaching were carried out by the Israeli military.

During the Intifada, the author was teaching at Birzeit University in the West Bank. I had to hide my books to avoid suspicion from the Israeli soldiers in the streets. If they discovered my teaching materials, I was at risk of being investigated and arrested. I also participated in the organization of popular teaching in my own community. My personal tension and stress, as well as that of my students', was particularly high during this period.

The leadership of the Intifada recognized the long term effects of denied education for an entire generation of Palestinians. Therefore, they requested students and teachers to return to the schools against Israeli policy. Although many clashes with soldiers followed this action, which included subsequent deaths, injuries, and imprisonment of participants, the community succeeded in forcing the reopening of educational institutions. The Israelis gave in to this pressure on the condition that there would be no signs of resistance to the occupation in these institutions. The Intifada leadership instructed the institutions to give no pretext to the Israelis for reclosing them.

In spite of this, the educational institutions continued for years to be the target of Israeli attacks and students and faculty suffered through the chronic closures. Weary of these threats, many students left the West Bank and Gaza to continue their studies in foreign countries. The Israeli authorities attempted to use this opportunity to reduce the number of educated Palestinians reentering the country by asking departing students to sign documents prohibiting their return for at least three years. Indeed, many Palestinian students attempting to return home were denied visas by the Israeli Embassy.

Women

Women carried out multiple roles during the Intifada years, both continuing with their traditional family role, and participating in the struggle against the Israeli army. Women who had previously been in a submissive role in terms of gender relations were now in direct physical confrontation with Israeli soldiers. They played a leading role in providing information about the location of the soldiers and passing this information to the demonstrators and youth in the streets. Many women were beaten, attacked, arrested, or killed when attempting to rescue youth or children captured or injured by Israeli soldiers. Women were also active in confronting the soldiers during home raids. The Intifada leadership appealed to women in the community to manage the economic crisis and food shortages resulting from the long curfews and strikes, and many women cultivated unused areas of land near their houses for produce. Women played an important part in the education of their children, and were often soley responsible for managing the traumas of their children and family members, particularly as many families had lost fathers and husbands as a result of Israeli imprisonments and killings. Generally, women provided the critical moral and social support needed in the face of extreme crisis and personal and community tragedies, as well as physical support in caring for the injured in the homes and hospitals.

☐ Coping and Resilience

Any discussion of trauma and the Palestinian community must take into account the conditions and characteristics of life under military occupation. Psychological conditions are a result of an intricate web of experiences, social conditions, interpersonal relations, community norms, and one's own experiences as a child. Military occupation affects all areas of life. It is a methodical and carefully planned process through which the occupier attempts to destroy the resilience and character of the occupied and to rob them of their most basic freedoms. The consequent turbulence in the lives of the occupied may often result in social and psychological difficulties. New psychoemotional conditions emerge which correspond with the new sociopolitical conditions.

The grandparents of today's generation in Palestine—the children of 1948—lived through decades of occupation and disasters, including the massacres of Dir Yassin and Jaffa in 1948 and the later massacres of Al-Qubeiba, Al-Samoua, Al-Tire, Qalqilia, and Nabra, during which hundreds of Palestinians were killed and thousands were forced to leave their homeland at gunpoint or to flee from the violence. Raya Punamaki, a Finnish researcher (1987), believes that the children of 1948 developed a panic complex revolving around the loss of their homeland and loss of hope for a normal life in the future, and that this has passed into the Palestinian national psyche as a collective inheritance of pain and sorrow. As traumatic experiences accumulate they reactivate and feed into this memory, keeping the painful experiences alive.

The children of 1967—parents of the current generation—were psychologically affected by the Israeli occupation of the remains of Palestine—the West Bank and Gaza—and the mass migration of Palestinians to escape the violence and oppression.

Today's generation is suffering from the effects of the Israeli attempts to crush the Intifada. They continue to experience closures, violence, travel restrictions, and more recently, the expansion of settlements and attempts to Judaize East Jerusalem's institutions, thereby reducing the Palestinian population to a minority.

The Palestinian peoples' ability to survive throughout these continued traumas is formidable. Before the Intifada, predominant response feelings in the community were those of helplessness and anxiety, because the socioeconomic structure of society was severely affected by the Israeli occupation. Palestinians witnessed amplification of social problems and violence. However, the Intifada created an outlet for feelings of oppression and had a healing affect within the community as people began to feel empowered through taking action. Community self-esteem, pride, and confidence grew. Self interests were transposed by public interests and people unified, creating new coping mechanisms and purpose. As such, coping and resilience resulted from a number of factors:

- the level of family, social, and emotional support
- faith in the ability of Palestinian people as survivors
- assertive action in place of passivity
- religious beliefs
- collective numbness to pain and suffering
- existential perception of life
- learning from similar experiences of occupied people in the world
- hope
- unity
- ideology
- achievement of short term objectives
- community, legal, financial, and moral support and protection
- altruism in the community
- catharsis through shared experience
- creativity in response to a situation
- concern over negative social responses to stress
- changes in social roles

☐ Children and Trauma

The major traumatic experiences of the Palestinians resulted from living in an environment full of violence and stress. Political, economical, and psychosocial disturbances have erupted in the West Bank including East Jerusalem and the Gaza Strip since 1967 until now. Palestinians have been suffering for over 30 years from loss of personal freedoms, humiliation, physical injuries, detentions, tear gas exposure, beatings, house demolitions, deaths, deportations, family disunion, and other forms of violence. Psychological studies on the mental health of those personally traumatized in World War II by destruction, family separation, and loss of loved ones found that these experiences led to various types of mental disturbances (Punamaki,1987). One important consequence of violence has been that normal childhood development, so necessary for a healthy and productive future for both the individual and society, has been denied to thousands of Palestinian children. Even when children are not directly exposed to violence, knowledge of traumatic events are threatening, painful, and cause damage to their development. Furthermore, their faith in the good intention of people and their faith in their own security and safety is destroyed (UNICEF, 1994).

According to the National Health Plan for the Palestinian people (1994), it was estimated that 60% of the population in 1992 were below 19 years old, including 47% older than 15 years old. These percentages were the same in all the districts of the West Bank and the Gaza Strip. Furthermore, it was predicted that these percentages will continue to be the same during the coming ten years. Palestinian children represent the majority of the population and are one of the most vulnerable groups.

Since the Intifada started, many of these children were shot at, detained, injured, exposed to verbal and physical abuse, deformed, and even killed. Many witnessed the killing of others, the demolition of houses, arrests, surprise attacks at homes, family disunion, and other forms of intimidating violence. From this perspective children can be seen as both primary victims of violence as well as covictims. Throughout the years of occupation, Palestinian children have been targets of various traumatic events, with each event varying in its developmental point of entry, intensity, duration, and psychological result.

Several studies indicate the adverse effects of Palestinian children's exposure to Israeli violence, confrontation, and collective punishments. For example, the documentation of Radda Barren (Nixon, 1990a; 1990b) extensively demonstrated these effects on Palestinian children's physical and emotional well being. Punamaki and Suleiman (1990) showed that exposure to political hardships increased Palestinian children's psychological symptoms and that none of the children's psychological coping modes were effective in decreasing this relationship. Similarly, Baker (1990) found that fears and depression symptoms increased 15% to 25% among Palestinian children one year after the beginning of the Intifada. In another study (1991), he reported that children in the West Bank were suffering from conduct and psychosomatic problems. Intense fears of leaving the house and encountering Israeli soldiers were the most pressing psychological problems facing these children. Khamis (1992) found various behavioral symptoms in response to stress in elementary school children, including bedwetting and stuttering. It should be noted that the trauma experienced by Palestinian children has also been observed to effect children's vocabulary, their values, and their choice of composition of toys and paintings. For example, the Israeli most commonly appears as the subject of the child's hostile behavior and source of fear. Such fears are also transferred onto other objects which represent old fears (Punamaki, 1987).

In the Gaza Strip, Abu Hein (1993) studied the impact of security closures on the psychological life of Palestinian families. He found that as a result of closures, children aged 6–12 years old were suffering from irritability, fear, fidgeting, hyperactivity, and fighting with others. Abu Hein and Raundalen (1993) studied the impact of Israeli deportations of Palestinians on children in the community aged 2–17 years old. They found a high level of emotional, psychological, and behavioral difficulties among the children of the deportees. They argue that these results show that children of deportees were more severely affected than the children who experienced imposed curfews, as indicated by Quota and El Sarraj's study in 1993 in the Gaza Strip. Case studies were also reported about the tremendous negative impact of night home raids by the Israeli soldiers on the emotional well being of children in the Gaza Strip (Abu Hein, 1993). In another study by Elbedour, Bensel, and Maruyama in 1993, a comparison was made between three samples of junior and senior high school children: Israeli-Arabs (from the Negev, the southern part of Israel) children, children from the West Bank, and children of Gaza. Results indicated that the highest posttraumatic stress disorder (PTSD) symptoms were recorded for children from Gaza, followed by children from the West Bank, and finally by the Israeli-Arabs.

Garbarino, Kostelny, and Dubrow (1991) interviewed a number of families in the West Bank and Gaza during the Intifada, and concluded that research did not find any children who had no direct contact with or experience of violence. This included cases of children who had been shot, detained, arrested, beaten, and tear gassed.

Surviving Palestinian children do not possess the necessary knowledge and skills to tackle severe and prolonged traumatic events, and the vast majority of them suffer in silence. A manifestation of this damage may take the form of violence directed towards each other (Awwad, 1996). It may also negatively affect their conceptualization of themselves and the future of their country in contrast to Israeli and Arab Israeli children. Findings of a recent study (Awwad, 1997a) showed that Israeli students (n = 1,144) expect their lives to be more peaceful than the Arab-Israelis (n = 356) and the Palestinian students (n = 1,099) respectively. This may result from a more realistic perspective by the Palestinians who have taken into consideration the daily confrontation and violence between the Israeli army and the Palestinian community in the Palestinian areas. Palestinian students expect that their country will be exploited by a foreign country state even after 40 years from now, to the expectations of Israeli and Arab Israeli students. Accordingly, the Palestinian sample does not expect life in Palestine to be prosperous and wealthy, like the Arab-Israelis and Israelis. They also do not expect democracy to prevail in their country, unlike the other two groups. It appears from these responses that the Palestinian students' involvements in the daily political struggle affects their perception of possible positive future events. Yet again the Israeli students are more optimistic than the Palestinian students about the coming 40 years in terms of securing meaningful employment, having good friends, and achieving personal and political freedom. The Arab-Israelis scored the highest on having a happy and harmonious family life and the Palestinians scored the highest on their expected participation in the political process within Palestine. However, they scored the lowest on expectations of political freedom from Israel. These results need to be seriously addressed by educators and mental health professionals in future interventions. In addition, adults have become accustomed to reducing the physical and psychosocial impacts of these human induced disasters. Such denial on the part of the parents, and the repression on the part of the child, may cause deep disturbances in the child's normal development. It may produce physical, mental, emotional, and social scars and injuries which can be difficult to heal unless immediate and serious attention is provided that guarantees the child's care and protection (UNICEF, 1994). The evidence that these types of adverse experiences can play a large part in causing cognitive disturbance is now substantial (Bowlby, 1992).

☐ Palestinian Women

It is necessary to state here that Palestinian parents, who are to provide care, protection, and safety to their children, have been victims of violence for many years. For example, Palestinian women who are considered to be the backbone of the Palestinian family and the primary care givers for children have been found to suffer from psychological difficulties due to the hardships of their lives, particularly under the occupation. Women in Gaza were found to have a higher rate of psychological disorders than men (Gaza Community Mental Health Program, 1992). The same was demonstrated in the West Bank (Awwad, 1989). Punamaki (1990) conducted a study on Palestinian women during 1982 (N = 40) and during 1985 (N = 40), before and after the June 1982 Israeli invasion of Lebanon. Results indicated that Palestinian women appraised their environment as more concerning, and exhibited a greater degree of personal helplessness after the 1985 Lebanon war, compared with their scores on these issues in 1982. Women in the 1985 sample were exposed to increased political hardships, and were generally less happy in their marriages than the 1982 sample. They expressed more political worries than the 1982 sample group. The greater the woman's exposure to political violence, and the younger her age, the more she expressed political worries. The study showed that a woman's expression of political worries was lessened according to the number of children she had. However, the children of larger families expressed more personal worries. In terms of coping mechanisms used, the 1985 group employed aggressive behavior more often than the 1982 sample, while the 1982 sample coped with stress by avoiding and retreating behavior more than the 1985 group. Punamaki concluded that these results demonstrated that after the Lebanon war women perceived their social environment as more threatening and dangerous, and themselves as more helpless in their personal lives than before the war.

In a recent study conducted by the Child and Family Consultation Center (Sansur, 1995) of 1,500 Palestinian women aged 18–60 from the West Bank and the Gaza Strip, findings show that these women suffer from various psychiatric symptoms ranging from mild to moderate to severe degrees on the Symptom Checklist 90 (Derogatis, 1983). It was found that:

51.3% suffered from obsessive compulsive disorder
44.5% suffered from depression
40.1% suffered from interpersonal sensitivity
39.9% suffered from anxiety
34.2% suffered from hostility
34.2% suffered from paranoid ideation
33.1% suffered from somatization

It was clear from the results that while reduction in household income is the most commonly occurring life event, experienced by over 68% of the respondents, it is by no means among the most stressful. The death of a husband and bigamy are among the life events causing more severe stress for women who experience them than any other life event. Of the 5.4% of the women who lost their husbands, 81.3% stated they experience severe distress, and of the 3.3% whose husbands remarried, 66.7% acknowledged experiencing severe distress.

☐ Political Prisoners

Palestinian men suffer as much as women, in similar and in different ways. They share the same social and physical environment and are often more directly exposed to stressful situations and violence related to living under military occupation.

Palestinian political prisoners are a specific group suffering from the effects of Israeli violence. When imprisoned, most Palestinian detainees are brutally and inhumanely treated. As with other countries where one people suppress another, political prisoners are detained without trial, beaten, interrogated, tortured, and held in inhumane conditions.

Following are examples of what occurs when a Palestinian, male or female, is detained. A black bag is placed over the head of the person so that they are unable to breathe and suffer from disorientation. The person may be beaten continually to increase their pain and vulnerability. Sleep deprivation is often employed, in extreme cases for up to ten days at a time. Another form of torture has become known internationally as the Palestinian Hanging. The victim is suspended from the arms, which are bent backwards and tortured with electricity to the most sensitive areas of the body (Prip, 1993). Detainees are repeatedly subjected to violence and bodily harm, and with threats of this to their families or loved ones. Detainees are often put into tiny cells with no freedom or basic rights for many years. During this time most prisoners feel frustrated at their inability to protect or provide for their families.

These methods, among others, are used by the Israeli military to coerce confessions from Palestinian political prisoners. The use of physical and mental torture against Palestinians by the Israelis, and their refusal to abide by the Geneva Convention on Torture, have been well documented. In 1992, the Palestinian Human Rights Information Centre issued an extensive report on the use of electric shocks applied to heads and organs. B'Tselem, the Israeli Information Centre for Human Rights in the Occupied Territories, documented the consistent use by the Israeli military of illegal methods for obtaining confessions (Docker, 1995). AlHaq Law in the Service of Man published affidavits describing the various types of torture used (AL-HAQ Law in the Service of Man, 1991).

When political prisoners are released—and there are many still held captive by the Israelis—they return to a continuing situation of difficulty. Many of them need medical treatment for the severe effects of torture and long imprisonment. This can include problems such as dental, muscular, and skin diseases due to lack of adequate medical care. In addition, they face ongoing political harassment from the Israelis, the possibility of rearrest or detainment and the continuing political situation.

In terms of rehabilitation in the community, the exdetainees face a job market where a severe unemployment crisis has prevailed for several years. This crisis is intensified by the ongoing Israeli closures of the West Bank and Gaza, which means many workers are unable to reach their workplaces in Israel, even if they have permits from the Israeli authorities. Younger exdetainees are further disadvantaged as many arrested at a young age were unable to finish their education, and lack vocational skills.

Soren Bojholm, MD, Chief Psychiatrist at the International Rehabilitation Council for Torture Victims (IRCT), studied the prevalence of mental symptoms amongst torture victims reported by several studies. These six studies found that torture victims suffer from, among other things, self-isolation, social withdrawal, emotional liability, depression, anxiety, irritability, aggressiveness, insomnia, impaired memory, impaired concentration, and sexual dysfunction. Many exdetainees and torture victims fall into the category of PTSD. For many, the trauma is being continually reactivated and despite a national Rehabilitation Programme for Ex Detainees, there remain insufficient skills and resources in the country to cope with these effects. No psychological assistance for ex-detainees and their families is yet provided in the program. Many prisoners were forced to make confessions and provide information under torture, and are unable to allieve their trauma and shame; they suffer in silence. Many exdetainees are further frustrated by the present political situation and feel that they sacrificed themselves for nothing (Awwad, 1997b).

☐ Mental Health Care

In order to respond to the numerous mental health needs of the Palestinian community it is necessary to introduce a summary of existing care systems. The mental health service system in the West Bank and Gaza is comprised of one mental hospital in Palestine located in Bethlehem and 11 practicing psychiatrists in the West Bank. Only 5 of them are officially registered by the Medical Union (B. Ashab, personal communication, Oct. 1996). Nine of those psychiatrists have private psychiatric clinics. There are also nine community psychiatric clinics that provide services to the public. Besides these psychiatric services there is only one nongovernmental mental health center in East Jerusalem that specializes mainly in research and training. Mental health services offered to refugee camp residents through UNWRA in the West Bank, has decreased tremendously. Currently there is only one psychologist who is responsible for providing services for 19 refugee camps. In Bethlehem there are 2 nongovernmental mental health clinics and a newly established child care and community development center.

In the Gaza Strip, there are 11 psychiatrists, 6 of them work in the Gaza community mental health program, and 5 work at the psychiatric unit at Optic Hospital. However, only one psychiatrist provides services at the UNRWA clinic that serves people in 8 refugee camps (F. Abu Hein, personal communication, Oct. 1996). The psychiatric hospital in Bethlehem, as well as the community psychiatric clinics in the West Bank, fall within the mental health department of the Ministry of Health in the West Bank. The psychiatric unit of Optic Hospital comes under the authority of the Mental Health Department of the Ministry of Health in Gaza City.

Psychosocial services in Palestine suffer from the following (Awwad, 1995):

1. Lack of qualified and trained mental health professionals. The qualifications of many of those who have been providing services to the public do not fit with the nature of their roles and functions. Many service providers who hold a baccalaureate degree in sociology or psychology are practicing counseling, psychology, or social work. It should be noted that Najah University in Nablus, and Birzeit University in the West Bank are the only local universities offering a B.A. degree in psychology and even that is mainly theoretical in nature.

   The findings of a study conducted by the Child and Family Consultation Center in 1993, showed that 56.5% of those employed in psychosocial services and programs in the West Bank and the Gaza Strip have a high school diploma or less; 35.3% have a baccalaureate degree and few have masters degrees (5%) or doctorate degrees (3%). These results indicate that more than half of the employees are not qualified to provide the services that they do to the public. They need training in areas such as psychological trauma, counseling skills, and community mental health.

2. Little clinical supervision for the employees—including those involved in diagnosis and intervention—who provide these services to the public.

3. Role conflicts among psychologists and psychiatrists who also work as administrators in mental health facilities. In the general health sector physicians may work as directors of hospitals or clinics.

4. Lack of financial resources that hinder development plans. Mental health services occupy a marginal segment in the health sector, and currently almost all of the Nongovernmental Organizations (NGOs) and institutions for mental health are suffering from financial difficulties due to the prevailing political conditions, in general, and the instability of the peace process, in particular.

5. Lack of public awareness of the needs and problems of people with mental, emotional, and psychological difficulties. There often are neg-

ative attitudes toward seeking professional assistance. These conditions have been aggravated by the lack of qualified and trained professionals. However, it should be noted that treatment offered by both the mental hospital in Bethlehem and the private psychiatric clinics is mainly individual and physiologically oriented, e.g., electroconvulsive treatment (ECT) and psychoactive medication.

6. Weakness of the administrative structure of existing services. Many mental health services are functioning as charitable societies, with the role and responsibility of their boards of directors or trustees unclear.

Awwad (1987), also demonstrated that there are no epidemiological studies which show the prevalence and the incidence of the Palestinians' mental health disorders. The diagnosis of the clients is often incorrect, therefore drugs prescribed are ineffective and sometimes harmful. Traumatic symptoms cannot be properly treated if they are not properly diagnosed. Preventative programs or public awareness campaigns are insufficient. There is no specialized national library in mental health or social sciences.

These conditions are aggravated when one realizes that the majority of people consult a medical doctor for emotional stress or psychosomatic complaints. Consulting with a mental health professional is considered a last resort. Therefore, the mental health status of the Palestinians becomes even more critical if we take into account the following:

1. Assessment and diagnosis: Physicians are not trained to conduct clinical assessments and make decisions about the use of medication in the treatment of patients who are suffering from emotional traumas. Physicians are not trained to make decisions on whether the person's suffering results from anxiety and/or psychosomatic complaints, to prescribe medication, or to refer them to a mental health facility.

2. Treatment: Physicians often prescribe psychoactive medication for patients they believe are suffering from mental health problems. They often lack accurate information about the chemical components of psychoactive medications, and there are a variety of local and foreign medications on the market which differ in quality and effectiveness. Physicians do not have full knowledge of the hazardous impact of psychoactive medications or their effects and contraindications. This is further complicated when the patient is prescribed a number of different medications. If the mental health status of the patient does not improve, the physician may change the prescription, increase or decrease the dose, and may not refer the patient to a mental health professional. In general, physicians do not have the clinical skills to recognize if the patient's condition becomes worse and whether the

prescribed medication is effective or not in treating the disorder or difficulty.

3. Follow up and referral: There is often no follow up from physicians with their patients to check if they are using their medications correctly. There is a general trend that biological treatment (e.g., medication and ECT), should be used as a last resort in the treatment of psychiatric or emotional disorders. However, since the establishment of mental health services in the occupied territories in the 1920s, Palestinian psychiatrists depend almost totally on the individual biological treatment for various psychological disorders and even for dealing with clients who are suffering from life stress symptoms. Often there are no referrals by physicians or psychiatrists to counseling services.

4. Nurses: Nurses, particularly in hospitals, play a key role in the treatment process of patients. Nurses are in daily direct contact with their patients and their families as well as with physicians. During their work, they may deal with patients who are suffering from psychiatric disorders, drug addictions, or stress. In many cases, Palestinian nurses are not trained to deal with emotional difficulties and differentiate between mental illness and stress disorders. Nurses often lack crisis intervention and communication skills. Additionally, nurses are responsible for monitoring a patient's use of medication and need to know the side effects of psychoactive medications and the proper use of medication dosage when a physician prescribes them.

Observations About the Patients and Their Families

1. In the last 30 years of occupation there has been no control over the dispensing of medication from pharmacies; i.e., the patient, the family, or even the patient's friends can obtain medications from pharmacies and repeat the prescription several times without the consultation of the physician. This may cause dependency on certain medications.

2. The patient does not often follow the instructions of the physician regarding the proper dosage. An increase or decrease in the dosage may take place by the patient or the family, who often stops taking the medication without consulting the physician.

3. Patients may visit more than one physician and may take more than one medication to relieve them from their symptoms.

4. Patients and their families expect improvement when medication is prescribed by a physician. Improvement is expected to take place immediately after the patient takes the medication.

5. There is no clear picture about the role of the family in the monitoring process of the patients who are using a drug therapy. This is besides the fact that the physicians do not involve family in the treatment, management, and in rehabilitation process.
6. Patients do not learn to relieve their psychological sufferings by finding within themselves new resources. They think that the solution is outside of themselves, in the medication. Thus, they never feel personally responsible for any improvement of their state and become more and more dependent rather than autonomous.
7. With only medication, the patient cannot have the feeling that he is a person meriting attention, consideration, and personal treatment.

Observations About the General Public

1. The public seeks nonmental health professionals, particularly physicians, to relieve them from the symptoms of psychiatric disorders, believing that these symptoms are a result of a physical illness. Though these physical complaints are caused by emotional stress or difficulties, the public is using tranquilizers and other kinds of medications to deal with such complaints as headaches, insomnia, and anxiety.
2. The public lacks needed information about the negative effects of medication. The family may experience anxiety or fear if they notice negative effects after taking the medication.
3. The public lacks needed information that a patient who is treated by psychoactive medications needs a certain amount of time before signs of improvement will be noticed.
4. Some people seek assistance from cup readers and other traditional healers to release them from emotional, personal, social, and financial difficulties. Healers who prepare prescriptions charge high amounts of money.
5. There is a popular negative stigma toward people seeking professional assistance from ps. Thus, they are caught between their psychological needs and their fear of losing their sense of belonging and inclusion in community life.

☐ Basic Cultural Beliefs

Parallel to this critical analysis of the present mental health system there exists a traditional system of mental health. The author conducted a pilot study where he asked eight social workers to interview a convenient sample of 118 Palestinians from the West Bank, including East Jerusalem. This sample consisted of 67 males and 51 females between the ages of 24 and 50 years of age. Since the Palestinian community includes Muslims,[1] Christians and Jews,[2] this sample therefore includes people from each of those religious communities. Furthermore, interviews were comprised of people from cities, villages, a refugee camp in the north of the West Bank (Askar), and the Israeli-Jordanian border (Bedouins). The Palestinian society is patriarchal, male dominated, and generally conservative and religious.

The basic cultural beliefs of Muslims are their beliefs in God's will and destiny. Based on that philosophy they believe that one should bear the hardships of life without complaining and that only God—not human beings—can assist people. Therefore, many religious Muslims refuse to seek the assistance of mental health professionals when they need help. Instead, they pray to God for assistance. In this sense, praying is a means of communication with God and it should be done at fixed times. Besides praying from the Quran (the Muslim Holy Book), some people use prayer beads for seeking forgiveness from Him. As a ritual it is practiced after each prayer to help them seek forgiveness. Some people even isolate themselves and pray when they are in a crisis or facing a serious problem. Admitting one's wrong deeds to God has another healing value as it reduces the believer's sense of fear and anxiety.

Christians also believe in God's will and in destiny. They pray for forgiveness and some admit their mistakes to a priest. They believe that by writing a prayer on a piece of paper and placing it under one's pillow, they will be protected against nightmares. Placing pictures of Jesus Christ, the Virgin Mary, and saints in the house has a protective value and can assist in maintaining a calming state of mind. In some of the old monasteries there is a holy relic of a metal chain similar to a halter. Christians believe that by putting this on and taking it off three times and kissing it, they will be protected from diseases and catastrophes. This ritual is also believed to cure epilepsy and hyperactivity in children. In many Christian homes one can find a picture of St. George carved in stone and placed over the entrance of the house to protect the home and everyone in it. The same thing could be said about wearing a gold cross around one's neck.

Samarians (also known as Samaritans) pray from another holy book called Al-Werrd. Like the Muslims and Christians they use a Holy Relic called Joseph's Higgab when someone is suffering from a loss or a mental health disorder. Jews also believe that it helps as a remedy and also solves one's problems.

Some Palestinians also believe in coffee cup and palm reading, superstitions, and in horoscopes. The findings in Figure 1 show the strength of traditional cultural beliefs.

The majority of the people like to share and express their feelings to their families or friends. Crying is believed to be helpful. Home visits among people is a normal thing and providing financial and social support can occur when a person is facing a crisis. Visits to sick people at home are very much appreciated as are visits on other social occasions such as births, marriages, and high school and college graduations. All these social visits are encouraged and valued by all socioeconomic classes and religious groups.

FIGURE 1. Percent distribution of traditional cultural beliefs

		Yes	No
Fate	1	92.30%	7.60%
Reading Quran	2	90.60%	9.30%
Prayer	3	94.40%	5.08%
Superstitions	4	15.30%	84.70%
Higgab Paper	5	22.10%	77.90%
Cup Reading	6	13.60%	86.40%
Spiritual Healing	7	38.90%	61.00%
Magic	8	22.00%	78.80%
Confessions	9	21.20%	78.80%
Reading Palm	10	5.90%	94.90%

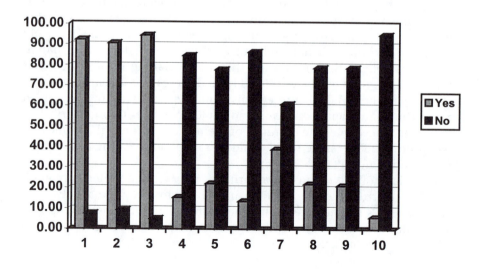

Relatedly, respect for the elderly is highly valued and many Palestinians do not accept sending elderly persons to institutions for care. They believe it is the right of an elderly person to stay at home and be taken care of by their sons and daughters, even when it is difficult for an elderly person to receive medical care in the home. This is a Palestinian value and some believe that if you care for elderly people and keep them at home God will reward you later on.

Though the family has an important therapeutic role for its members, the results of this study indicated that mentally disabled persons were still looked at as meriting sympathy, and should be helped. See Figure 2 for distribution of attitudes towards mentally disabled persons.

FIGURE 2. Percent distribution of attitudes towards mentally disabled persons

		Yes	No
Provide assistance	1	94.90%	5.90%
Hospitalization	2	91.50%	9.30%
Stay at home	3	39.80%	60.10%
Self determination	4	55.00%	47.50%
Other determine	5	44.70%	53.30%
Referred to doctors	6	97.50%	2.50%

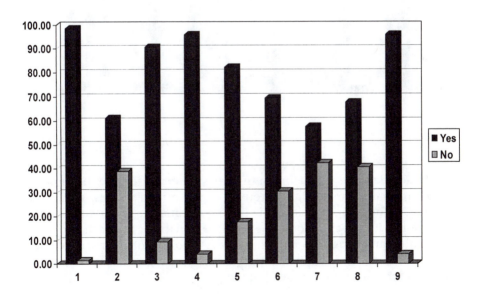

FIGURE 3. Percent distribution of healing methods

		Yes	No
Fate	1	98.30%	1.60%
Reading Quran	2	61.00%	39.00%
Prayer	3	90.60%	9.30%
Superstitions	4	95.80%	4.20%
Higgab Paper	5	82.20%	17.80%
Cup Reading	6	69.50%	30.50%
Spiritual Healing	7	57.63%	42.40%
Magic	8	67.80%	40.68%
Confessions	9	95.76%	4.23%

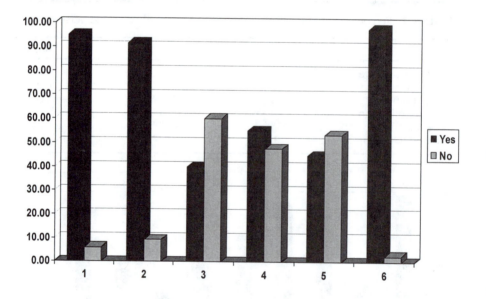

Additional means of healing in the Palestinian culture are the desire of people to walk, dance, sing, listen to music, attend parties, write, and watch T.V. Touching people while talking to them or to comfort them is often done. However, among the negative impacts of violence and stress are alcohol and drug addiction and heavy smoking of cigarettes. Generally, there is a lack of cultural and recreational programs and places. See Figure 3 for distribution of healing methods.

☐ Death and Dying

Raphael (1989) referred to the fear of death as death anxiety or death avoidance, death denial, and reluctance to interact with the dying. She stated that, "the death of a loved one means not only the loss, but also the nearness of personal death, the threat to the self. One is close to death and may be touched or contaminated by it. All the personalised and internalised meanings of death will be invoked by the death of a loved one. All the personal vulnerabilities associated with death will be aroused by its closeness to the self" (p. 23).

During the Intifada, Palestinians suffered a great deal in response to the many who were physically injured or killed. It is well documented that to overcome grief and the pain of loss one needs to pass through the normal stages of mourning. Bowlby's (1992) attachment theory clearly demonstrates the impact of loss and the human reaction associated with it. According to Worden (1992) mourning is the adaptation to loss which involves the following four tasks: 1) accept the reality of the loss; 2) work through the pain of grief; 3) adjust to an environment in which the deceased is missing; and 4) emotionally relocate the deceased and move on with life. It is essential that the grieving person accomplishes these tasks before mourning can be completed. Incompleted grief tasks can impair further growth and development (Worden 1992).

Looking again to the Palestinian past experiences of sudden death as a result of confrontation with the Israeli army, their traumatic experiences with issues of death and dying are exceptional when compared to the people of the Arab countries as well as many other parts of the world. Almost all of the Palestinians killed during confrontations were buried either without the presence of their relatives or with the presence of their parents and very few others, depending on the military order given to the family on that event. Usually, Israeli soldiers hold the body and send it to an Israeli autopsy. After a few days, the body is returned to the family under two conditions : that no public funeral is allowed so that no demonstrations can take place; and that very few persons, no more than ten, are allowed to bury the dead person. In almost all cases a curfew is issued, and the funeral takes place during the night, secretly and silently, under the careful observations of the soldiers.

However, in many cases, youth managed to retrieve the body from the hospital or the site of the shooting, and hide it from the Israeli soldiers. After the killing takes place, the army announces a curfew and starts a search operation for the dead body—including chasing youth, attacking houses, and demolishing homes, furniture, and assets.

The author worked as a general supervisor of the YMCA program for the psychosocial rehabilitation of the physically injured youth during the first two years of the Intifada, and also with mothers who lost their sons in the struggle. In one therapy session, a mother told me that the youth put her son's body in a car after he was shot dead. During the chase by Israeli soldiers, those youth entered her home and hid her son's body under her bed. Though the soldiers searched the home of many others in the neighborhood, they failed to find it. The youth succeeded during the night to secretly take the body out of the home and to bury it without letting the family or anyone else know its location. Full of risk, this event took place under strict curfew conditions when soldiers were everywhere in town. Palestinians believe that taking the body to an Israeli autopsy clinic in Tel Aviv is done only for purposes of harassment and to steal the internal body organs—not to conduct a medical examination as the cause of death is known and clear.

What is important is how this mother was reacting to this traumatic and very painful event. It is not only the task of therapy to assist her to accept the reality of death intellectually, but also to help her to accept this fact emotionally. Without exception, these events were taking place contrary to normal grieving. Parkes stated, "If it is necessary for the bereaved person to go through the pain of grief in order to get the grief work done, then anything that continually allows the person to avoid or suppress this pain can be expected to prolong the course of mourning" (cited in Worden, 1992).

It is also important to note how the Palestinians perceive different types of death—they call a person who has been killed by the Israelis a martyr. On many occasions Palestinian mothers could be seen dancing while crying after hearing of the killing. Grieving during the Intifada was viewed by Palestinians as unhealthy, which led to a denial of the need to grieve. As a martyr, it is believed that the dead person is alive in heaven, therefore there is no need for mourning or grieving. In other words, there was a cultural force that worked against the feeling of pain and anger. More important is the impact of this force against survivors working through the normal tasks of mourning and the blocking of ways of feeling the trauma. From a therapeutic point of view this force hinders the process of normal healing by avoiding painful feelings and thoughts. This unconscious motive to protect the bereaved from experiencing the distress of the traumatic event may protect them in the short term, bearing in mind the tremendous social support which the family receives after the event. However, with the increased number of killings and demolished social support, the shield protecting the traumatized families gradually diminishes, leaving them to carry this pain with them throughout their lives.

The stress of chronic trauma has added yet another destructive phenomena: the number of Palestinians, particularly youth, who commit suicide. According to reports by the Palestinian police, during April 1997, 21 persons attempted suicide, although only one actually died. The Gaza district reported the highest suicide rate, followed by Nablus, Jericho, and Tulkarem respectively in the West Bank. During 1997, 67 people attempted suicide and 16 died (Jerusalem Newspaper, 1997).

Worden (1992) indicated that if task 2 of mourning—working through the pain of grief—is not adequately completed, therapy may be needed later on, at which point it can be more difficult for the person to go back and work through the pain he or she has been avoiding. This is very often a more complex and difficult experience than dealing with it at the time of the loss. Also, it can be complicated by having a less supportive social system than would have been available at the time of the original loss. In John Bowlby's (1980) words, "sooner or later, some of those who avoid all conscious grieving breakdown—usually with some form of depression" (cited in Worden, 1992, p. 14).

The impact of loss is aggravated more when we remember that this culture encourages denial and that there is a lack of services for trauma survivors. To reduce the terrible impact of traumatic events caused by killing or other deaths, physicians prescribe tranquillizers. This is especially the case for women. Worden (1992) indicated that drugs might be beneficial at the time of the loss when some sedation or help managing anxiety is useful. However, such administrations are usually of short duration and unnecessary.

In this study, three religious groups indicated fears surrounding issues of death and dying although they believe that death is a right. They believe in life after death and are therefore concerned with completing the dead person's ritual rights. Palestinians care greatly for close members of the family. Food is delivered to the family from relatives, neighbors, or friends after a death takes place. The custom is that the dead person stays in one room with grieving women while the men are invited to another neighbor's or relative's house. Muslim women do not participate in the funeral; it is restricted to men. On the contrary, Christian men and women participate in the funeral but only men bury the deceased. Christian women are allowed to visit the cemetery the next day and can then express their feelings freely. This is done with other women providing emotional support and empathy. Normally, the mourning period is for three days. People from the city, camp, or village come to visit the grieving family to offer their condolences and support. Food or sweets are served on those days. These have a calming effect because it is believed to be for the forgiveness of the dead person. This practice is repeated again after 40 days and after one year from the anniversary of the death. Additionally, Christians have another mourning day which takes place after six months of the death date. Although Muslim women believe that intense expression of feelings during and after the death (such as wailing) is against Islam and that it causes torture for the deceased as well as for the bereaved, they still do it—especially when the deceased is a parent or a young individual.

Many women believe that intense expressions of feelings such as crying, renting one's garments, slapping one's face, dressing in black, and visiting for the 40 day anniversary of the death are unacceptable practices because it causes discomfort to the deceased. What is most important is the psychosocial support which the grieving family receives from others. Both Muslims and Christians believe that death is a means of reward or punishment. While some Sumarians, however, believe that death is the only means of reward or punishment, others do not. Still others do not believe in either of these because they do not accept the belief in life after death. On the other hand, Samarians believe that crying after death is an emotional catharsis that is normal. However, Samarians are against some practices such as wailing, renting one's garments, crying in cemeteries, and slapping one's face. Some refuse these practices because they believe it is against their religion. Others refuse them because they think it is against logic and reason. But, like the Muslims and Christians, they encourage the serving of food and mourning periods as a means of providing psychosocial support for the close family members of the deceased.

The issue of how children experience death and dying in the Palestinian community is extremely important. In many cases young children are removed from their bereaved parents, as it is believed that it is better for them to not witness their parents' crying and grieving. In my own experience, this is what happened to me and my sister when my uncle, who was a soldier, was killed in the late 1950s during a surprise attack by the Israeli army on Hussan, a Jordanian border point that is a small village near Bethlehem. We were extremely scared at the sight of the body which was covered by a blanket and surrounded by crowds of people who were gathered at my uncle's house. My sister and I were forced to separate from my mother, who was in a state of shock. We were taken to join other crying children in a house far away and we were not allowed to leave despite our fears and screaming. We, therefore, did not attend the funeral or go to the church. I still remember this frightening and painful experience, particularly when my mother recollects this traumatic event.

Similar norms are still applied today. Children are left without the support they badly need to help them resolve the pain of loss and cope with their anxieties and fears. However, on some occasions we find that mothers allow the children to remain with her and others at the house where the dead body is located or to participate in the funeral. Whether children are separated or not is often dependent on the parents or family's level of education, religious beliefs, and the nature of the death, customs of the locality, and the emotional well being of the parents at the time of the event.

During the Intifada, when thousands of Palestinians were killed by Israeli soldiers, the author and a Canadian specialist on death and dying, B. Shahbaklian, published a manual (1992) to help parents cope with the psychological impact of the death of their children. Copies were distributed and explained to mothers in different locations of the West Bank and Gaza, particularly in the refugee camps.

☐ Gender Issues

Palestinian women have been and are active in the National Liberation Movement. They currently play an important role in the political, educational, and business spheres as part of the capacity building of the Palestinian nation. Representing approximately 50% of the population, women need to fully participate for real change to occur. Throughout the West Bank and Gaza diversity in traditional and nontraditional roles can be observed. There are, for example, extremes in dress from women who wear typical western style clothing to those who are completely veiled representative of extreme Muslim culture and religion. Most women work inside the home, however, some women operate businesses and hold high level positions in all stratas of society. Palestinian women are among the most educated in the Arab world. Some hold degrees in medicine, engineering, and education.

Women in Palestine struggle for equal rights as do women in all of the world. They have always been a strength in society, however, as discussed earlier in this chapter, the Intifada placed women in leadership roles outside of the home as well as inside. With many husbands, older sons, and relatives incarcerated as political prisoners protecting children and ensuring family stability and security fell to them. Palestinian women contributed greatly to keeping the family and community strong so that Palestinians could continue the struggle against occupation.

Respect for the cultural and traditional practices of the Palestinian people is best practiced by observation of the particular setting in which you will work.

☐ Working with Trauma in Palestine

It is important that foreign aide workers intending to work in Palestine on mental health or psychosocial issues be aware of the often contradictory position in which they may find themselves. On the one hand they will be viewed as experts with access to information and techniques of working perhaps not available in country. In this respect their support will be eagerly sought. However, in addition to the problematic areas of dependency and paternalism, they will be severely limited by cultural barriers and stigmas as mentioned previously, and may have minimal effectiveness in direct service. Additionally, because, to date, there are no policies, regulations, or standards in the mental health field, and therefore no protection of titles, foreign aide workers may be encouraged to work beyond their strict professional remit, and sometimes in ways that are not ethically appropriate. There is occasional evidence of professional double standard in Palestine, where foreign workers become involved in areas for which they are not fully qualified, or in activities such as counseling through a translator as a means of overcoming language barriers, something that would rarely be acceptable in their own countries. Therefore it is important to balance the needs of a situation with limited resources with professionally appropriate and focused behavior that is based on sustainability. In particular, opportunities for training and professional development in the field of counseling and medical and mental health are both required and requested, and experience has demonstrated that greater efficiency lies in the remit of knowledge and skills transference through direct training and developing long term, focused coaching and supervision relationships.

Regardless of the professional capacity or field in which foreign workers may be operating, it is strongly advised that they establish a system of supervision or mentoring for themselves from a Palestinian coprofessional. Particularly in the field of mental health, cultural protocols and issues may severely challenge Western models of intervention techniques.

Generally, groupwork is not productive for certain traumas such as political imprisonment and torture, as the purpose of revisiting the moments of extreme powerlessness and helplessness will be hindered by concepts of information giving and collaboration. Community reliance on medical and biological interventions will also be a source of frustration, as will the lack of alternative resources such as referral systems and service providers.

Foreign workers also need to be aware of gender relations and roles within the community and how these will affect their own professional and social interactions as foreign men and foreign women.

An ability for managing and seeking support for personal stresses of adaptation and shared situational stressors is essential, as is an understanding and awareness of overidentification, transference, and countertransference of trauma, and methods of working with learned helplessness and depression in a community where concepts of freedom, choice, personal authority, and human rights are consistently challenged.

☐ Stress and the Community

In closing, since the peace negotiations between the Palestinians and the Israelis started, the Palestinians have been living within a contradictory conscious state of peace and conflict. Regardless, the Palestinians are achieving self-rule for the first time in over 1,000 years of conflicts and wars. This present generation has memories of military occupation under Turkish, British, Jordanian, and Israeli rule. The trauma caused by this long term occupation and violence has had a continuous and accumulative effect on the Palestinian people for at least the past three generations. Most of the present day traumatic experiences of Palestinians living in the West Bank and Gaza Strip are a result of living in an environment full of violence and stress. The most recent political, economical, and psychosocial disturbances within the Palestinian society have been the result of the Israeli occupation in the West Bank and Gaza Strip since 1967. Exposure to prolonged violent activities was experienced by the entire population on individual, familial, and societal levels.

The consequences of high levels of stress increase the likelihood of people's vulnerability. It is well documented that "whereby the greater the exposure to traumatic events, the greater the percentage of the population with symptoms of post traumatic stress disorder" (Herman, 1992, p. 57). But as was previously mentioned, the mental health system in Palestine is still underdeveloped, therefore, one cannot expect clinical interventions as ways of helping people cope more effectively with stress. The difficult question, which remains unanswered is: how can the Palestinian community be assisted to adapt to the ever changing conditions of peace and conflict while taking into consideration the nature of the situations and challenges that confront them? The answer to this question will determine whether the Palestinians in the long run will survive and prosper or whether they will fall by the wayside. Additionally, one should also remember that neither the Palestinians nor the conditions they live in will stay the same for very long. This means that as the stress accumulates and continues, vulnerability increases, and adaptation must take place all the time. However, successful adaptation to one set of conditions is not a guarantee of successful adaptation to others (Sarason & Sarason, 1984). Moreover, is the question of whether the Palestinian society is going to enter the 21st century dependent on drugs and ECT. These practices began in Palestine in 1920 to help Palestinians deal with their suffering, pain, and maladaptive behavior.

If high risk groups among the Palestinians who seek psychiatric care are ordered to take medication to suppress symptoms, they are once again disempowered. This is contrary to therapy for PTSD survivors. According to Herman (1992, p. 50),

> "Traumatic events call into question basic human relationships. They breach the attachments of family, friendship, love and community. They shatter the construction of the self that is formed and sustained in relation to others. They undermine the belief systems that give meaning to human experience. They violate the victim's faith in a natural or divine order and cast the victim into a state of existential crisis. . . . Traumatic events have primary effects not only on the psychological structures of the self but also on the systems of attachment and meaning that link individual and community."

This kind of disconnection between the victim and the community is very damaging to both of them. Therefore, future work with the Palestinians should be directed toward increasing the role of primary sources of support where people can sense in their relationship with each other safety, protection, and trust. These are basic ingredients to recovery. Establishing a healing relationship is a way toward empowerment of the survivor and a creation for a new connection. Developing nontraditional clinical interventions where people can learn better ways to deal with human induced disasters as well as natural disasters is another dimension toward recovery.

The more we understand what causes people to feel stress and the more we can identify the factors that produce vulnerability, the clearer the sources of their behavior will be and the more likely that we will be able to develop effective treatment procedures (Sarason & Sarason, 1984).

Palestinian trauma is both historical, ongoing, reinforced, reactivated, and anticipated. The pressure of living with constant uncertainty is insidious and debilitating and the need for developed and effective methods of intervention and support is critical for a society that is coping with a violent past while trying to build for an unknown future.

☐ Endnotes

[1]Based upon unofficial resources, it was estimated that Muslims represent 97% of the Palestinians in the West Bank, including East Jerusalem and the Gaza Strip, while Christians represent 3% (PASSIA, 1996).

[2]Jews called the Samarians or Samaritans in Nablus, North of the West Bank were 569 persons in 1994 (Samaritan pamphlet, no date provided). However, during data collection this number reached 650 persons.

☐ References

Abu Hein, F. (1993). *Clinical psychological effects of Israeli home raids on children in the Gaza Strip.* Unpublished manuscript.

Abu Hein, F., & Raundalen, M. (1993). *Deportation and its effects on the Palestinian children in Gaza.* Unpublished manuscript.

Awwad, E. (1987). *Institutions and services of mental health in the West Bank and Gaza Strip.* Birzeit: Documentation and Research Center, Birzeit University.

Awwad, E. (1989). *Children in the shadow of war: A psychological study on attitudes and emotional life of Israeli and Palestinian children.* Temper Peace Research Institute (Research Report 23).

Awwad, E. (June 5–6, 1995). *Mental health in Palestine: Standardization and accreditation.* Jerusalem: The Second Convention Promoting Regional Dialogue in the NGO Health Sector - Standardization. Medical Aid for Palestine.

Awwad, E. (1996). Violence in the schools. In *Violence phenomenon in the schools and methods of prevention* (pp. 10–21). Ramallah: The Center for Applied Research (CARE) and the Palestinian National Committee for Education, Science and Culture. UNICEF.

Awwad, E. (1997a). Historical consciousness under special circumstances: The case of the young Palestinians. In M. Angvik, & B. V. Borries (Eds.), *Youth and history: A comparative European survey on historical consciousness and political attitudes among adolescents* (pp. 322–327). Hamburg: Korber - Stiftung.

Awwad, E. (1997b). Identity reconstruction of young Palestinians, Israeli Palestinians and Israeli Jews in the light of the peace process. In D. S. Halperin (Ed.), *To live together: Shaping new attitudes to peace through education* (pp. 69–75). Paris: International Bureau of Education, UNESCO.

Awwad E., & Shahbaklian, B. (1992). *Child facing the death event.* Division of Illiteracy and Adult Education: Birzeit University.

Baker, A. M. (1990). The psychological impact of the Intifada on Palestinian children in the occupied West Bank and Gaza: An exploratory study. *American Journal of Orthopsychiatry, 60,* 496–504.

Baker, A. M. (1991). Psychological responses of Palestinian children to environmental stress associated with military occupation. *Journal of Refugee Studies, 4*(3), 237–247.

Bisan for Research and Development (1990). *The Intifada and some social issues.* Jerusalem: Author.

Bowlby, J. (1992). *A secure base: Clinical applications of attachment theory.* London: Tavistook Routledge.

Child and Family Consultation Center. (1993). *A description of mental health services.* Unpublished manuscript.

Derogates, L. (1983). *Symptom checklist–90: Administration, scoring and procedures manual II for the revised version.* Towson, MD: Clinical Psychometric Research.

Elbedour, S., Bensel, R., & Maruyama, G. (1993). Children at risk: Psychological coping with war and conflict in the Middle East. *International Journal of Mental Health, 22,*(3), 33–52.

Garbarino, J., Kostelny, K., & Dubrow, N. (1991). *No place to be a child: Growing up in a war zone.* Lexington, MA: Lexington Books.

Gaza Community Mental Health Program. (1992). *Epidemiological study of mental health in the Gaza Strip.* Unpublished manuscript.

Herman, J. L. (1992). *Trauma and recovery.* New York: Basic Books.

Khamis, V. (1992). *Behavioral problems among school–aged Palestinian children as perceived by their teachers.* Unpublished manuscript, Bethlehem University, West Bank.

Nixon, A. E. (January 1990a). *The status of Palestinian children during the uprising in the occupied territories: Child death and injury* (Part 1, vol. 1: A Chronology). Radda Barner, Swedish Save the Children: Author.

Nixon, A. E. (January, 1990b). *The status of Palestinian children during the uprising in the occupied territories: Child death and injury* (Part 1, vol. 2: Appendices). Radda Barner, Swedish Save the Children: Author.

Nixon, A. E., Goldring, B. A., & Bing–Canar, J. (January, 1990). *The status of Palestinian children during the uprising in the occupied territories: Collective punishment and education.* Part 2. Radda Barner, Swedish Save the Children: Author.

Palestinian Central Bureau of Statistics (1996). *Small area population in the West Bank and Gaza Strip: Revised estimate.* Palestine: Ramallah.

The phantom of suicide conquers the Palestinian society: Are suicidals victims or criminals. (1997, May 29). *Jerusalem Newspaper,* p. 5.

Prip, K. (1993). European committee for the prevention of torture and inhuman degrading treatment or punishment. *Torture, 3*(3), 87–90.

Punamaki, R-L. (1987). *Children in the shadow of war: A psychological study on attitudes and emotional life of Israeli and Palestinian children.* Temper Peace Research Institute (Research Report 23).

Punamaki, R-L. (1990). Impact of political change on the psychological stress among West Bank Palestinian women. *Journal of Medicine and War, 6,* 169–181.

Punamaki, R-L., & Suleiman, R. (1990). Predictors and effectiveness of coping with political violence among Palestinian children. *British Journal of Social Psychology, 29,* 67–77.

Quiet deportation in East Jerusalem. (1997, Mid-June). *Palestine & The UN,* p. 1.

Quota, S., & El Sarraj, E. (1993). *Palestinian children under curfew.* Unpublished manuscript.

Raphael, B. (1989). *The anatomy of bereavement: A handbook for the caring professions.* Winchester, MA: Union Hyman.

Sarason, I. G., & Sarason, B. R. (1984). *Abnormal psychology: The problem of maladaptive behavior* (4th ed.). Englewood, NJ: Prentice Hall.

Sansur, M. (1995). *Mental health and Palestinian women: A survey of mental health conditions of Palestinian women in the West Bank and Gaza Strip.* Jerusalem: Child and Family Consultation Center.

The Palestinian Academic Society for the Study of International Affairs. (1996). *Passia diary.* Jerusalem: Author.

UNICEF (1994). *Helping the child who suffers from a psychological trauma: A manual for social and health workers and pre–school teachers.* Amman: Author.

Worden, W. (1992). *Grief counseling and grief therapy: A handbook for mental health practitioners* (2nd ed.). New York: Springer Publishing Company.

CHAPTER

11

Michael G. Wessells

Culture, Power, and Community: Intercultural Approaches to Psychosocial Assistance and Healing

Worldwide, enormous needs exist for psychosocial assistance in addressing problems such as trauma and loss. Natural disasters, terrorism, the HIV/AIDS pandemic, technological accidents, and violence at levels from the familial to the international produce the most conspicuous needs (International Federation of Red Cross and Red Crescent Societies, 1996). Many people face chronic, complex emergencies that are rooted in histories of colonialism, oppression, poverty, and environmental degradation. Although emergencies are frequently identified by country, they transcend national boundaries. Similarly, profound psychosocial needs often exist within national boundaries for particular, disadvantaged cultural groups such as Kurds in Iraq, Native Americans in the United States, or Aboriginal people in Australia.

Nowhere is the global scale of the psychosocial needs more apparent than in situations of armed conflict (Garbarino, Kostelny, & Dubrow, 1991; UNICEF, 1996; Wessells, 1998a) which are fought increasingly along lines of ethnic identity (Gurr, 1993). Since the end of the Cold War, there have been 103 armed conflicts fought overwhelmingly within states, with an average of 25–35 conflicts occurring at any point in time (Wallensteen & Sollenberg, 1998). As illustrated by the wars in the former Yugoslavia and the 1994 Rwandan genocide, contemporary armed conflicts kill mostly civilians in fighting at the community level; use rape, ethnic cleansing, and mutilation as instruments of war; pit neighbor against neighbor; shatter social trust; and implant searing memories of victimization that plant seeds of future conflict. Problems of land mines, displaced people, and a shift from political to criminal violence remain long after the signing of a ceasefire, blurring the distinction between war and peace. Without work on healing and other tasks of psychosocial assistance, significant numbers of people may be at risk of future violence. In this sense, work on healing is part of comprehensive programs of postconflict reconstruction and conflict prevention (Wessells & Monteiro, in press).

Psychologists have contributed to, and will no doubt continue contributing to, the international response to crisis situations (Danieli, Rodley, & Weisaeth, 1996; Wessells, 1998b). Serious problems, however, confront psychologists in this work. Often they are invited by nongovernmental organizations (NGOs), by governments, or by UN agencies to work in cultural settings with which they are unfamiliar and in which the tools of Western psychology have not been validated. Significant risks exist of oversimplification, culturally biased approaches, and construction of unsustainable programs. Worse yet, damage may be done through the marginalization of local voices and traditions, the use of tools that heighten stress excessively or that place people at risk in other ways, and squandering human and financial resources that are precious in situations of extreme poverty and need (Bracken & Petty, 1998). In addition, when psychologists enter other cultural settings, they have an opportunity to learn from the local understandings of mental health, resources, practices of healing. But if they enter the situation as experts, they may be inclined to teach and to practice rather than to listen, to learn, and to work in partnership.

For these and other reasons, it is vital to place culture at the center in arranging psychosocial assistance of all kinds. The editors and authors of this book have done this in regard to work on trauma, loss, and healing. Rather than assuming the universality of Western psychology, they have taken as their point of departure the more appropriate view that concepts of mental health and illness exhibit significant cultural variability, as do practices of healing (Adler & Mukherji, 1995; Murdock, 1980; Swartz, 1998). In many respects, each chapter following the introduction provides a map of a particular cultural system of belief and practice. Collectively, the chapters shatter any myths that Western concepts and methods can be taken off the shelf and used in every cultural context in an effective, ethically appropriate manner. They also provide a wealth of useful contextual information and practical advice for psychologists who plan to work across cultural boundaries on how to help design and implement culturally relevant programs of psychosocial assistance.

In this final chapter, it is valuable to identify cross cutting themes, systematize what has been learned, and extract some key lessons for consultants. This chapter aims to integrate the main insights into a broad conceptual framework centered around issues of context, culture, power, and community. Its point of departure is the idea that loss of hope, meaning, and perceived control are pivotal aspects of trauma (Herman, 1992). Recovery from trauma and loss requires the reconstruction of meaning, the rebuilding of hope, and the sense of empowerment needed to regain control of one's being and life. The imposition of Western, decontextualized views marginalizes local voices and cultural traditions, disempowers communities, and limits healing. Conversely, the use of consultants' power to situate problems in historic context and to learn about and valorize local cultural traditions, when appropriate, empowers the community and brings into play culturally appropriate, sustainable healing resources. Community empowerment and local capacity building are vital for regaining control, healing wounds, and building a bridge from a difficult past to a more positive future (Dubrow, in press). This framework has far reaching implications for how one works as a consultant, views and works with local people in need, and disposes oneself toward other cultures. Having developed the integrative framework, I will summarize some of the key practical implications that emerge from the preceding chapters.

☐ Trauma and Healing in Context

Psychological stresses and trauma often occur in contexts of abject poverty, chronic oppression and discrimination, extreme physical need, and political, ecological, and social disruption. In these contexts, psychological wounds cannot be separated from collective wounds—they are psychosocial with an emphasis on the social. As Stamm and Stamm (this volume) point out, the psychological stresses and problems in Native North American communities are inextricably interwoven with an historic context of genocide, discrimination, and marginalization. Similarly, as Vélez-Ibáñez (this volume) points out, the problems of Mexicans in the Southwest U.S. are connected with problems of poverty, unemployment, and oppression. These stressors are chronic and historically rooted.

In a war zone or disaster situation, many local people may experience problems such as sleep disturbances, flashbacks, social isolation, substance abuse, and so on. For clinical psychologists trained in Western universities, it is quite natural to view these problems through the lens of concepts of trauma and posttraumatic stress disorder (PTSD; for useful reviews, see Friedman & Marsella, 1996; Stamm & Friedman, in press; van der Kolk, McFarlane, & Weisaeth, 1996). It is tempting in such circumstances to set up mental health clinics or to arrange other venues for delivering psychological services to address traumas.

Although beneficial in some respects, this trauma emphasis encounters serious difficulties when narrowly applied. First, it individualizes the problem. Dominant conceptual frameworks construct trauma as an individual phenomenon, distracting attention from the wider, social elements of the situation. But in war situations, the impact of trauma on individuals cannot be separated from the devastation of families and communities (Reichenberg & Friedman, 1996). Further, in collectivist societies, individualistic approaches may be at odds with the local culture. Second, a trauma emphasis encourages fragmentation of multifaceted problems. Although psychologists naturally look for and address psychological issues, the immediate problems may have more to do with food, security, housing, and survival (Dawes, 1994). It is vital for psychologists to view human problems holistically (Wessells & Kostelny, 1996).

Third, emphasis on trauma encourages an ahistorical conceptualization that overlooks the stresses imposed by racism, economic domination, or political oppression. The failure to situate problems historically may lead to oversimplification, diagnostic problems (Dubrow & Nader, this volume), and the misdirection of resources. To talk about war affected populations as traumatized, for example, can pathologize the people and medicalize problems that are political and economic. As Vélez-Ibáñez & García Parra (this volume) notes, profound psychological stress often arises from economic disadvantages. When consultants fail to talk about the historic context of problems, local people often feel demeaned and misunderstood. Consider, for example, the problems associated with focusing narrowly on problems of trauma in the Palestinian context, where victimization has become woven into the fabric of group identity by virtue of the historic situation. In focusing on the trauma of youths who have nightmares and related problems by virtue of having been arrested or shot, a psychologist overlooks the connection between mental health and sociopolitical context (Punamaki, 1989) and tacitly denies the historic oppression that many Palestinians view as the defining feature of their social reality (Awwad, this volume). Similarly, focus on trauma in the Israeli context may draw attention from the culture of dying, which is grounded in problems of the Holocaust, repeated attacks, and chronic insecurity (Bar-On, this volume).

In regard to intervention, equally difficult problems confront a single minded emphasis on trauma. Ethically, it is questionable to address traumas in contexts of political oppression without also working to support human rights and constructive political change. Ultimately, psychologists fail to improve human well being if their interventions serve to heal lambs for the slaughter, to enable people to endure oppression without ending it, or to silence rebellion in the face of tyranny. Further, trauma interventions alone cannot address the wider human needs that have great urgency in many crises. Healing requires hope and empowerment, and these cannot flower in situations of extreme poverty, oppression, and armed conflict. Access to jobs and education, physical reconstruction, and the resumption of culturally appropriate patterns of living may contribute very significantly to psychosocial well being (Gibbs, 1997).

To advance psychosocial well being, one must work holistically, bridge the macro- and micro-social levels, and integrate psychosocial work into comprehensive, multidisciplinary programs (Wessells & Kostelny, 1996). For psychologists working as consultants, this may require much new learning and a willingness to go beyond the boundaries of one's discipline. On the ground, it requires listening to communities in a manner conducive to holistic understanding and analysis of their situation and problems. It may also mean talking at length with economists, political analysts, and people from NGOs and government agencies who can help to construct a holistic perspective and with whom one might partner in implementing comprehensive strategies.

☐ Putting Culture at the Center

Western psychology reflects the values and beliefs dominant in the wider cultural system (Smith, 1986). In the US, a mechanistic world view prevails, and society is saturated with values of individualism, freedom, pragmatism, and material wealth. These values find expression in the myth of the self-made person who, despite a difficult background, rises above his or her circumstances and succeeds through hard work and a can-do attitude. Since US psychology embodies these values and beliefs, it seems natural for American psychologists to seek scientific explanations, to focus on individual healing, to empower individuals to rise above the limits imposed by their material circumstances, and to encourage healing through free exploration and expression of emotions and ideas.

Spiritual Cosmologies

Although this orientation is appropriate in many Western settings and is grounded on a solid base of research, it is by no means universal. In other cultures, this orientation may be inappropriate and may fit poorly with local cosmology, norms, and values. As Peddle et al. (this volume) note, it is particularly incongruent with the spiritually centered cosmology that pervades Angola, Sierra Leone, and most of sub-Saharan Africa. There, the visible world and the spiritual realm are united, and the living community is viewed as an extension of the ancestral community. Since people attribute events in the visible world to spiritual causes, it is the spiritual meanings and dimensions of their life experiences that are most important and that have greatest psychological impact. Local cosmology has powerful implications for both diagnosis and treatment. To succeed in the sub-Saharan context, work on healing must step beyond Western boundaries and include local, culturally defined understanding and practice (Swartz, 1998).

For example, if an Angolan village was attacked and a boy's parents were killed, the boy might have fled the village before he had conducted the culturally appropriate burial rituals. Outwardly, the boy might exhibit signs of trauma. The larger problem, however, might be the boy's belief that he is haunted by the unavenged spirits of his parents, who cannot make transition to the ancestor's realm unless the rituals have been conducted. The boy's stress is less a matter of what had happened than of the culturally constructed meanings he assigned to his experiences. In Angolan cosmology, this is not an individual problem since it entails a rupture between the living and the ancestors, who have not been honored properly. Outside consultants need not accept the validity of this spiritual interpretation, but they should recognize the power of the beliefs in shaping local behavior and views of social reality. Without taking into account the local belief system, a Western psychologist might misunderstand the problem and would be poorly positioned to take steps to address it. Arguably, talking and processes of emotionally working through would not be effective in such a case. What is needed is an appropriate burial ritual that communalizes the bereavement process and is believed to restore spiritual harmony. Following the conduct of the appropriate rituals, talking about the deceased may be dangerous since it enables bad spirits to revisit (Honwana, 1997; also see Gerber et al., this volume).

Spiritually oriented cosmologies guide thought and practice on mental health and illness in many parts of the world, as emphasized in the chapters in this book on Africa, Native North Americans, and Southeast Asians. Accordingly, one of the first steps to be taken by practitioners who will work in non–Western cultures is to learn about the local cosmology of the system they are about to enter. Often this can be accomplished by talking with anthropologists who study the area or by interviewing elders and other local people about their beliefs. This first step is useful in tailoring Western approaches to fit local cultures and in avoiding the use of methods that, although beneficial in Western contexts, may cause damage in non–Western cultures (see Dubrow & Nader, this volume). But this tailoring of Western approaches is only a first step. To construct culturally relevant approaches, it is essential to use and to learn from local approaches, placing culture at the center of one's psychosocial work.

Local Cultural Resources

Local communities, although often viewed by outside consultants and donor agencies as recipients of aid, are more appropriately seen as actors who bring creativity and a rich array of cultural resources to the tasks of psychosocial assistance. A partial list of resources is as follows.

Traditions

Local communities are repositories of centuries-old traditions and of the accumulated wisdom and understanding of the culture. Traditional beliefs color the meaning and interpretation of one's life experiences and provide the foundation for traditional methods of healing. In addition, traditions themselves provide a sense of meaning, continuity, and psychosocial support in difficult circumstances.

Human Resources

Traditional healers and herbalists often provide consultation and services related to health and healing at the local level. Elders, concerned parents, women's groups, teachers, and influentials in the religious communities may contribute expertise and may also become involved in community based projects. Local family and village networks may help to identify key people who already work on the issues to be addressed by the project. These networks also provide useful venues for the delivery of psychosocial assistance.

Community Processes

At the community level, traditional and official power structures regulate access, influence the distribution of resources, and provide legitimacy and moral support for work in the community. There are norms of dialogue and consultation, rules for entering the community and communicating respect, different constituencies to be heard and negotiated with, and key players who are respected and know how to get things done in the community. Respecting and working with these local processes is an integral part of cultural sensitivity and increases the likely impact of one's psychosocial work.

Tools

Local communities have specific methods and tools for healing such as rituals, ceremonies, and practices of remembrance. Since they are grounded in the beliefs, values, and traditions of the local culture, they are both culturally appropriate and more sustainable than methods brought in from the outside.

Wise consultants recognize the value of these cultural resources and will learn from and work with them in all phases of situation analysis, needs assessment, planning and program design, training and program implementation, and monitoring and evaluation. Following decades of war and community dislocation, these resources may be weakened or disrupted. In these extreme situations, outside donors and consultants may play an important role in aiding the recovery of traditions, enabling fragile community processes, and providing resources and space in which communities can begin the process of rebuilding. In this work, it is vital to remember that local people, even in desperate circumstances, are not passive victims but survivors who have much resilience and internal capacity to shape their own future. In this sense, the role of outside consultants is to assist in building local capacity (Anderson & Woodrow, 1998).

Despite their importance, local cultural resources should be viewed critically. As illustrated by female genital mutilation, local practices and traditions may be harmful and ethically objectionable in some cases. Premature rejection of local methods should be avoided, but so should romanticized images of traditional approaches (Dawes, 1997). Like all approaches, traditional approaches to healing need to be assessed carefully, and consultants' expertise and outsiders' perspectives may be valuable in this process. Further, the valorization or use of local cultural resources may privilege some local groups over others. One may not assume that the use of a particular traditional method of healing is a psychological matter—it is equally a political act that serves to strengthen some interests in the local power structure over others. It is vital for consultants to ask whose interests are being served.

A related point is that cultures are incomplete social constructions that are dynamic and evolving. Traditional healing methods, for example, are not fossilized but evolve in new ways and adapt to changing circumstances. In Angola, for example, traditional healers are planning to conduct mass rituals for people who had died during the war but for whom it had been impossible to conduct burial rituals (Carlinda Monteiro, personal communication, September 16, 1998). Often, constructive change may arise through interaction with other cultures. Since no known cultural system provides comprehensive resources for healing, coping, and resilience, there is always a need for cultural growth and expansion of resources. In important respects, outside consultants are agents of cultural interaction and interpenetration, which now occurs globally on a very extensive scale owing to changes in transportation and communications technologies. The door is open for an increased mixture of Western and traditional approaches in ways that enrich multiple cultural systems and help to build a multicultural psychology. Although the potential for improving psychosocial assistance is great, significant challenges also arise in regard to asymmetries of power.

☐ Power and Consultation

In emergency situations, psychologists hired by NGOs or UN agencies often play a lead role in defining the situation, identifying the psychological dimensions of the problems, and suggesting interventions. When Western-trained psychologists go as consultants to a developing country, often in very difficult circumstances, they enter a situation in which there is a large power asymmetry (Wessells & Kostelny, 1996). Viewed as experts, they tacitly carry the imprimatur of Western science and of Western psychology, regarded globally as embodying the highest standards of research, education, training, and practice. A huge wealth gap contributes to the asymmetry, as consultants often serve donor agencies that have resources that dwarf those of impoverished communities. Local people may view consultants as gateways to precious funding, jobs, and other material resources.

Use of outside psychological consultants can be beneficial in bringing into play the powerful knowledge and tools of Western psychology and in getting the advice of outsiders who may be able to see the situation in fresh perspective. Unfortunately, the dynamics of the situation invite a tyranny of Western expertise. The multitude of problems involved usually stems not from any conspiracy or conscious intent but rather from hidden power dynamics and the tacit assumption that Western knowledge trumps local knowledge. The consultants, viewed as highly prestigious by local people, may wield influence that extends well beyond what the consultants themselves want, or think, is appropriate. Out of desperation, local people may look to the experts for solutions when the situation admits no easy answers. The power wielded by consultants may privilege some groups over others. In many regions, it is customary for outside consultants to talk mostly with male elders and elite members of the community. In this situation, following the cultural rules can contribute to problems of gender and class discrimination.

Eager to address urgent human needs, the outside consultants may apply their own belief systems and use the methods they believe to have the strongest scientific grounding. Unintentionally, consultants may encourage excessive confidence in Western approaches even in cultural contexts in which the approaches have not been validated properly. These methods, despite their culture bias, may be seized upon by local communities badly in need of hope. Alternately, local people, although doubtful of the efficacy or sustainability of a Western approach, may play along with the outsiders' ideas in hopes of obtaining jobs or food. This situation can be difficult to detect for outsiders who do not know the local rules. As Stamm and Stamm (this volume) note, consultants may take the apparent agreement of community leaders with the proposed psychosocial work at face value, when in fact the agreement may reflect norms of politeness and courtesy to visitors. Subtly, Western views may be imposed.

In many situations, this imposition process is bolstered by self-silencing. Local people may be reluctant to talk about local beliefs and methods out of embarrassment and a desire to avoid appearing backward. Unwary consultants may be misled into believing that there are no local approaches to healing in use, when in fact they are used widely but only in the presence of family and people regarded as insiders. If traditional beliefs and approaches are brought up, local people may dismiss them as inferior since they are not grounded in rigorous scientific research. Sadly, it is often local people who view their own approaches as inferior. This deeply ingrained sense of inferiority is one of the worst residues of colonialism and is itself a major form of psychological damage.

The dynamics of this situation marginalize local methods and disempower local communities. The problems go well beyond cultural insensitivity and unsustainability—they have more to do with psychology being used as an instrument of cultural imperialism (Dawes, 1997; Wessells, 1992). When this occurs, well intentioned intervention efforts inflict psychological damage through the continuation of historic patterns of oppression and external domination. In addition, there may be an erosion of local cultural beliefs and practices that are key resources for healing, and communities may be increasingly cut off from the traditions in which their sense of meaning and identity are grounded. As communities lose their voice, they slide further into passivity and silently give up hope in their own ability.

Fortunately, this scenario is preventable. Although the power asymmetry is inherent, it can be negotiated through critical consciousness in which consultants reflect with key informants on who benefits from the use of particular approaches, whether local people feel they have a voice, what the consultants' and donors' motives are, and how the decision making process may reflect historic patterns of privileging. In addition, consultants can work with a partnership orientation in which communities have a voice and in which outsiders and insiders share power in program design, implementation, and evaluation. This is the core idea behind community based approaches.

☐ Community Based Approaches

Community based approaches focus etiology and treatment resources not on individuals but on the community itself. Analyzing communities as the life support systems for individuals assumes that individual mental health and family well being cannot be achieved in community contexts where there are profound problems such as poverty, crime, unemployment, and discrimination. Taking a holistic approach assumes that communal wounds require communal healing. Accordingly, community based approaches seek to integrate psychosocial assistance with economic development and political reconstruction. This orientation fits well with collectivist societies where group oriented cosmology dominates and where it is inappropriate and ineffective to arrange individual mental health services. Community based approaches embody the insights that communities are key sources of emotional and social support; that connection with community is a source of identity, meaning, and resilience (see Tully, this volume); and that reestablishment of control often occurs best in a group context.

As Peddle et al. (this volume) discuss, community based strategies emphasize local participation, community mobilization and empowerment, and use of local, culturally appropriate resources. Ideally, the programs are led by local people who understand the culture, language, and situation. Since local people are key players, they develop a sense of ownership in the program, the success of which may impact their immediate families. Often with the assistance of training, community members become sensitized to issues of mental health and learn methods of psychosocial assistance for groups in need. In this respect, community based programs are not elitist or aimed at skimming off the cream of the community to assume exalted positions. Rather, the emphasis is on building broad participation and on mobilizing everyone—individuals, families, women, elders, teachers, etc.—in the service of advancing psychosocial well being. Some of the methods used will likely be familiar to psychologists. For example, in the Angolan project discussed by Peddle et al., war affected children may be invited to engage in free drawing or participate in dramatic productions as a means of expressing and coming to terms with their war experiences. The work also includes projects (such as rebuilding schools) that do not look like the forms of psychosocial assistance that many psychologists learned in graduate school. Here it is wise to remember that especially in difficult circumstances, healing is linked with physical reconstruction and development. Quite often, a new school becomes a symbol of hope and positive future orientation. The construction process itself helps to mobilize and empower the community and serves as a tangible embodiment of the process of self-transformation that is needed. Ultimately, community based approaches seek to achieve change from the inside out.

Community based work entails a significant redefinition of the consultant's role. Normatively, Western consultants are viewed as experts who apply scientific concepts and methods to local problems. Positioned in the driver's seat, Western consultants frequently play a directive role in leading the planning of interventions and in either implementing programs themselves or training others to implement following a prescribed model. In community based approaches, on the other hand, outside consultants share power and play a much more facilitative role. Although they bring valuable knowledge and tools to the table, they fundamentally seek to partner with local people, agencies, and communities. Realizing their lack of understanding of the culture and situation, they often view themselves as learners rather than experts. Fundamentally, they may view their role as one of empowering the community, assisting it in shaping its own future. Understanding the power asymmetry in the situation, they may use methods of elicitation and joint problem solving (Lederach, 1995), which demonstrate respect for local cultural traditions and help to incorporate local resources into psychosocial programs. Working effectively in this mode entails staying in the background, avoiding dependency, building local capacity, and helping to advance processes of internal change while remaining on the outside.

A particularly valuable role for outside consultants is to assist in the integration of Western and traditional approaches. Through dialogue with community people, consultants may assist in selecting and tailoring Western approaches to the local context. At the same time, they can valorize, learn about, and support appropriate local approaches to healing. The emphasis is on creating a joint community of practice (Gilbert, 1997) that synthesizes the values, perspectives, understandings, and tools of both the consultant and the local actors. In this integrationist project, the attempt is to combine the tools and insights from diverse cultural traditions in advancing psychosocial well being (Wessells & Monteiro, in press). As ways of interweaving Western and local practices are constructed, they are then tested jointly, and the results may stimulate new questions and define emergent goals. These become the focus of additional discourse and action research aimed at increasing the socially transformative power of the knowledge and practice (Brydon-Miller & Tolman, 1997; Fals-Borda & Rahman, 1991). Using their understanding of methodology, Western consultants may contribute significantly to processes of evaluation and research. In many situations, traditional healing practices and their psychosocial impacts have never been documented carefully. In addition, they may help to encourage the flow of information across cultural boundaries. Just as they bring Western ideas into the local setting, they may through writing and presentations bring ideas from local communities into the discourse of mainstream psychology. Both global and local psychologies stand to be enriched by this cultural interchange.

☐ Practical Suggestions

This framework illustrates the complexity of the work of outside psychological consultants. Although seldom stated in their contracts, it is vital for consultants to be conscious of the ever present temptation toward hubris, to be aware of the complexities that exist on the ground, and to reflect carefully on their own orientation, values, and influence. Although the magnitude of the task may seem daunting, one may take heart in knowing that, as illustrated in the preceding chapters, it is possible to structure one's work in ways that are psychologically sophisticated, culturally grounded, sensitive to the needs and situation of local people, oriented toward partnership and power sharing, and successful in advancing human well being. Specific suggestions that follow from this framework and that have been emphasized in previous chapters may be summarized as follows.

1. Analyze your own preconceptions and stereotypes about the culture, people, problems, and likely interventions in the context you are entering.
2. Recognize that your knowledge, values, methods, and approach are extensions of a cultural system that may be very different from the one you are entering.
3. Honor and respect local people, who have much to teach about survival and the meaning of resilience.
4. Listen and learn from local communities and their traditions, talking frequently with elders and other key informants.
5. Ask what you have done to actively invite discussion and sharing of local beliefs and practices.
6. Center programs around local leaders rather than expatriates, remembering that you are an outsider.

7. Analyze in a systems perspective the local power structure and social processes of the community, appreciating the wealth of different actors within it, the norms and customs, the change agents, and the obstacles to constructive change.

8. Situate the current community orientation and problems in historic context, connecting psychological issues with problems of colonialism, poverty, racism, and discrimination, among others.

9. Be conscious of the power and influence you potentially yield in various roles as trained psychologist, Ph.D., NGO or UN representative, and so on.

10. Analyze the impact of your own gender, ethnicity, religious orientation, social class, and national origin on the people and projects you work with; also analyze more broadly how these factors play out in the wider program.

11. Understand the diversity that exists within a community and a culture, which seldom exhibit the monolithic quality that the terms suggest.

12. Ask on a continuing basis "who benefits" and "who's excluded" in the project work, being mindful of historic inequities and the potential of projects to amplify destructive conflict by privileging some groups over others.

13. Learn to work effectively with different subgroups, building bridges between different constituencies within the community.

14. Whenever appropriate, support the use of local resources, aiming to build local capacity, cultural relevance, and sustainability.

15. If you are entering a war zone, remember that this is itself a political act, and ask how your presence and action are likely to be appropriated by different parties to the conflict.

16. Before visiting, read up on the history and the culture of the area to see the situation in a broader context.

17. To build comprehensive programs, collaborate with NGOs, government agencies, and network with people from various disciplines.

In acting on these and related suggestions, it is beneficial to take a long term perspective, seeking not only to address the immediate needs, but also to advance peace, social justice, and constructive societal transformation.

☐ **References**

Adler, L., & Mukherji, B. (Eds.). (1995). *Spirit versus scalpel: Traditional healing and modern psychotherapy.* Westport, CT: Bergin & Garvey.

Anderson, M. B., & Woodrow, P. J. (1998). *Rising from the ashes: Development strategies in times of disaster.* Boulder, CO: Lynne Rienner.

Bracken, P. J., & Petty, C. (Eds.). (1998). *Rethinking the trauma of war.* London: Free Association Books.

Brydon-Miller, M., & Tolman, D. (Eds.). (1997). Transforming psychology: Interpretive and participatory research methods. *Journal of Social Issues, 53(4),*

Danieli, Y. I., Rodley, N. S., & Weisaeth, L. (Eds.). (1996). *International responses to traumatic stress.* Amityville, NY: Baywood.

Dawes, A. (1994). The emotional impact of political violence. In A. Dawes & D. Donald (Eds.), *Childhood & adversity: Psychological perspectives from South African research* (pp. 177–199). Cape Town: David Philip.

Dawes, A. (1997, July). *Cultural imperialism in the treatment of children following political violence and war: A Southern African perspective.* Paper presented at the Fifth International Symposium on the Contributions of Psychology to Peace, Melbourne.

Dubrow, N. (in press). The role of the mental health professional in building bridges of peace. In A. Shalev, R. Yehuda, & A. McFarlane (Eds.), *International handbook of human response to trauma.* New York: Plenum.

Fals-Borda, O., & Rahman, M. A. (1991). *Action and knowledge: Breaking the monopoly with participatory action research.* New York: Apex.

Friedman, M. J., & Marsella, A. J. (1996). Posttraumatic stress disorder: An overview of the concept. In A. J. Marsella, M. J. Friedman, E. T. Gerrity, & R. M. Scurfield (Eds.), *Ethnocultural aspects of posttraumatic stress disorder: Issues, research, and clinical applications* (pp. 11–32). Washington, DC: American Psychological Association.

Garbarino, J., Kostelny, K., & Dubrow, N. (1991). *No place to be a child: Growing up in a war zone.* Lexington, MA: Lexington Books.

Gibbs, S. (1997). Postwar social reconstruction in Mozambique: Reframing children's experiences of trauma and healing. In K. Kumar (Ed.), *Rebuilding war-torn societies: Critical areas for international assistance* (pp. 227–238). Boulder, CO: Lynne Rienner.

Gilbert, A. (1997). Small voices against the wind: Local knowledge and social transformation. *Peace and Conflict: Journal of Peace Psychology, 3,* 275–292.

Gurr, T. R. (1993). *Minorities at risk: A global view of ethnopolitical conflicts.* Washington, DC: U.S. Institute of Peace Press.

Herman, J. (1992). *Trauma and recovery.* New York: HarperCollins.

Honwana, A. (1997). Healing for peace: Traditional healers and postwar reconstruction in Southern Mozambique. *Peace and conflict: Journal of Peace Psychology, 3,* 293–305.

International Federation of Red Cross and Red Crescent Societies (1996). *World Disasters Report 1996.* New York: Oxford University Press.

Lederach, J. P. (1995). *Preparing for peace.* Syracuse, NY: Syracuse University Press.

Murdock, G. (1980). *Theories of illness: A world survey.* Pittsburgh, PA: University of Pittsburgh Press.

Punamäki, R. (1989). Political violence and mental health. *International Journal of Mental Health, 17,* 3–15.

Reichenberg, D., & Friedman, S. (1996). Traumatized children. Healing the invisible wounds of war: A rights approach. In Y. Danieli, N. S. Rodley, & L. Weisaeth (Eds.), *International responses to traumatic stress* (pp. 307–326). Amityville, NY: Baywood.

Smith, M. B. (1986). War, peace and psychology. *Journal of Social Issues, 42,* 23–38.

Stamm, B. H., & Friedman, M. J. (in press). Cultural diversity in the appraisal & expression of traumatic exposure. In A. Shalev, R. Yehuda, & A. McFarlane (Eds.), *International Handbook of Human Response to Trauma.* New York: Plenum Press.

Swartz, L. (1998). *Culture and mental health: A Southern African view.* Cape Town: Oxford University Press.

UNICEF (1996). *The state of the world's children 1996.* New York: UNICEF.

van der Kolk, V. A., McFarlane, A. C., & Weisaeth, L. (Eds.). (1996). *Traumatic stress: The effects of overwhelming experience on mind, body, and society.* New York: Guilford.

Wallensteen, P., & Sollenberg, M. (1998). Armed conflict and regional conflict complexes, 1989–97. *Journal of Peace Research, 35(5),* 621–634.

Wessells, M. G. (1992). Building peace psychology on a global scale: Challenges and opportunities. *The Peace Psychology Bulletin, 1,* 32–44.

Wessells, M. G. (1998a). The changing nature of armed conflict and its implications for children: The Graca Machel/UN Study. *Peace and Conflict: Journal of Peace Psychology, 4(4),* 321–334.

Wessells, M. G. (1998b). Humanitarian intervention, psychosocial assistance, and peacekeeping. In H. Langholtz (Ed.), *The psychology of peacekeeping* (pp. 131–152). Westport, CT: Praeger.

Wessells, M. G., & Kostelny, K. (1996). *The Graça Machel/UN Study on the Impact of Armed Conflict on Children: Implications for early child development.* New York: UNICEF.

Wessells, M., & Monteiro, C. (in press). Psychosocial intervention and post-war reconstruction in Angola: Interweaving Western and traditional approaches. In D. Christie, R. Wagner, & D. Winter (Eds.), *Peace, conflict, and violence: Peace psychology for the 21st century.* Englewood Cliffs, NJ: Prentice Hall.

AUTHOR INDEX

SUBJECT INDEX